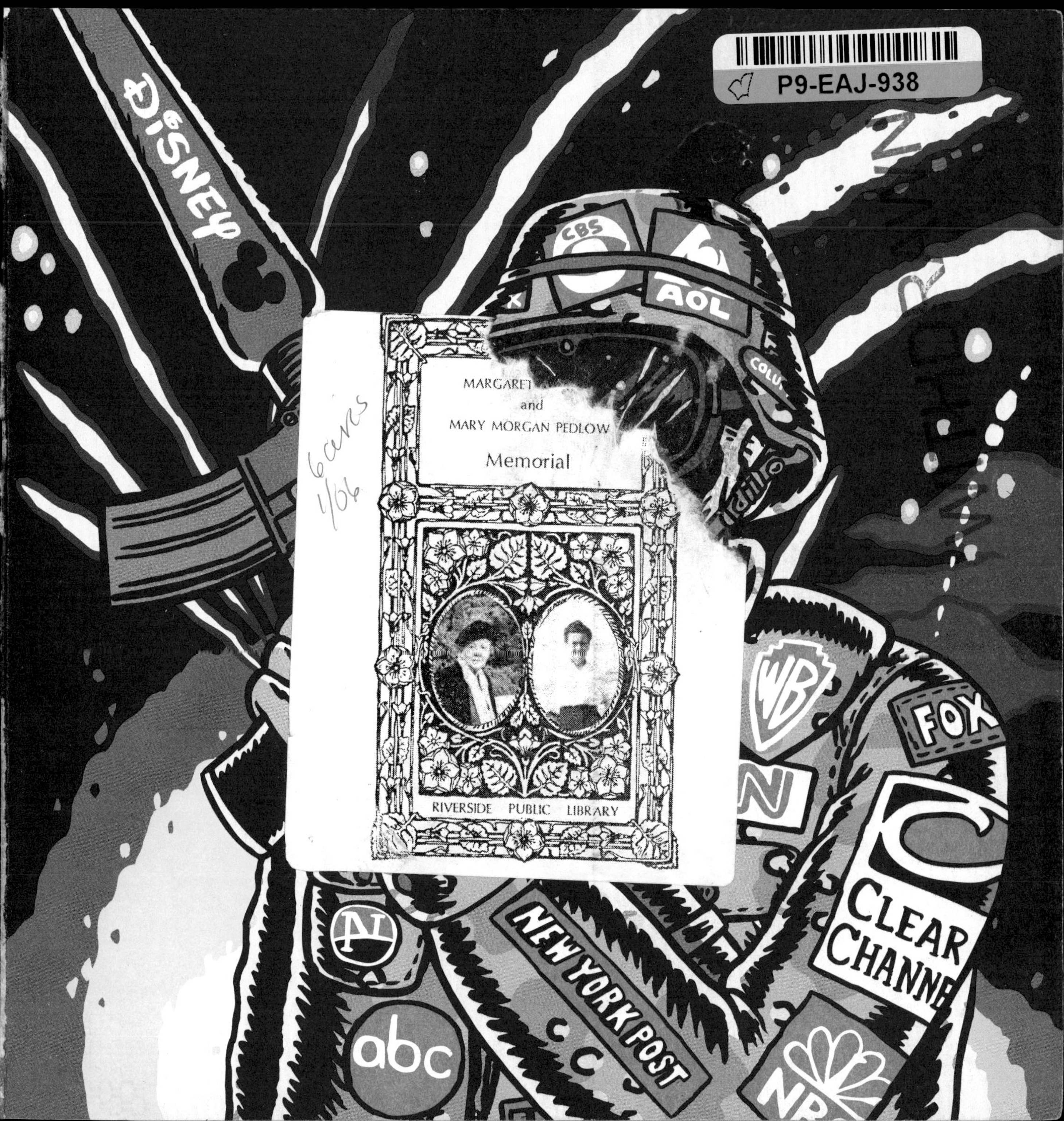
DISNEY
CBS
AOL
WB
FOX
CLEAR
CHANNE
NEW YORK POST
abc

VERY SPECIAL THANKS TO:

**Ted Keller**

and everyone at the *Village Voice*
for publishing my comic strip since 1998 with no restrictions, just unwavering support.

Greg, Ria, Crystal, Jon, Phoebe and everyone at Seven Stories Press
for your enthusiasm and hard work in publishing this book.

SPECIAL THANKS TO EVERYONE WHO HAS SUPPORTED MY CARTOONING OVER THE YEARS INCLUDING:

Nicholas Blechman and the *New York Times*; Maxine Davidowitz, Steve Reddicliffe and *TV Guide*; Peter Gorman, John Holmstrom and *High Times*; Charlie Cross, Stewart Williams and the *Rocket* where "Schlock 'n' Roll" began; Scott Gillespie, Beth Ewen and *Citybusiness*; Doug Tice, Glen Warchol, David Carr, Claude Peck, Marcia Wright Roepke and the *Twin Cities Reader* where I got my professional start; staff and friends from the *Manitou Messenger* and the *Zephyrus*; all the weekly papers that currently run "Sutton Impact" and the people who read it each week – THANK YOU!

EXTRA SPECIAL THANKS TO: Sue, Yineth, Mom and Dad, Mark, Lee, Jim, family and friends.



www.suttonimpactstudio.com

A Seven Stories Press First Edition



Seven Stories Press
140 Watts Street
New York, NY 10013
http://www.sevenstories.com

In Canada:
Publishers Group Canada, 250A Carlton Street, Toronto, ON M5A 2L1

In the U.K.:
Turnaround Publisher Services Ltd., Unit 3, Olympia Trading Estate, Coburg Road, Wood Green, London N22 6TZ

In Australia:
Palgrave Macmillan, 627 Chapel Street, South Yarra VIC 3141

Sutton, Ward.
Sutton impact : the political cartoons of Ward Sutton / Ward Sutton.-- A Seven Stories Press 1st ed.
p. cm.
ISBN-13: 978-1-58322-677-3 (alk. paper)
ISBN-10: 1-58322-677-X (alk. paper)
1. United States--Politics and government--2001---Caricatures and cartoons. 2. United States--Social conditions--1980---Caricatures and cartoons. 3. Editorial cartoons--New York (State)--New York. 4. American wit and humor, Pictorial. I. Title.

E902.S88 2005
741.5 973--dc22

2005045054

9 8 7 6 5 4 3 2 1

College professors may order examination copies of Seven Stories Press titles for a free six-month trial period. To order, visit www.sevenstories.com/textbook, or fax on school letterhead to (212) 226-1411.

Book design by Ward Sutton Printed in the USA

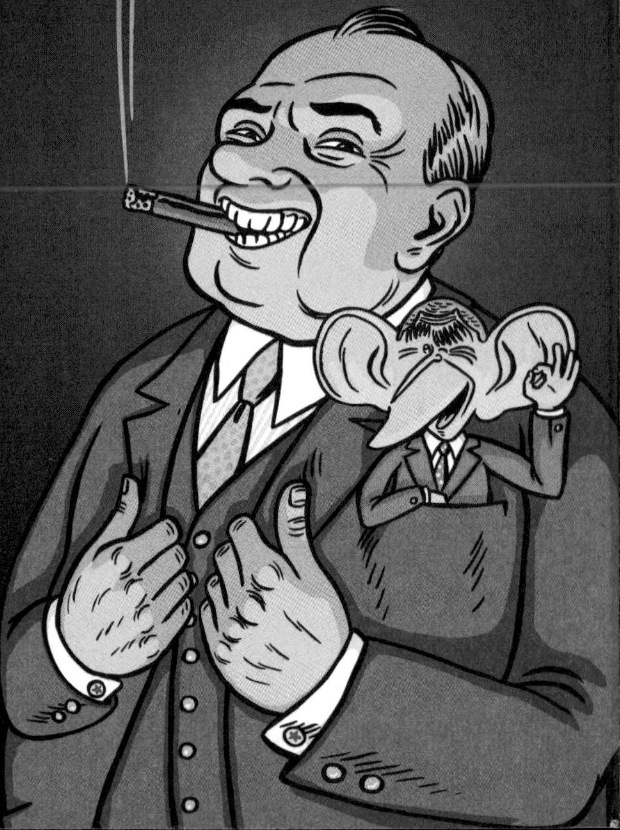

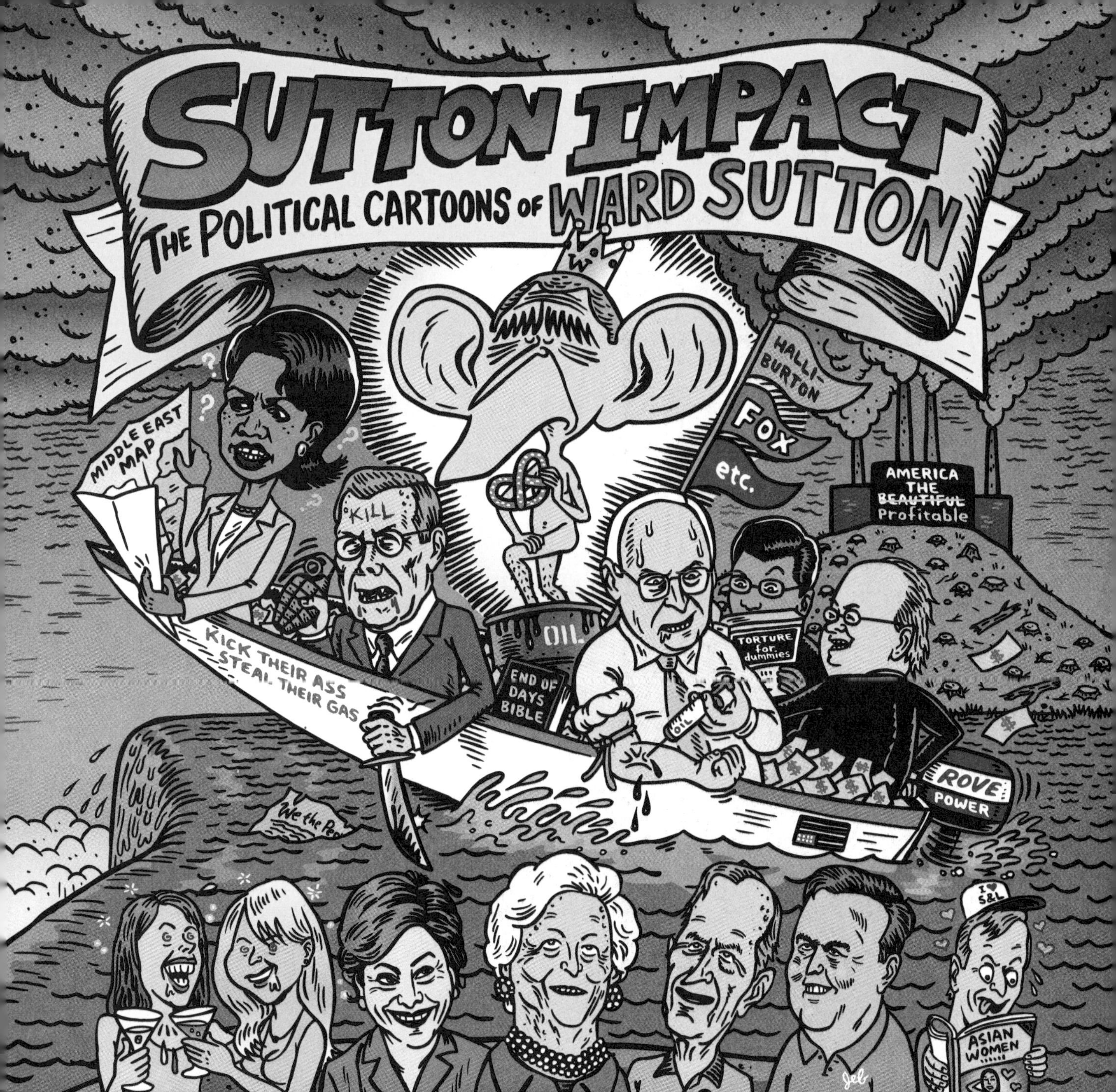
SUTTON IMPACT
THE POLITICAL CARTOONS OF WARD SUTTON
W
MIDDLE EAST MAP
KILL
HALLI-BURTON
FOX
etc.
AMERICA THE ~~BEAUTIFUL~~ Profitable
OIL
TORTURE for dummies
KICK THEIR ASS STEAL THEIR GAS
END OF DAYS BIBLE
OIL
ROVE POWER
We the Peo
I ♥ S&L
ASIAN WOMEN
Jeb

SEVEN STORIES PRESS • NEW YORK

Dedicated to the memory, the legacy, and the inspiration of

# Paul Wellstone

IT'S HARD TO IMAGINE AN ELECTION AS EXCITING AS THE 1990 MINNESOTA SENATE RACE BETWEEN OUTSIDER PAUL WELLSTONE, A PROUDLY LIBERAL COLLEGE PROFESSOR ...

... AND REPUBLICAN INCUMBENT RUDY BOSCHWITZ, AN EN-TRENCHED, TWO-TERM, MONEY-BAGS CONSERVATIVE.

KONK!

$

IT WAS A REAL DAVID-AND-GOLIATH MATCH.

WHEN BOSCHWITZ REFUSED TO DEBATE, WELLSTONE MADE A MICHAEL MOORE-STYLE AD TITLED, "WHERE'S RUDY?" IT WAS A HUGE, HILARIOUS HIT.

WHY WON'T RUDY RETURN MY CALLS?

BOSCHWIT CAMPAIGN OFFICE

!

HIS CAMPAIGN WAS OUTSPENT 7-1, YET WELLSTONE PULLED OFF AN AMAZING UPSET WIN. HE BEAT BOSCHWITZ IN '96, TOO.

WHEN HE WAS SWORN IN, HE HANDED VICE-PRESIDENT DAN QUAYLE A TAPE OF MINNESOTANS EXPRESSING OPPOSITION TO THE GULF WAR. MANY CALLED PAUL RUDE AND AN EMBARASSMENT.

???

TO DAN

I CALLED HIM A HERO.

JUST WEEKS BEFORE HIS TRAGIC DEATH IN A 2002 PLANE CRASH, PAUL VOTED AGAINST THE IRAQ WAR RESOLUTION. DESPITE HIS TOUGH RE-ELECTION BATTLE, HE VOTED HIS CONSCIENCE AS ALWAYS.

HE WASN'T PERFECT (NO ONE IS) BUT HE WAS PRINCIPLED.

HE WAS HONEST, SINCERE, AND A NICE GUY.

HERE'S TO YOU, PAUL.

1944-2002

"STAND UP, KEEP FIGHTING!"

## CONTENTS



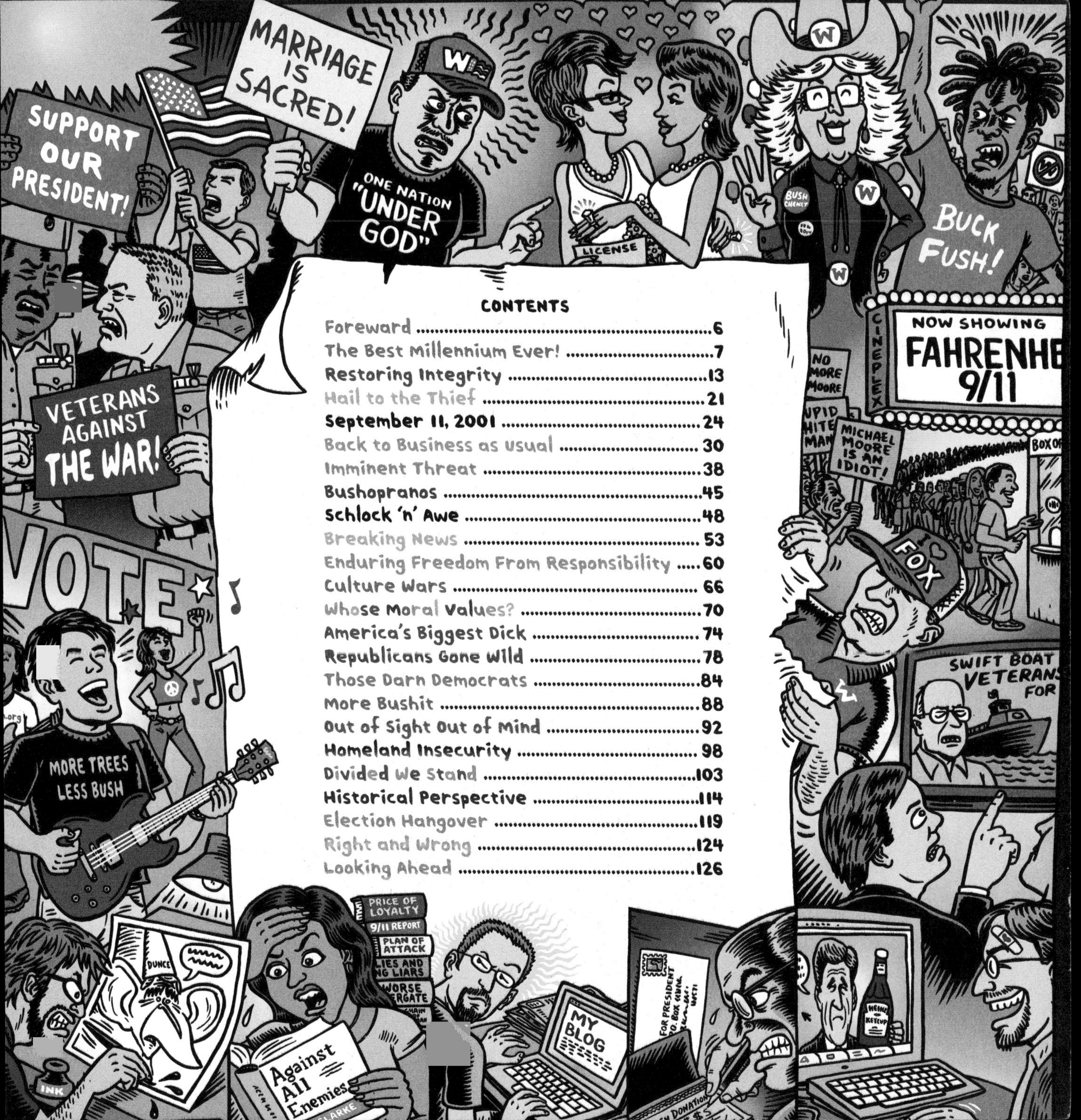

SUPPORT OUR PRESIDENT!
MARRIAGE IS SACRED!
ONE NATION "UNDER GOD"
LICENSE
BUSH CHENEY
BUCK FUSH!
NOW SHOWING
FAHRENHE
9/11
CINEPLEX
NO MORE MOORE
MICHAEL MOORE IS AN IDIOT!
VETERANS AGAINST THE WAR!
VOTE
FOX
SWIFT BOAT VETERANS FOR
MORE TREES LESS BUSH
PRICE OF LOYALTY
9/11 REPORT
PLAN OF ATTACK
DUNCE
INK
Against All Enemies
CLARKE
MY BLOG
FOR PRESIDENT

# Foreward

### (In a world going backwards)

"Nobody knows what kind of trouble we're in.
Nobody seems to think it all might happen again."
— Gram Parsons/The Byrds ("100 Years From Now")

You know those movies where only the main character knows about an impending danger? Something terrible is about to happen but no one will listen? It all seems so clear and obvious but for some reason the warning signs are invisible or being ignored? And for his/her efforts, the main character is branded a kook or a criminal?

It's 2005 and I feel like I'm in that movie. Maybe you do, too.

Back at college in the mid-1980s, I asked a bunch of friends at lunch one day whether they believed the United States as we knew it would still exist through the end of our lifetimes. Everyone said yes. Then I asked if they thought the United States would just simply last forever, or at least for as long as the earth and humans existed. People sort of shrugged with ambivalence and continued eating.

If the United States were to end, how would it occur? Would it be through aggression by an outside force? Or would it be an implosion from within? Another Civil War? Would the end come in a flash or slowly over time as a gradual degradation?

Back in college, this all seemed hypothetical. But the 2000 "election" gave me the sinking feeling that something was seriously wrong. Could the United States, as we know it, be fading away at this moment?

These days if you challenge the mainstream narrative broadcast by the media, you're labeled a conspiracy nut. I say if you believe their narrative you're a nut.

Pollution is "clear skies." Prejudice is a "moral value." War is "freedom." And if you try to use the word "Orwellian" (as John Kerry did in a Presidential debate) you get mocked for it (as he was on "Saturday Night Live").

As that wise man Mick Jagger once asked, "What can a poor boy do, except to sing for a rock'n'roll band?" Good question. I can't sing that well, though, so I draw cartoons instead. If our nation is going down the toilet, I want to spell out the truth. With drawings. And hopefully make people laugh.

This isn't a movie. I'm not alone. You're not alone. Thanks for reading.

## Ward

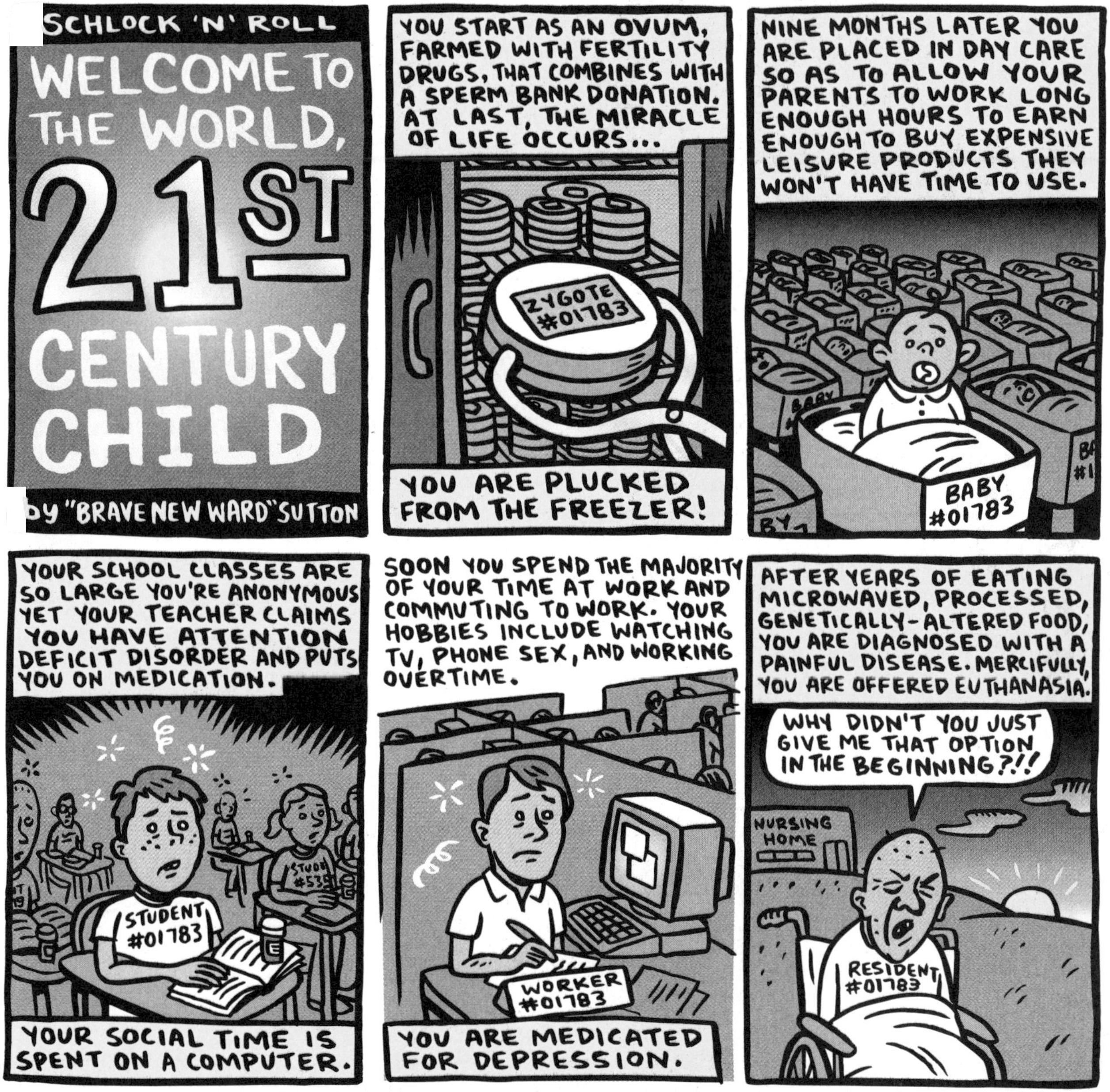
SCHLOCK 'N' ROLL
WELCOME TO THE WORLD, 21ST CENTURY CHILD
by "BRAVE NEW WARD" SUTTON
YOU START AS AN OVUM, FARMED WITH FERTILITY DRUGS, THAT COMBINES WITH A SPERM BANK DONATION. AT LAST, THE MIRACLE OF LIFE OCCURS...
ZYGOTE #01783
YOU ARE PLUCKED FROM THE FREEZER!
NINE MONTHS LATER YOU ARE PLACED IN DAY CARE SO AS TO ALLOW YOUR PARENTS TO WORK LONG ENOUGH HOURS TO EARN ENOUGH TO BUY EXPENSIVE LEISURE PRODUCTS THEY WON'T HAVE TIME TO USE.
BABY #01783
YOUR SCHOOL CLASSES ARE SO LARGE YOU'RE ANONYMOUS YET YOUR TEACHER CLAIMS YOU HAVE ATTENTION DEFICIT DISORDER AND PUTS YOU ON MEDICATION.
STUDENT #01783
YOUR SOCIAL TIME IS SPENT ON A COMPUTER.
SOON YOU SPEND THE MAJORITY OF YOUR TIME AT WORK AND COMMUTING TO WORK. YOUR HOBBIES INCLUDE WATCHING TV, PHONE SEX, AND WORKING OVERTIME.
WORKER #01783
YOU ARE MEDICATED FOR DEPRESSION.
AFTER YEARS OF EATING MICROWAVED, PROCESSED, GENETICALLY-ALTERED FOOD, YOU ARE DIAGNOSED WITH A PAINFUL DISEASE. MERCIFULLY, YOU ARE OFFERED EUTHANASIA.
WHY DIDN'T YOU JUST GIVE ME THAT OPTION IN THE BEGINNING?!!
NURSING HOME
RESIDENT #01783

When I was in grade school, we were constantly being asked to envision the year 2000 and all the progress that would be made in society by then. I foresaw all the different people of the world living in civilized harmony with a better understanding of what life is really all about. Imagine my embarrassment!

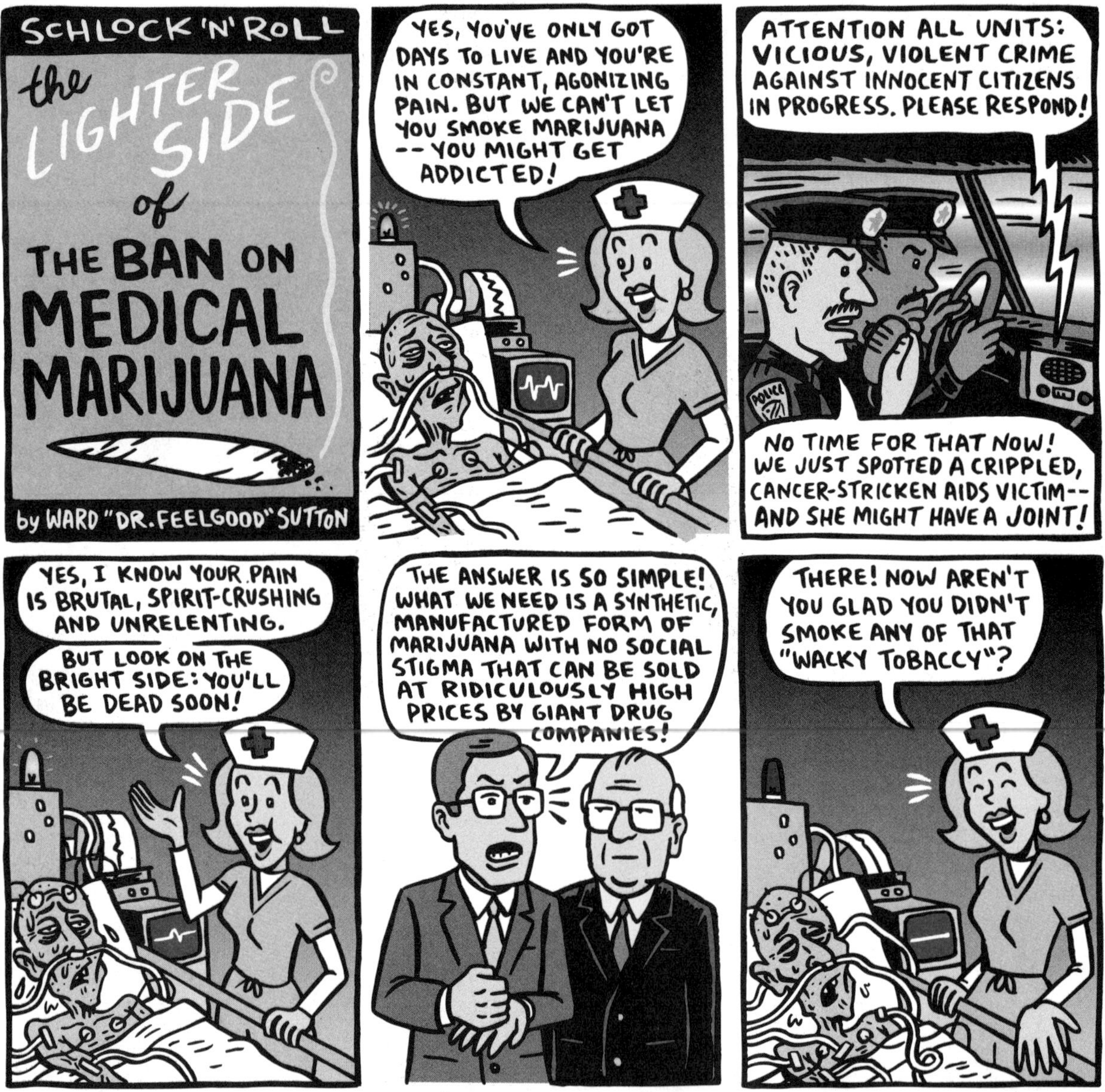
SCHLOCK 'N' ROLL
the LIGHTER SIDE of THE BAN ON MEDICAL MARIJUANA
by WARD "DR. FEELGOOD" SUTTON
YES, YOU'VE ONLY GOT DAYS TO LIVE AND YOU'RE IN CONSTANT, AGONIZING PAIN. BUT WE CAN'T LET YOU SMOKE MARIJUANA -- YOU MIGHT GET ADDICTED!
ATTENTION ALL UNITS: VICIOUS, VIOLENT CRIME AGAINST INNOCENT CITIZENS IN PROGRESS. PLEASE RESPOND!
POLICE
NO TIME FOR THAT NOW! WE JUST SPOTTED A CRIPPLED, CANCER-STRICKEN AIDS VICTIM-- AND SHE MIGHT HAVE A JOINT!
YES, I KNOW YOUR PAIN IS BRUTAL, SPIRIT-CRUSHING AND UNRELENTING.
BUT LOOK ON THE BRIGHT SIDE: YOU'LL BE DEAD SOON!
THE ANSWER IS SO SIMPLE! WHAT WE NEED IS A SYNTHETIC, MANUFACTURED FORM OF MARIJUANA WITH NO SOCIAL STIGMA THAT CAN BE SOLD AT RIDICULOUSLY HIGH PRICES BY GIANT DRUG COMPANIES!
THERE! NOW AREN'T YOU GLAD YOU DIDN'T SMOKE ANY OF THAT "WACKY TOBACCY"?

Throughout much of the 1990s, I was the cartoonist for *High Times* magazine. They have what must be one of the last non-smoke-free office spaces in the country. They were very supportive and I think working for them gave me a clear sense that in my cartoons I could really say **ANYTHING** I wanted to. But eventually I decided it was high time to move on from *High Times* because there are only so many times you can say, "Marijuana should be legal."

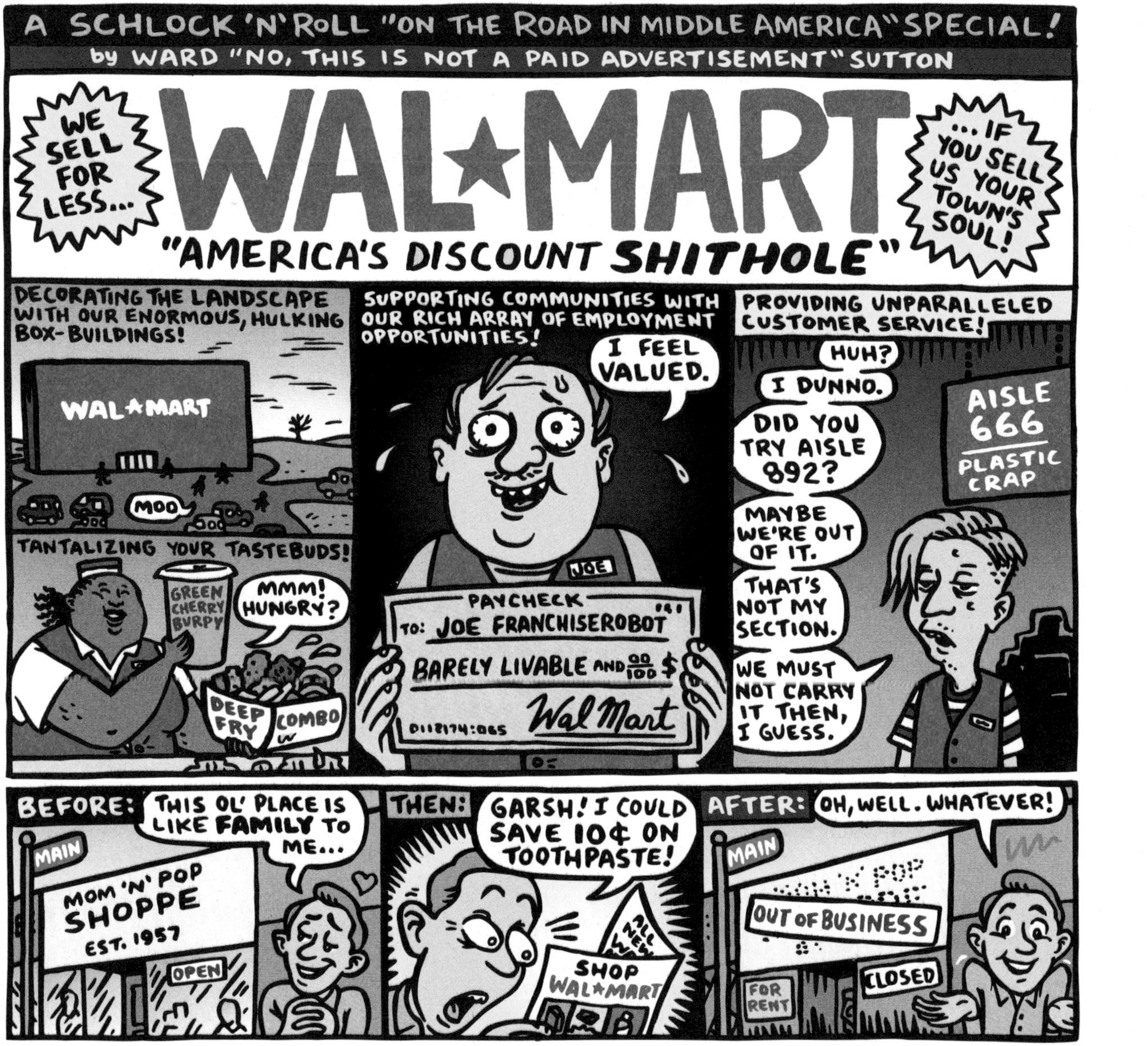
A SCHLOCK 'N' ROLL "ON THE ROAD IN MIDDLE AMERICA" SPECIAL!
by WARD "NO, THIS IS NOT A PAID ADVERTISEMENT" SUTTON
WE SELL FOR LESS...
WAL★MART
...IF YOU SELL US YOUR TOWN'S SOUL!
"AMERICA'S DISCOUNT SHITHOLE"
DECORATING THE LANDSCAPE WITH OUR ENORMOUS, HULKING BOX-BUILDINGS!
WAL★MART
MOO
TANTALIZING YOUR TASTEBUDS!
GREEN CHERRY BURPY
MMM! HUNGRY?
DEEP FRY
COMBO
SUPPORTING COMMUNITIES WITH OUR RICH ARRAY OF EMPLOYMENT OPPORTUNITIES!
I FEEL VALUED.
JOE
PAYCHECK
TO: JOE FRANCHISEROBOT
BARELY LIVABLE AND 00/100 $
Wal Mart
0118174:065
PROVIDING UNPARALLELED CUSTOMER SERVICE!
HUH?
I DUNNO.
DID YOU TRY AISLE 892?
MAYBE WE'RE OUT OF IT.
THAT'S NOT MY SECTION.
WE MUST NOT CARRY IT THEN, I GUESS.
AISLE 666
PLASTIC CRAP
BEFORE:
THIS OL' PLACE IS LIKE FAMILY TO ME...
MAIN
MOM 'N' POP SHOPPE
EST. 1957
OPEN
THEN:
GARSH! I COULD SAVE 10¢ ON TOOTHPASTE!
SHOP WAL★MART
AFTER:
OH, WELL. WHATEVER!
MAIN
OUT OF BUSINESS
CLOSED
FOR RENT

I visited a good friend of mine who is a pastor in a small town in Minnesota. A new Wal Mart had opened there and, predictably, a number of smaller stores owned and run by people in the community had to shut down. When the community had it's annual summer parade, Wal Mart drove a huge semi-truck down the route in lieu of a float and threw candy out the back. As the former small business owners (now out of work) looked on, their kids scrambled to pick up the pieces of candy falling on the pavement.

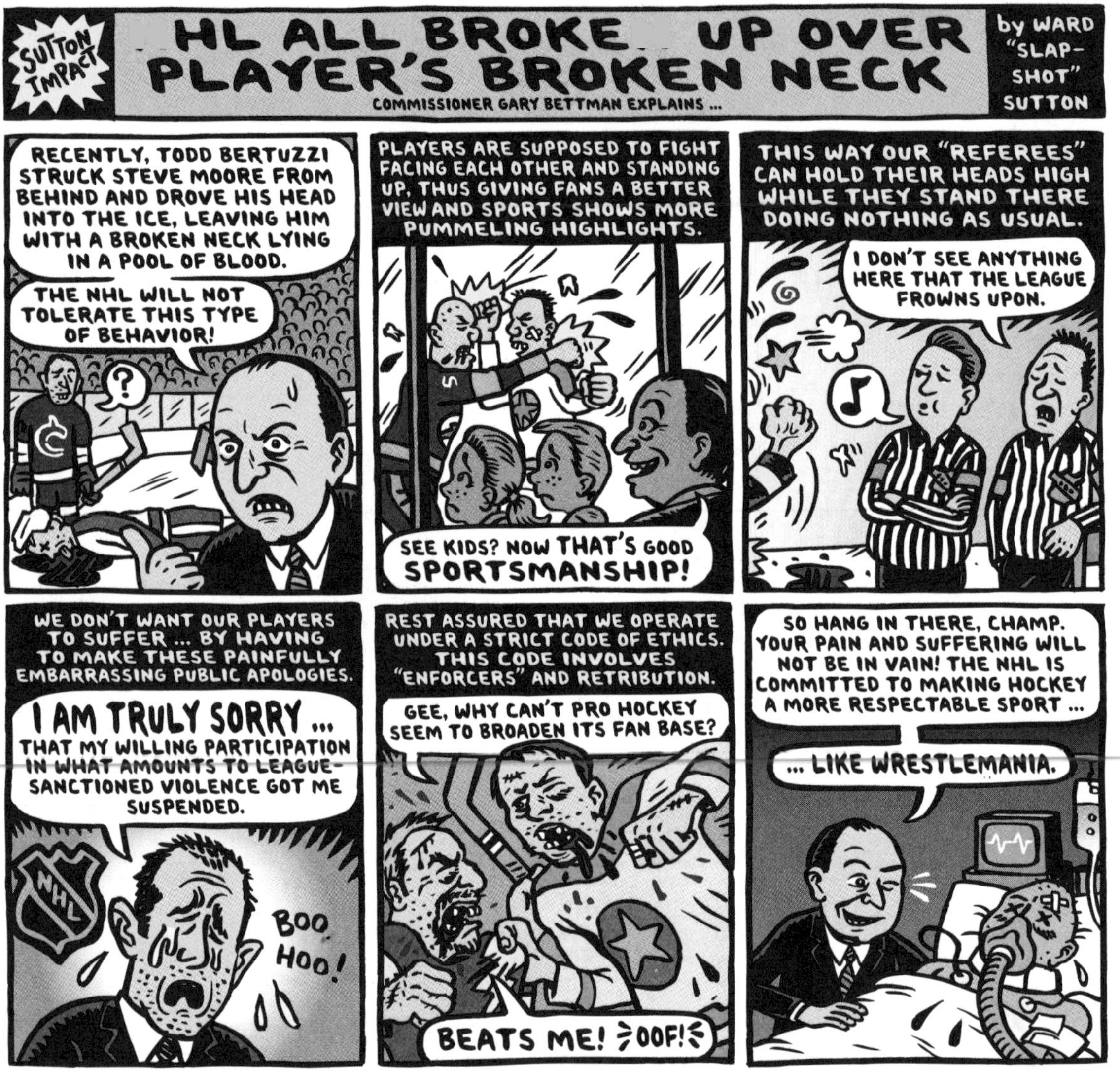
SUTTON IMPACT
HL ALL BROKE UP OVER PLAYER'S BROKEN NECK
COMMISSIONER GARY BETTMAN EXPLAINS ...
by WARD "SLAP-SHOT" SUTTON
RECENTLY, TODD BERTUZZI STRUCK STEVE MOORE FROM BEHIND AND DROVE HIS HEAD INTO THE ICE, LEAVING HIM WITH A BROKEN NECK LYING IN A POOL OF BLOOD.
THE NHL WILL NOT TOLERATE THIS TYPE OF BEHAVIOR!
?
PLAYERS ARE SUPPOSED TO FIGHT FACING EACH OTHER AND STANDING UP, THUS GIVING FANS A BETTER VIEW AND SPORTS SHOWS MORE PUMMELING HIGHLIGHTS.
SEE KIDS? NOW THAT'S GOOD SPORTSMANSHIP!
THIS WAY OUR "REFEREES" CAN HOLD THEIR HEADS HIGH WHILE THEY STAND THERE DOING NOTHING AS USUAL.
I DON'T SEE ANYTHING HERE THAT THE LEAGUE FROWNS UPON.
WE DON'T WANT OUR PLAYERS TO SUFFER ... BY HAVING TO MAKE THESE PAINFULLY EMBARRASSING PUBLIC APOLOGIES.
I AM TRULY SORRY ... THAT MY WILLING PARTICIPATION IN WHAT AMOUNTS TO LEAGUE-SANCTIONED VIOLENCE GOT ME SUSPENDED.
NHL
BOO HOO!
REST ASSURED THAT WE OPERATE UNDER A STRICT CODE OF ETHICS. THIS CODE INVOLVES "ENFORCERS" AND RETRIBUTION.
GEE, WHY CAN'T PRO HOCKEY SEEM TO BROADEN ITS FAN BASE?
BEATS ME! OOF!
SO HANG IN THERE, CHAMP. YOUR PAIN AND SUFFERING WILL NOT BE IN VAIN! THE NHL IS COMMITTED TO MAKING HOCKEY A MORE RESPECTABLE SPORT ...
... LIKE WRESTLEMANIA.

As a kid, I saw a made-for-TV movie about a pro hockey player who died on the ice after being beaten by another player. It freaked me out, but the film's tidy ending led me to believe that this kind of incident was a thing of the past. Soon after, when a friend invited me along to an NHL game, I was shocked by how the crowd would rise to their feet like a mob and cheer on any kind of fight (or boo if a player refused to fight). Even my friend's dad was going along with this. Years later, I followed high school hockey where there are actual rules against fighting and the skill of the players really shines -- it's compelling to watch. I sometimes wonder if any of those guys from high school are now in the NHL, obligated to perform like a bunch of roosters in a cock fight, attacking each other for the crowd's entertainment.

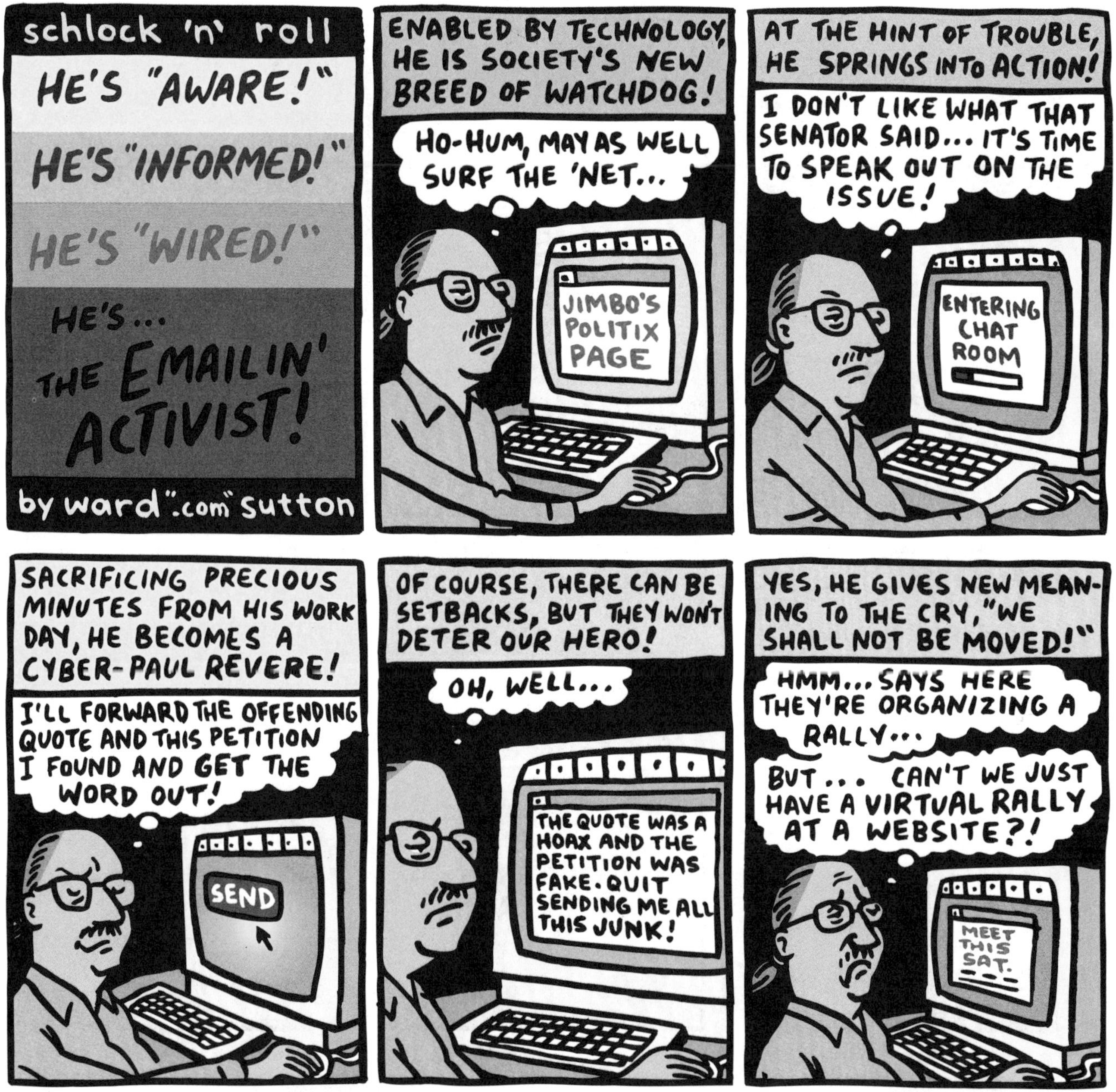
schlock 'n' roll
HE'S "AWARE!"
HE'S "INFORMED!"
HE'S "WIRED!"
HE'S... THE EMAILIN' ACTIVIST!
by ward ".com" sutton
ENABLED BY TECHNOLOGY, HE IS SOCIETY'S NEW BREED OF WATCHDOG!
HO-HUM, MAY AS WELL SURF THE 'NET...
JIMBO'S POLITIX PAGE
AT THE HINT OF TROUBLE, HE SPRINGS INTO ACTION!
I DON'T LIKE WHAT THAT SENATOR SAID... IT'S TIME TO SPEAK OUT ON THE ISSUE!
ENTERING CHAT ROOM
SACRIFICING PRECIOUS MINUTES FROM HIS WORK DAY, HE BECOMES A CYBER-PAUL REVERE!
I'LL FORWARD THE OFFENDING QUOTE AND THIS PETITION I FOUND AND GET THE WORD OUT!
SEND
OF COURSE, THERE CAN BE SETBACKS, BUT THEY WON'T DETER OUR HERO!
OH, WELL...
THE QUOTE WAS A HOAX AND THE PETITION WAS FAKE. QUIT SENDING ME ALL THIS JUNK!
YES, HE GIVES NEW MEANING TO THE CRY, "WE SHALL NOT BE MOVED!"
HMM... SAYS HERE THEY'RE ORGANIZING A RALLY...
BUT... CAN'T WE JUST HAVE A VIRTUAL RALLY AT A WEBSITE?!
MEET THIS SAT.

The internet gets a lot of credit for getting people more involved in the political process. But it also deserves credit for making people FEEL like they're more involved in the political process.

Schlock 'n' Roll

HE CAPTURED OUR HEARTS WITH *THE GREATEST GENERATION, THE GREATEST GENERATION SPEAKS,* AND *AN ALBUM OF MEMORIES... FROM THE GREATEST GENERATION.*

NOW ENJOY THESE NEW BOOKS FROM

TOM BROKAW

by WARD "ANCHOR AWAY!" SUTTON

"In Our Day, Women and Coloreds knew their place and shut up about it."

A Portfolio of the Thoughtful Reflections of the Greatest Generation

by Tom Brokaw

From Saving the Free World from the Krauts and the Japs to Setting the VCR to tape *Murder She Wrote*

A Chronicle of Achievement of the GREATEST GENERATION by Tom Brokaw

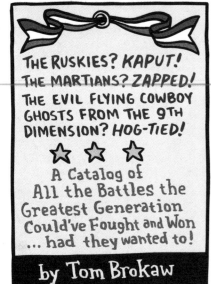

THE RUSKIES? *KAPUT!* THE MARTIANS? *ZAPPED!* THE EVIL FLYING COWBOY GHOSTS FROM THE 9TH DIMENSION? *HOG-TIED!*

A Catalog of All the Battles the Greatest Generation Could've Fought and Won ... had they wanted to!

by Tom Brokaw

If I Close My Eyes, I Can Imagine I'm one of Them

My Greatest Generation MASTURBATION FANTASIES by Tom Brokaw

"After all they've done for us, let's Ruin the National Mall in their Honor."

So what if it's ill-conceived? It's the Greatest Generation WWII Memorial

by Tom Brokaw
FOREWORD BY TOM HANKS

The anointing of sainthood on the "Silent Generation," transforming them into the "Greatest Generation" (as well-intentioned as some of it may have been), seemed merely misguided, simplistic and annoying at the time. In retrospect, I believe it laid the groundwork for redirecting public opinion in a tragically regressive direction. (see the following page ...)

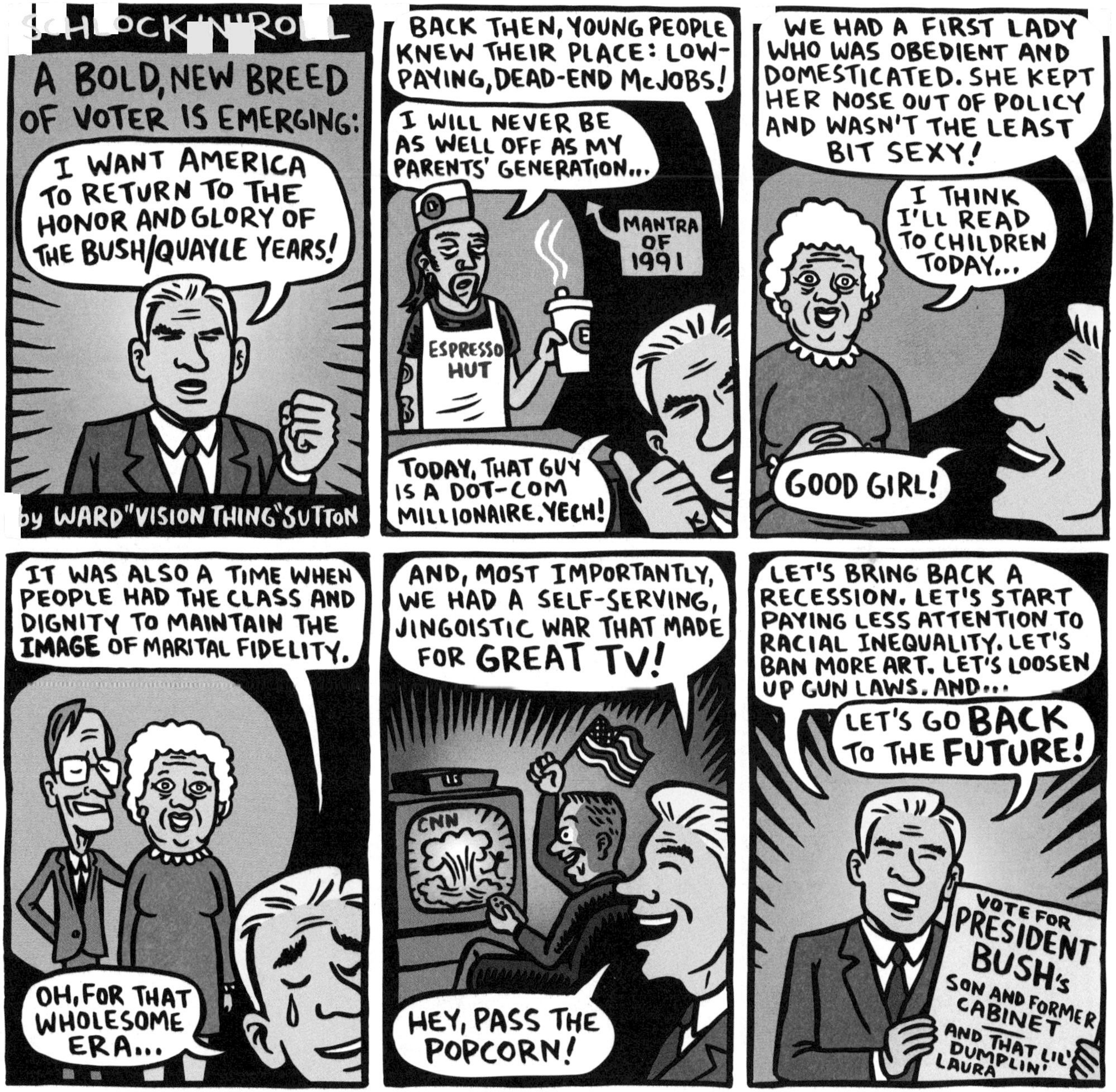
SCHLOCK'N'ROLL
A BOLD, NEW BREED OF VOTER IS EMERGING:
I WANT AMERICA TO RETURN TO THE HONOR AND GLORY OF THE BUSH/QUAYLE YEARS!
by WARD "VISION THING" SUTTON
BACK THEN, YOUNG PEOPLE KNEW THEIR PLACE: LOW-PAYING, DEAD-END McJOBS!
I WILL NEVER BE AS WELL OFF AS MY PARENTS' GENERATION...
MANTRA OF 1991
ESPRESSO HUT
TODAY, THAT GUY IS A DOT-COM MILLIONAIRE. YECH!
WE HAD A FIRST LADY WHO WAS OBEDIENT AND DOMESTICATED. SHE KEPT HER NOSE OUT OF POLICY AND WASN'T THE LEAST BIT SEXY!
I THINK I'LL READ TO CHILDREN TODAY...
GOOD GIRL!
IT WAS ALSO A TIME WHEN PEOPLE HAD THE CLASS AND DIGNITY TO MAINTAIN THE IMAGE OF MARITAL FIDELITY.
OH, FOR THAT WHOLESOME ERA...
AND, MOST IMPORTANTLY, WE HAD A SELF-SERVING, JINGOISTIC WAR THAT MADE FOR GREAT TV!
CNN
HEY, PASS THE POPCORN!
LET'S BRING BACK A RECESSION. LET'S START PAYING LESS ATTENTION TO RACIAL INEQUALITY. LET'S BAN MORE ART. LET'S LOOSEN UP GUN LAWS. AND...
LET'S GO BACK TO THE FUTURE!
VOTE FOR PRESIDENT BUSH's SON AND FORMER CABINET AND THAT LIL' DUMPLIN' LAURA

I remain shocked by the way the public seems to have forgotten what a lousy president George H. W. Bush was. Maybe it's because he was such a dull guy that people lost interest in thinking about him critically after he got his ass trounced by Clinton in 1992.

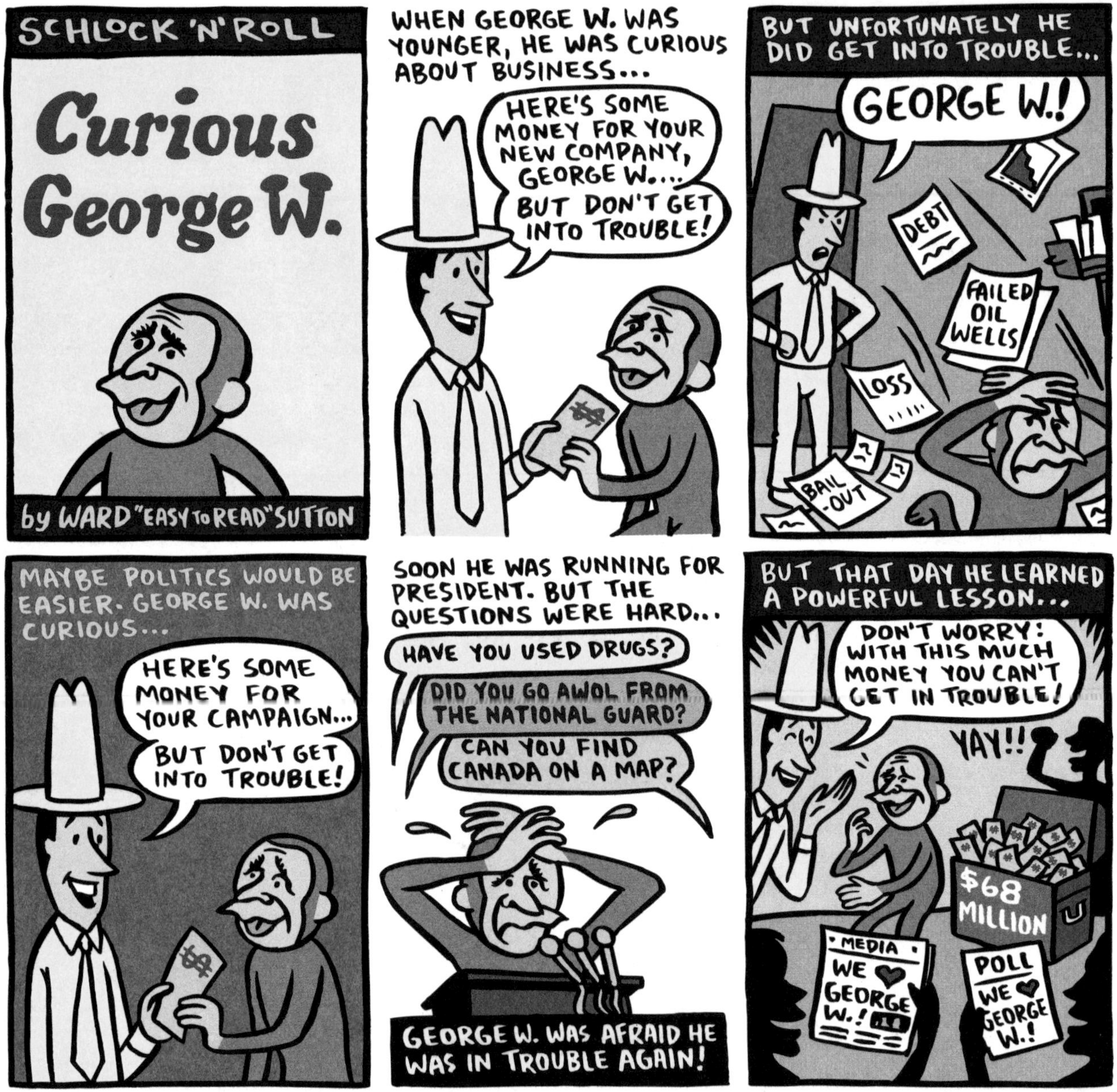
SCHLOCK 'N' ROLL
Curious George W.
by WARD "EASY TO READ" SUTTON
WHEN GEORGE W. WAS YOUNGER, HE WAS CURIOUS ABOUT BUSINESS...
HERE'S SOME MONEY FOR YOUR NEW COMPANY, GEORGE W....
BUT DON'T GET INTO TROUBLE!
BUT UNFORTUNATELY HE DID GET INTO TROUBLE...
GEORGE W.!
DEBT
FAILED OIL WELLS
LOSS
BAIL-OUT
MAYBE POLITICS WOULD BE EASIER. GEORGE W. WAS CURIOUS...
HERE'S SOME MONEY FOR YOUR CAMPAIGN...
BUT DON'T GET INTO TROUBLE!
SOON HE WAS RUNNING FOR PRESIDENT. BUT THE QUESTIONS WERE HARD...
HAVE YOU USED DRUGS?
DID YOU GO AWOL FROM THE NATIONAL GUARD?
CAN YOU FIND CANADA ON A MAP?
GEORGE W. WAS AFRAID HE WAS IN TROUBLE AGAIN!
BUT THAT DAY HE LEARNED A POWERFUL LESSON...
DON'T WORRY: WITH THIS MUCH MONEY YOU CAN'T GET IN TROUBLE!
YAY!!
$68 MILLION
MEDIA
WE ♥ GEORGE W.!
POLL
WE ♥ GEORGE W.!

In the spring of 1999, I was in Austin, Texas. A cab driver took me past the state capitol and bragged that their governor "just might become our next president."
"What an idiot," I thought, repressing that awful feeling I had that he might be right.

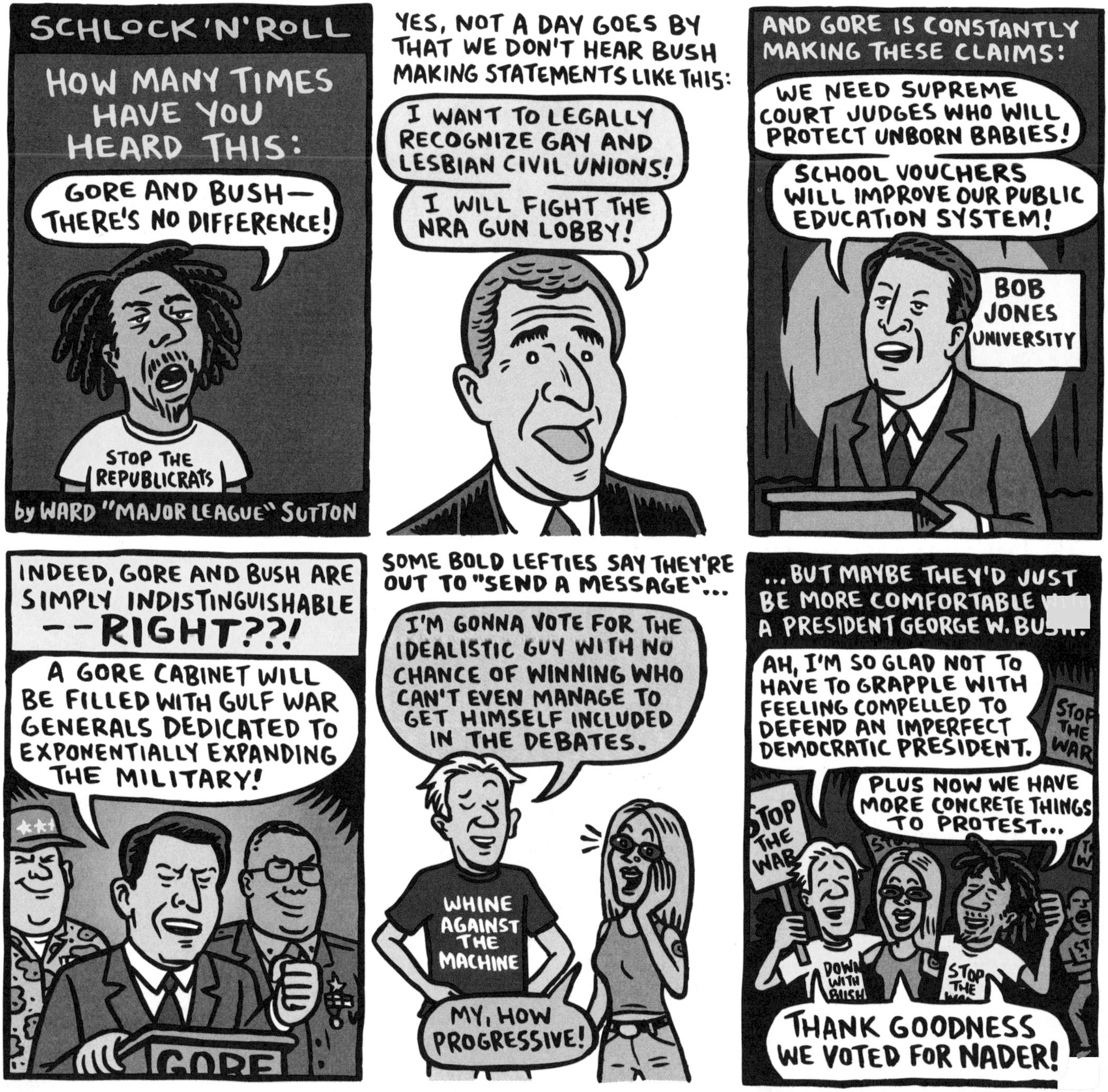
SCHLOCK'N'ROLL
HOW MANY TIMES HAVE YOU HEARD THIS:
GORE AND BUSH— THERE'S NO DIFFERENCE!
STOP THE REPUBLICRATS
by WARD "MAJOR LEAGUE" SUTTON
YES, NOT A DAY GOES BY THAT WE DON'T HEAR BUSH MAKING STATEMENTS LIKE THIS:
I WANT TO LEGALLY RECOGNIZE GAY AND LESBIAN CIVIL UNIONS!
I WILL FIGHT THE NRA GUN LOBBY!
AND GORE IS CONSTANTLY MAKING THESE CLAIMS:
WE NEED SUPREME COURT JUDGES WHO WILL PROTECT UNBORN BABIES!
SCHOOL VOUCHERS WILL IMPROVE OUR PUBLIC EDUCATION SYSTEM!
BOB JONES UNIVERSITY
INDEED, GORE AND BUSH ARE SIMPLY INDISTINGUISHABLE --RIGHT??!
A GORE CABINET WILL BE FILLED WITH GULF WAR GENERALS DEDICATED TO EXPONENTIALLY EXPANDING THE MILITARY!
GORE
SOME BOLD LEFTIES SAY THEY'RE OUT TO "SEND A MESSAGE"...
I'M GONNA VOTE FOR THE IDEALISTIC GUY WITH NO CHANCE OF WINNING WHO CAN'T EVEN MANAGE TO GET HIMSELF INCLUDED IN THE DEBATES.
WHINE AGAINST THE MACHINE
MY, HOW PROGRESSIVE!
...BUT MAYBE THEY'D JUST BE MORE COMFORTABLE
A PRESIDENT GEORGE W. BU
AH, I'M SO GLAD NOT TO HAVE TO GRAPPLE WITH FEELING COMPELLED TO DEFEND AN IMPERFECT DEMOCRATIC PRESIDENT.
STOP THE WAR
PLUS NOW WE HAVE MORE CONCRETE THINGS TO PROTEST...
STOP THE WAR
DOWN WITH BUSH
THANK GOODNESS WE VOTED FOR NADER!

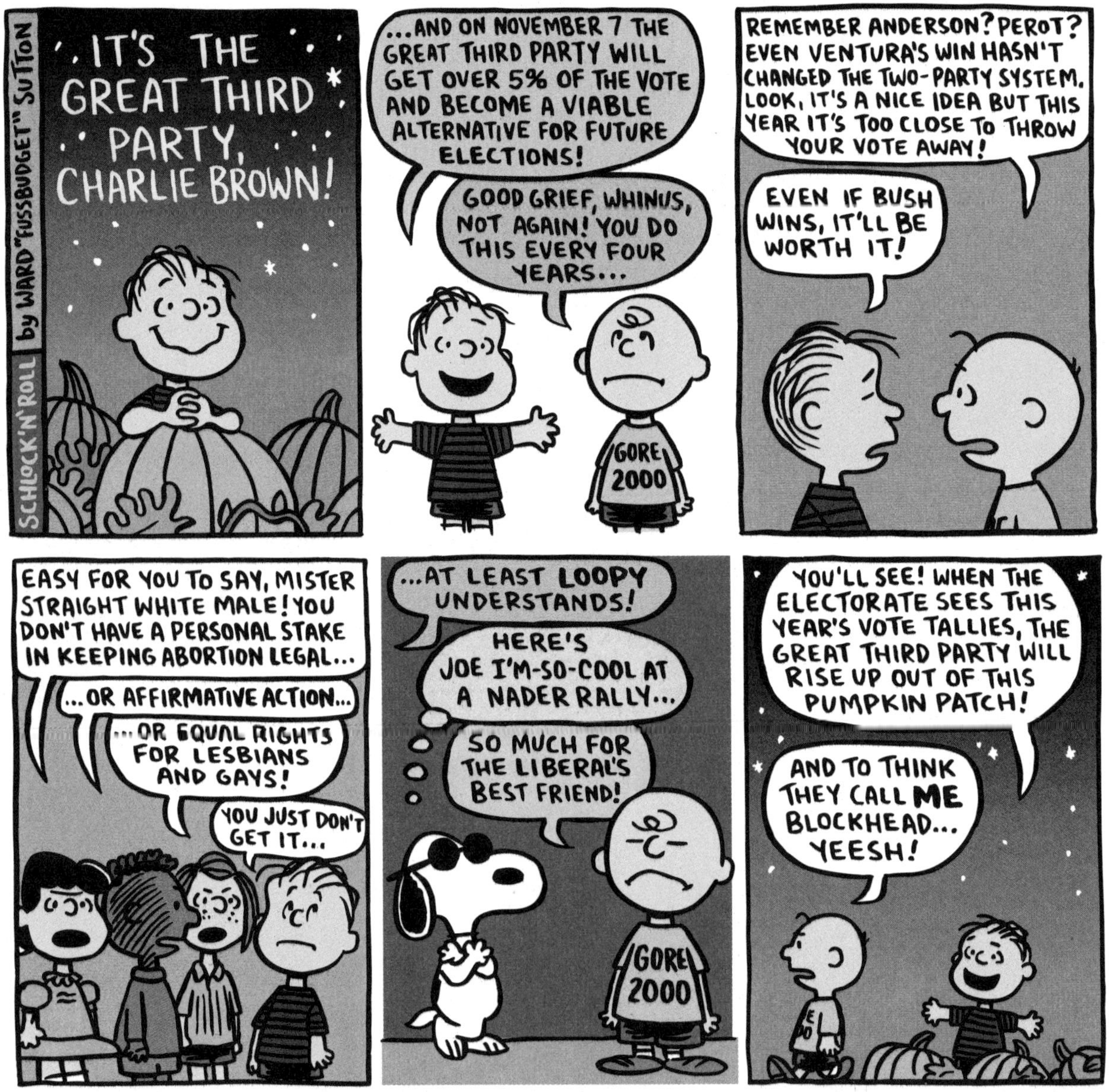
SCHLOCK'N'ROLL by WARD "FUSSBUDGET" SUTTON
IT'S THE GREAT THIRD PARTY, CHARLIE BROWN!
...AND ON NOVEMBER 7 THE GREAT THIRD PARTY WILL GET OVER 5% OF THE VOTE AND BECOME A VIABLE ALTERNATIVE FOR FUTURE ELECTIONS!
GOOD GRIEF, WHINUS, NOT AGAIN! YOU DO THIS EVERY FOUR YEARS...
GORE 2000
REMEMBER ANDERSON? PEROT? EVEN VENTURA'S WIN HASN'T CHANGED THE TWO-PARTY SYSTEM. LOOK, IT'S A NICE IDEA BUT THIS YEAR IT'S TOO CLOSE TO THROW YOUR VOTE AWAY!
EVEN IF BUSH WINS, IT'LL BE WORTH IT!
EASY FOR YOU TO SAY, MISTER STRAIGHT WHITE MALE! YOU DON'T HAVE A PERSONAL STAKE IN KEEPING ABORTION LEGAL...
...OR AFFIRMATIVE ACTION...
...OR EQUAL RIGHTS FOR LESBIANS AND GAYS!
YOU JUST DON'T GET IT...
...AT LEAST LOOPY UNDERSTANDS!
HERE'S JOE I'M-SO-COOL AT A NADER RALLY...
SO MUCH FOR THE LIBERAL'S BEST FRIEND!
GORE 2000
YOU'LL SEE! WHEN THE ELECTORATE SEES THIS YEAR'S VOTE TALLIES, THE GREAT THIRD PARTY WILL RISE UP OUT OF THIS PUMPKIN PATCH!
AND TO THINK THEY CALL ME BLOCKHEAD... YEESH!

On election night 2000, I was part of a performance where cartoonists projected their work and read it aloud. I had some people help me with the voices, including my brother, who was a Nader supporter. When we got to the above tip-of-the-hat to Charles Schulz, my brother pulled off his sweater to reveal a Nader T-shirt and proclaimed, with a smile and a wink, that he would not be participating in reading this one. Everyone laughed – the crowd loved it. The night was fun ... until everything went to hell, that is.

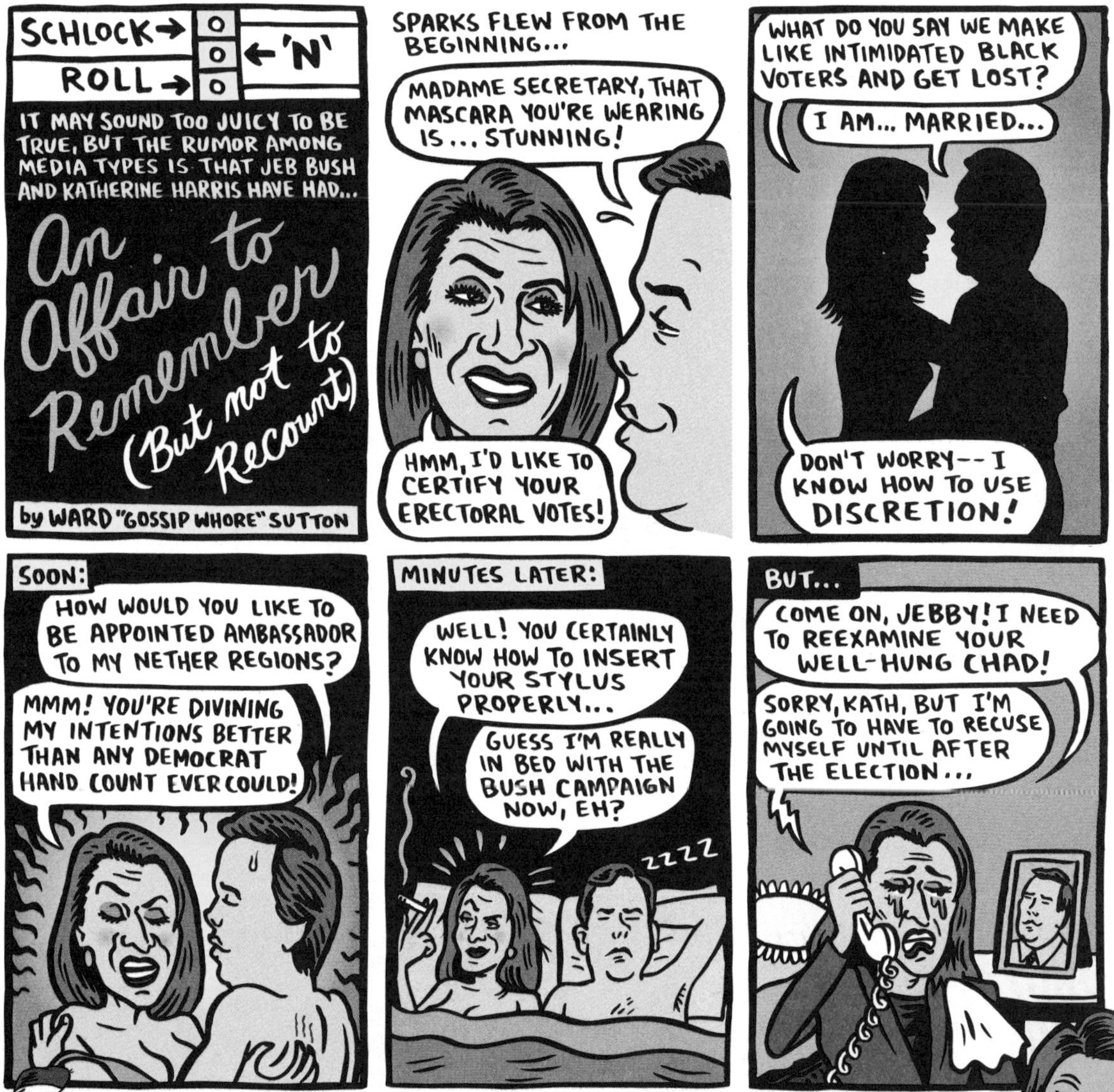
SCHLOCK → 'N' ← ROLL →
IT MAY SOUND TOO JUICY TO BE TRUE, BUT THE RUMOR AMONG MEDIA TYPES IS THAT JEB BUSH AND KATHERINE HARRIS HAVE HAD...
An Affair to Remember (But not to Recount)
by WARD "GOSSIP WHORE" SUTTON
SPARKS FLEW FROM THE BEGINNING...
MADAME SECRETARY, THAT MASCARA YOU'RE WEARING IS... STUNNING!
HMM, I'D LIKE TO CERTIFY YOUR ERECTORAL VOTES!
WHAT DO YOU SAY WE MAKE LIKE INTIMIDATED BLACK VOTERS AND GET LOST?
I AM... MARRIED...
DON'T WORRY-- I KNOW HOW TO USE DISCRETION!
SOON:
HOW WOULD YOU LIKE TO BE APPOINTED AMBASSADOR TO MY NETHER REGIONS?
MMM! YOU'RE DIVINING MY INTENTIONS BETTER THAN ANY DEMOCRAT HAND COUNT EVER COULD!
MINUTES LATER:
WELL! YOU CERTAINLY KNOW HOW TO INSERT YOUR STYLUS PROPERLY...
GUESS I'M REALLY IN BED WITH THE BUSH CAMPAIGN NOW, EH?
ZZZZ
BUT...
COME ON, JEBBY! I NEED TO REEXAMINE YOUR WELL-HUNG CHAD!
SORRY, KATH, BUT I'M GOING TO HAVE TO RECUSE MYSELF UNTIL AFTER THE ELECTION...

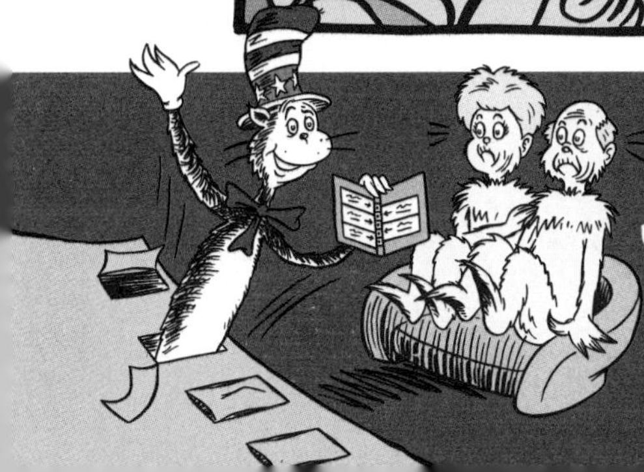

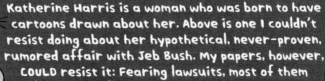

Katherine Harris is a woman who was born to have cartoons drawn about her. Above is one I couldn't resist doing about her hypothetical, never-proven, rumored affair with Jeb Bush. My papers, however, COULD resist it: Fearing lawsuits, most of them declined to publish this one. At right is Katherine as the Grinch, part of *TV Guide's* "Cat in the Chad" parody I was hired to illustrate.

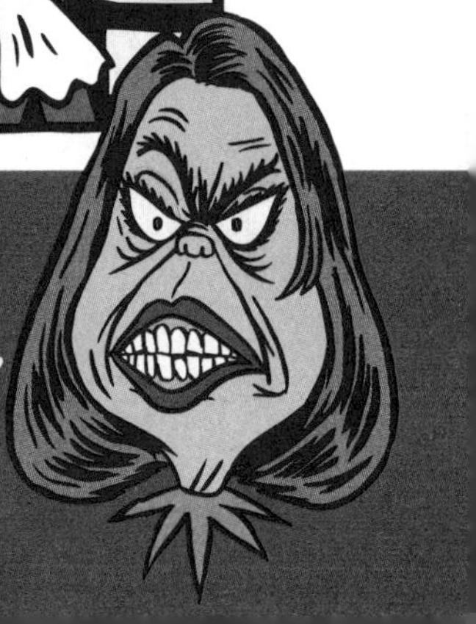

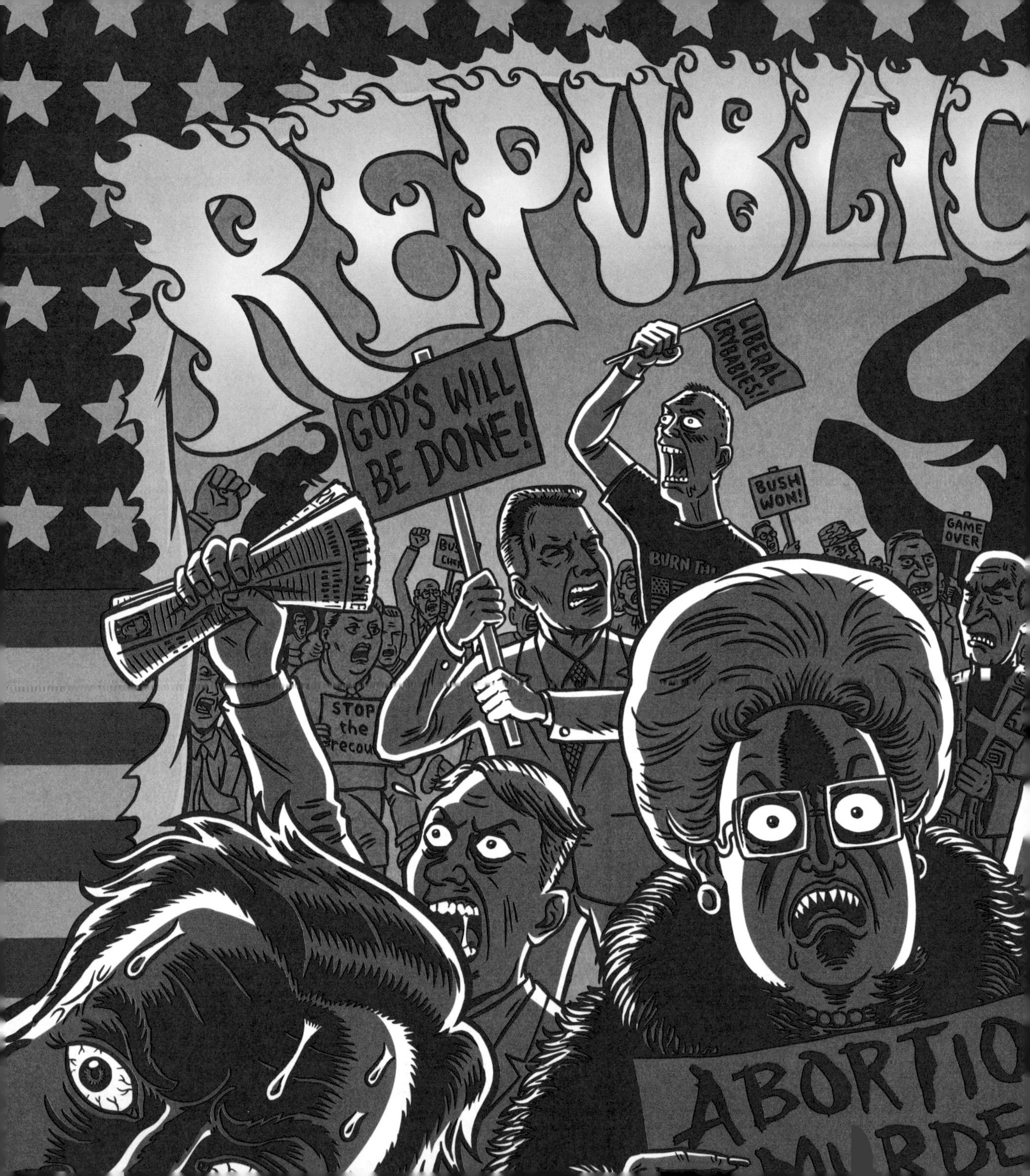
REPUBLIC
GOD'S WILL BE DONE!
LIBERAL CRYBABIES!
BUSH WON!
GAME OVER
STOP the

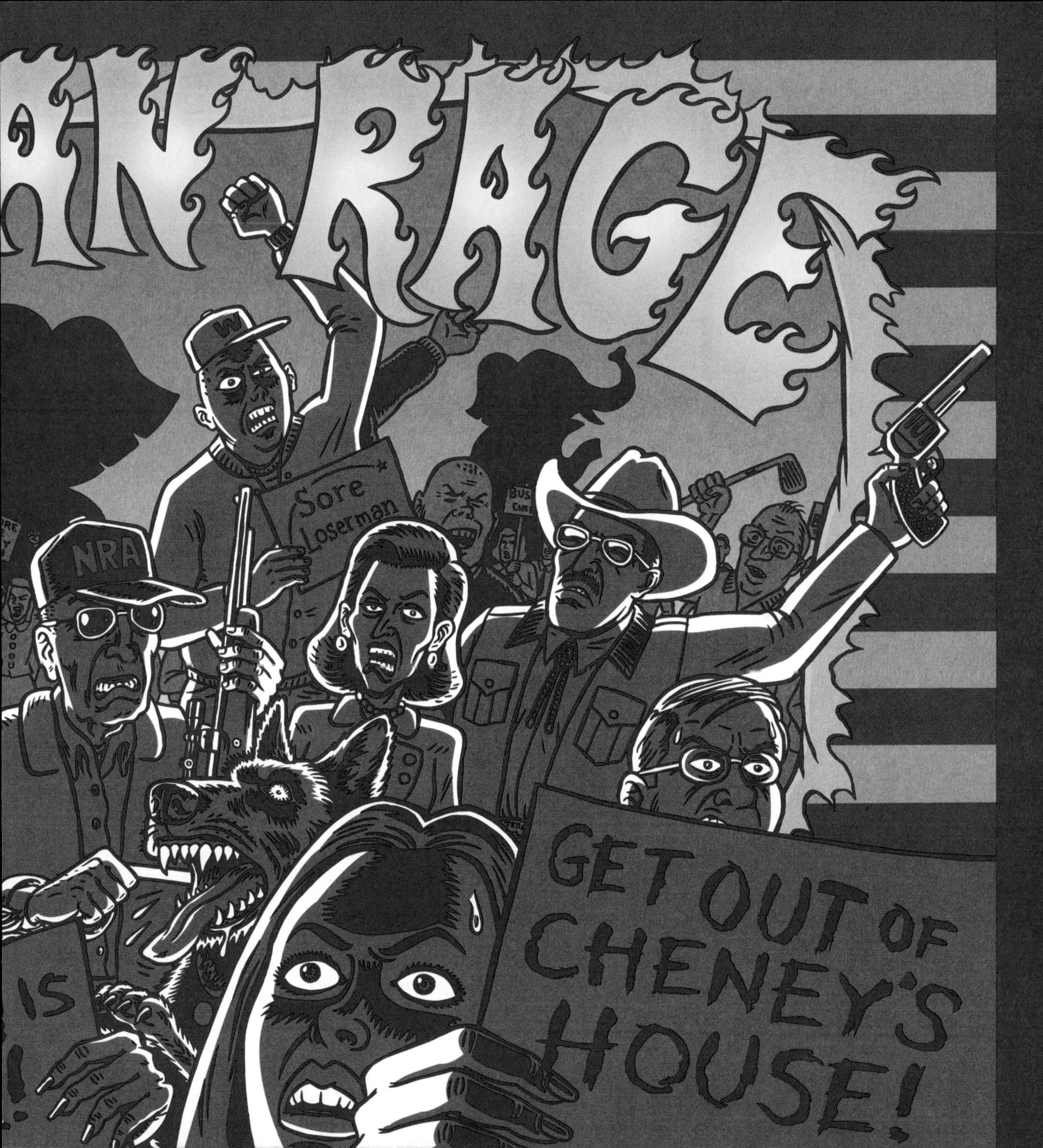
NRA
Sore Loserman
GET OUT OF CHENEY'S HOUSE!
IS

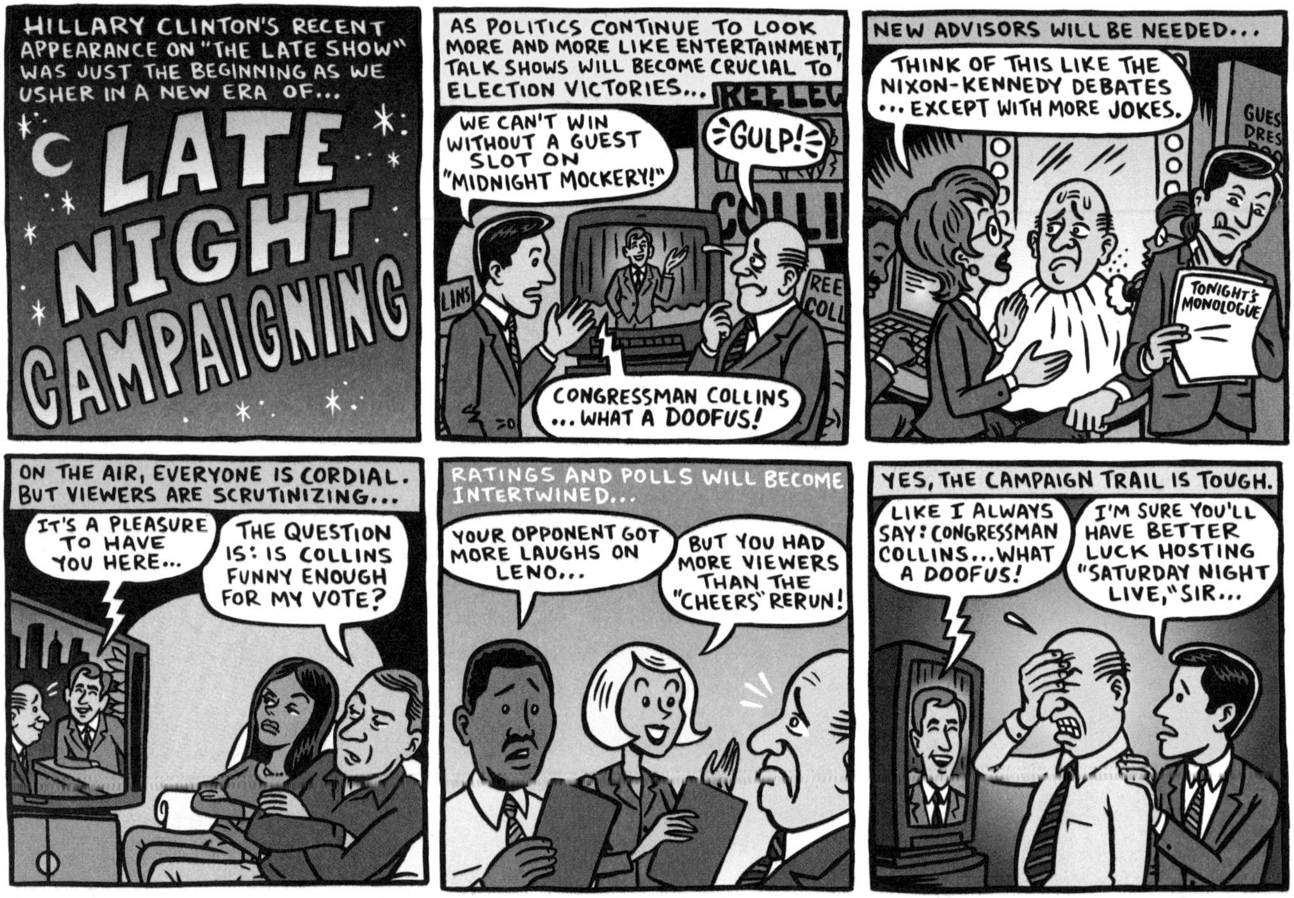
HILLARY CLINTON'S RECENT APPEARANCE ON "THE LATE SHOW" WAS JUST THE BEGINNING AS WE USHER IN A NEW ERA OF...
LATE NIGHT CAMPAIGNING
AS POLITICS CONTINUE TO LOOK MORE AND MORE LIKE ENTERTAINMENT, TALK SHOWS WILL BECOME CRUCIAL TO ELECTION VICTORIES...
WE CAN'T WIN WITHOUT A GUEST SLOT ON "MIDNIGHT MOCKERY!"
GULP!
CONGRESSMAN COLLINS ... WHAT A DOOFUS!
NEW ADVISORS WILL BE NEEDED...
THINK OF THIS LIKE THE NIXON-KENNEDY DEBATES ... EXCEPT WITH MORE JOKES.
TONIGHT'S MONOLOGUE
ON THE AIR, EVERYONE IS CORDIAL. BUT VIEWERS ARE SCRUTINIZING...
IT'S A PLEASURE TO HAVE YOU HERE...
THE QUESTION IS: IS COLLINS FUNNY ENOUGH FOR MY VOTE?
RATINGS AND POLLS WILL BECOME INTERTWINED...
YOUR OPPONENT GOT MORE LAUGHS ON LENO...
BUT YOU HAD MORE VIEWERS THAN THE "CHEERS" RERUN!
YES, THE CAMPAIGN TRAIL IS TOUGH.
LIKE I ALWAYS SAY: CONGRESSMAN COLLINS... WHAT A DOOFUS!
I'M SURE YOU'LL HAVE BETTER LUCK HOSTING "SATURDAY NIGHT LIVE," SIR...

It's a thrill to work for the *New York Times*, but they are very specific about what they want from artists, especially on the Op-Ed page. The editors don't want graphics that single out politicians for criticism. Instead they prefer pieces that focus on political trends (see above) and/or make a point of satirizing both sides of a debate. During the election recounts of 2000, I pitched the idea of a double portrait of the eventual winner looking both jubilant in victory but also anxious over the country's divisiveness. When Bush prevailed, they gave me the go-ahead to create the piece (see right), but at the last minute they requested the beads of sweat be removed from his forehead.

(In retrospect, there's an unintended irony to this piece, since Bush is so smug and deliberately polarizing, never one to worry about divisiveness.)

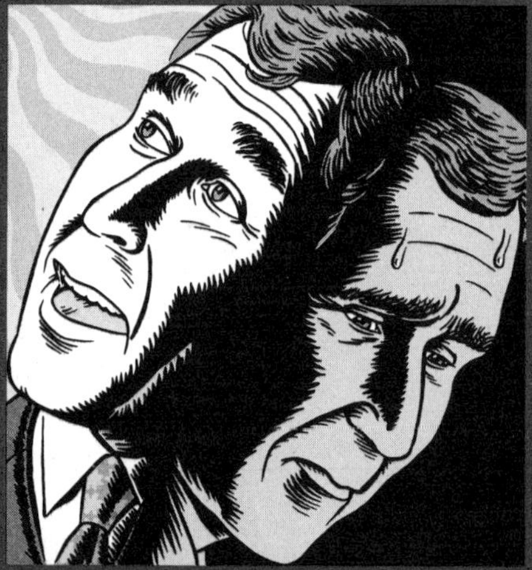

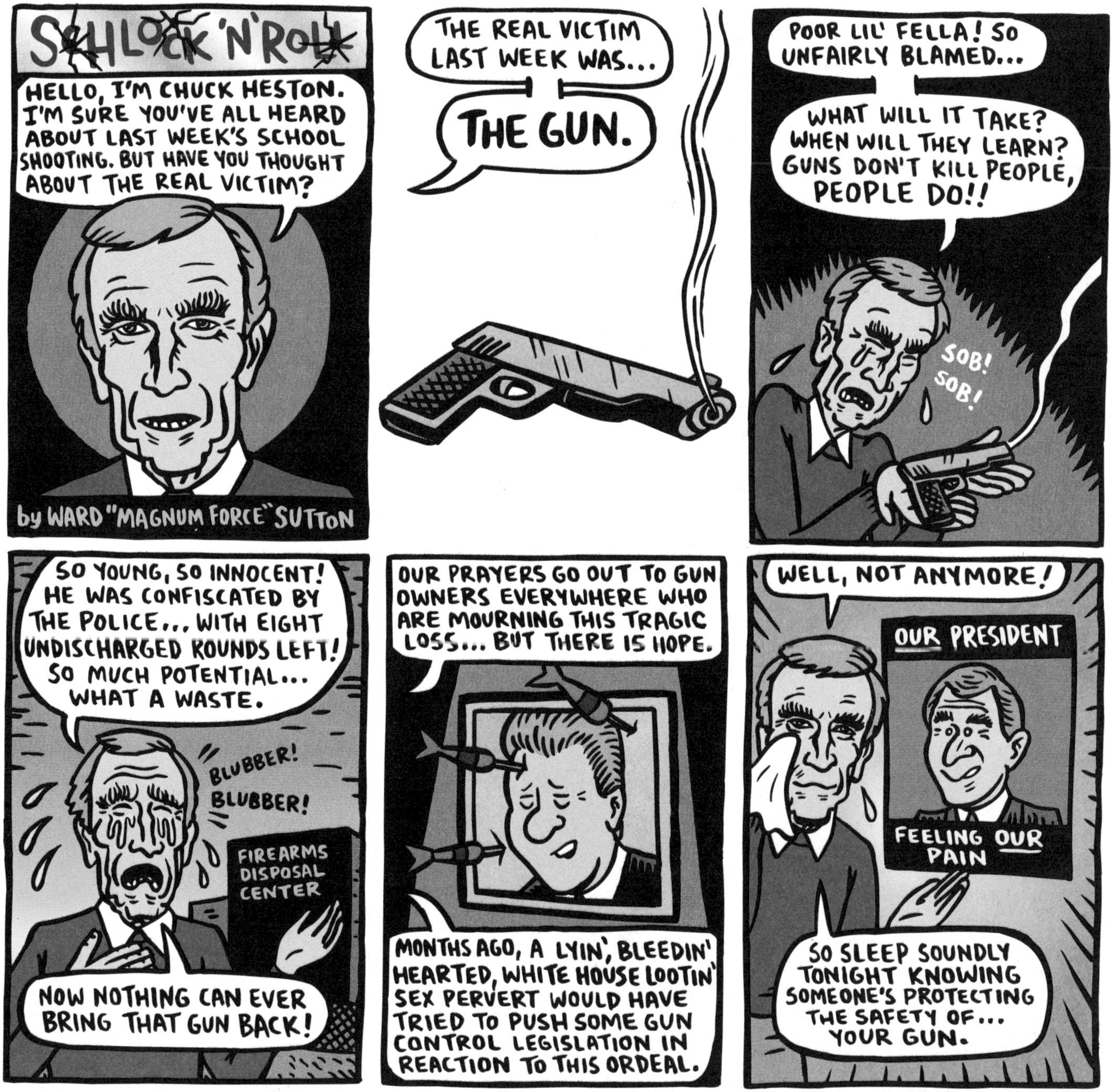
SCHLOCK 'N' ROLL
HELLO, I'M CHUCK HESTON. I'M SURE YOU'VE ALL HEARD ABOUT LAST WEEK'S SCHOOL SHOOTING. BUT HAVE YOU THOUGHT ABOUT THE REAL VICTIM?
by WARD "MAGNUM FORCE" SUTTON
THE REAL VICTIM LAST WEEK WAS...
THE GUN.
POOR LIL' FELLA! SO UNFAIRLY BLAMED...
WHAT WILL IT TAKE? WHEN WILL THEY LEARN? GUNS DON'T KILL PEOPLE, PEOPLE DO!!
SOB! SOB!
SO YOUNG, SO INNOCENT! HE WAS CONFISCATED BY THE POLICE... WITH EIGHT UNDISCHARGED ROUNDS LEFT! SO MUCH POTENTIAL... WHAT A WASTE.
BLUBBER! BLUBBER!
FIREARMS DISPOSAL CENTER
NOW NOTHING CAN EVER BRING THAT GUN BACK!
OUR PRAYERS GO OUT TO GUN OWNERS EVERYWHERE WHO ARE MOURNING THIS TRAGIC LOSS... BUT THERE IS HOPE.
MONTHS AGO, A LYIN', BLEEDIN' HEARTED, WHITE HOUSE LOOTIN' SEX PERVERT WOULD HAVE TRIED TO PUSH SOME GUN CONTROL LEGISLATION IN REACTION TO THIS ORDEAL.
WELL, NOT ANYMORE!
OUR PRESIDENT
FEELING OUR PAIN
SO SLEEP SOUNDLY TONIGHT KNOWING SOMEONE'S PROTECTING THE SAFETY OF... YOUR GUN.

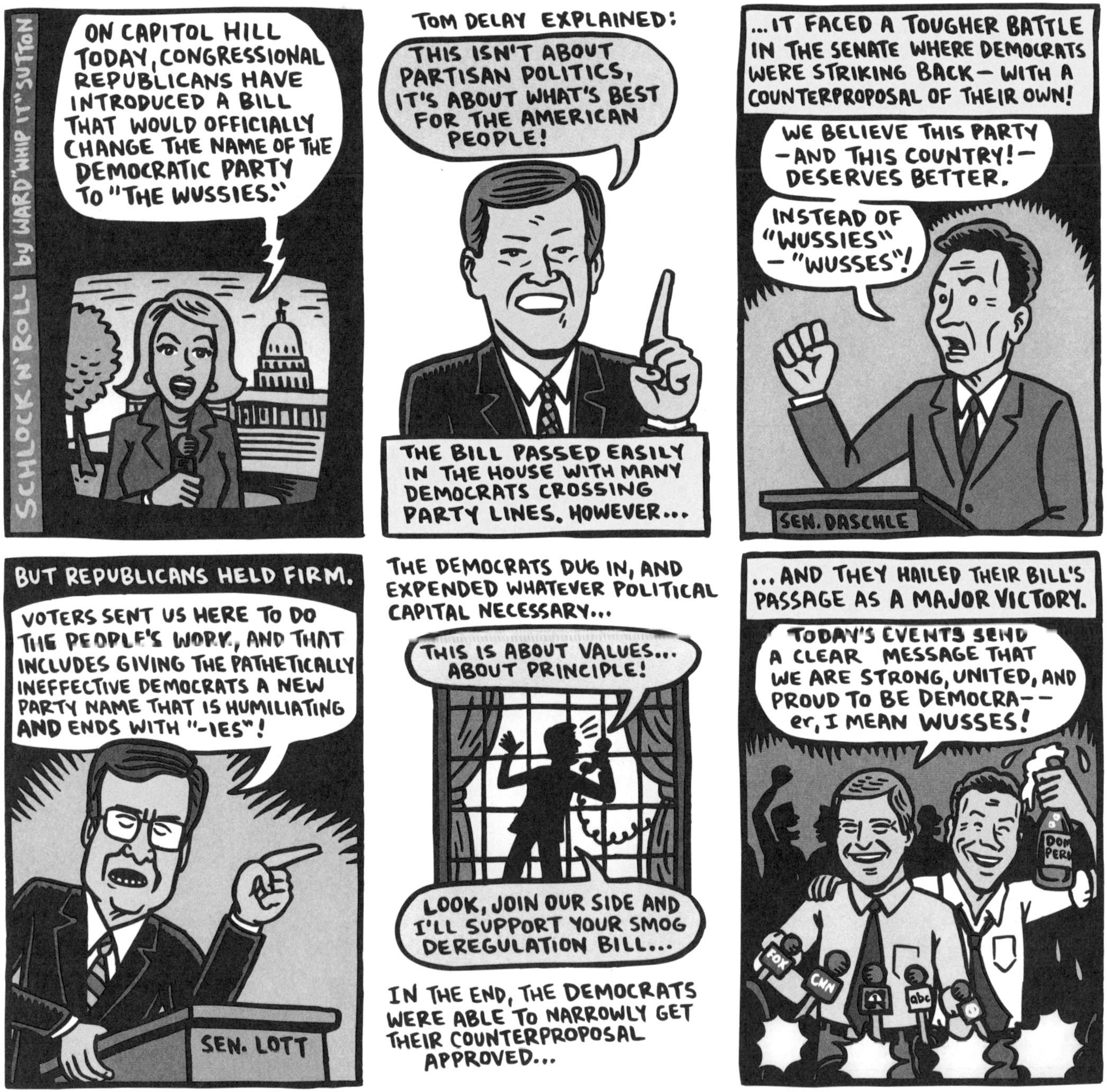
SCHLOCK 'N' ROLL by WARD "WHIP IT" SUTTON
ON CAPITOL HILL TODAY, CONGRESSIONAL REPUBLICANS HAVE INTRODUCED A BILL THAT WOULD OFFICIALLY CHANGE THE NAME OF THE DEMOCRATIC PARTY TO "THE WUSSIES."
TOM DELAY EXPLAINED:
THIS ISN'T ABOUT PARTISAN POLITICS, IT'S ABOUT WHAT'S BEST FOR THE AMERICAN PEOPLE!
THE BILL PASSED EASILY IN THE HOUSE WITH MANY DEMOCRATS CROSSING PARTY LINES. HOWEVER...
...IT FACED A TOUGHER BATTLE IN THE SENATE WHERE DEMOCRATS WERE STRIKING BACK — WITH A COUNTERPROPOSAL OF THEIR OWN!
WE BELIEVE THIS PARTY — AND THIS COUNTRY! — DESERVES BETTER.
INSTEAD OF "WUSSIES" — "WUSSES"!
SEN. DASCHLE
BUT REPUBLICANS HELD FIRM.
VOTERS SENT US HERE TO DO THE PEOPLE'S WORK, AND THAT INCLUDES GIVING THE PATHETICALLY INEFFECTIVE DEMOCRATS A NEW PARTY NAME THAT IS HUMILIATING AND ENDS WITH "-IES"!
SEN. LOTT
THE DEMOCRATS DUG IN, AND EXPENDED WHATEVER POLITICAL CAPITAL NECESSARY...
THIS IS ABOUT VALUES... ABOUT PRINCIPLE!
LOOK, JOIN OUR SIDE AND I'LL SUPPORT YOUR SMOG DEREGULATION BILL...
IN THE END, THE DEMOCRATS WERE ABLE TO NARROWLY GET THEIR COUNTERPROPOSAL APPROVED...
...AND THEY HAILED THEIR BILL'S PASSAGE AS A MAJOR VICTORY.
TODAY'S EVENTS SEND A CLEAR MESSAGE THAT WE ARE STRONG, UNITED, AND PROUD TO BE DEMOCRA-- er, I MEAN WUSSES!
FOX
CNN
abc

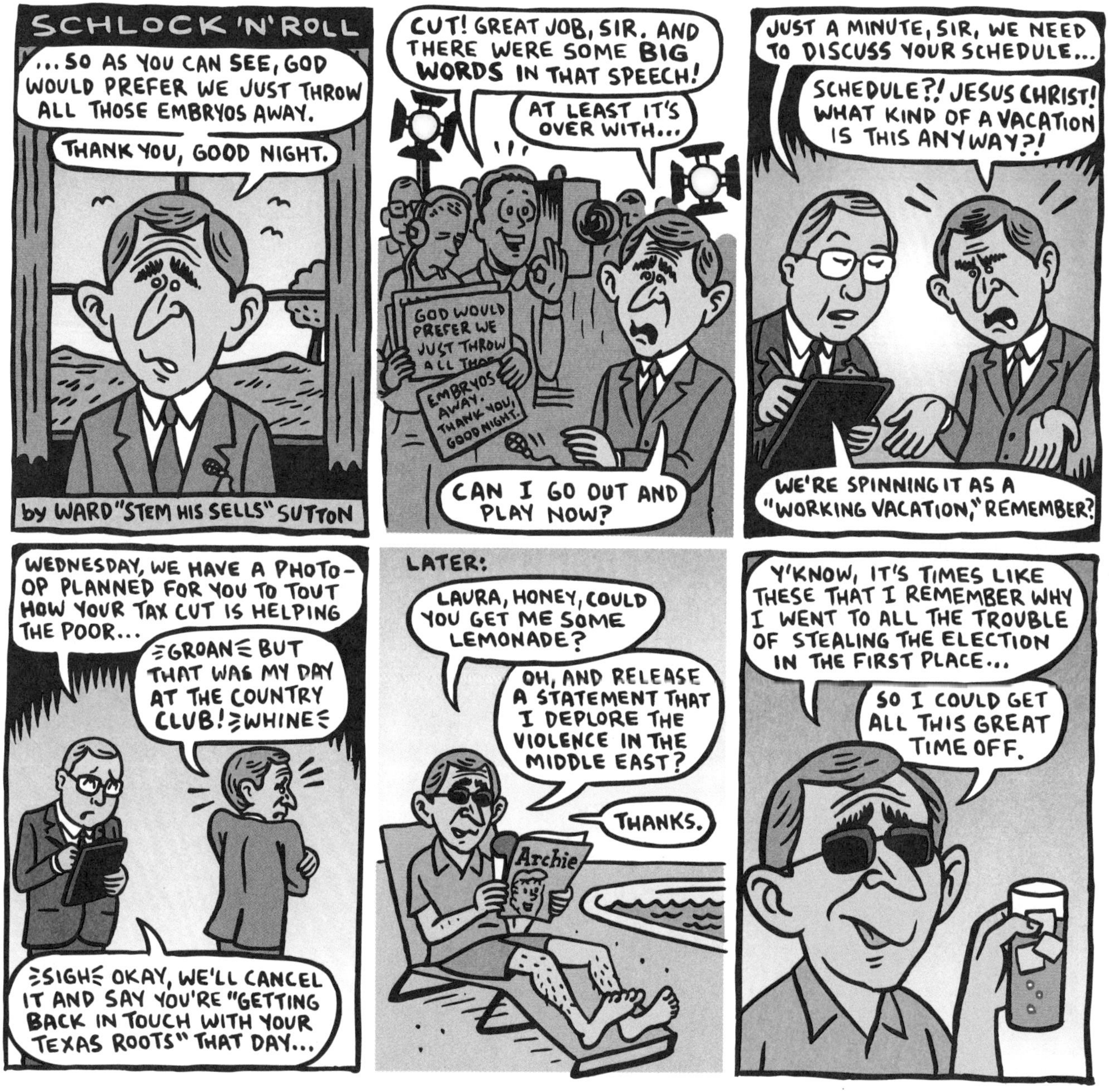
SCHLOCK 'N' ROLL
...SO AS YOU CAN SEE, GOD WOULD PREFER WE JUST THROW ALL THOSE EMBRYOS AWAY.
THANK YOU, GOOD NIGHT.
by WARD "STEM HIS SELLS" SUTTON
CUT! GREAT JOB, SIR. AND THERE WERE SOME BIG WORDS IN THAT SPEECH!
AT LEAST IT'S OVER WITH...
GOD WOULD PREFER WE JUST THROW ALL THOSE
EMBRYOS AWAY. THANK YOU, GOOD NIGHT.
CAN I GO OUT AND PLAY NOW?
JUST A MINUTE, SIR, WE NEED TO DISCUSS YOUR SCHEDULE...
SCHEDULE?! JESUS CHRIST! WHAT KIND OF A VACATION IS THIS ANYWAY?!
WE'RE SPINNING IT AS A "WORKING VACATION," REMEMBER?
WEDNESDAY, WE HAVE A PHOTO-OP PLANNED FOR YOU TO TOUT HOW YOUR TAX CUT IS HELPING THE POOR...
≋GROAN≋ BUT THAT WAS MY DAY AT THE COUNTRY CLUB! ≋WHINE≋
≋SIGH≋ OKAY, WE'LL CANCEL IT AND SAY YOU'RE "GETTING BACK IN TOUCH WITH YOUR TEXAS ROOTS" THAT DAY...
LATER:
LAURA, HONEY, COULD YOU GET ME SOME LEMONADE?
OH, AND RELEASE A STATEMENT THAT I DEPLORE THE VIOLENCE IN THE MIDDLE EAST?
THANKS.
Archie
Y'KNOW, IT'S TIMES LIKE THESE THAT I REMEMBER WHY I WENT TO ALL THE TROUBLE OF STEALING THE ELECTION IN THE FIRST PLACE...
SO I COULD GET ALL THIS GREAT TIME OFF.

I drew this cartoon in August 2001 during Bush's month-long vacation. The privileged, fratboy-style laziness of his record presidential time off was merely irritating at the time, before we all learned the nature of the work (and CIA terror warnings) he was actually avoiding.

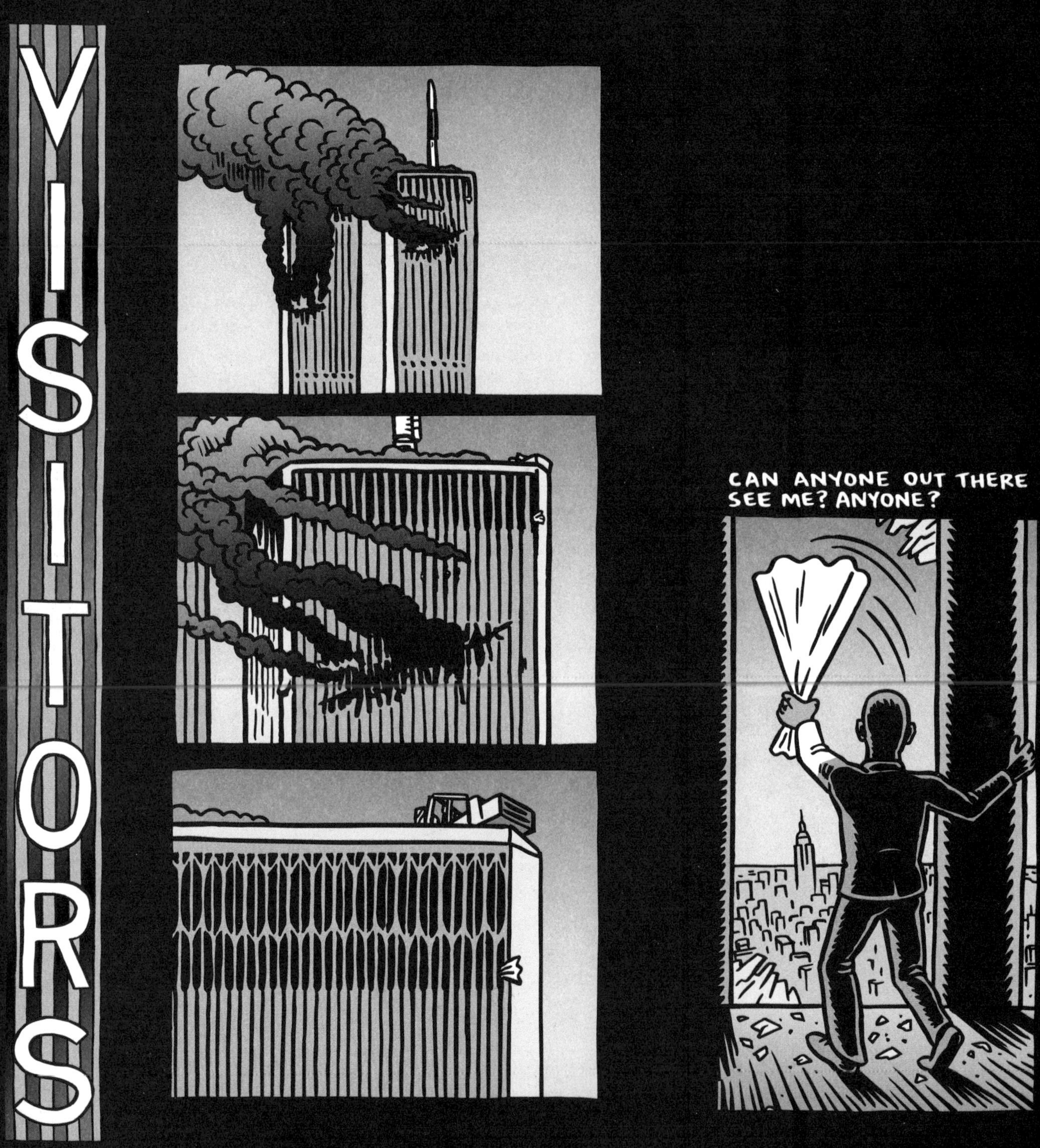
VISITORS
CAN ANYONE OUT THERE SEE ME? ANYONE?

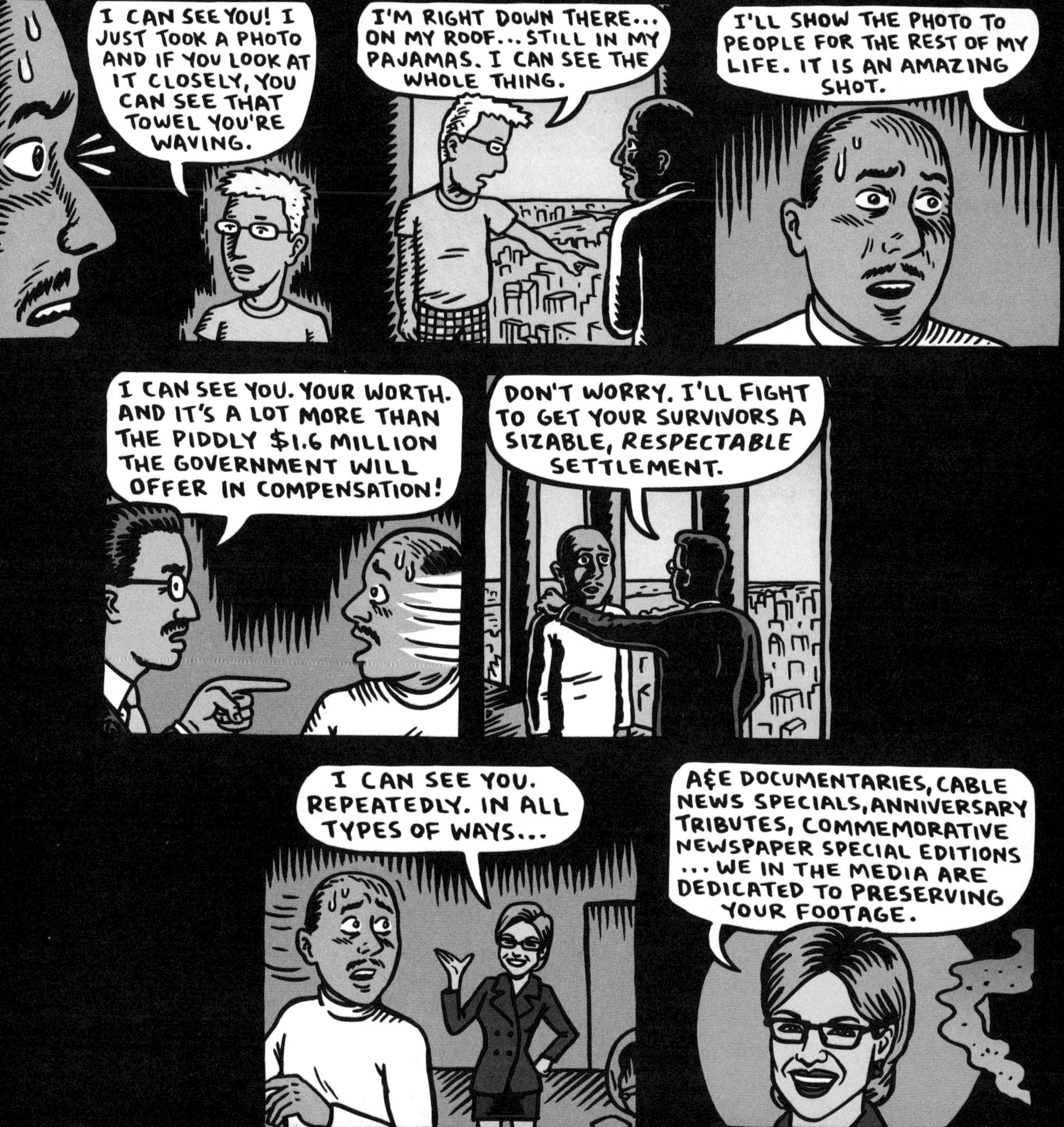
I CAN SEE YOU! I JUST TOOK A PHOTO AND IF YOU LOOK AT IT CLOSELY, YOU CAN SEE THAT TOWEL YOU'RE WAVING.
I'M RIGHT DOWN THERE... ON MY ROOF... STILL IN MY PAJAMAS. I CAN SEE THE WHOLE THING.
I'LL SHOW THE PHOTO TO PEOPLE FOR THE REST OF MY LIFE. IT IS AN AMAZING SHOT.
I CAN SEE YOU. YOUR WORTH. AND IT'S A LOT MORE THAN THE PIDDLY $1.6 MILLION THE GOVERNMENT WILL OFFER IN COMPENSATION!
DON'T WORRY. I'LL FIGHT TO GET YOUR SURVIVORS A SIZABLE, *RESPECTABLE* SETTLEMENT.
I CAN SEE YOU. REPEATEDLY. IN ALL TYPES OF WAYS...
A&E DOCUMENTARIES, CABLE NEWS SPECIALS, ANNIVERSARY TRIBUTES, COMMEMORATIVE NEWSPAPER SPECIAL EDITIONS ... WE IN THE MEDIA ARE DEDICATED TO PRESERVING YOUR FOOTAGE.

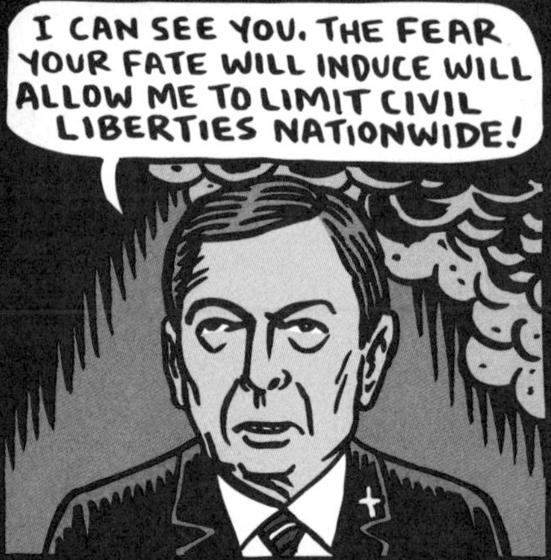
I CAN SEE YOU. THE FEAR YOUR FATE WILL INDUCE WILL ALLOW ME TO LIMIT CIVIL LIBERTIES NATIONWIDE!

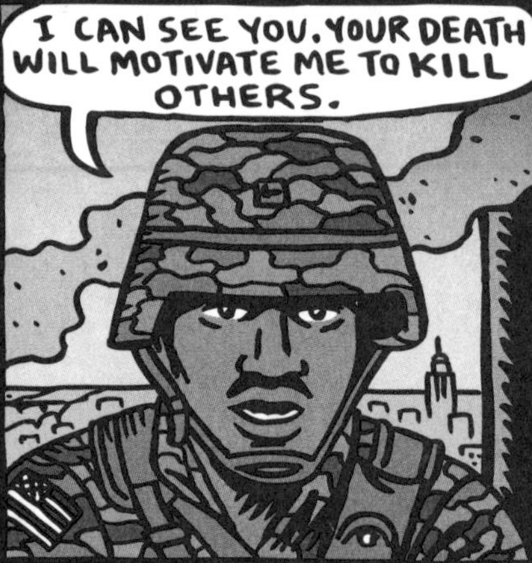
I CAN SEE YOU. YOUR DEATH WILL MOTIVATE ME TO KILL OTHERS.

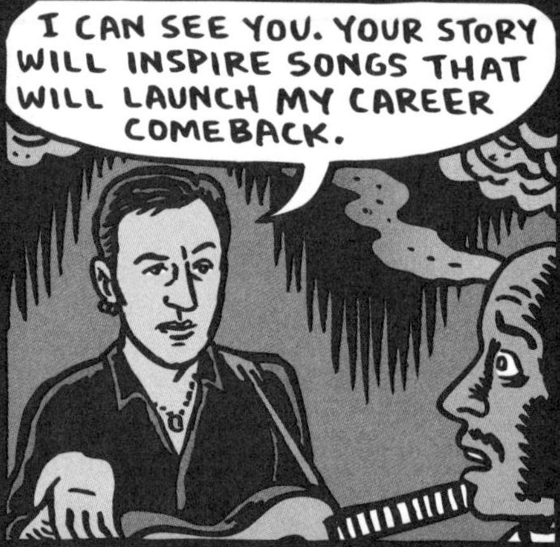
I CAN SEE YOU. YOUR STORY WILL INSPIRE SONGS THAT WILL LAUNCH MY CAREER COMEBACK.

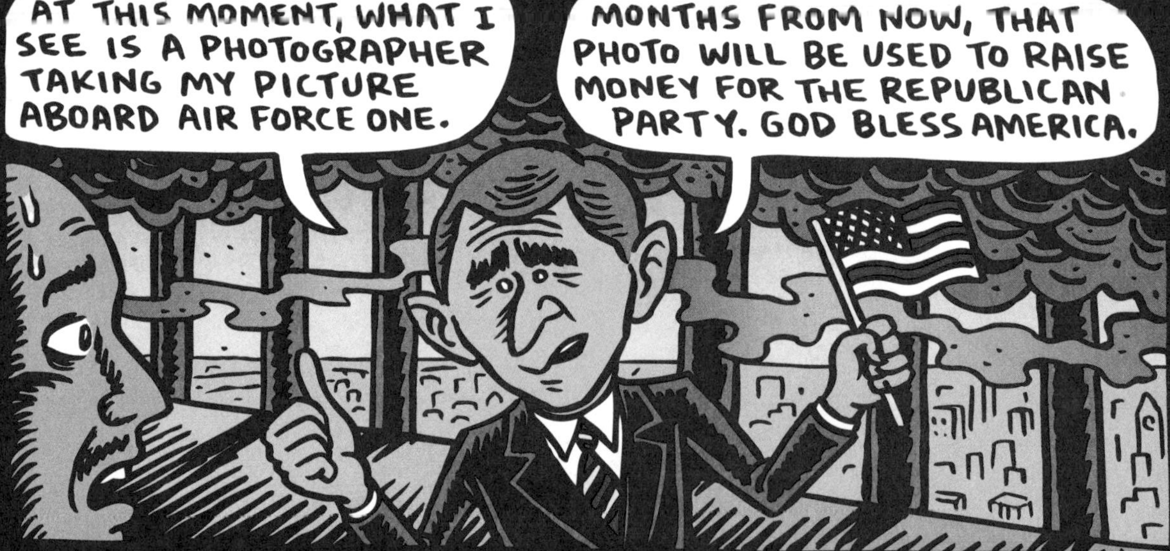
AT THIS MOMENT, WHAT I SEE IS A PHOTOGRAPHER TAKING MY PICTURE ABOARD AIR FORCE ONE.
MONTHS FROM NOW, THAT PHOTO WILL BE USED TO RAISE MONEY FOR THE REPUBLICAN PARTY. GOD BLESS AMERICA.

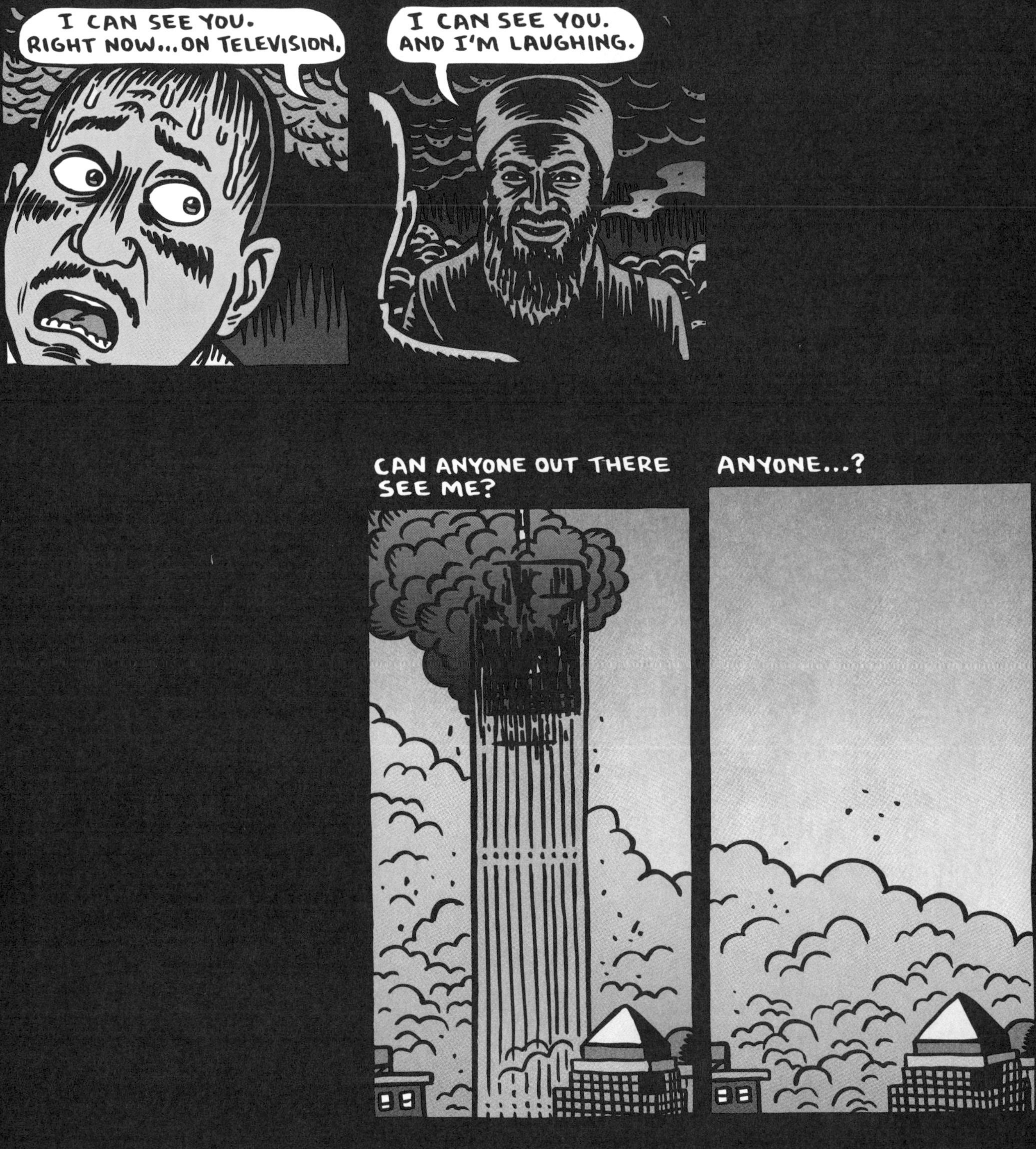
I CAN SEE YOU.
RIGHT NOW...ON TELEVISION.
I CAN SEE YOU.
AND I'M LAUGHING.
CAN ANYONE OUT THERE SEE ME?
ANYONE...?

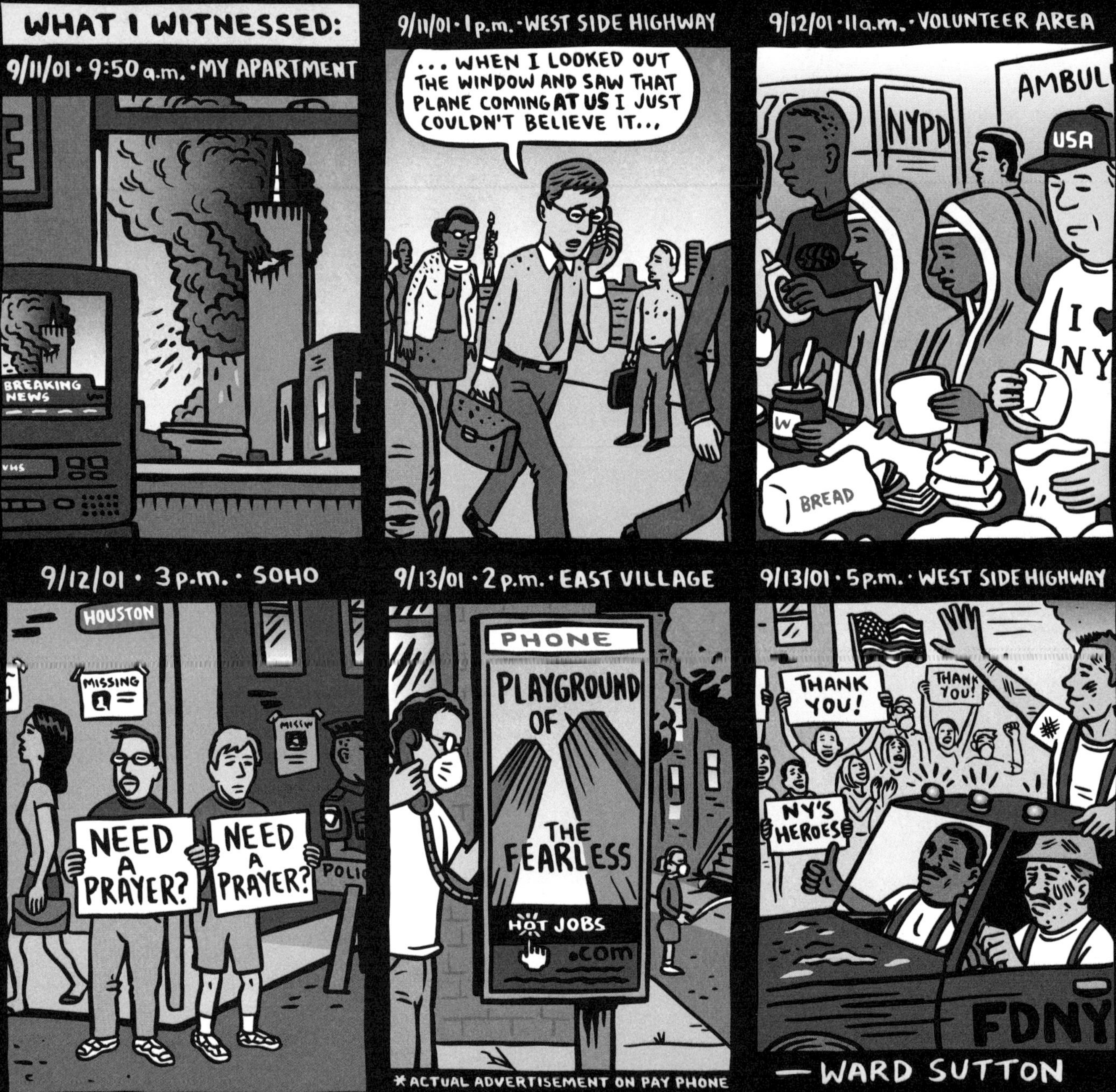
WHAT I WITNESSED:
9/11/01 • 9:50 a.m. • MY APARTMENT
BREAKING NEWS
VHS
9/11/01 • 1 p.m. • WEST SIDE HIGHWAY
...WHEN I LOOKED OUT THE WINDOW AND SAW THAT PLANE COMING AT US I JUST COULDN'T BELIEVE IT...,
9/12/01 • 11 a.m. • VOLUNTEER AREA
AMBUL
NYPD
USA
I ♥ NY
BREAD
9/12/01 • 3 p.m. • SOHO
HOUSTON
MISSING
NEED A PRAYER?
NEED A PRAYER?
POLIC
9/13/01 • 2 p.m. • EAST VILLAGE
PHONE
PLAYGROUND OF THE FEARLESS
HOT JOBS
.com
*ACTUAL ADVERTISEMENT ON PAY PHONE
9/13/01 • 5 p.m. • WEST SIDE HIGHWAY
THANK YOU!
THANK YOU!
NY'S HEROES
FDNY
—WARD SUTTON

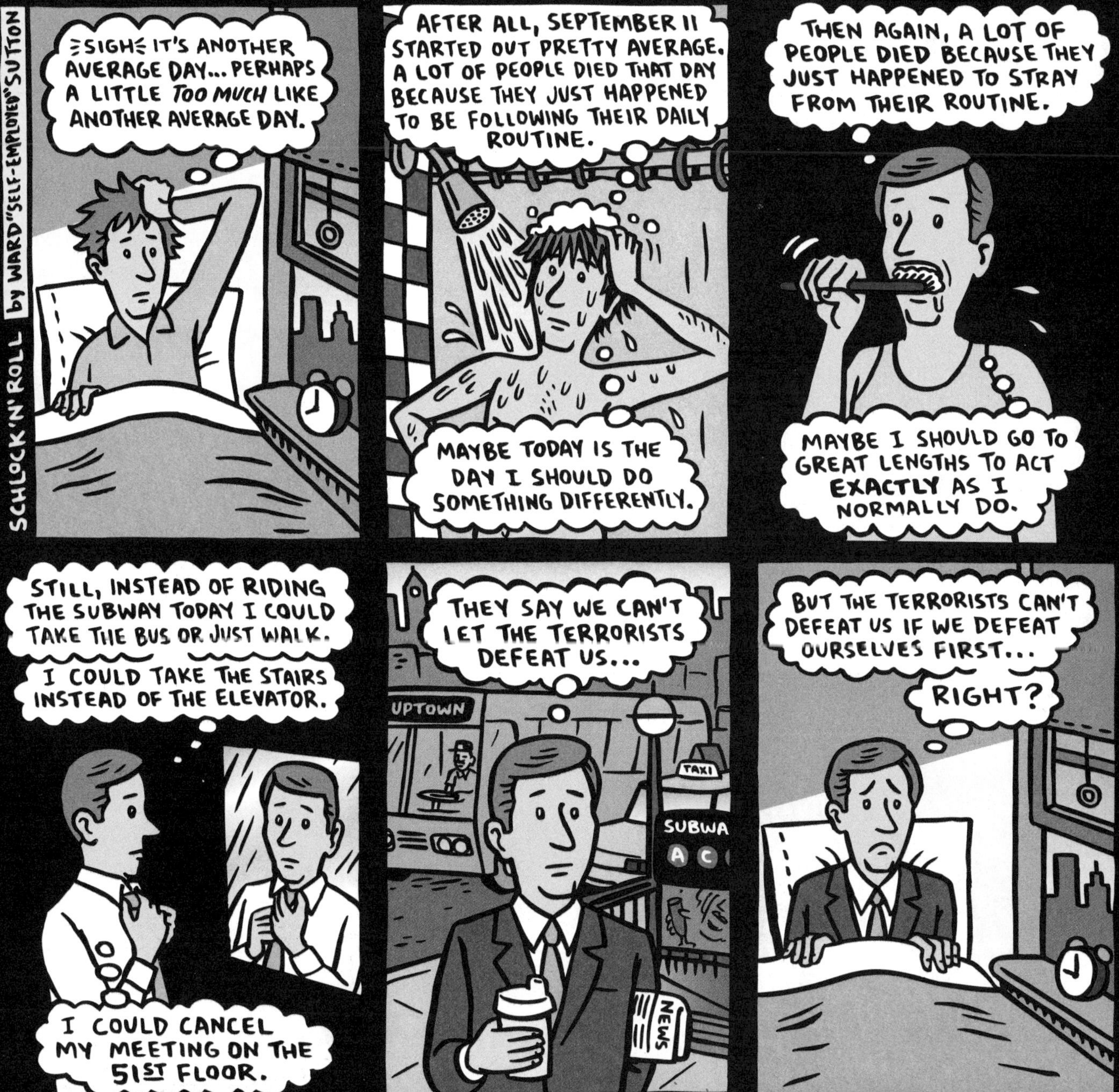
SCHLOCK 'N' ROLL by WARD "SELF-EMPLOYED" SUTTON
≶SIGH≶ IT'S ANOTHER AVERAGE DAY... PERHAPS A LITTLE TOO MUCH LIKE ANOTHER AVERAGE DAY.
AFTER ALL, SEPTEMBER 11 STARTED OUT PRETTY AVERAGE. A LOT OF PEOPLE DIED THAT DAY BECAUSE THEY JUST HAPPENED TO BE FOLLOWING THEIR DAILY ROUTINE.
MAYBE TODAY IS THE DAY I SHOULD DO SOMETHING DIFFERENTLY.
THEN AGAIN, A LOT OF PEOPLE DIED BECAUSE THEY JUST HAPPENED TO STRAY FROM THEIR ROUTINE.
MAYBE I SHOULD GO TO GREAT LENGTHS TO ACT EXACTLY AS I NORMALLY DO.
STILL, INSTEAD OF RIDING THE SUBWAY TODAY I COULD TAKE THE BUS OR JUST WALK.
I COULD TAKE THE STAIRS INSTEAD OF THE ELEVATOR.
I COULD CANCEL MY MEETING ON THE 51ST FLOOR.
THEY SAY WE CAN'T LET THE TERRORISTS DEFEAT US...
UPTOWN
TAXI
SUBWA
A C
NEWS
BUT THE TERRORISTS CAN'T DEFEAT US IF WE DEFEAT OURSELVES FIRST...
RIGHT?

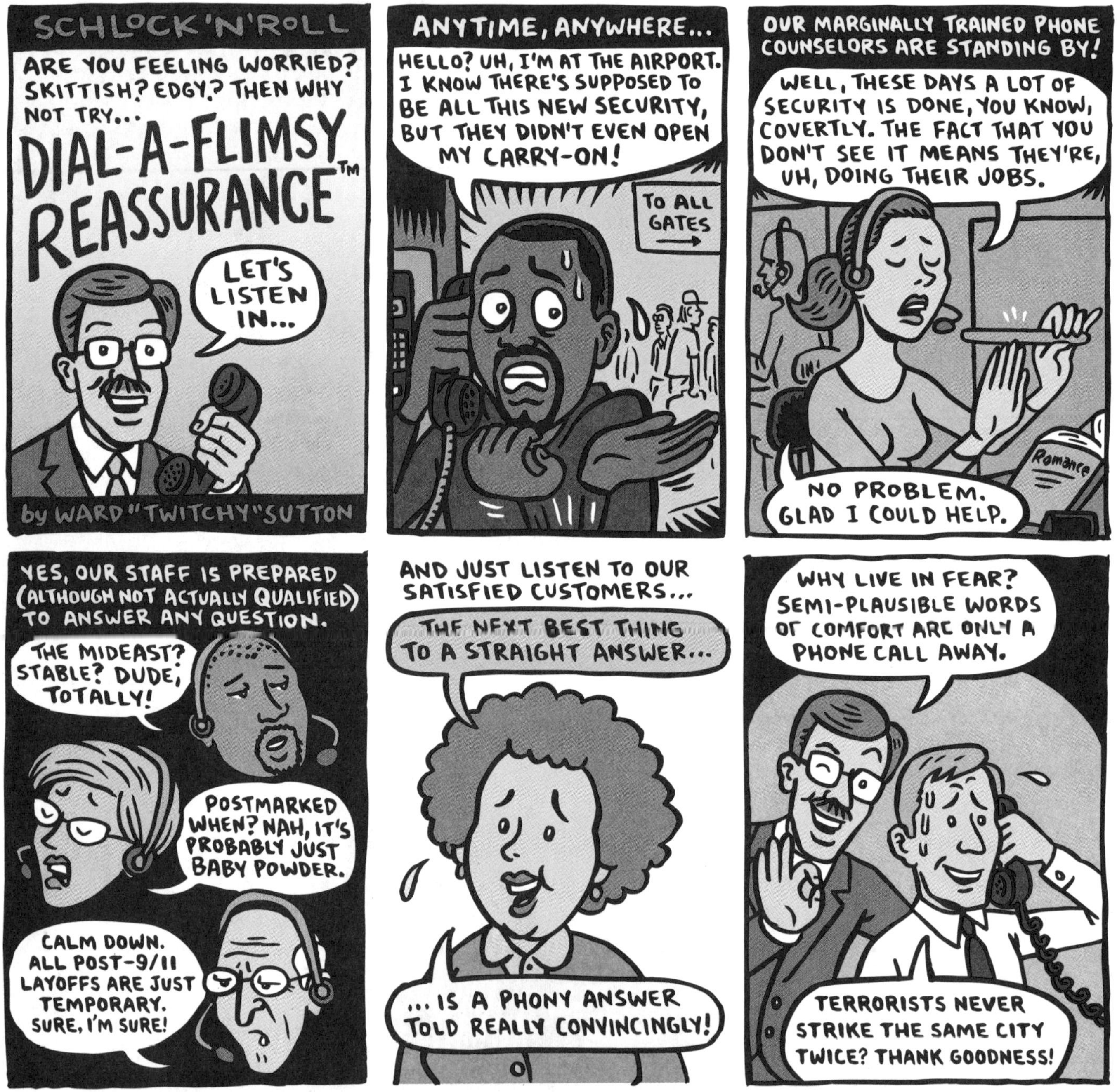
SCHLOCK'N'ROLL
ARE YOU FEELING WORRIED? SKITTISH? EDGY? THEN WHY NOT TRY...
DIAL-A-FLIMSY REASSURANCE™
LET'S LISTEN IN...
by WARD "TWITCHY" SUTTON
ANYTIME, ANYWHERE...
HELLO? UH, I'M AT THE AIRPORT. I KNOW THERE'S SUPPOSED TO BE ALL THIS NEW SECURITY, BUT THEY DIDN'T EVEN OPEN MY CARRY-ON!
TO ALL GATES
OUR MARGINALLY TRAINED PHONE COUNSELORS ARE STANDING BY!
WELL, THESE DAYS A LOT OF SECURITY IS DONE, YOU KNOW, COVERTLY. THE FACT THAT YOU DON'T SEE IT MEANS THEY'RE, UH, DOING THEIR JOBS.
Romance
NO PROBLEM. GLAD I COULD HELP.
YES, OUR STAFF IS PREPARED (ALTHOUGH NOT ACTUALLY QUALIFIED) TO ANSWER ANY QUESTION.
THE MIDEAST? STABLE? DUDE, TOTALLY!
POSTMARKED WHEN? NAH, IT'S PROBABLY JUST BABY POWDER.
CALM DOWN. ALL POST-9/11 LAYOFFS ARE JUST TEMPORARY. SURE, I'M SURE!
AND JUST LISTEN TO OUR SATISFIED CUSTOMERS...
THE NEXT BEST THING TO A STRAIGHT ANSWER...
...IS A PHONY ANSWER TOLD REALLY CONVINCINGLY!
WHY LIVE IN FEAR? SEMI-PLAUSIBLE WORDS OF COMFORT ARE ONLY A PHONE CALL AWAY.
TERRORISTS NEVER STRIKE THE SAME CITY TWICE? THANK GOODNESS!

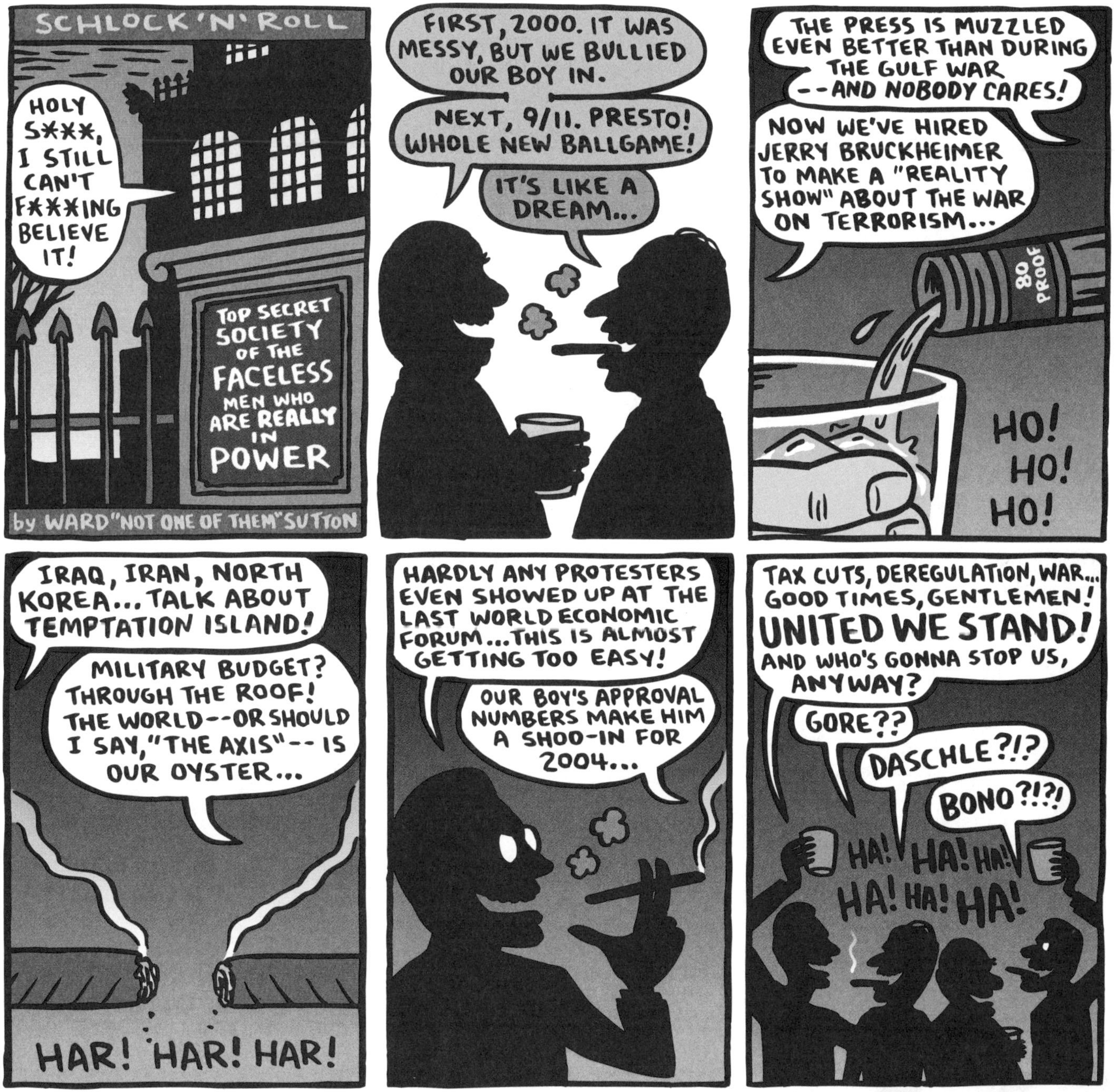
SCHLOCK 'N' ROLL
HOLY S***, I STILL CAN'T F***ING BELIEVE IT!
TOP SECRET SOCIETY OF THE FACELESS MEN WHO ARE REALLY IN POWER
by WARD "NOT ONE OF THEM" SUTTON
FIRST, 2000. IT WAS MESSY, BUT WE BULLIED OUR BOY IN.
NEXT, 9/11. PRESTO! WHOLE NEW BALLGAME!
IT'S LIKE A DREAM...
THE PRESS IS MUZZLED EVEN BETTER THAN DURING THE GULF WAR --AND NOBODY CARES!
NOW WE'VE HIRED JERRY BRUCKHEIMER TO MAKE A "REALITY SHOW" ABOUT THE WAR ON TERRORISM...
80 PROOF
HO! HO! HO!
IRAQ, IRAN, NORTH KOREA... TALK ABOUT TEMPTATION ISLAND!
MILITARY BUDGET? THROUGH THE ROOF! THE WORLD--OR SHOULD I SAY, "THE AXIS"-- IS OUR OYSTER...
HAR! HAR! HAR!
HARDLY ANY PROTESTERS EVEN SHOWED UP AT THE LAST WORLD ECONOMIC FORUM... THIS IS ALMOST GETTING TOO EASY!
OUR BOY'S APPROVAL NUMBERS MAKE HIM A SHOO-IN FOR 2004...
TAX CUTS, DEREGULATION, WAR... GOOD TIMES, GENTLEMEN!
UNITED WE STAND!
AND WHO'S GONNA STOP US, ANYWAY?
GORE??
DASCHLE?!?
BONO?!?!
HA! HA! HA! HA! HA! HA!

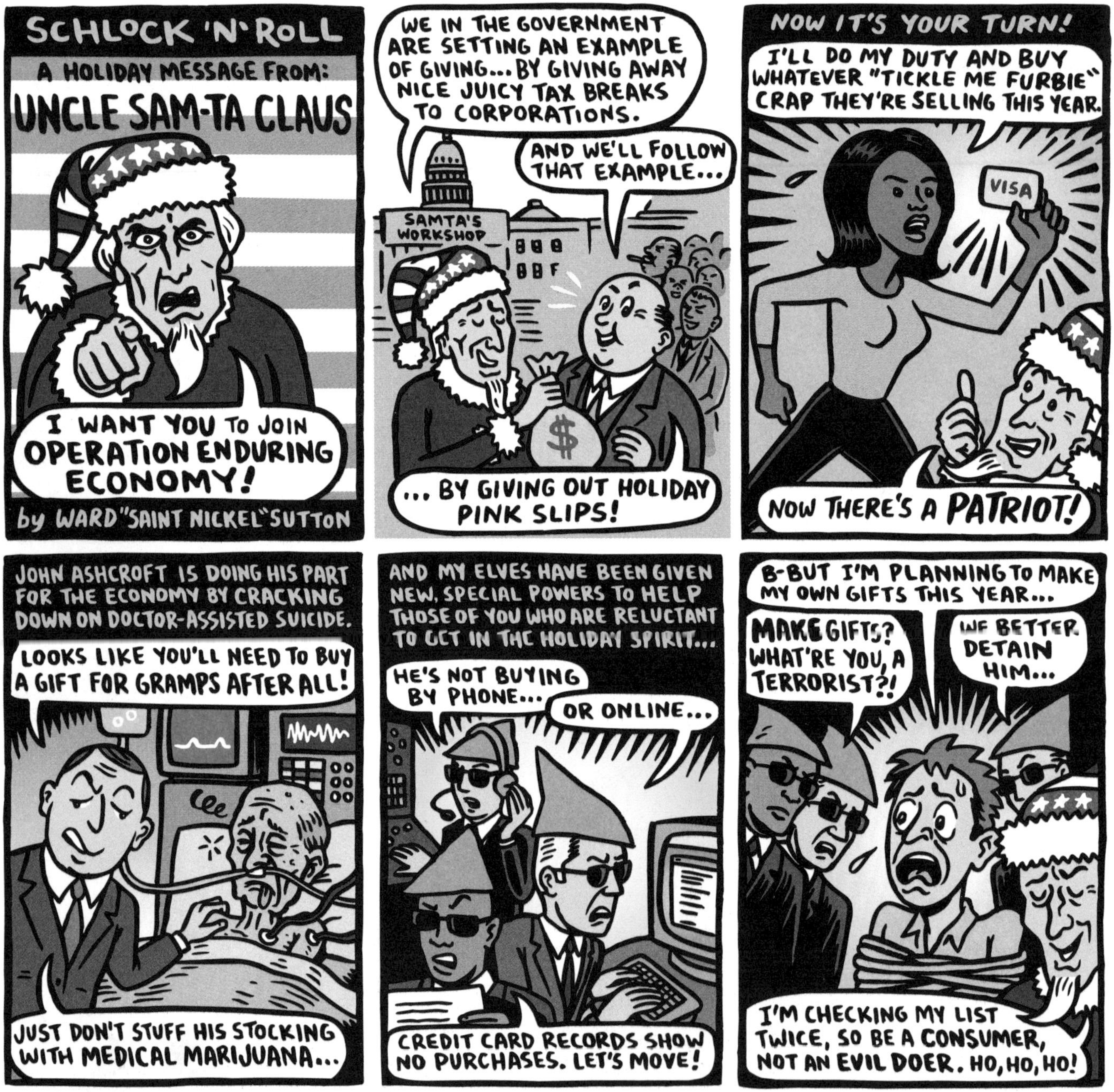
SCHLOCK 'N' ROLL
A HOLIDAY MESSAGE FROM:
UNCLE SAM-TA CLAUS
I WANT YOU TO JOIN OPERATION ENDURING ECONOMY!
by WARD "SAINT NICKEL" SUTTON
WE IN THE GOVERNMENT ARE SETTING AN EXAMPLE OF GIVING... BY GIVING AWAY NICE JUICY TAX BREAKS TO CORPORATIONS.
AND WE'LL FOLLOW THAT EXAMPLE...
SAMTA'S WORKSHOP
... BY GIVING OUT HOLIDAY PINK SLIPS!
NOW IT'S YOUR TURN!
I'LL DO MY DUTY AND BUY WHATEVER "TICKLE ME FURBIE" CRAP THEY'RE SELLING THIS YEAR.
VISA
NOW THERE'S A PATRIOT!
JOHN ASHCROFT IS DOING HIS PART FOR THE ECONOMY BY CRACKING DOWN ON DOCTOR-ASSISTED SUICIDE.
LOOKS LIKE YOU'LL NEED TO BUY A GIFT FOR GRAMPS AFTER ALL!
JUST DON'T STUFF HIS STOCKING WITH MEDICAL MARIJUANA...
AND MY ELVES HAVE BEEN GIVEN NEW, SPECIAL POWERS TO HELP THOSE OF YOU WHO ARE RELUCTANT TO GET IN THE HOLIDAY SPIRIT...
HE'S NOT BUYING BY PHONE...
OR ONLINE...
CREDIT CARD RECORDS SHOW NO PURCHASES. LET'S MOVE!
B-BUT I'M PLANNING TO MAKE MY OWN GIFTS THIS YEAR...
MAKE GIFTS? WHAT'RE YOU, A TERRORIST?!
WE BETTER DETAIN HIM...
I'M CHECKING MY LIST TWICE, SO BE A CONSUMER, NOT AN EVIL DOER. HO, HO, HO!

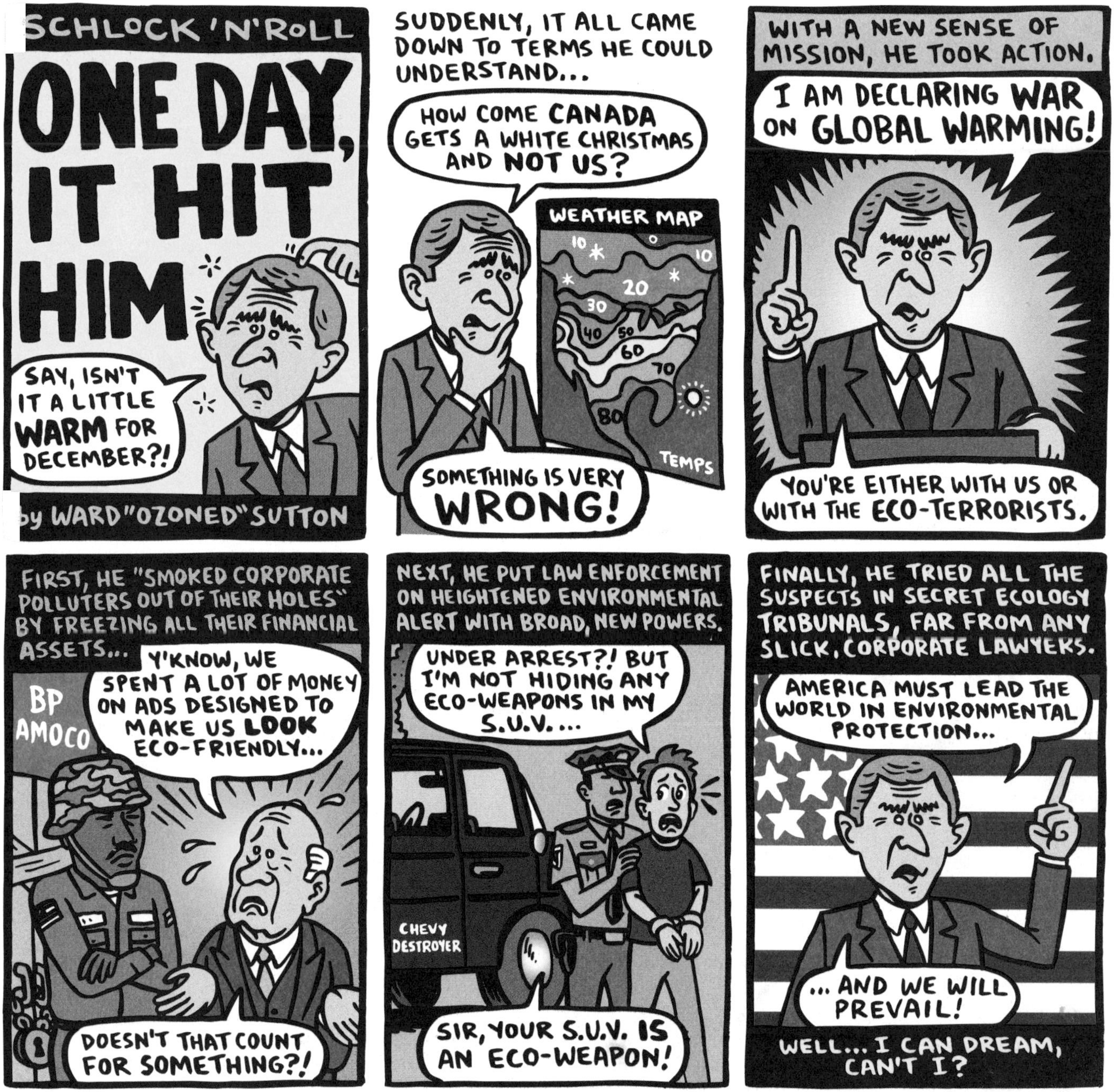
SCHLOCK 'N' ROLL
ONE DAY, IT HIT HIM
SAY, ISN'T IT A LITTLE WARM FOR DECEMBER?!
by WARD "OZONED" SUTTON
SUDDENLY, IT ALL CAME DOWN TO TERMS HE COULD UNDERSTAND...
HOW COME CANADA GETS A WHITE CHRISTMAS AND NOT US?
WEATHER MAP
10
10
20
30
40
50
60
70
80
TEMPS
SOMETHING IS VERY WRONG!
WITH A NEW SENSE OF MISSION, HE TOOK ACTION.
I AM DECLARING WAR ON GLOBAL WARMING!
YOU'RE EITHER WITH US OR WITH THE ECO-TERRORISTS.
FIRST, HE "SMOKED CORPORATE POLLUTERS OUT OF THEIR HOLES" BY FREEZING ALL THEIR FINANCIAL ASSETS...
BP AMOCO
Y'KNOW, WE SPENT A LOT OF MONEY ON ADS DESIGNED TO MAKE US LOOK ECO-FRIENDLY...
DOESN'T THAT COUNT FOR SOMETHING?!
NEXT, HE PUT LAW ENFORCEMENT ON HEIGHTENED ENVIRONMENTAL ALERT WITH BROAD, NEW POWERS.
UNDER ARREST?! BUT I'M NOT HIDING ANY ECO-WEAPONS IN MY S.U.V. ...
CHEVY DESTROYER
SIR, YOUR S.U.V. IS AN ECO-WEAPON!
FINALLY, HE TRIED ALL THE SUSPECTS IN SECRET ECOLOGY TRIBUNALS, FAR FROM ANY SLICK, CORPORATE LAWYERS.
AMERICA MUST LEAD THE WORLD IN ENVIRONMENTAL PROTECTION...
... AND WE WILL PREVAIL!
WELL... I CAN DREAM, CAN'T I?

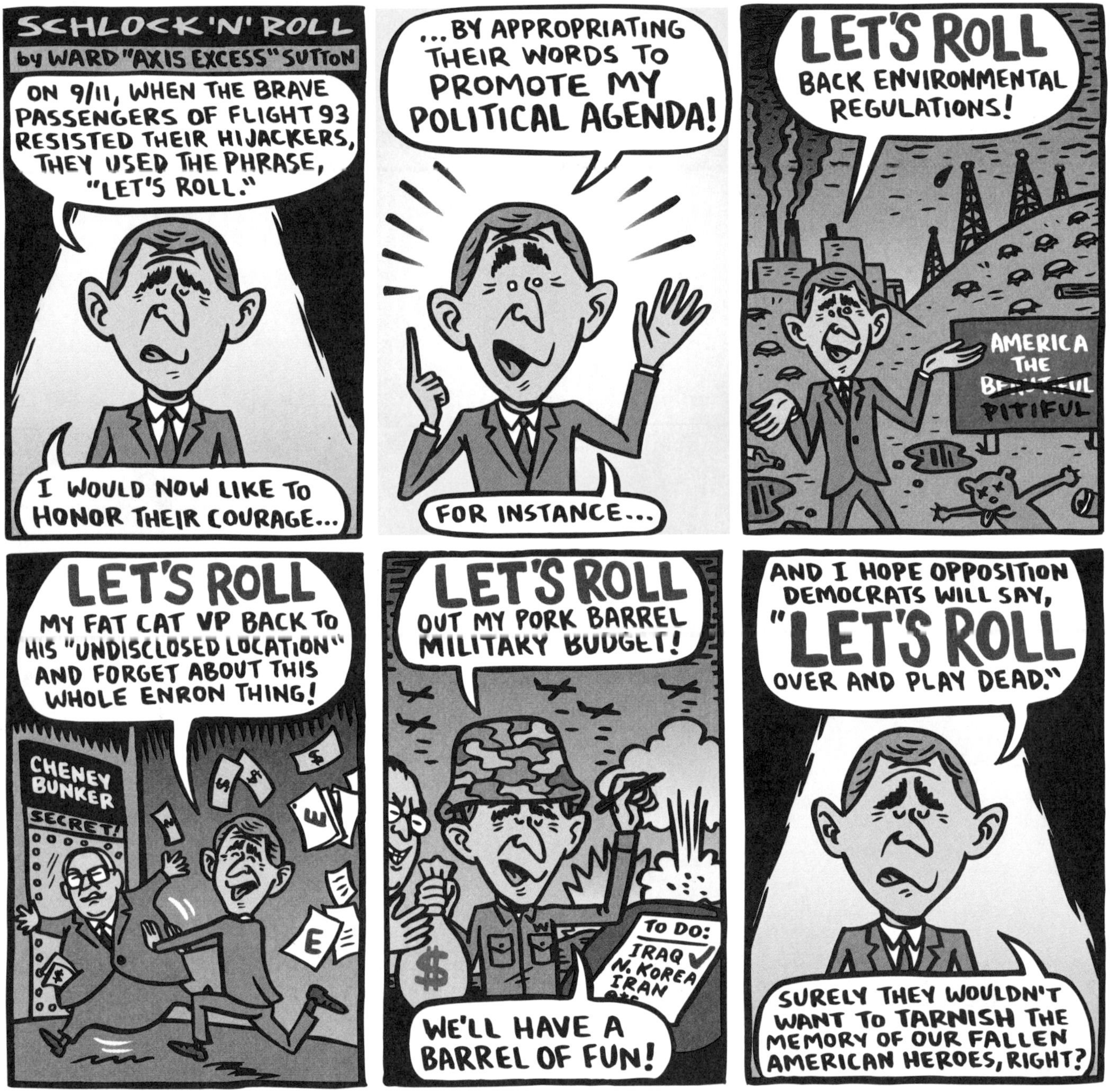
SCHLOCK 'N' ROLL
by WARD "AXIS EXCESS" SUTTON
ON 9/11, WHEN THE BRAVE PASSENGERS OF FLIGHT 93 RESISTED THEIR HIJACKERS, THEY USED THE PHRASE, "LET'S ROLL."
I WOULD NOW LIKE TO HONOR THEIR COURAGE...
...BY APPROPRIATING THEIR WORDS TO PROMOTE MY POLITICAL AGENDA!
FOR INSTANCE...
LET'S ROLL BACK ENVIRONMENTAL REGULATIONS!
AMERICA THE
PITIFUL
LET'S ROLL MY FAT CAT VP BACK TO HIS "UNDISCLOSED LOCATION" AND FORGET ABOUT THIS WHOLE ENRON THING!
CHENEY BUNKER
SECRET!
E
LET'S ROLL OUT MY PORK BARREL MILITARY BUDGET!
TO DO:
IRAQ ✔
N. KOREA
IRAN
WE'LL HAVE A BARREL OF FUN!
AND I HOPE OPPOSITION DEMOCRATS WILL SAY, "LET'S ROLL OVER AND PLAY DEAD."
SURELY THEY WOULDN'T WANT TO TARNISH THE MEMORY OF OUR FALLEN AMERICAN HEROES, RIGHT?

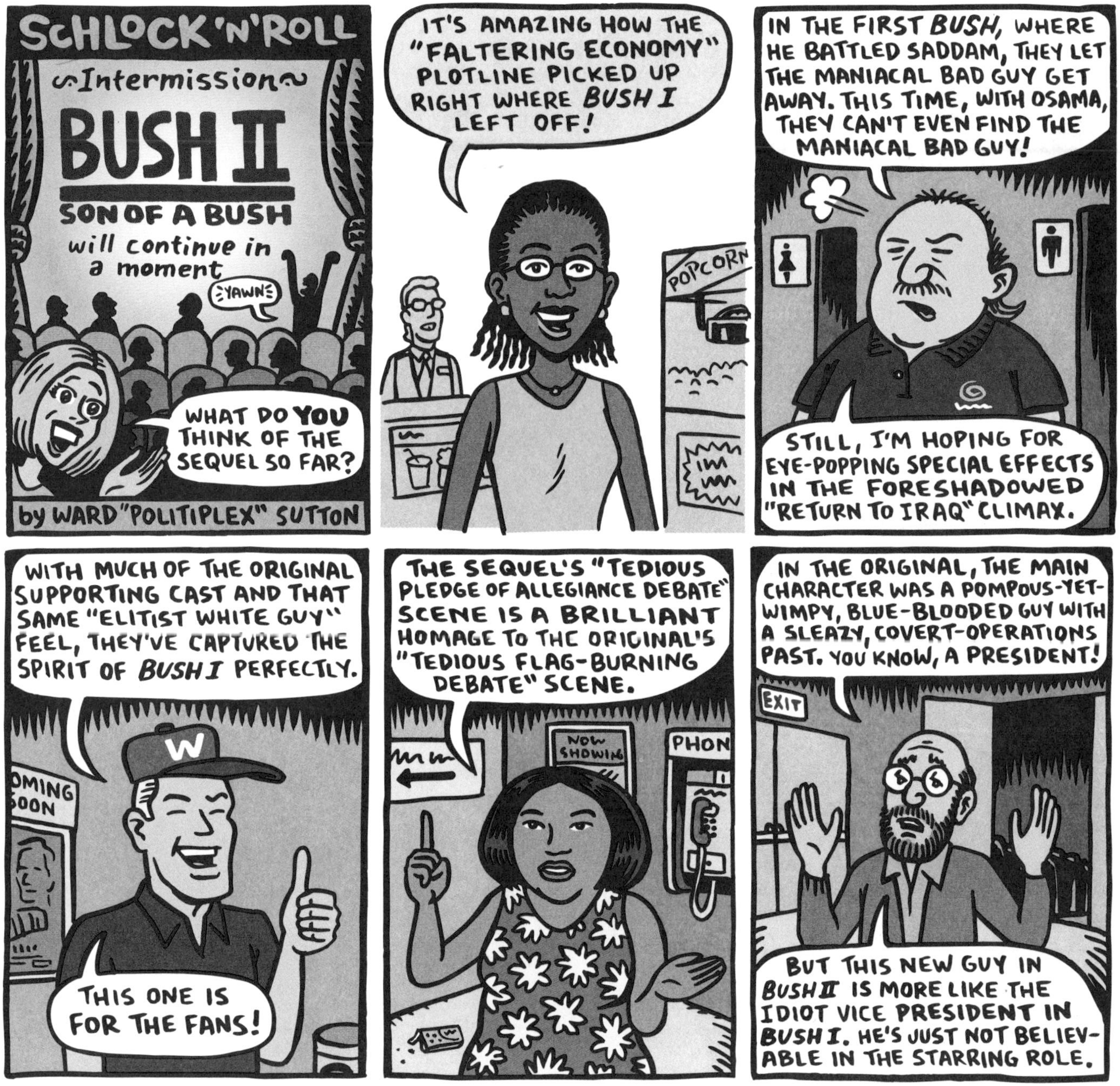
SCHLOCK 'N' ROLL
Intermission
BUSH II
SON OF A BUSH
will continue in a moment
YAWN
WHAT DO YOU THINK OF THE SEQUEL SO FAR?
by WARD "POLITIPLEX" SUTTON
IT'S AMAZING HOW THE "FALTERING ECONOMY" PLOTLINE PICKED UP RIGHT WHERE BUSH I LEFT OFF!
POPCORN
IN THE FIRST BUSH, WHERE HE BATTLED SADDAM, THEY LET THE MANIACAL BAD GUY GET AWAY. THIS TIME, WITH OSAMA, THEY CAN'T EVEN FIND THE MANIACAL BAD GUY!
STILL, I'M HOPING FOR EYE-POPPING SPECIAL EFFECTS IN THE FORESHADOWED "RETURN TO IRAQ" CLIMAX.
WITH MUCH OF THE ORIGINAL SUPPORTING CAST AND THAT SAME "ELITIST WHITE GUY" FEEL, THEY'VE CAPTURED THE SPIRIT OF BUSH I PERFECTLY.
W
OMING OON
THIS ONE IS FOR THE FANS!
THE SEQUEL'S "TEDIOUS PLEDGE OF ALLEGIANCE DEBATE" SCENE IS A BRILLIANT HOMAGE TO THE ORIGINAL'S "TEDIOUS FLAG-BURNING DEBATE" SCENE.
NOW SHOWING
PHON
IN THE ORIGINAL, THE MAIN CHARACTER WAS A POMPOUS-YET-WIMPY, BLUE-BLOODED GUY WITH A SLEAZY, COVERT-OPERATIONS PAST. YOU KNOW, A PRESIDENT!
EXIT
BUT THIS NEW GUY IN BUSH II IS MORE LIKE THE IDIOT VICE PRESIDENT IN BUSH I. HE'S JUST NOT BELIEVABLE IN THE STARRING ROLE.

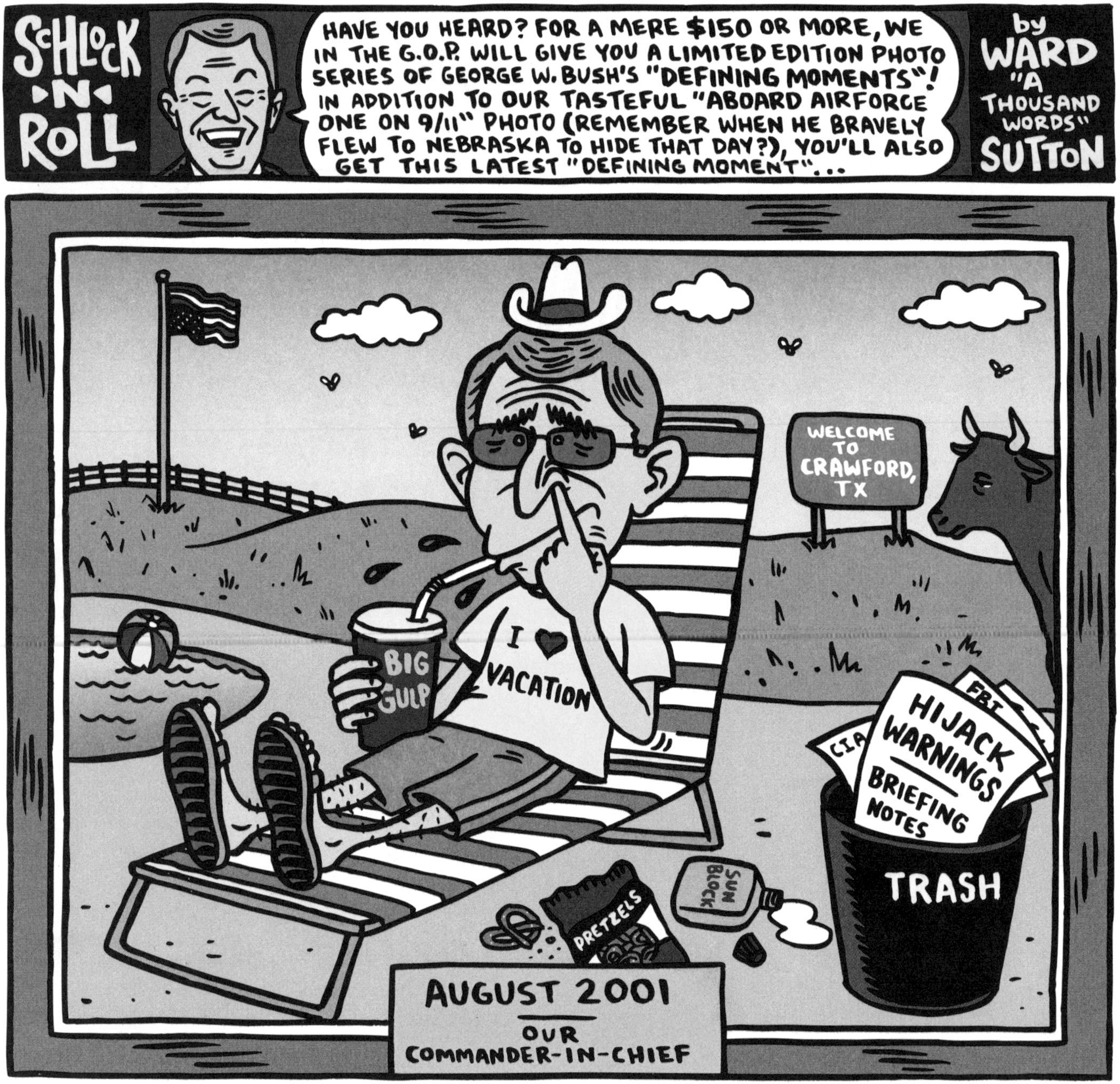
SCHLOCK N ROLL
HAVE YOU HEARD? FOR A MERE $150 OR MORE, WE IN THE G.O.P. WILL GIVE YOU A LIMITED EDITION PHOTO SERIES OF GEORGE W. BUSH'S "DEFINING MOMENTS"! IN ADDITION TO OUR TASTEFUL "ABOARD AIRFORCE ONE ON 9/11" PHOTO (REMEMBER WHEN HE BRAVELY FLEW TO NEBRASKA TO HIDE THAT DAY?), YOU'LL ALSO GET THIS LATEST "DEFINING MOMENT"...
by WARD "A THOUSAND WORDS" SUTTON
WELCOME TO CRAWFORD, TX
BIG GULP
I ♥ VACATION
FBI
CIA
HIJACK WARNINGS
BRIEFING NOTES
TRASH
SUN BLOCK
PRETZELS
AUGUST 2001
OUR COMMANDER-IN-CHIEF

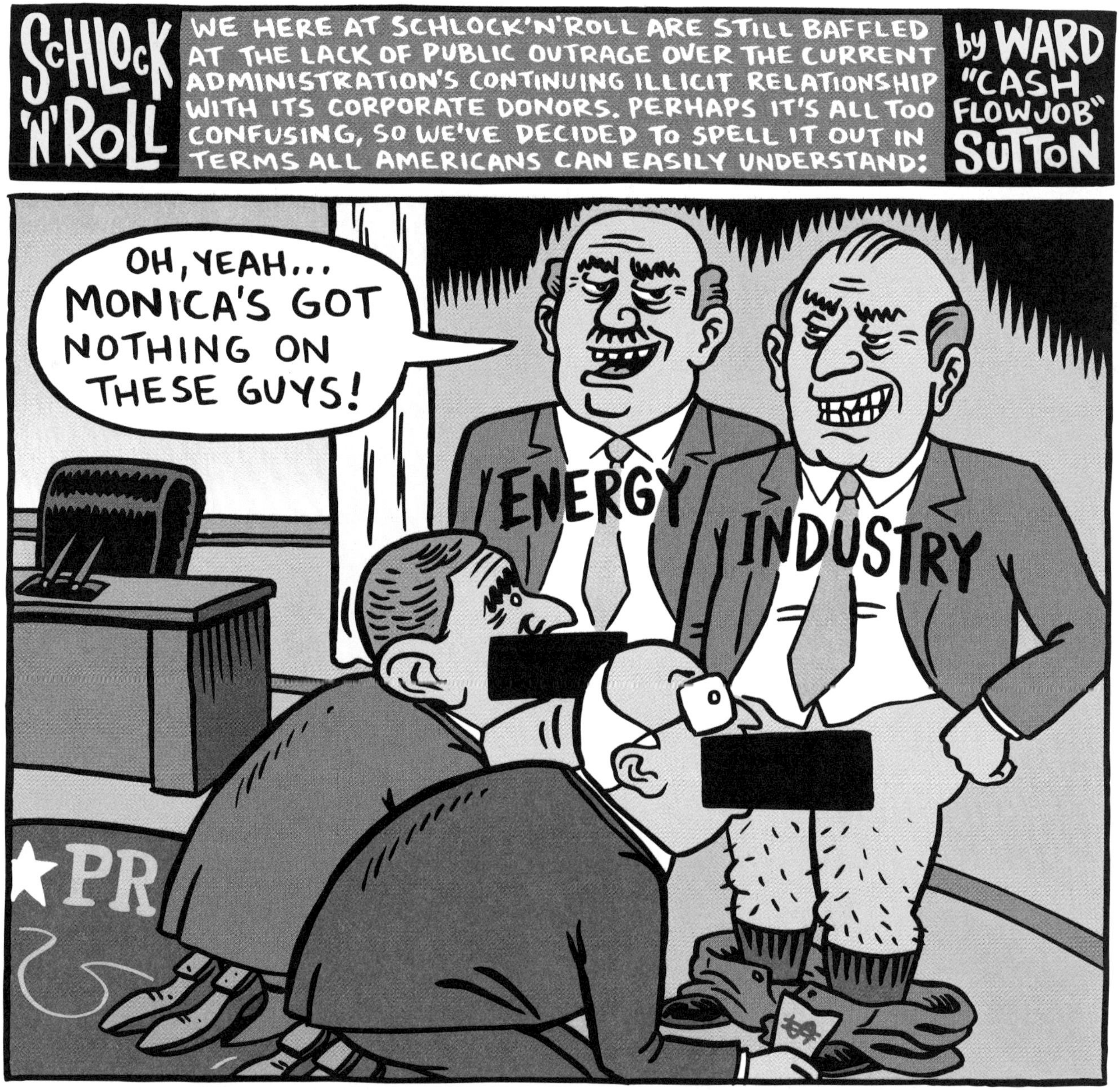
SCHLOCK 'N' ROLL
WE HERE AT SCHLOCK'N'ROLL ARE STILL BAFFLED AT THE LACK OF PUBLIC OUTRAGE OVER THE CURRENT ADMINISTRATION'S CONTINUING ILLICIT RELATIONSHIP WITH ITS CORPORATE DONORS. PERHAPS IT'S ALL TOO CONFUSING, SO WE'VE DECIDED TO SPELL IT OUT IN TERMS ALL AMERICANS CAN EASILY UNDERSTAND:
by WARD "CASH FLOWJOB" SUTTON
OH, YEAH... MONICA'S GOT NOTHING ON THESE GUYS!
ENERGY
INDUSTRY
PR

After I created this cartoon, I had a moment where I thought, "Have I finally gone too far?" A minute or two later I answered myself, "Of course not!" And I was pleasantly surprised that none of my papers had the slightest problem with it.

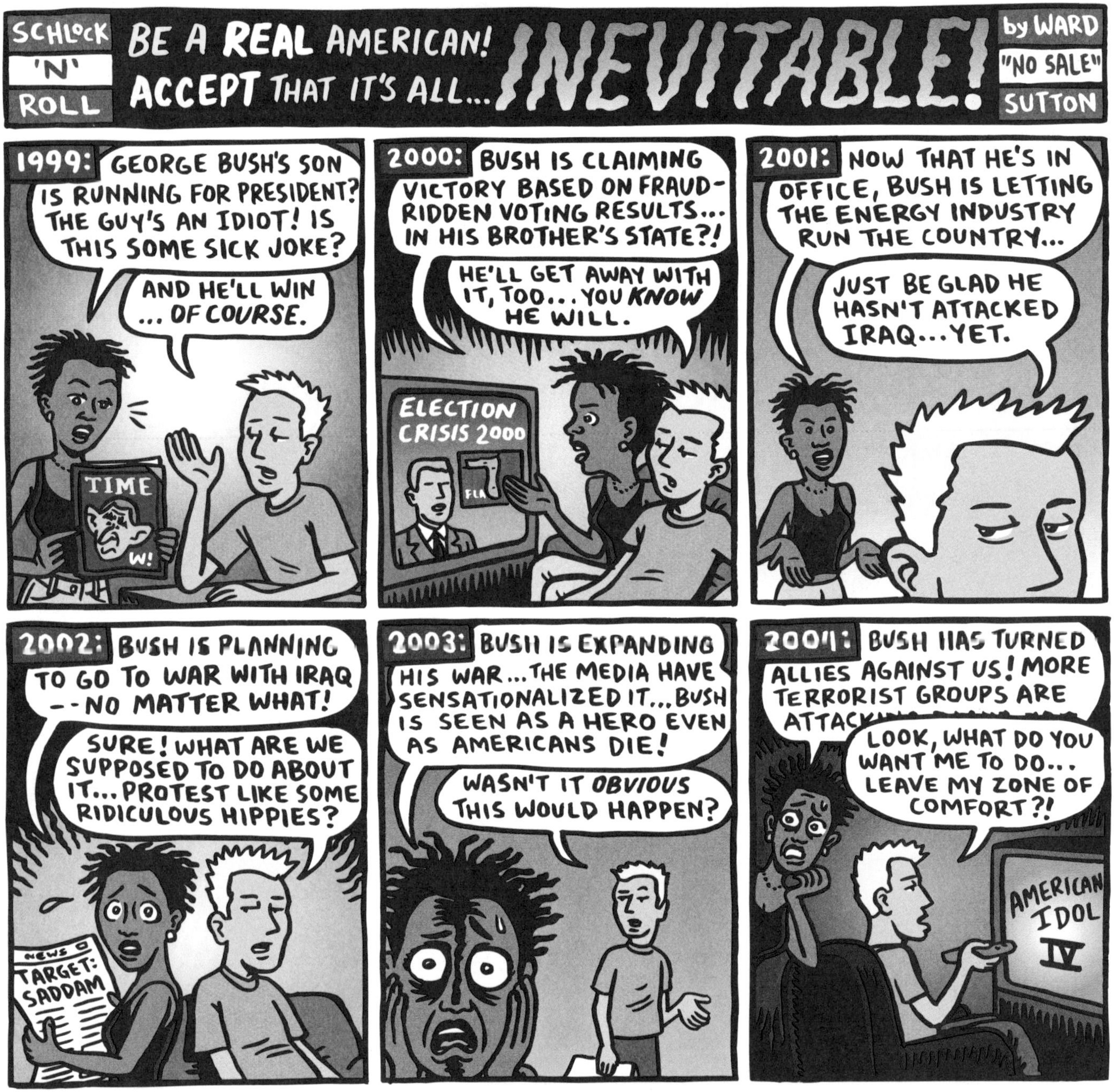
SCHLOCK 'N' ROLL
BE A REAL AMERICAN! ACCEPT THAT IT'S ALL... INEVITABLE!
by WARD "NO SALE" SUTTON
1999:
GEORGE BUSH'S SON IS RUNNING FOR PRESIDENT? THE GUY'S AN IDIOT! IS THIS SOME SICK JOKE?
AND HE'LL WIN ... OF COURSE.
TIME
W!
2000:
BUSH IS CLAIMING VICTORY BASED ON FRAUD-RIDDEN VOTING RESULTS... IN HIS BROTHER'S STATE?!
HE'LL GET AWAY WITH IT, TOO... YOU KNOW HE WILL.
ELECTION CRISIS 2000
FLA
2001:
NOW THAT HE'S IN OFFICE, BUSH IS LETTING THE ENERGY INDUSTRY RUN THE COUNTRY...
JUST BE GLAD HE HASN'T ATTACKED IRAQ... YET.
2002:
BUSH IS PLANNING TO GO TO WAR WITH IRAQ --NO MATTER WHAT!
SURE! WHAT ARE WE SUPPOSED TO DO ABOUT IT... PROTEST LIKE SOME RIDICULOUS HIPPIES?
NEWS
TARGET: SADDAM
2003:
BUSH IS EXPANDING HIS WAR... THE MEDIA HAVE SENSATIONALIZED IT... BUSH IS SEEN AS A HERO EVEN AS AMERICANS DIE!
WASN'T IT OBVIOUS THIS WOULD HAPPEN?
2004:
BUSH HAS TURNED ALLIES AGAINST US! MORE TERRORIST GROUPS ARE ATTAC
LOOK, WHAT DO YOU WANT ME TO DO... LEAVE MY ZONE OF COMFORT?!
AMERICAN IDOL IV

## SCHLOCK 'N' ROLL by WARD "AXIS OF EVEL KNIEVEL" SUTTON

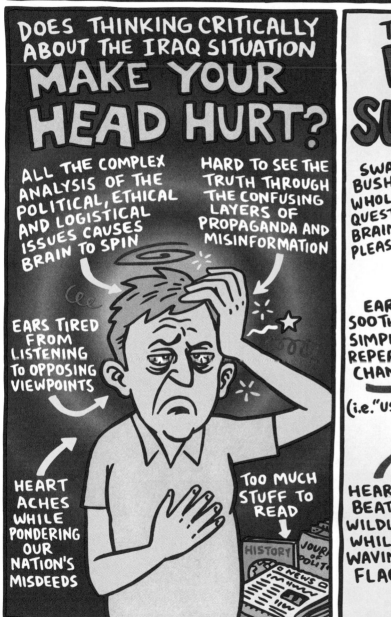

**DOES THINKING CRITICALLY ABOUT THE IRAQ SITUATION MAKE YOUR HEAD HURT?**

ALL THE COMPLEX ANALYSIS OF THE POLITICAL, ETHICAL AND LOGISTICAL ISSUES CAUSES BRAIN TO SPIN

HARD TO SEE THE TRUTH THROUGH THE CONFUSING LAYERS OF PROPAGANDA AND MISINFORMATION

EARS TIRED FROM LISTENING TO OPPOSING VIEWPOINTS

HEART ACHES WHILE PONDERING OUR NATION'S MISDEEDS

TOO MUCH STUFF TO READ

**THEN WHY NOT BLINDLY SUPPORT WAR?**

SWALLOWING BUSH RATIONALE WHOLE WITHOUT QUESTION ALLOWS BRAIN TO REMAIN PLEASANTLY DORMANT

EASY TO SEE IT ALL THEIR WAY WHEN REFUSING TO LOOK BELOW THE SURFACE

EARS SOOTHED BY SIMPLISTIC, REPEATED CHANTS

(i.e. "USA! USA!")

HEART BEATS WILDLY WHILE WAVING FLAG

WE'RE #1

THAT'S BETTER!

FOX NEWS

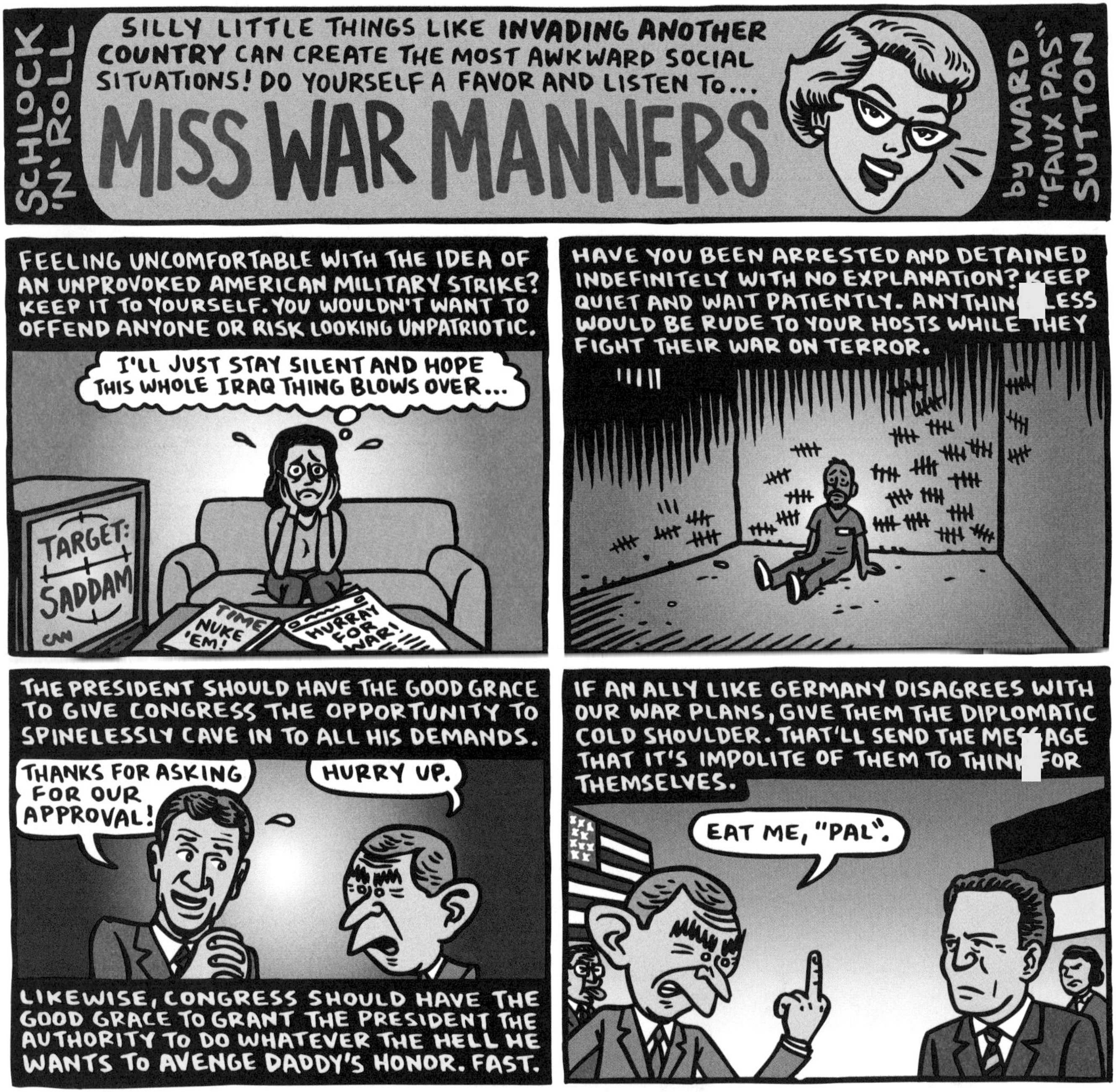
SCHLOCK 'N' ROLL
SILLY LITTLE THINGS LIKE INVADING ANOTHER COUNTRY CAN CREATE THE MOST AWKWARD SOCIAL SITUATIONS! DO YOURSELF A FAVOR AND LISTEN TO...
MISS WAR MANNERS
by WARD "FAUX PAS" SUTTON
FEELING UNCOMFORTABLE WITH THE IDEA OF AN UNPROVOKED AMERICAN MILITARY STRIKE? KEEP IT TO YOURSELF. YOU WOULDN'T WANT TO OFFEND ANYONE OR RISK LOOKING UNPATRIOTIC.
I'LL JUST STAY SILENT AND HOPE THIS WHOLE IRAQ THING BLOWS OVER...
TARGET: SADDAM
CNN
TIME
NUKE 'EM!
HURRAY FOR WAR!
HAVE YOU BEEN ARRESTED AND DETAINED INDEFINITELY WITH NO EXPLANATION? KEEP QUIET AND WAIT PATIENTLY. ANYTHING LESS WOULD BE RUDE TO YOUR HOSTS WHILE THEY FIGHT THEIR WAR ON TERROR.
THE PRESIDENT SHOULD HAVE THE GOOD GRACE TO GIVE CONGRESS THE OPPORTUNITY TO SPINELESSLY CAVE IN TO ALL HIS DEMANDS.
THANKS FOR ASKING FOR OUR APPROVAL!
HURRY UP.
LIKEWISE, CONGRESS SHOULD HAVE THE GOOD GRACE TO GRANT THE PRESIDENT THE AUTHORITY TO DO WHATEVER THE HELL HE WANTS TO AVENGE DADDY'S HONOR. FAST.
IF AN ALLY LIKE GERMANY DISAGREES WITH OUR WAR PLANS, GIVE THEM THE DIPLOMATIC COLD SHOULDER. THAT'LL SEND THE MESSAGE THAT IT'S IMPOLITE OF THEM TO THINK FOR THEMSELVES.
EAT ME, "PAL".

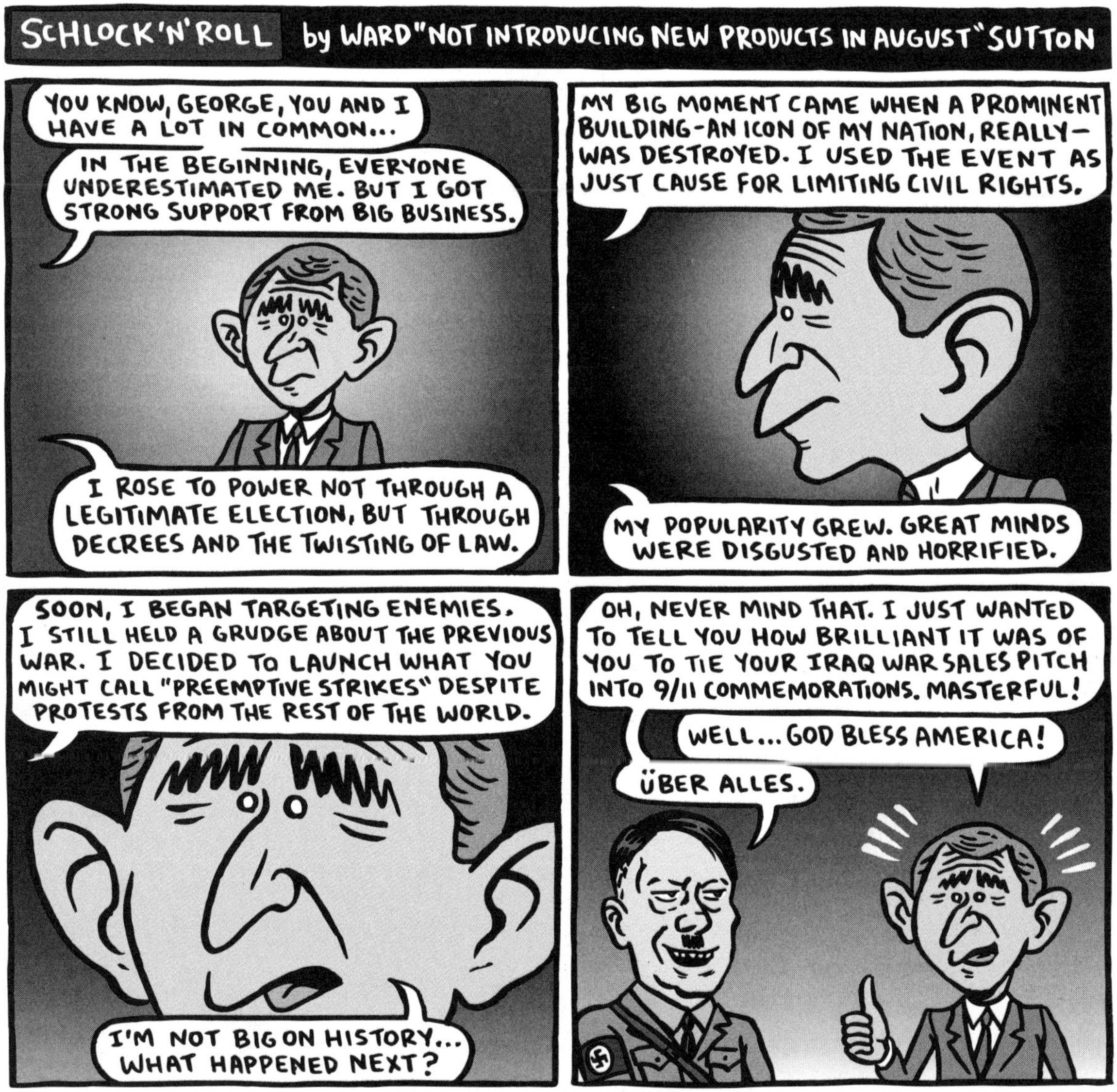
SCHLOCK'N'ROLL by WARD "NOT INTRODUCING NEW PRODUCTS IN AUGUST" SUTTON
YOU KNOW, GEORGE, YOU AND I HAVE A LOT IN COMMON...
IN THE BEGINNING, EVERYONE UNDERESTIMATED ME. BUT I GOT STRONG SUPPORT FROM BIG BUSINESS.
I ROSE TO POWER NOT THROUGH A LEGITIMATE ELECTION, BUT THROUGH DECREES AND THE TWISTING OF LAW.
MY BIG MOMENT CAME WHEN A PROMINENT BUILDING-AN ICON OF MY NATION, REALLY-WAS DESTROYED. I USED THE EVENT AS JUST CAUSE FOR LIMITING CIVIL RIGHTS.
MY POPULARITY GREW. GREAT MINDS WERE DISGUSTED AND HORRIFIED.
SOON, I BEGAN TARGETING ENEMIES. I STILL HELD A GRUDGE ABOUT THE PREVIOUS WAR. I DECIDED TO LAUNCH WHAT YOU MIGHT CALL "PREEMPTIVE STRIKES" DESPITE PROTESTS FROM THE REST OF THE WORLD.
I'M NOT BIG ON HISTORY... WHAT HAPPENED NEXT?
OH, NEVER MIND THAT. I JUST WANTED TO TELL YOU HOW BRILLIANT IT WAS OF YOU TO TIE YOUR IRAQ WAR SALES PITCH INTO 9/11 COMMEMORATIONS. MASTERFUL!
WELL... GOD BLESS AMERICA!
ÜBER ALLES.

Just weeks after this cartoon ran, Herta Daubler-Gmelin, the German justice minister, set off an international firestorm of controversy when she said, "Bush wants to divert attention from domestic problems. It's a classic tactic. It's one that Hitler used."

Many people consider the mention of Hitler to mean the end of rational debate. But is it really rational to put Nazi history in a box and keep it off limits when critiquing modern politics? Pretending Hitler and the Nazis were anything other than human does a service to no one. Obviously, Bush is not Hitler, but I believe it's valid and crucial to examine the similarities of their tactics and rise to power.

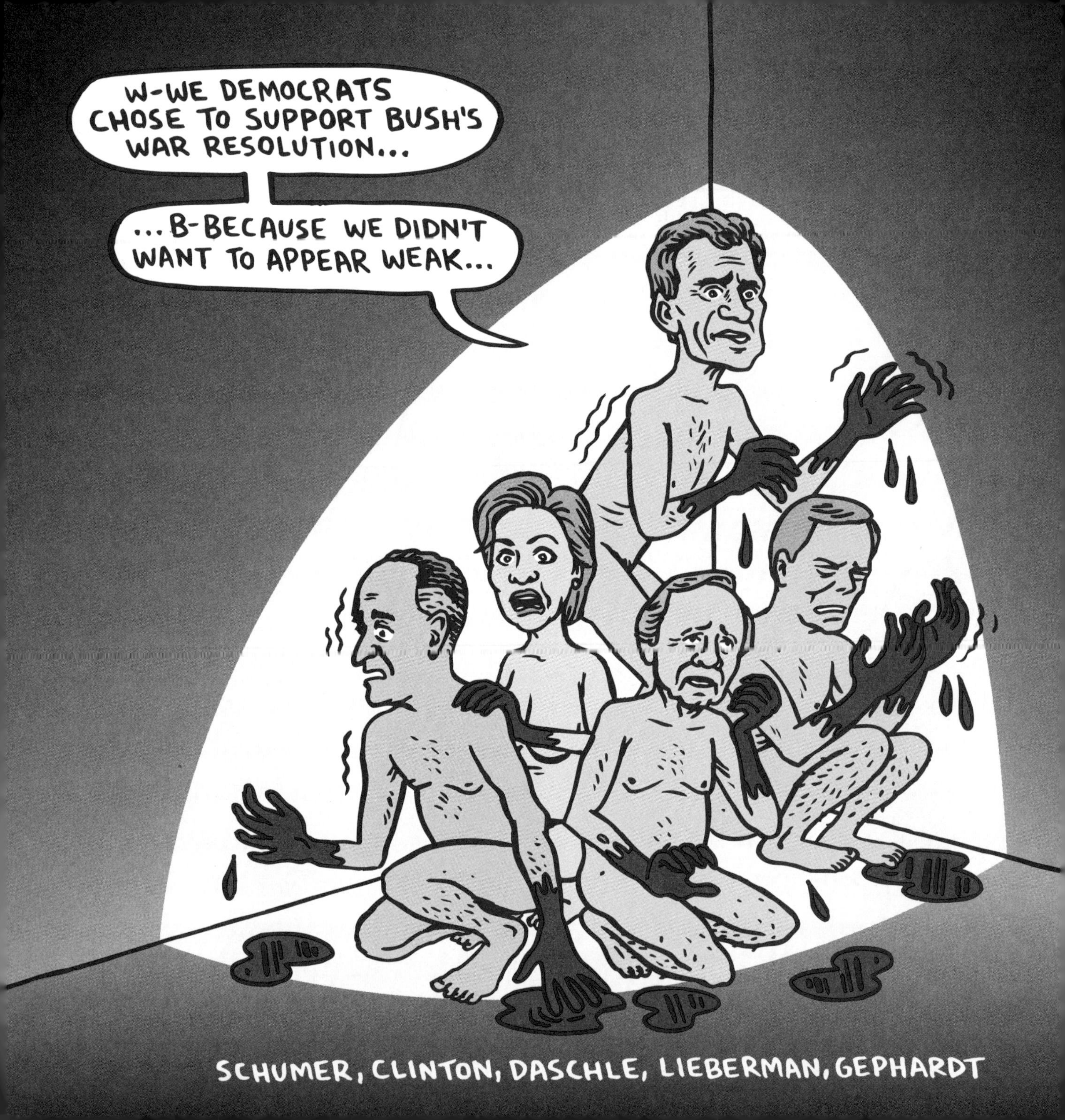
W-WE DEMOCRATS CHOSE TO SUPPORT BUSH'S WAR RESOLUTION...
...B-BECAUSE WE DIDN'T WANT TO APPEAR WEAK...
SCHUMER, CLINTON, DASCHLE, LIEBERMAN, GEPHARDT

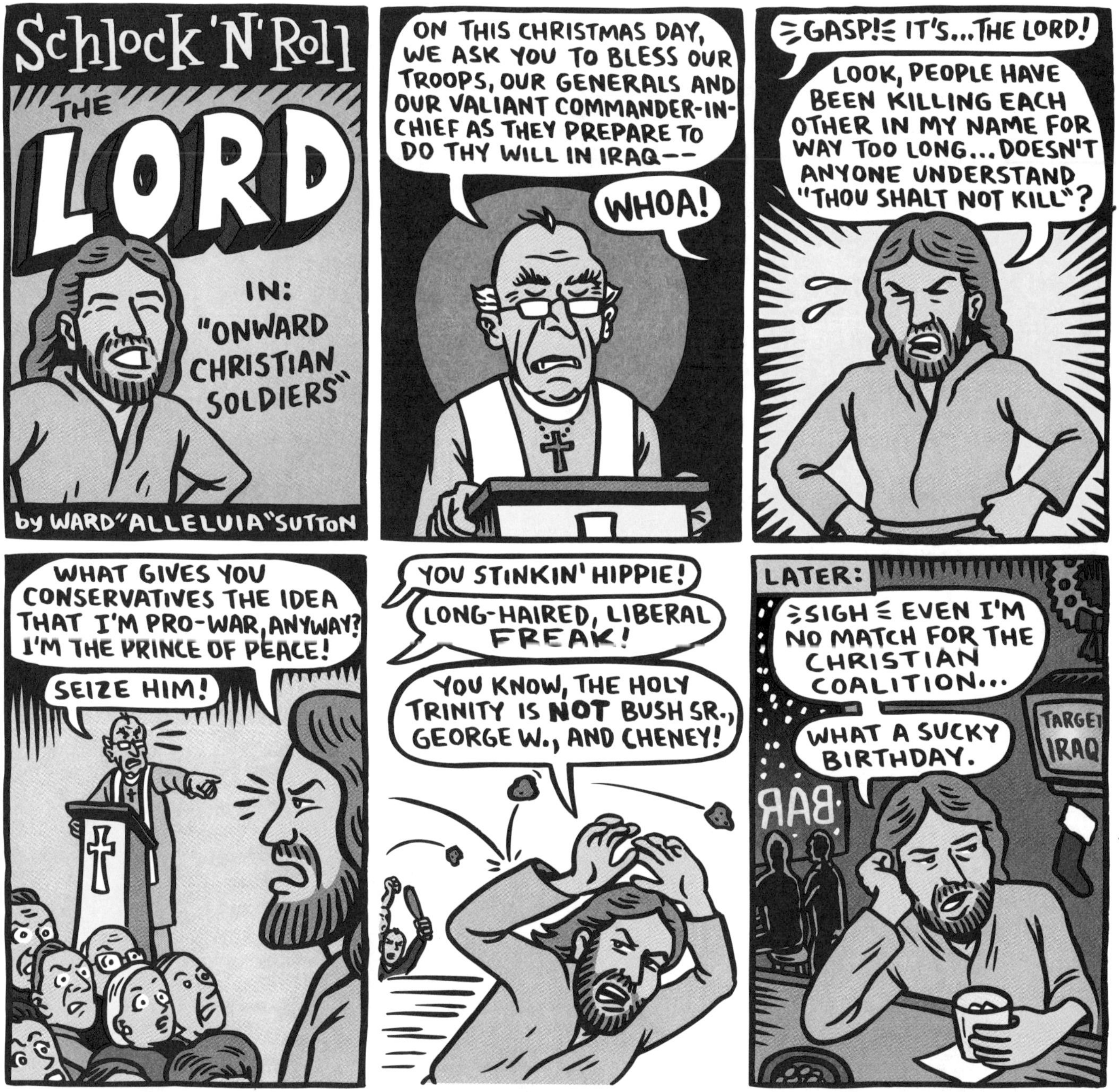
Schlock 'N' Roll
THE LORD
IN: "ONWARD CHRISTIAN SOLDIERS"
by WARD "ALLELUIA" SUTTON
ON THIS CHRISTMAS DAY, WE ASK YOU TO BLESS OUR TROOPS, OUR GENERALS AND OUR VALIANT COMMANDER-IN-CHIEF AS THEY PREPARE TO DO THY WILL IN IRAQ--
WHOA!
≡GASP!≡ IT'S...THE LORD!
LOOK, PEOPLE HAVE BEEN KILLING EACH OTHER IN MY NAME FOR WAY TOO LONG... DOESN'T ANYONE UNDERSTAND "THOU SHALT NOT KILL"?
WHAT GIVES YOU CONSERVATIVES THE IDEA THAT I'M PRO-WAR, ANYWAY? I'M THE PRINCE OF PEACE!
SEIZE HIM!
YOU STINKIN' HIPPIE!
LONG-HAIRED, LIBERAL FREAK!
YOU KNOW, THE HOLY TRINITY IS NOT BUSH SR., GEORGE W., AND CHENEY!
LATER:
≡SIGH≡ EVEN I'M NO MATCH FOR THE CHRISTIAN COALITION...
WHAT A SUCKY BIRTHDAY.
TARGE
IRAQ

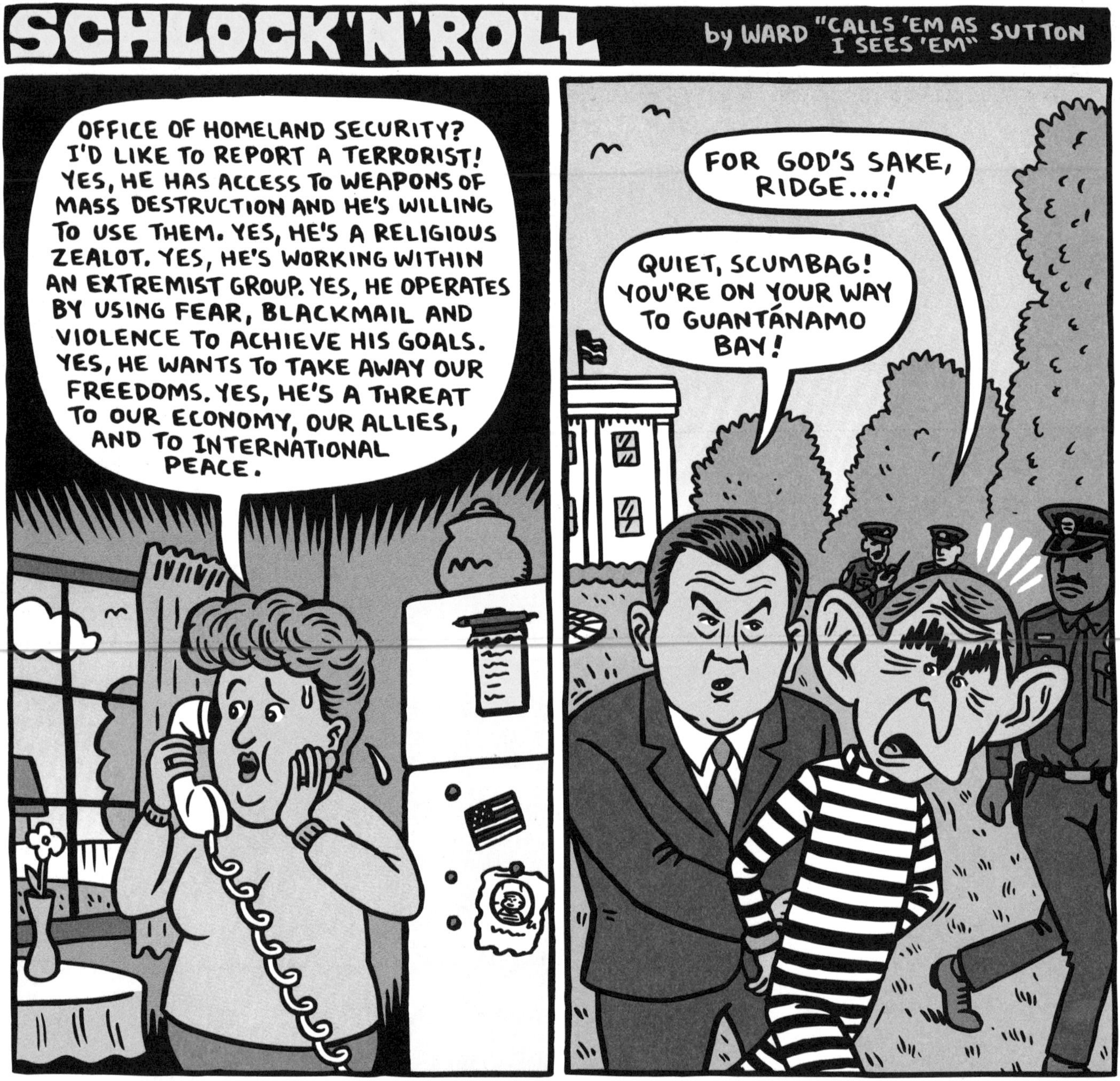
SCHLOCK'N'ROLL
by WARD "CALLS 'EM AS I SEES 'EM" SUTTON
OFFICE OF HOMELAND SECURITY? I'D LIKE TO REPORT A TERRORIST! YES, HE HAS ACCESS TO WEAPONS OF MASS DESTRUCTION AND HE'S WILLING TO USE THEM. YES, HE'S A RELIGIOUS ZEALOT. YES, HE'S WORKING WITHIN AN EXTREMIST GROUP. YES, HE OPERATES BY USING FEAR, BLACKMAIL AND VIOLENCE TO ACHIEVE HIS GOALS. YES, HE WANTS TO TAKE AWAY OUR FREEDOMS. YES, HE'S A THREAT TO OUR ECONOMY, OUR ALLIES, AND TO INTERNATIONAL PEACE.
FOR GOD'S SAKE, RIDGE...!
QUIET, SCUMBAG! YOU'RE ON YOUR WAY TO GUANTÁNAMO BAY!

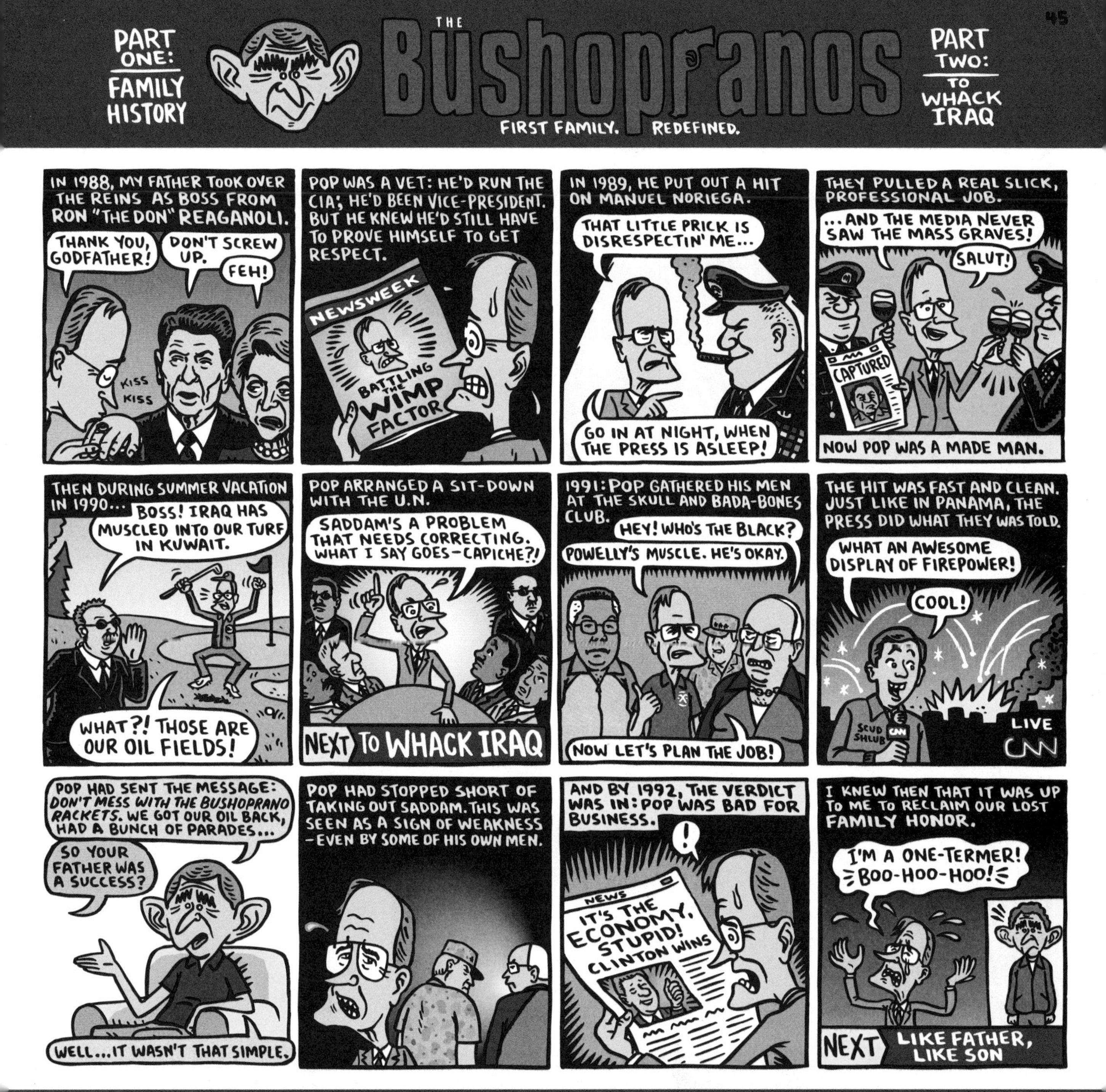
PART ONE: FAMILY HISTORY
THE Bushopranos
FIRST FAMILY. REDEFINED.
PART TWO: TO WHACK IRAQ
IN 1988, MY FATHER TOOK OVER THE REINS AS BOSS FROM RON "THE DON" REAGANOLI.
THANK YOU, GODFATHER!
DON'T SCREW UP.
FEH!
KISS KISS
POP WAS A VET: HE'D RUN THE CIA; HE'D BEEN VICE-PRESIDENT. BUT HE KNEW HE'D STILL HAVE TO PROVE HIMSELF TO GET RESPECT.
NEWSWEEK
BATTLING THE WIMP FACTOR
IN 1989, HE PUT OUT A HIT ON MANUEL NORIEGA.
THAT LITTLE PRICK IS DISRESPECTIN' ME...
GO IN AT NIGHT, WHEN THE PRESS IS ASLEEP!
THEY PULLED A REAL SLICK, PROFESSIONAL JOB.
...AND THE MEDIA NEVER SAW THE MASS GRAVES!
SALUT!
CAPTURED
NOW POP WAS A MADE MAN.
THEN DURING SUMMER VACATION IN 1990...
BOSS! IRAQ HAS MUSCLED INTO OUR TURF IN KUWAIT.
WHAT?! THOSE ARE OUR OIL FIELDS!
POP ARRANGED A SIT-DOWN WITH THE U.N.
SADDAM'S A PROBLEM THAT NEEDS CORRECTING. WHAT I SAY GOES—CAPICHE?!
NEXT TO WHACK IRAQ
1991: POP GATHERED HIS MEN AT THE SKULL AND BADA-BONES CLUB.
HEY! WHO'S THE BLACK?
POWELLY'S MUSCLE. HE'S OKAY.
NOW LET'S PLAN THE JOB!
THE HIT WAS FAST AND CLEAN. JUST LIKE IN PANAMA, THE PRESS DID WHAT THEY WAS TOLD.
WHAT AN AWESOME DISPLAY OF FIREPOWER!
COOL!
SCUD SHLUB
LIVE
CNN
POP HAD SENT THE MESSAGE: *DON'T MESS WITH THE BUSHOPRANO RACKETS.* WE GOT OUR OIL BACK, HAD A BUNCH OF PARADES...
SO YOUR FATHER WAS A SUCCESS?
WELL... IT WASN'T THAT SIMPLE.
POP HAD STOPPED SHORT OF TAKING OUT SADDAM. THIS WAS SEEN AS A SIGN OF WEAKNESS —EVEN BY SOME OF HIS OWN MEN.
AND BY 1992, THE VERDICT WAS IN: POP WAS BAD FOR BUSINESS.
!
NEWS
IT'S THE ECONOMY, STUPID! CLINTON WINS
I KNEW THEN THAT IT WAS UP TO ME TO RECLAIM OUR LOST FAMILY HONOR.
I'M A ONE-TERMER! BOO-HOO-HOO!
NEXT LIKE FATHER, LIKE SON

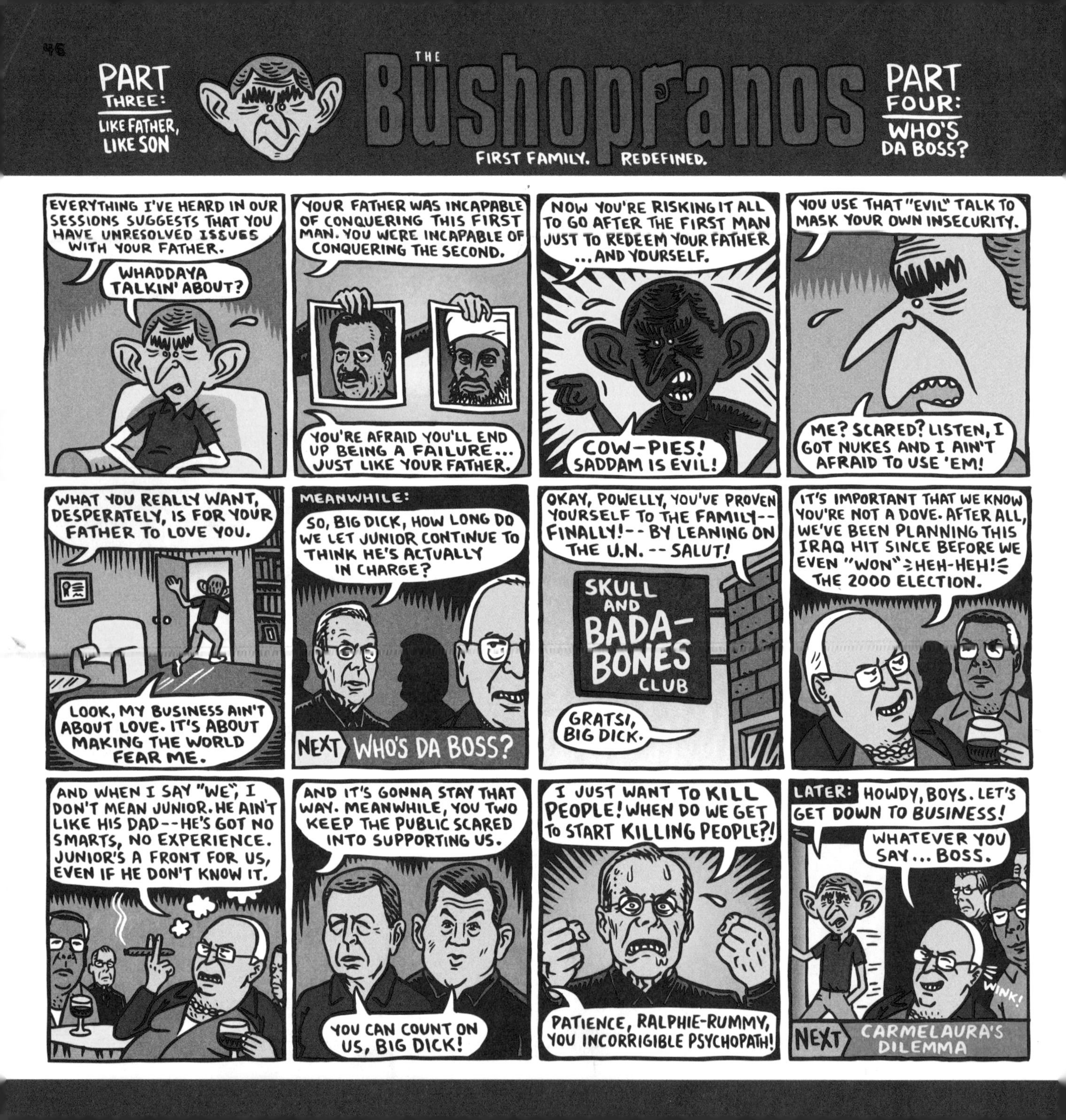
PART THREE: LIKE FATHER, LIKE SON
THE Bushopranos
FIRST FAMILY. REDEFINED.
PART FOUR: WHO'S DA BOSS?
EVERYTHING I'VE HEARD IN OUR SESSIONS SUGGESTS THAT YOU HAVE UNRESOLVED ISSUES WITH YOUR FATHER.
WHADDAYA TALKIN' ABOUT?
YOUR FATHER WAS INCAPABLE OF CONQUERING THIS FIRST MAN. YOU WERE INCAPABLE OF CONQUERING THE SECOND.
YOU'RE AFRAID YOU'LL END UP BEING A FAILURE... JUST LIKE YOUR FATHER.
NOW YOU'RE RISKING IT ALL TO GO AFTER THE FIRST MAN JUST TO REDEEM YOUR FATHER ...AND YOURSELF.
COW-PIES! SADDAM IS EVIL!
YOU USE THAT "EVIL" TALK TO MASK YOUR OWN INSECURITY.
ME? SCARED? LISTEN, I GOT NUKES AND I AIN'T AFRAID TO USE 'EM!
WHAT YOU REALLY WANT, DESPERATELY, IS FOR YOUR FATHER TO LOVE YOU.
LOOK, MY BUSINESS AIN'T ABOUT LOVE. IT'S ABOUT MAKING THE WORLD FEAR ME.
MEANWHILE:
SO, BIG DICK, HOW LONG DO WE LET JUNIOR CONTINUE TO THINK HE'S ACTUALLY IN CHARGE?
NEXT WHO'S DA BOSS?
OKAY, POWELLY, YOU'VE PROVEN YOURSELF TO THE FAMILY--FINALLY!--BY LEANING ON THE U.N. --SALUT!
SKULL AND BADA-BONES CLUB
GRATSI, BIG DICK.
IT'S IMPORTANT THAT WE KNOW YOU'RE NOT A DOVE. AFTER ALL, WE'VE BEEN PLANNING THIS IRAQ HIT SINCE BEFORE WE EVEN "WON" HEH-HEH! THE 2000 ELECTION.
AND WHEN I SAY "WE", I DON'T MEAN JUNIOR. HE AIN'T LIKE HIS DAD--HE'S GOT NO SMARTS, NO EXPERIENCE. JUNIOR'S A FRONT FOR US, EVEN IF HE DON'T KNOW IT.
AND IT'S GONNA STAY THAT WAY. MEANWHILE, YOU TWO KEEP THE PUBLIC SCARED INTO SUPPORTING US.
YOU CAN COUNT ON US, BIG DICK!
I JUST WANT TO KILL PEOPLE! WHEN DO WE GET TO START KILLING PEOPLE?!
PATIENCE, RALPHIE-RUMMY, YOU INCORRIGIBLE PSYCHOPATH!
LATER: HOWDY, BOYS. LET'S GET DOWN TO BUSINESS!
WHATEVER YOU SAY... BOSS.
WINK!
NEXT CARMELAURA'S DILEMMA

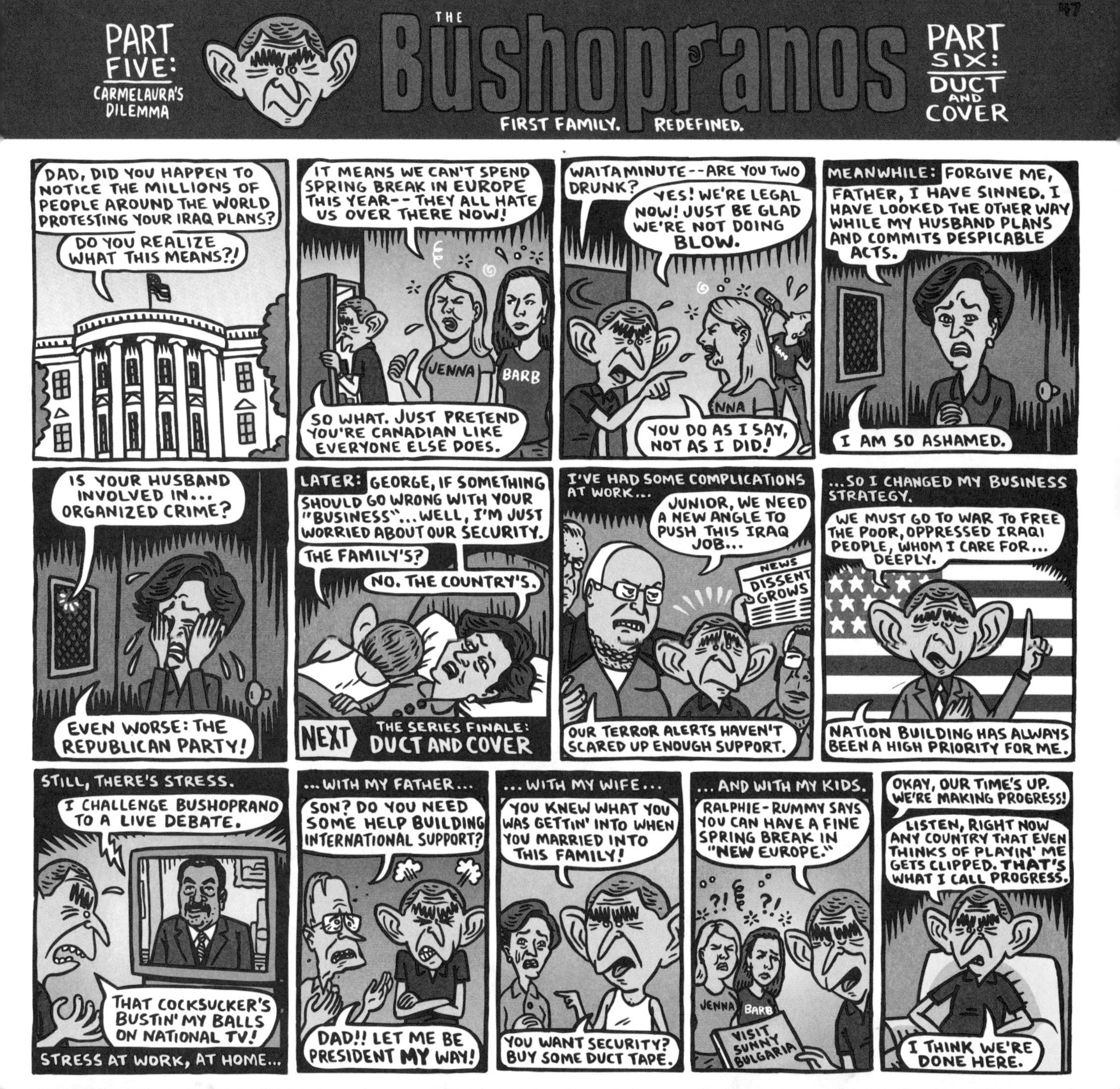
PART FIVE:
CARMELAURA'S DILEMMA
THE Bushopranos
FIRST FAMILY. REDEFINED.
PART SIX:
DUCT AND COVER
DAD, DID YOU HAPPEN TO NOTICE THE MILLIONS OF PEOPLE AROUND THE WORLD PROTESTING YOUR IRAQ PLANS?
DO YOU REALIZE WHAT THIS MEANS?!
IT MEANS WE CAN'T SPEND SPRING BREAK IN EUROPE THIS YEAR-- THEY ALL HATE US OVER THERE NOW!
JENNA
BARB
SO WHAT. JUST PRETEND YOU'RE CANADIAN LIKE EVERYONE ELSE DOES.
WAITA MINUTE--ARE YOU TWO DRUNK?
YES! WE'RE LEGAL NOW! JUST BE GLAD WE'RE NOT DOING BLOW.
NNA
YOU DO AS I SAY, NOT AS I DID!
MEANWHILE: FORGIVE ME, FATHER, I HAVE SINNED. I HAVE LOOKED THE OTHER WAY WHILE MY HUSBAND PLANS AND COMMITS DESPICABLE ACTS.
I AM SO ASHAMED.
IS YOUR HUSBAND INVOLVED IN... ORGANIZED CRIME?
EVEN WORSE: THE REPUBLICAN PARTY!
LATER: GEORGE, IF SOMETHING SHOULD GO WRONG WITH YOUR "BUSINESS"... WELL, I'M JUST WORRIED ABOUT OUR SECURITY.
THE FAMILY'S?
NO. THE COUNTRY'S.
NEXT THE SERIES FINALE: DUCT AND COVER
I'VE HAD SOME COMPLICATIONS AT WORK...
JUNIOR, WE NEED A NEW ANGLE TO PUSH THIS IRAQ JOB...
NEWS DISSENT GROWS
OUR TERROR ALERTS HAVEN'T SCARED UP ENOUGH SUPPORT.
...SO I CHANGED MY BUSINESS STRATEGY.
WE MUST GO TO WAR TO FREE THE POOR, OPPRESSED IRAQI PEOPLE, WHOM I CARE FOR... DEEPLY.
NATION BUILDING HAS ALWAYS BEEN A HIGH PRIORITY FOR ME.
STILL, THERE'S STRESS.
I CHALLENGE BUSHOPRANO TO A LIVE DEBATE.
THAT COCKSUCKER'S BUSTIN' MY BALLS ON NATIONAL TV!
STRESS AT WORK, AT HOME...
...WITH MY FATHER...
SON? DO YOU NEED SOME HELP BUILDING INTERNATIONAL SUPPORT?
DAD!! LET ME BE PRESIDENT MY WAY!
...WITH MY WIFE...
YOU KNEW WHAT YOU WAS GETTIN' INTO WHEN YOU MARRIED INTO THIS FAMILY!
YOU WANT SECURITY? BUY SOME DUCT TAPE.
...AND WITH MY KIDS.
RALPHIE-RUMMY SAYS YOU CAN HAVE A FINE SPRING BREAK IN "NEW EUROPE."
JENNA
BARB
VISIT SUNNY BULGARIA
OKAY, OUR TIME'S UP. WE'RE MAKING PROGRESS!
LISTEN, RIGHT NOW ANY COUNTRY THAT EVEN THINKS OF PLAYIN' ME GETS CLIPPED. THAT'S WHAT I CALL PROGRESS.
I THINK WE'RE DONE HERE.

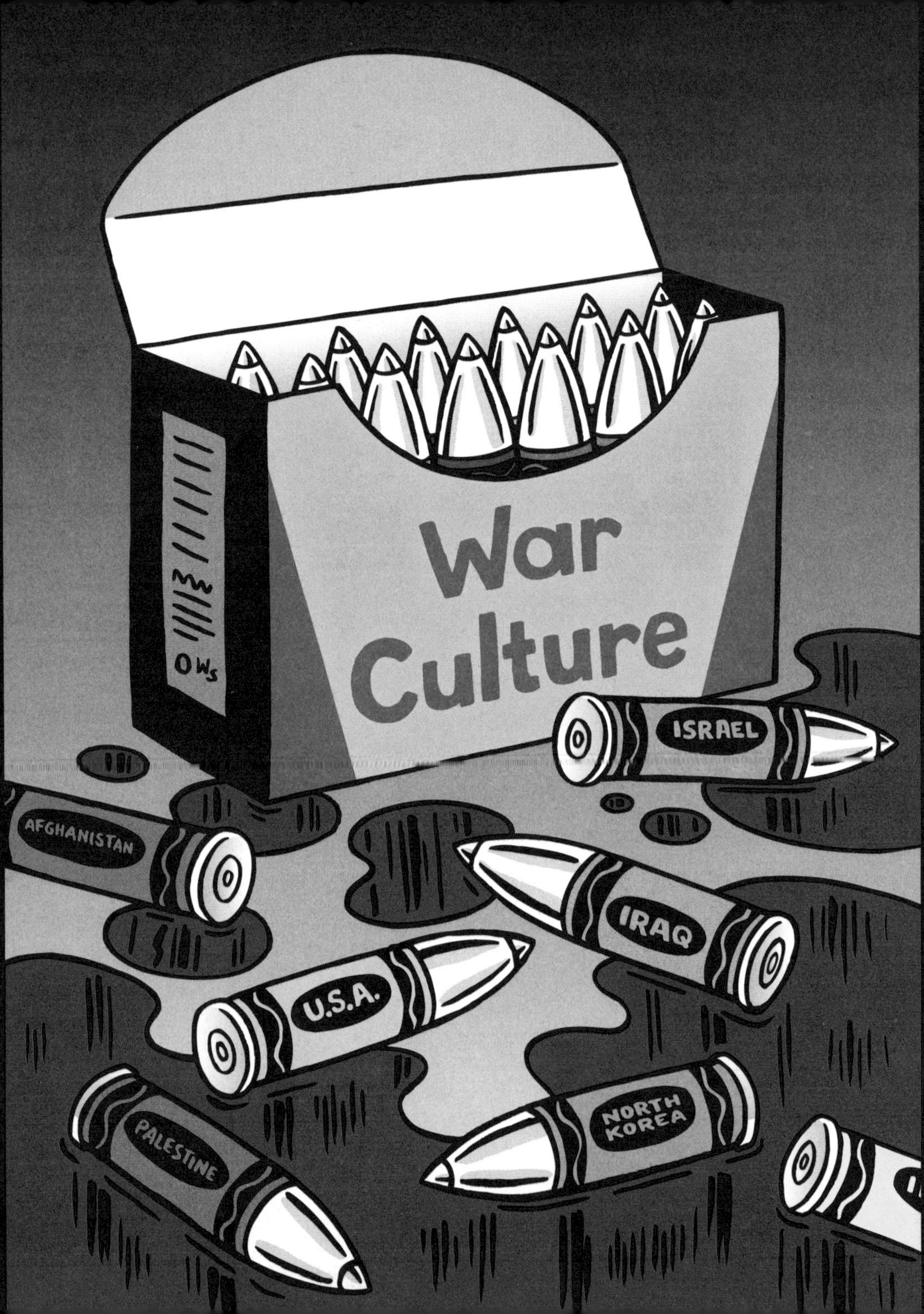

War
Culture
ISRAEL
AFGHANISTAN
IRAQ
U.S.A.
NORTH KOREA
PALESTINE

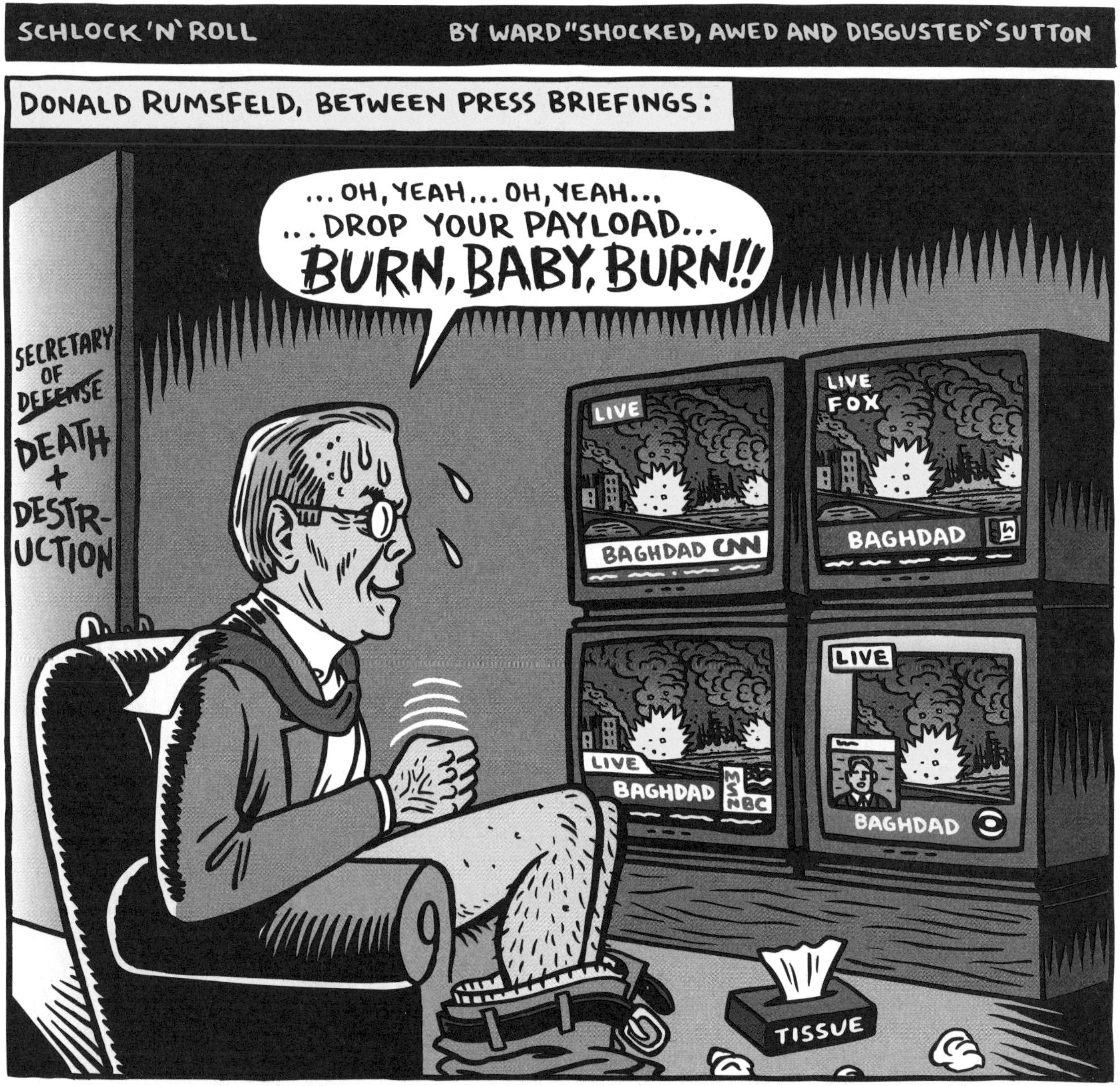
SCHLOCK 'N' ROLL
BY WARD "SHOCKED, AWED AND DISGUSTED" SUTTON
DONALD RUMSFELD, BETWEEN PRESS BRIEFINGS:
...OH, YEAH... OH, YEAH... ...DROP YOUR PAYLOAD... BURN, BABY, BURN!!
SECRETARY OF DEFENSE
DEATH + DESTR-UCTION
LIVE
BAGHDAD CNN
LIVE FOX
BAGHDAD
LIVE
BAGHDAD MSNBC
LIVE
BAGHDAD
TISSUE

The *Village Voice* ran a letter from an angry reader who thought this cartoon was disgusting. It was exactly the kind of response I wanted to provoke. Why do some people react more strongly to seeing masturbation than to seeing our bombs kill thousands of people?

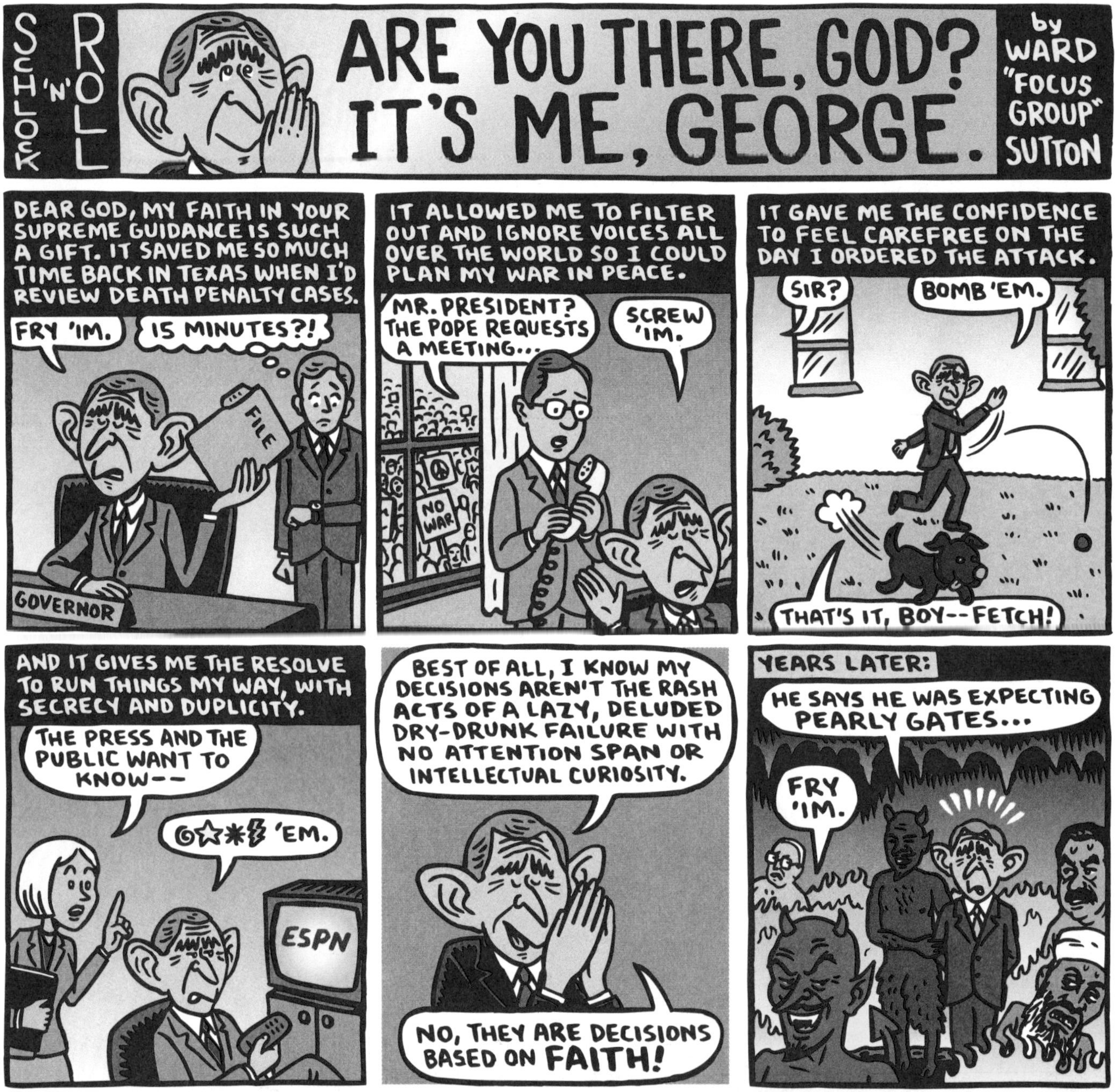
SCHLOCK 'N' ROLL
ARE YOU THERE, GOD? IT'S ME, GEORGE.
by WARD "FOCUS GROUP" SUTTON
DEAR GOD, MY FAITH IN YOUR SUPREME GUIDANCE IS SUCH A GIFT. IT SAVED ME SO MUCH TIME BACK IN TEXAS WHEN I'D REVIEW DEATH PENALTY CASES.
FRY 'IM.
15 MINUTES?!
FILE
GOVERNOR
IT ALLOWED ME TO FILTER OUT AND IGNORE VOICES ALL OVER THE WORLD SO I COULD PLAN MY WAR IN PEACE.
MR. PRESIDENT? THE POPE REQUESTS A MEETING...
SCREW 'IM.
NO WAR
IT GAVE ME THE CONFIDENCE TO FEEL CAREFREE ON THE DAY I ORDERED THE ATTACK.
SIR?
BOMB 'EM.
THAT'S IT, BOY--FETCH!
AND IT GIVES ME THE RESOLVE TO RUN THINGS MY WAY, WITH SECRECY AND DUPLICITY.
THE PRESS AND THE PUBLIC WANT TO KNOW--
@☆*# 'EM.
ESPN
BEST OF ALL, I KNOW MY DECISIONS AREN'T THE RASH ACTS OF A LAZY, DELUDED DRY-DRUNK FAILURE WITH NO ATTENTION SPAN OR INTELLECTUAL CURIOSITY.
NO, THEY ARE DECISIONS BASED ON FAITH!
YEARS LATER:
HE SAYS HE WAS EXPECTING PEARLY GATES...
FRY 'IM.

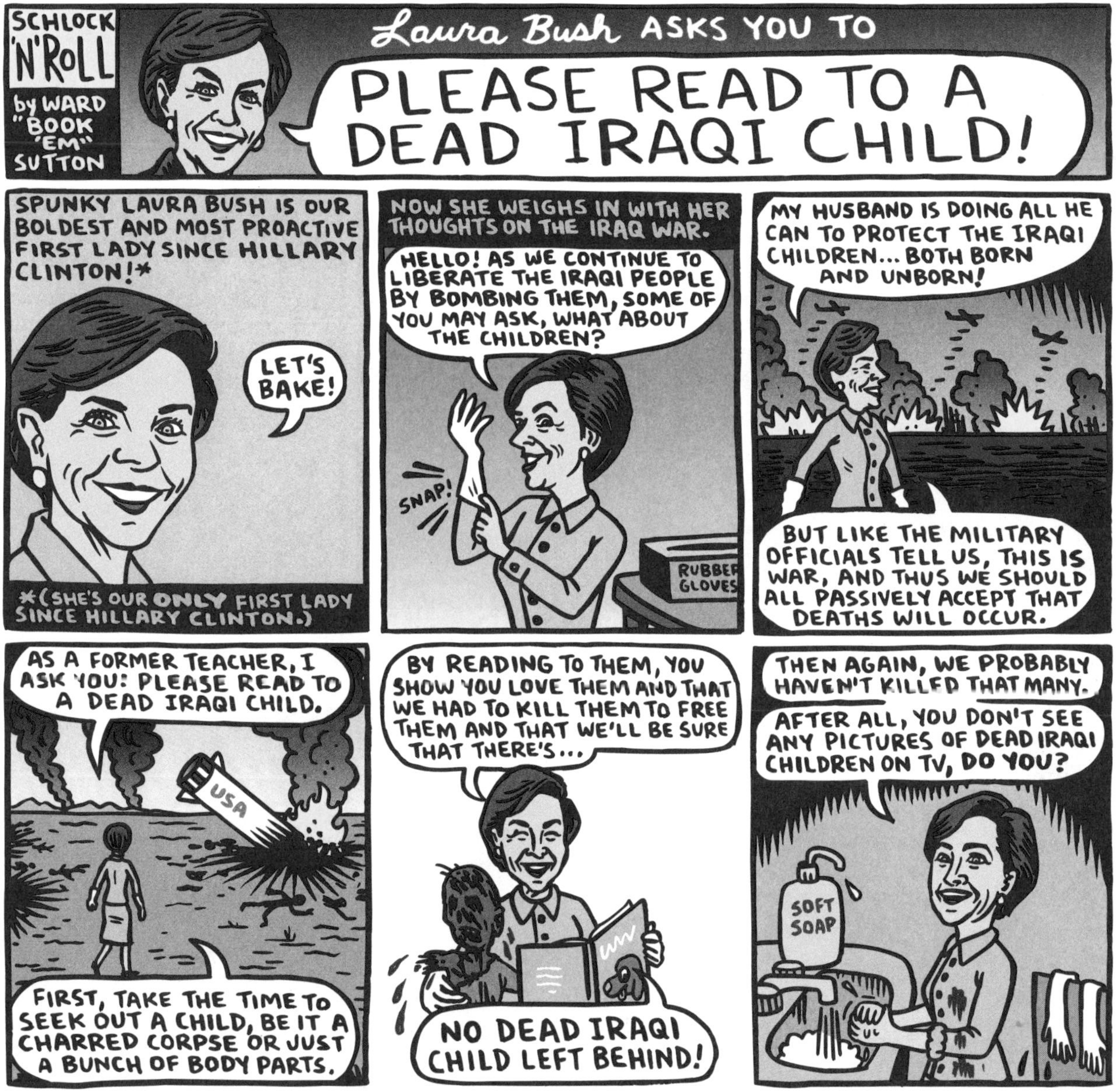
SCHLOCK 'N' ROLL
by WARD "BOOK 'EM" SUTTON
Laura Bush ASKS YOU TO
PLEASE READ TO A DEAD IRAQI CHILD!
SPUNKY LAURA BUSH IS OUR BOLDEST AND MOST PROACTIVE FIRST LADY SINCE HILLARY CLINTON!*
LET'S BAKE!
*(SHE'S OUR ONLY FIRST LADY SINCE HILLARY CLINTON.)
NOW SHE WEIGHS IN WITH HER THOUGHTS ON THE IRAQ WAR.
HELLO! AS WE CONTINUE TO LIBERATE THE IRAQI PEOPLE BY BOMBING THEM, SOME OF YOU MAY ASK, WHAT ABOUT THE CHILDREN?
SNAP!
RUBBER GLOVES
MY HUSBAND IS DOING ALL HE CAN TO PROTECT THE IRAQI CHILDREN... BOTH BORN AND UNBORN!
BUT LIKE THE MILITARY OFFICIALS TELL US, THIS IS WAR, AND THUS WE SHOULD ALL PASSIVELY ACCEPT THAT DEATHS WILL OCCUR.
AS A FORMER TEACHER, I ASK YOU: PLEASE READ TO A DEAD IRAQI CHILD.
USA
FIRST, TAKE THE TIME TO SEEK OUT A CHILD, BE IT A CHARRED CORPSE OR JUST A BUNCH OF BODY PARTS.
BY READING TO THEM, YOU SHOW YOU LOVE THEM AND THAT WE HAD TO KILL THEM TO FREE THEM AND THAT WE'LL BE SURE THAT THERE'S...
NO DEAD IRAQI CHILD LEFT BEHIND!
THEN AGAIN, WE PROBABLY HAVEN'T KILLED THAT MANY.
AFTER ALL, YOU DON'T SEE ANY PICTURES OF DEAD IRAQI CHILDREN ON TV, DO YOU?
SOFT SOAP

In the spring of 2003, I was asked to be on a panel at MTV Studios on the topic of "Art in a Time of Fear." When I showed this cartoon, the audience recoiled in reaction. Tony Kushner was also on the panel and we realized we'd created work on the same theme: He had written a play that was published in the *Nation* about Laura Bush reading to dead Iraqi children (a stage version of the play was later produced).

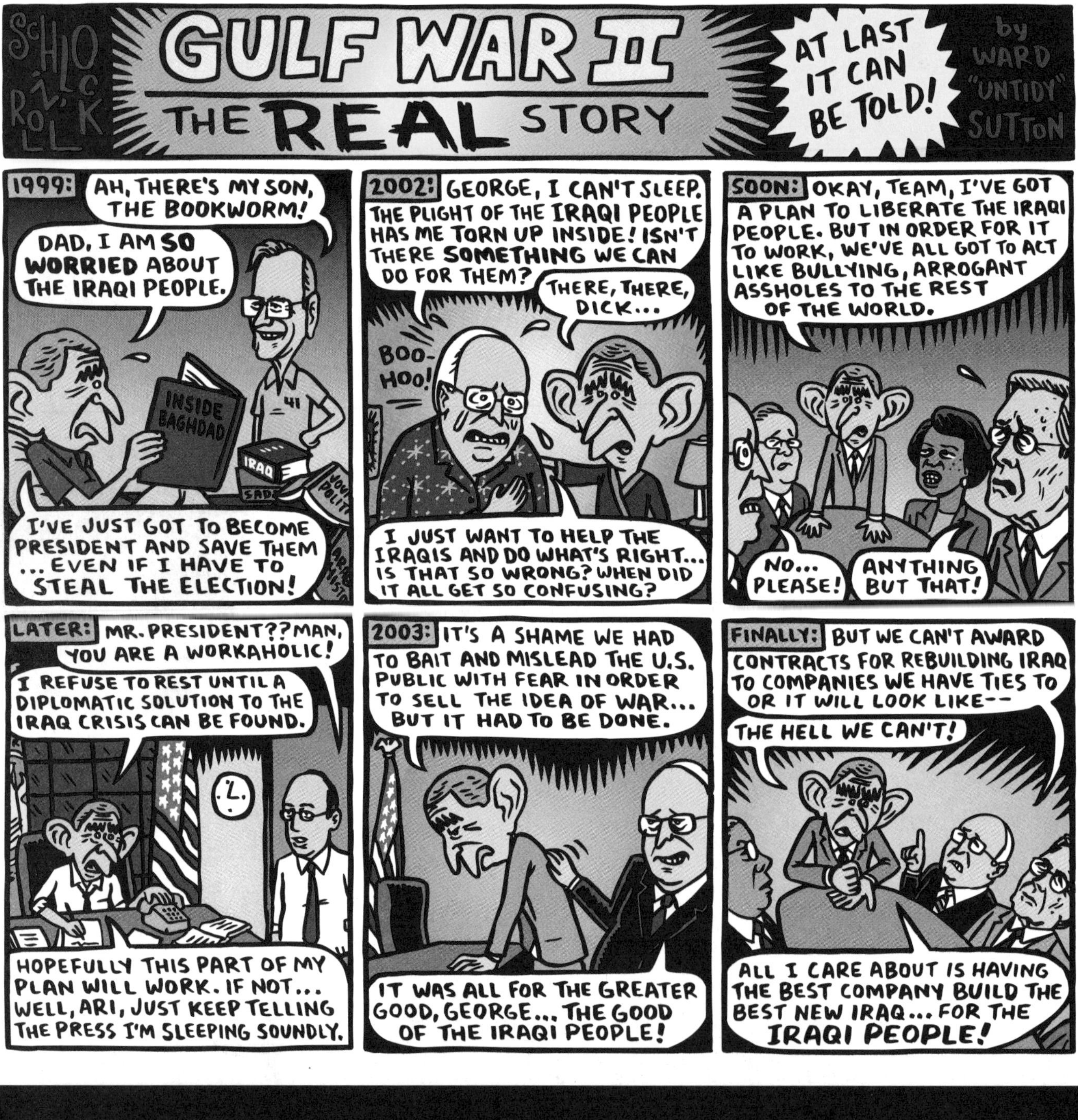
SCHLOCK 'N' ROLL
GULF WAR II
THE REAL STORY
AT LAST IT CAN BE TOLD!
by WARD "UNTIDY" SUTTON
1999:
AH, THERE'S MY SON, THE BOOKWORM!
DAD, I AM SO WORRIED ABOUT THE IRAQI PEOPLE.
INSIDE BAGHDAD
41
IRAQ
I'VE JUST GOT TO BECOME PRESIDENT AND SAVE THEM ... EVEN IF I HAVE TO STEAL THE ELECTION!
2002:
GEORGE, I CAN'T SLEEP. THE PLIGHT OF THE IRAQI PEOPLE HAS ME TORN UP INSIDE! ISN'T THERE SOMETHING WE CAN DO FOR THEM?
THERE, THERE, DICK...
BOO-HOO!
I JUST WANT TO HELP THE IRAQIS AND DO WHAT'S RIGHT... IS THAT SO WRONG? WHEN DID IT ALL GET SO CONFUSING?
SOON:
OKAY, TEAM, I'VE GOT A PLAN TO LIBERATE THE IRAQI PEOPLE. BUT IN ORDER FOR IT TO WORK, WE'VE ALL GOT TO ACT LIKE BULLYING, ARROGANT ASSHOLES TO THE REST OF THE WORLD.
NO... PLEASE!
ANYTHING BUT THAT!
LATER:
MR. PRESIDENT?? MAN, YOU ARE A WORKAHOLIC!
I REFUSE TO REST UNTIL A DIPLOMATIC SOLUTION TO THE IRAQ CRISIS CAN BE FOUND.
HOPEFULLY THIS PART OF MY PLAN WILL WORK. IF NOT... WELL, ARI, JUST KEEP TELLING THE PRESS I'M SLEEPING SOUNDLY.
2003:
IT'S A SHAME WE HAD TO BAIT AND MISLEAD THE U.S. PUBLIC WITH FEAR IN ORDER TO SELL THE IDEA OF WAR... BUT IT HAD TO BE DONE.
IT WAS ALL FOR THE GREATER GOOD, GEORGE... THE GOOD OF THE IRAQI PEOPLE!
FINALLY:
BUT WE CAN'T AWARD CONTRACTS FOR REBUILDING IRAQ TO COMPANIES WE HAVE TIES TO OR IT WILL LOOK LIKE--
THE HELL WE CAN'T!
ALL I CARE ABOUT IS HAVING THE BEST COMPANY BUILD THE BEST NEW IRAQ... FOR THE IRAQI PEOPLE!

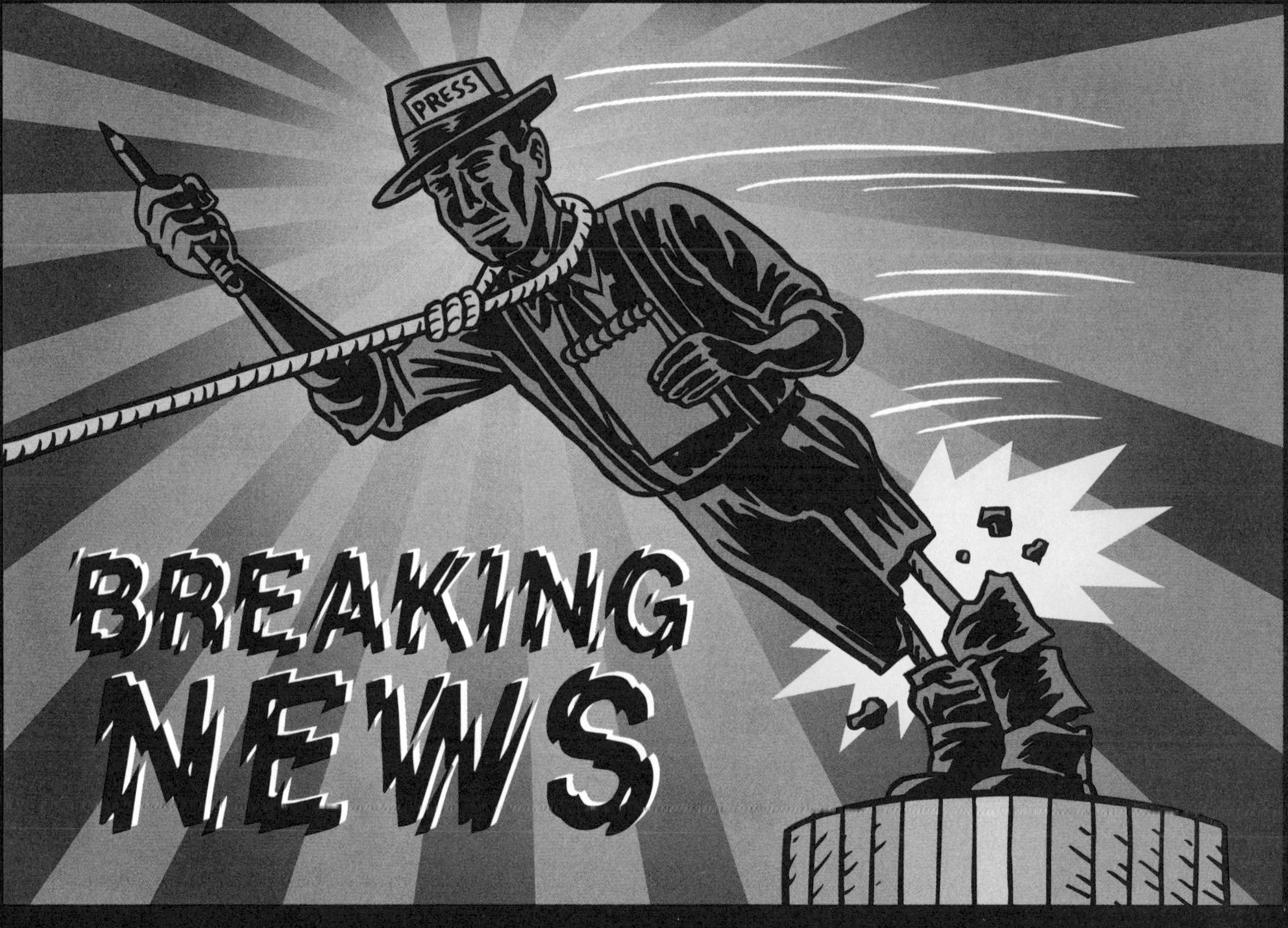
PRESS
BREAKING
NEWS

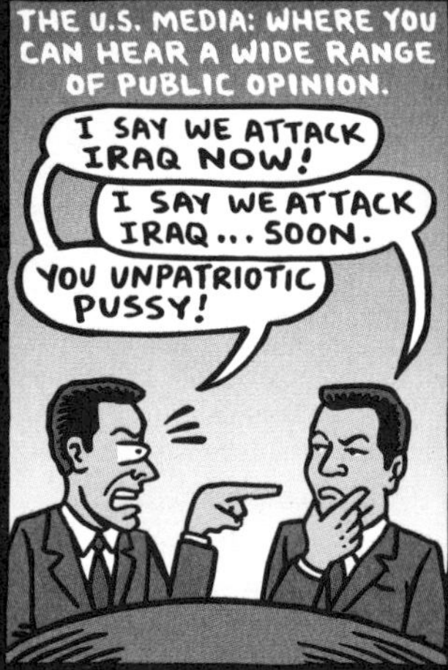
THE U.S. MEDIA: WHERE YOU CAN HEAR A WIDE RANGE OF PUBLIC OPINION.
I SAY WE ATTACK IRAQ NOW!
I SAY WE ATTACK IRAQ... SOON.
YOU UNPATRIOTIC PUSSY!

In 2003, I co-organized two multi-disciplinary arts events on political themes at Judson Memorial Church in New York City. "War Culture" (see page 48) took place as the Iraq war was just starting and examined how perpetual war is affecting our society. "Breaking News" (above) occurred the following fall and took a critical look at America's media industrial complex and all its failings. Each event featured visual art, installations, dance, comedy, film, animation, performance art, music, political cartoons and, last but not least, free drinks.

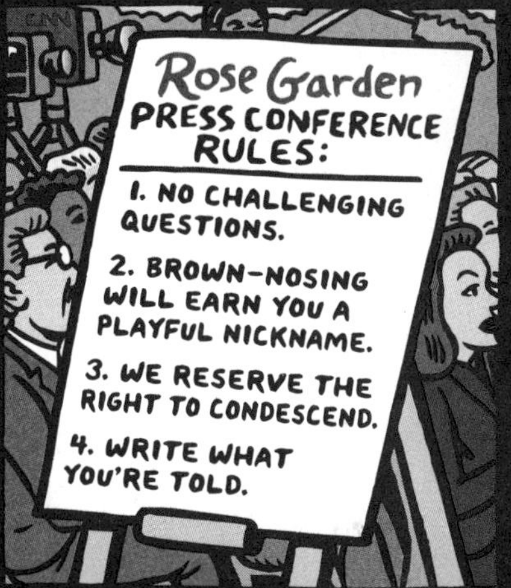
Rose Garden
PRESS CONFERENCE RULES:
1. NO CHALLENGING QUESTIONS.
2. BROWN-NOSING WILL EARN YOU A PLAYFUL NICKNAME.
3. WE RESERVE THE RIGHT TO CONDESCEND.
4. WRITE WHAT YOU'RE TOLD.

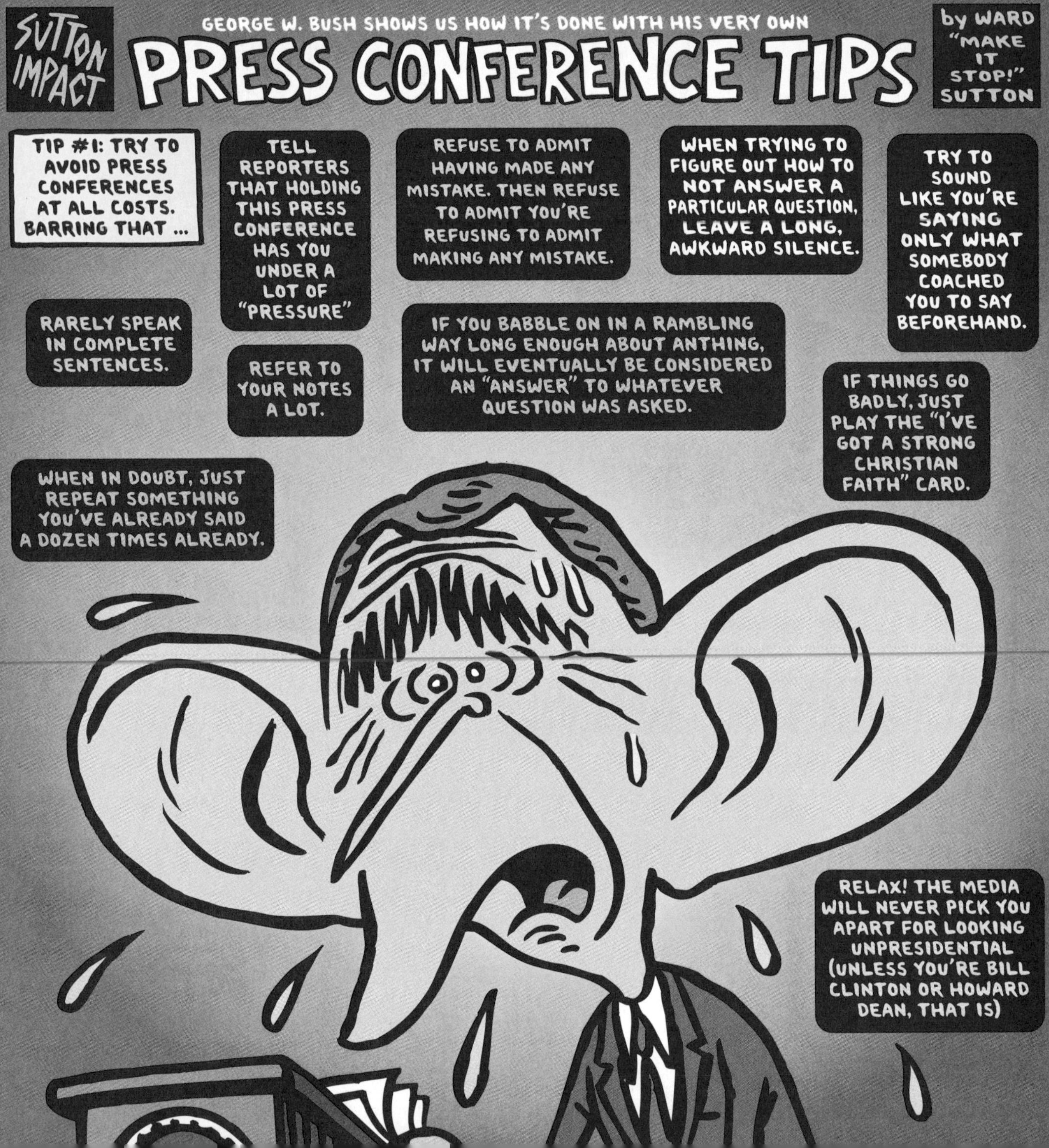
SUTTON IMPACT
GEORGE W. BUSH SHOWS US HOW IT'S DONE WITH HIS VERY OWN
PRESS CONFERENCE TIPS
by WARD "MAKE IT STOP!" SUTTON
TIP #1: TRY TO AVOID PRESS CONFERENCES AT ALL COSTS. BARRING THAT ...
TELL REPORTERS THAT HOLDING THIS PRESS CONFERENCE HAS YOU UNDER A LOT OF "PRESSURE"
REFUSE TO ADMIT HAVING MADE ANY MISTAKE. THEN REFUSE TO ADMIT YOU'RE REFUSING TO ADMIT MAKING ANY MISTAKE.
WHEN TRYING TO FIGURE OUT HOW TO NOT ANSWER A PARTICULAR QUESTION, LEAVE A LONG, AWKWARD SILENCE.
TRY TO SOUND LIKE YOU'RE SAYING ONLY WHAT SOMEBODY COACHED YOU TO SAY BEFOREHAND.
RARELY SPEAK IN COMPLETE SENTENCES.
REFER TO YOUR NOTES A LOT.
IF YOU BABBLE ON IN A RAMBLING WAY LONG ENOUGH ABOUT ANTHING, IT WILL EVENTUALLY BE CONSIDERED AN "ANSWER" TO WHATEVER QUESTION WAS ASKED.
IF THINGS GO BADLY, JUST PLAY THE "I'VE GOT A STRONG CHRISTIAN FAITH" CARD.
WHEN IN DOUBT, JUST REPEAT SOMETHING YOU'VE ALREADY SAID A DOZEN TIMES ALREADY.
RELAX! THE MEDIA WILL NEVER PICK YOU APART FOR LOOKING UNPRESIDENTIAL (UNLESS YOU'RE BILL CLINTON OR HOWARD DEAN, THAT IS)

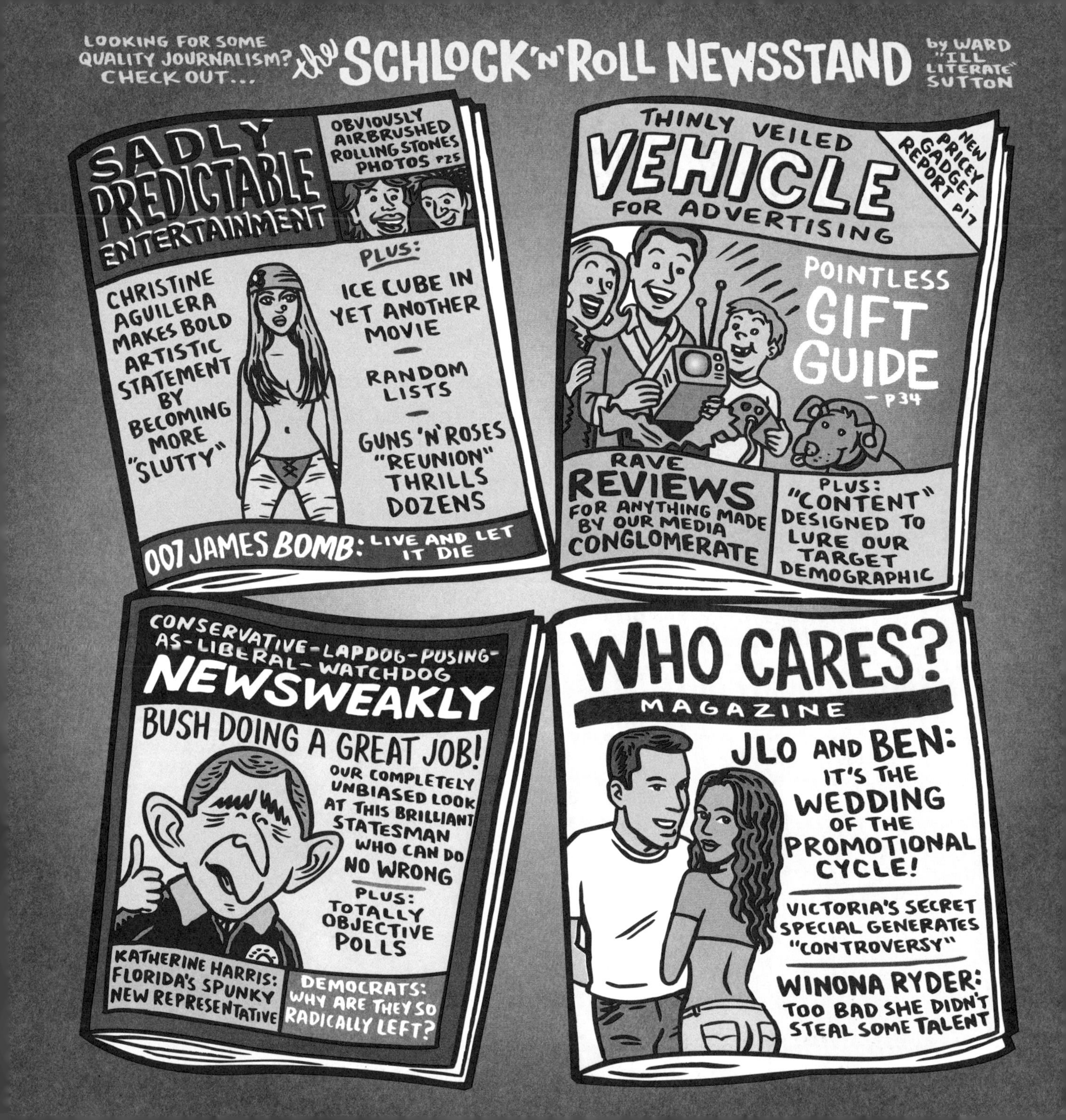

LOOKING FOR SOME QUALITY JOURNALISM? CHECK OUT...
the SCHLOCK 'N' ROLL NEWSSTAND
by WARD "ILL LITERATE" SUTTON
SADLY PREDICTABLE ENTERTAINMENT
OBVIOUSLY AIRBRUSHED ROLLING STONES PHOTOS P25
CHRISTINE AGUILERA MAKES BOLD ARTISTIC STATEMENT BY BECOMING MORE "SLUTTY"
PLUS:
ICE CUBE IN YET ANOTHER MOVIE
RANDOM LISTS
GUNS 'N' ROSES "REUNION" THRILLS DOZENS
007 JAMES BOMB: LIVE AND LET IT DIE
THINLY VEILED VEHICLE FOR ADVERTISING
NEW PRICEY GADGET REPORT P17
POINTLESS GIFT GUIDE - P34
RAVE REVIEWS FOR ANYTHING MADE BY OUR MEDIA CONGLOMERATE
PLUS: "CONTENT" DESIGNED TO LURE OUR TARGET DEMOGRAPHIC
CONSERVATIVE-LAPDOG-POSING-AS-LIBERAL-WATCHDOG NEWSWEAKLY
BUSH DOING A GREAT JOB!
OUR COMPLETELY UNBIASED LOOK AT THIS BRILLIANT STATESMAN WHO CAN DO NO WRONG
PLUS: TOTALLY OBJECTIVE POLLS
KATHERINE HARRIS: FLORIDA'S SPUNKY NEW REPRESENTATIVE
DEMOCRATS: WHY ARE THEY SO RADICALLY LEFT?
WHO CARES? MAGAZINE
JLO AND BEN: IT'S THE WEDDING OF THE PROMOTIONAL CYCLE!
VICTORIA'S SECRET SPECIAL GENERATES "CONTROVERSY"
WINONA RYDER: TOO BAD SHE DIDN'T STEAL SOME TALENT

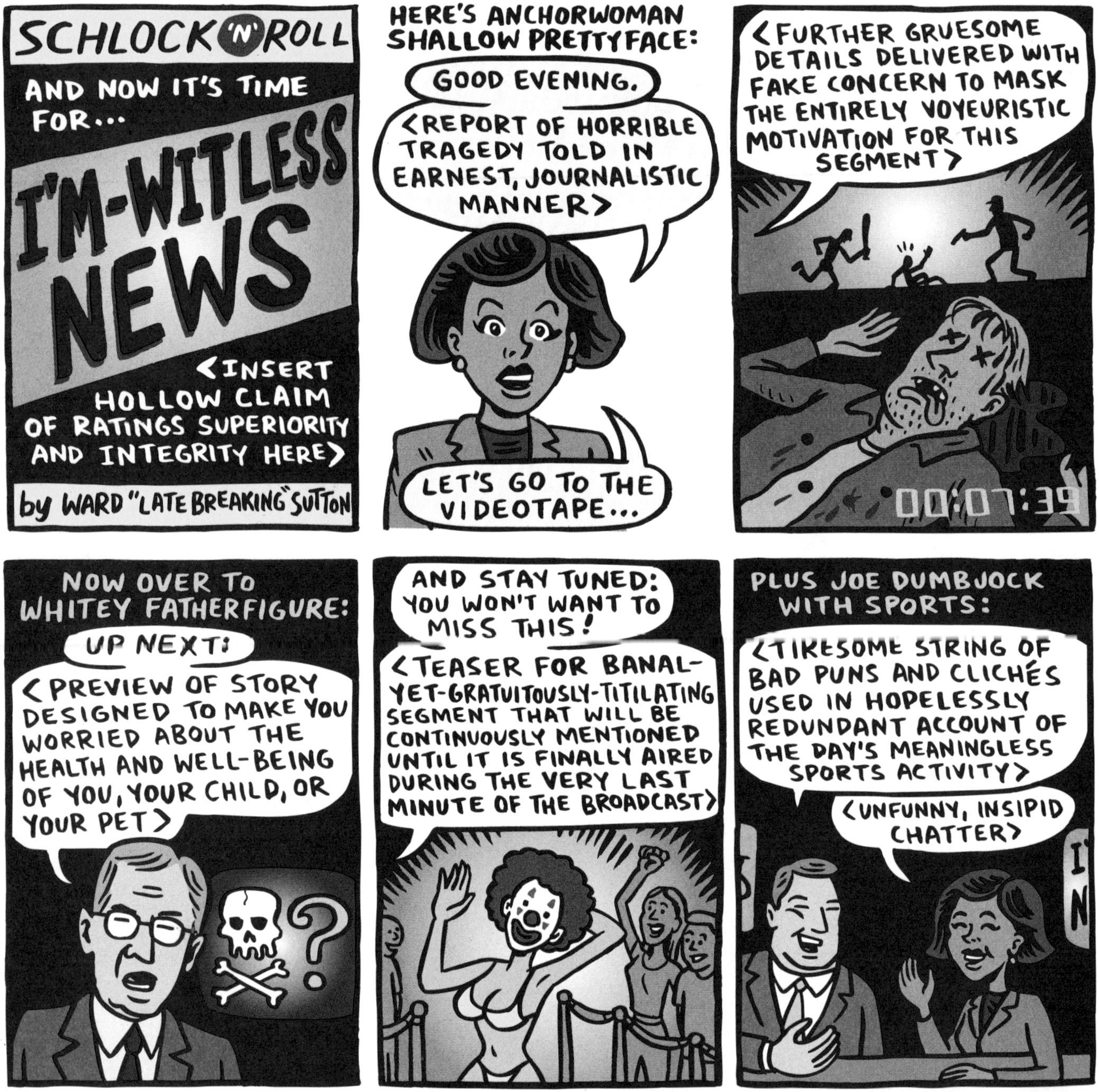
SCHLOCK 'N' ROLL
AND NOW IT'S TIME FOR...
I'M-WITLESS NEWS
<INSERT HOLLOW CLAIM OF RATINGS SUPERIORITY AND INTEGRITY HERE>
by WARD "LATE BREAKING" SUTTON
HERE'S ANCHORWOMAN SHALLOW PRETTYFACE:
GOOD EVENING.
<REPORT OF HORRIBLE TRAGEDY TOLD IN EARNEST, JOURNALISTIC MANNER>
LET'S GO TO THE VIDEOTAPE...
<FURTHER GRUESOME DETAILS DELIVERED WITH FAKE CONCERN TO MASK THE ENTIRELY VOYEURISTIC MOTIVATION FOR THIS SEGMENT>
00:07:39
NOW OVER TO WHITEY FATHERFIGURE:
UP NEXT:
<PREVIEW OF STORY DESIGNED TO MAKE YOU WORRIED ABOUT THE HEALTH AND WELL-BEING OF YOU, YOUR CHILD, OR YOUR PET>
AND STAY TUNED: YOU WON'T WANT TO MISS THIS!
<TEASER FOR BANAL-YET-GRATUITOUSLY-TITILATING SEGMENT THAT WILL BE CONTINUOUSLY MENTIONED UNTIL IT IS FINALLY AIRED DURING THE VERY LAST MINUTE OF THE BROADCAST>
PLUS JOE DUMBJOCK WITH SPORTS:
<TIRESOME STRING OF BAD PUNS AND CLICHÉS USED IN HOPELESSLY REDUNDANT ACCOUNT OF THE DAY'S MEANINGLESS SPORTS ACTIVITY>
<UNFUNNY, INSIPID CHATTER>

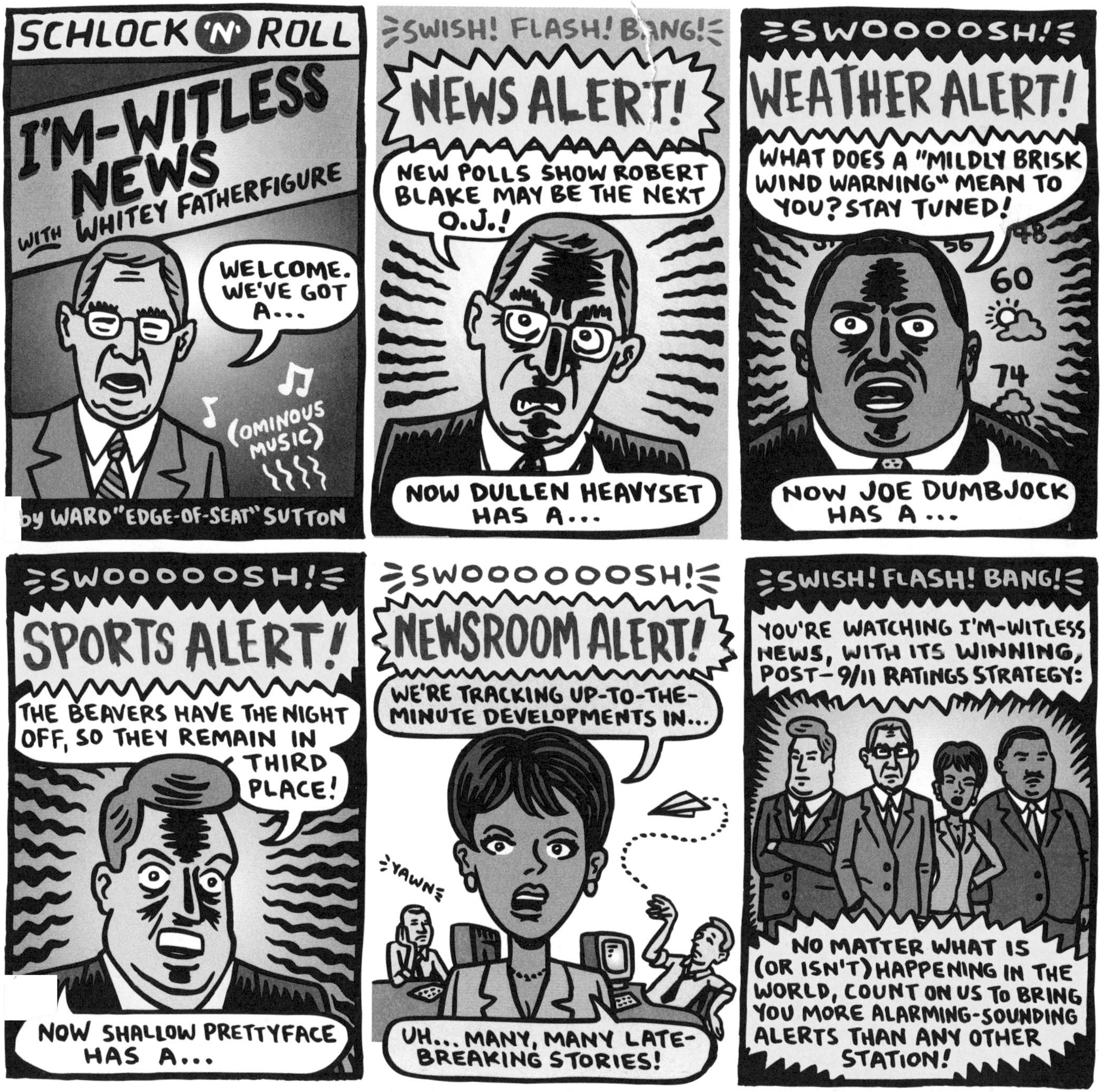
SCHLOCK 'N' ROLL
I'M-WITLESS NEWS
WITH WHITEY FATHERFIGURE
WELCOME. WE'VE GOT A...
(OMINOUS MUSIC)
by WARD "EDGE-OF-SEAT" SUTTON
SWISH! FLASH! BANG!
NEWS ALERT!
NEW POLLS SHOW ROBERT BLAKE MAY BE THE NEXT O.J.!
NOW DULLEN HEAVYSET HAS A...
SWOOOOSH!
WEATHER ALERT!
WHAT DOES A "MILDLY BRISK WIND WARNING" MEAN TO YOU? STAY TUNED!
56
48
60
74
NOW JOE DUMBJOCK HAS A...
SWOOOOOSH!
SPORTS ALERT!
THE BEAVERS HAVE THE NIGHT OFF, SO THEY REMAIN IN THIRD PLACE!
NOW SHALLOW PRETTYFACE HAS A...
SWOOOOOOOSH!
NEWSROOM ALERT!
WE'RE TRACKING UP-TO-THE-MINUTE DEVELOPMENTS IN...
YAWN
UH... MANY, MANY LATE-BREAKING STORIES!
SWISH! FLASH! BANG!
YOU'RE WATCHING I'M-WITLESS NEWS, WITH ITS WINNING, POST-9/11 RATINGS STRATEGY:
NO MATTER WHAT IS (OR ISN'T) HAPPENING IN THE WORLD, COUNT ON US TO BRING YOU MORE ALARMING-SOUNDING ALERTS THAN ANY OTHER STATION!

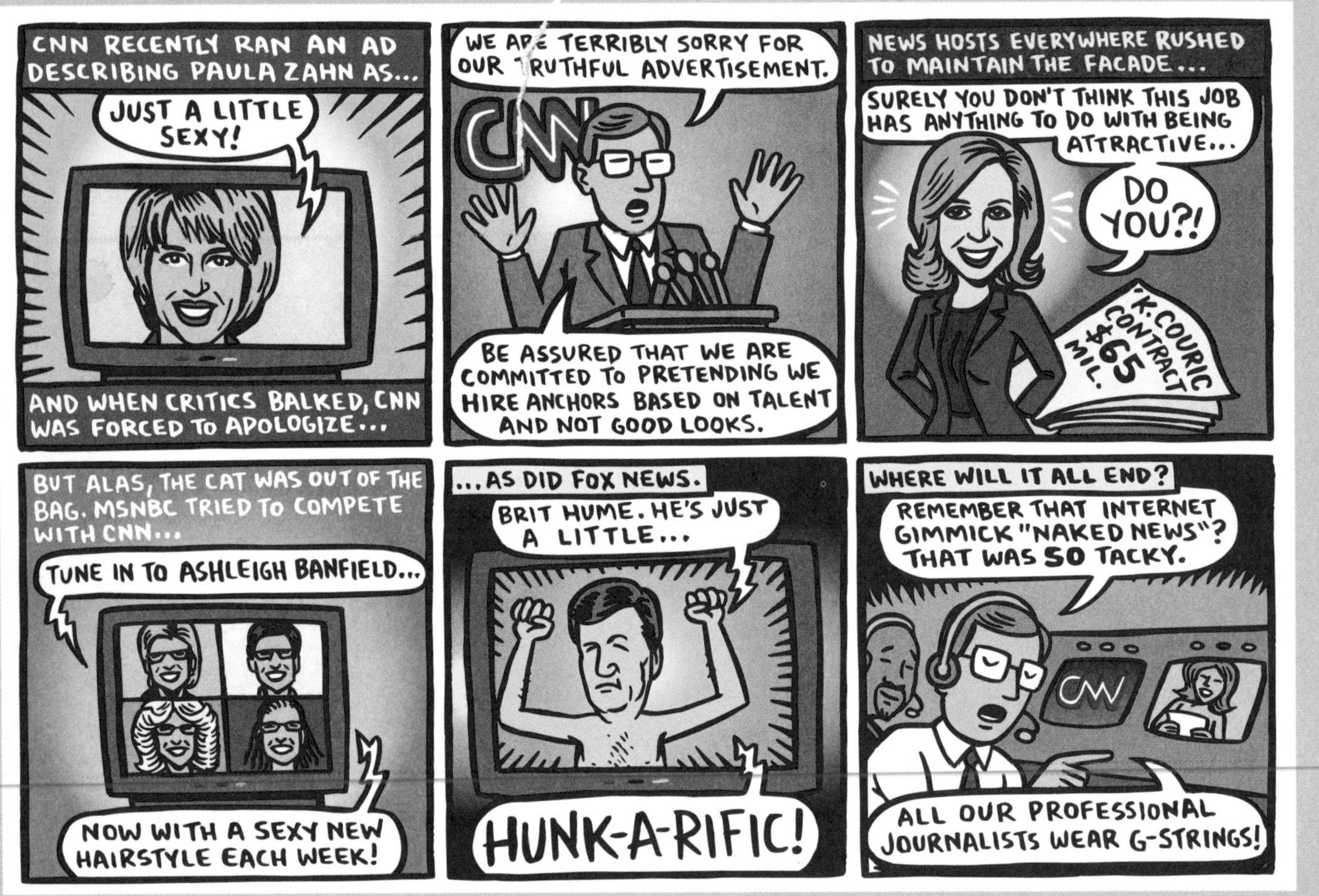
CNN RECENTLY RAN AN AD DESCRIBING PAULA ZAHN AS...
JUST A LITTLE SEXY!
AND WHEN CRITICS BALKED, CNN WAS FORCED TO APOLOGIZE...
WE ARE TERRIBLY SORRY FOR OUR TRUTHFUL ADVERTISEMENT.
BE ASSURED THAT WE ARE COMMITTED TO PRETENDING WE HIRE ANCHORS BASED ON TALENT AND NOT GOOD LOOKS.
NEWS HOSTS EVERYWHERE RUSHED TO MAINTAIN THE FACADE...
SURELY YOU DON'T THINK THIS JOB HAS ANYTHING TO DO WITH BEING ATTRACTIVE...
DO YOU?!
K. COURIC CONTRACT $65 MIL.
BUT ALAS, THE CAT WAS OUT OF THE BAG. MSNBC TRIED TO COMPETE WITH CNN...
TUNE IN TO ASHLEIGH BANFIELD...
NOW WITH A SEXY NEW HAIRSTYLE EACH WEEK!
...AS DID FOX NEWS.
BRIT HUME. HE'S JUST A LITTLE...
HUNK-A-RIFIC!
WHERE WILL IT ALL END?
REMEMBER THAT INTERNET GIMMICK "NAKED NEWS"? THAT WAS SO TACKY.
ALL OUR PROFESSIONAL JOURNALISTS WEAR G-STRINGS!

As cartoonist for TV Guide from 2000 – 2003, I rarely had the opportunity to be very political or controversial with my strip, "That's Entertoonment!" Still, I had fun. When CNN flaunted Paula Zahn's sex appeal and subsequently apologized (either a colossal blunder or a genius marketing strategy worthy of Karl Rove, depending on your point of view), I created the above cartoon. Shortly thereafter I got a call from Brit Hume's office at Fox News. They wanted a print of the cartoon and invited me to visit their studio. Brit's wife is the head of the Washington bureau and her office is decorated with large renderings of fighter jets. She was busy on the phone trying to get the Pentagon to return a videotape that was confiscated from one of their cameramen. She explained that the media couldn't let the government or the military push them around. I was pleasantly surprised to hear that Fox News was standing up for freedom of the press. Then she went on to enthusiastically defend Dick Cheney's refusal to release documents from his Energy Task Force. During the newscast, they came back to the confiscated videotape story four times and I began to think it was less about principle and more about self-referential sensationalism. Brit was polite, if mostly uninterested (his assistant had arranged my visit) and nobody seemed to think it was funny when I signed the print, "To Brit, Stay FOX-ey!"

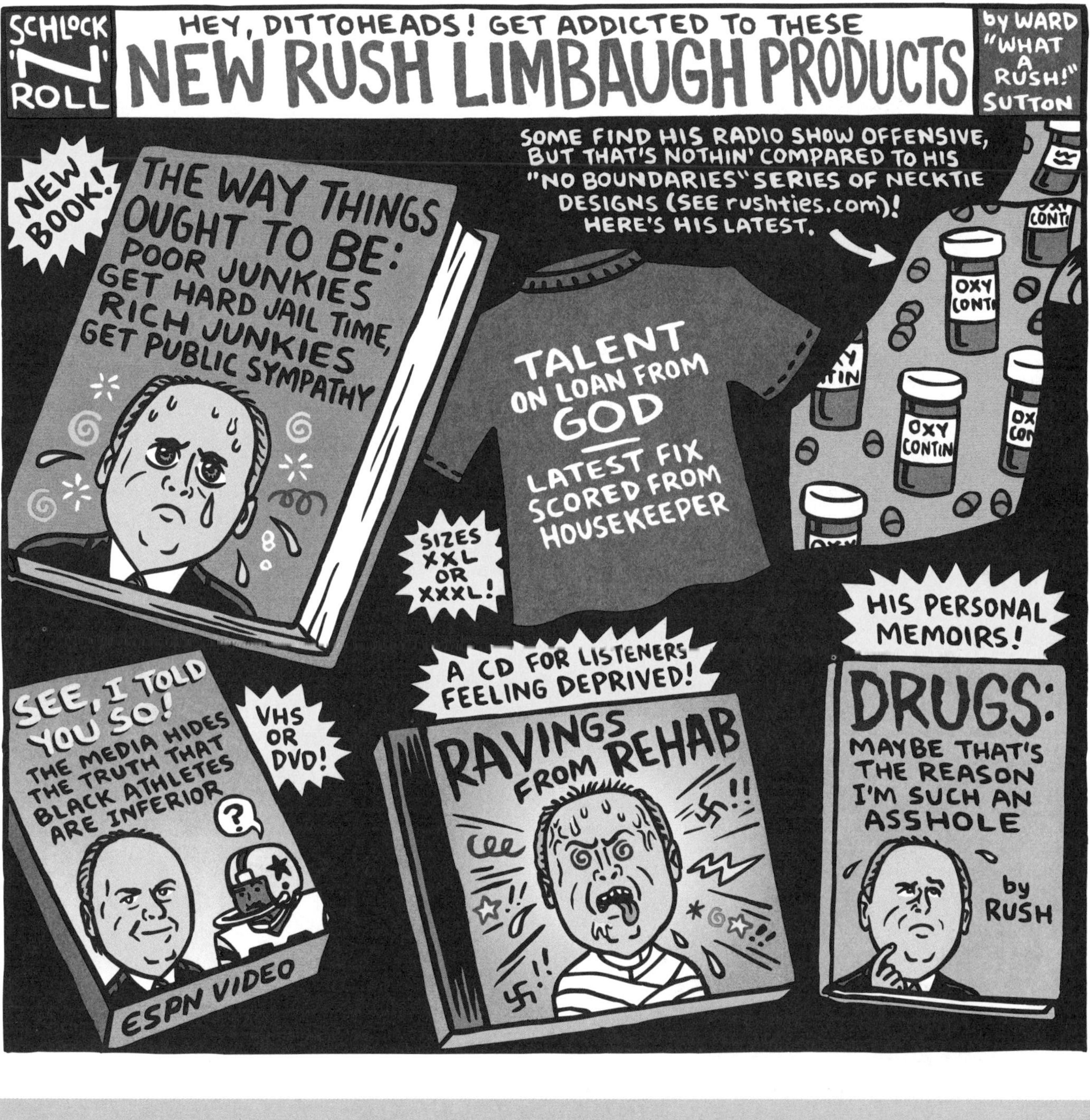
SCHLOCK 'N' ROLL
HEY, DITTOHEADS! GET ADDICTED TO THESE
NEW RUSH LIMBAUGH PRODUCTS
by WARD "WHAT A RUSH!" SUTTON
NEW BOOK!
THE WAY THINGS OUGHT TO BE: POOR JUNKIES GET HARD JAIL TIME, RICH JUNKIES GET PUBLIC SYMPATHY
SOME FIND HIS RADIO SHOW OFFENSIVE, BUT THAT'S NOTHIN' COMPARED TO HIS "NO BOUNDARIES" SERIES OF NECKTIE DESIGNS (SEE rushties.com)! HERE'S HIS LATEST.
OXY CONTIN
TALENT ON LOAN FROM GOD
LATEST FIX SCORED FROM HOUSEKEEPER
SIZES XXL OR XXXL!
HIS PERSONAL MEMOIRS!
SEE, I TOLD YOU SO! THE MEDIA HIDES THE TRUTH THAT BLACK ATHLETES ARE INFERIOR
?
ESPN VIDEO
VHS OR DVD!
A CD FOR LISTENERS FEELING DEPRIVED!
RAVINGS FROM REHAB
DRUGS: MAYBE THAT'S THE REASON I'M SUCH AN ASSHOLE
by RUSH

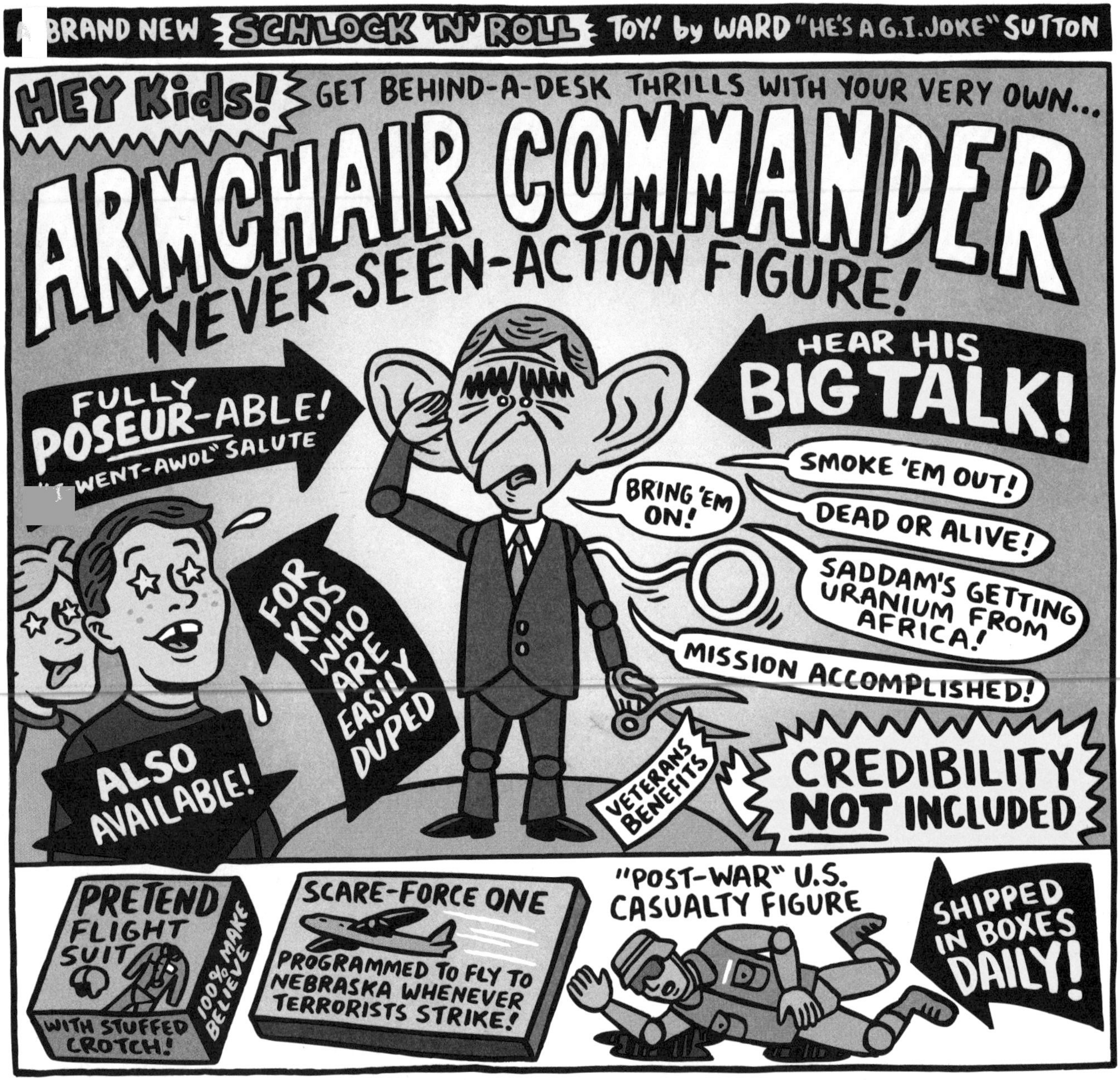
A BRAND NEW SCHLOCK 'N' ROLL TOY! by WARD "HE'S A G.I. JOKE" SUTTON
HEY Kids!
GET BEHIND-A-DESK THRILLS WITH YOUR VERY OWN...
ARMCHAIR COMMANDER
NEVER-SEEN-ACTION FIGURE!
FULLY POSEUR-ABLE!
WENT-AWOL" SALUTE
HEAR HIS BIG TALK!
BRING 'EM ON!
SMOKE 'EM OUT!
DEAD OR ALIVE!
SADDAM'S GETTING URANIUM FROM AFRICA!
MISSION ACCOMPLISHED!
FOR KIDS WHO ARE EASILY DUPED
ALSO AVAILABLE!
VETERANS BENEFITS
CREDIBILITY NOT INCLUDED
PRETEND FLIGHT SUIT
100% MAKE BELIEVE
WITH STUFFED CROTCH!
SCARE-FORCE ONE
PROGRAMMED TO FLY TO NEBRASKA WHENEVER TERRORISTS STRIKE!
"POST-WAR" U.S. CASUALTY FIGURE
SHIPPED IN BOXES DAILY!

About a week after this cartoon ran some company released a real Bush action figure (Irony not included). It probably looked like I was clairvoyant or had an advance inside scoop. In truth, I never thought anyone could be so stupid as to make a Bush action figure.

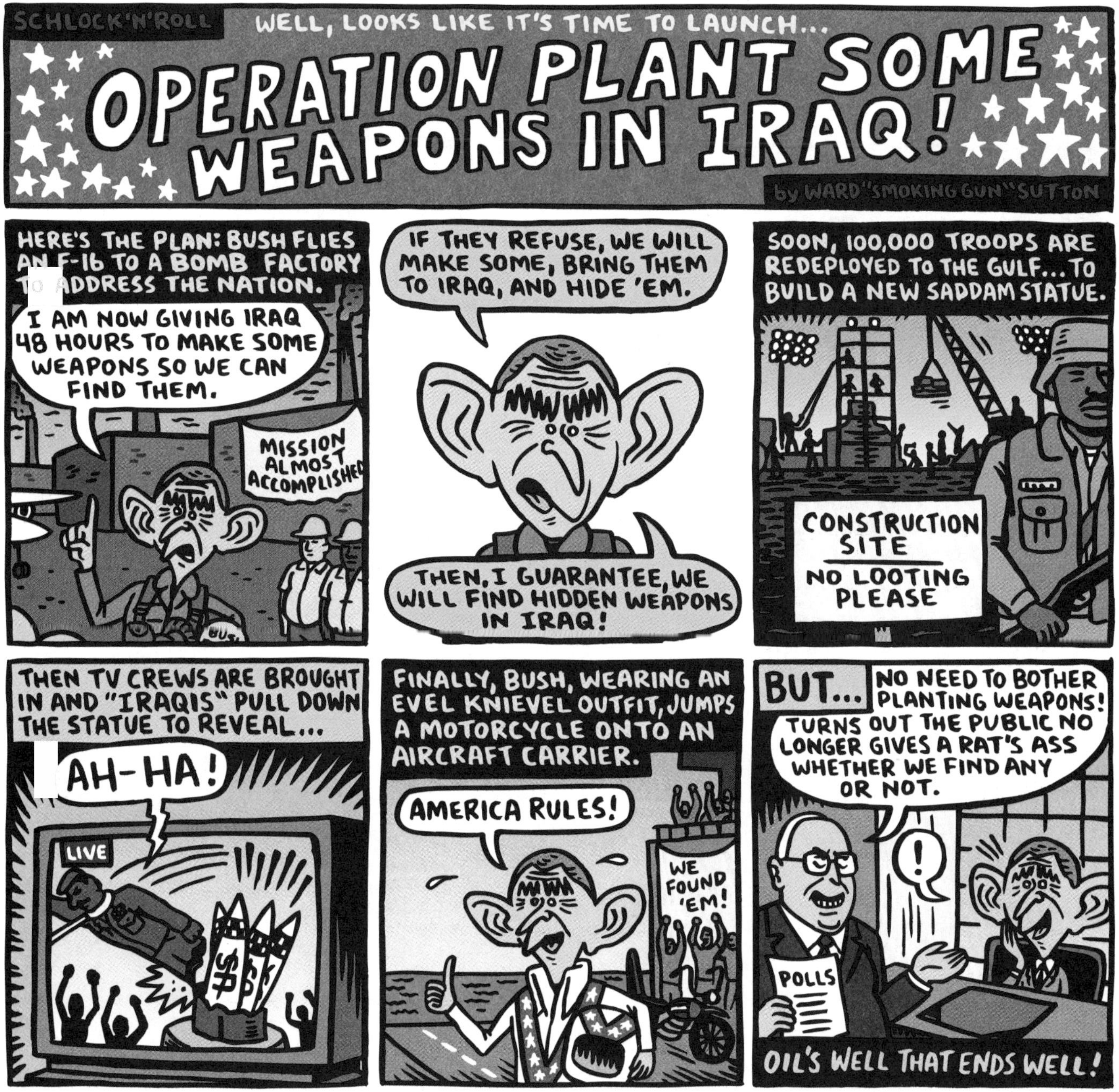
SCHLOCK'N'ROLL
WELL, LOOKS LIKE IT'S TIME TO LAUNCH...
OPERATION PLANT SOME WEAPONS IN IRAQ!
by WARD "SMOKING GUN" SUTTON
HERE'S THE PLAN: BUSH FLIES AN F-16 TO A BOMB FACTORY TO ADDRESS THE NATION.
I AM NOW GIVING IRAQ 48 HOURS TO MAKE SOME WEAPONS SO WE CAN FIND THEM.
MISSION ALMOST ACCOMPLISHED
IF THEY REFUSE, WE WILL MAKE SOME, BRING THEM TO IRAQ, AND HIDE 'EM.
THEN, I GUARANTEE, WE WILL FIND HIDDEN WEAPONS IN IRAQ!
SOON, 100,000 TROOPS ARE REDEPLOYED TO THE GULF... TO BUILD A NEW SADDAM STATUE.
CONSTRUCTION SITE
NO LOOTING PLEASE
THEN TV CREWS ARE BROUGHT IN AND "IRAQIS" PULL DOWN THE STATUE TO REVEAL...
AH-HA!
LIVE
FINALLY, BUSH, WEARING AN EVEL KNIEVEL OUTFIT, JUMPS A MOTORCYCLE ONTO AN AIRCRAFT CARRIER.
AMERICA RULES!
WE FOUND 'EM!
BUT...
NO NEED TO BOTHER PLANTING WEAPONS! TURNS OUT THE PUBLIC NO LONGER GIVES A RAT'S ASS WHETHER WE FIND ANY OR NOT.
!
POLLS
OIL'S WELL THAT ENDS WELL!

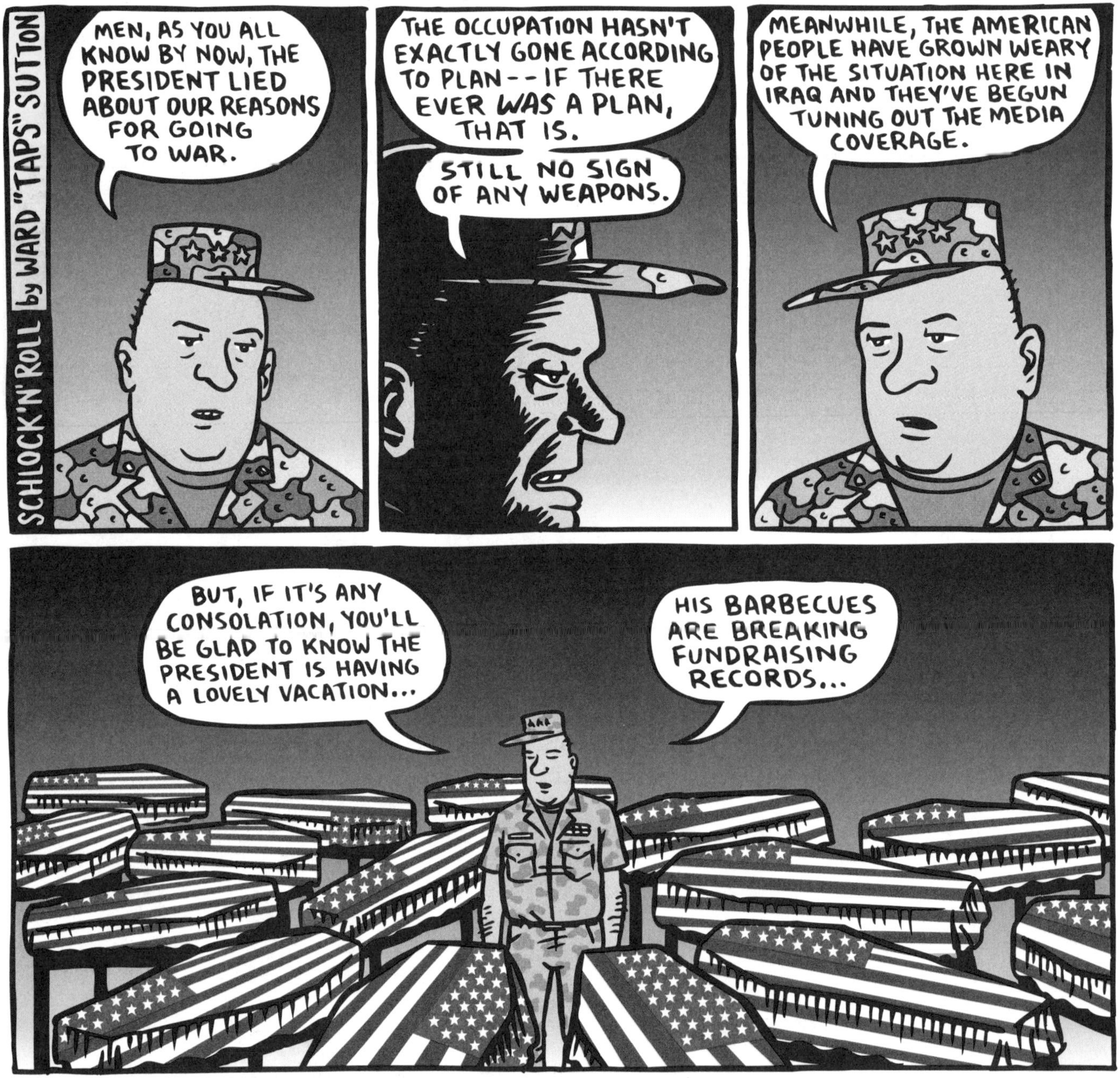
SCHLOCK'N'ROLL by WARD "TAPS" SUTTON
MEN, AS YOU ALL KNOW BY NOW, THE PRESIDENT LIED ABOUT OUR REASONS FOR GOING TO WAR.
THE OCCUPATION HASN'T EXACTLY GONE ACCORDING TO PLAN--IF THERE EVER WAS A PLAN, THAT IS.
STILL NO SIGN OF ANY WEAPONS.
MEANWHILE, THE AMERICAN PEOPLE HAVE GROWN WEARY OF THE SITUATION HERE IN IRAQ AND THEY'VE BEGUN TUNING OUT THE MEDIA COVERAGE.
BUT, IF IT'S ANY CONSOLATION, YOU'LL BE GLAD TO KNOW THE PRESIDENT IS HAVING A LOVELY VACATION...
HIS BARBECUES ARE BREAKING FUNDRAISING RECORDS...

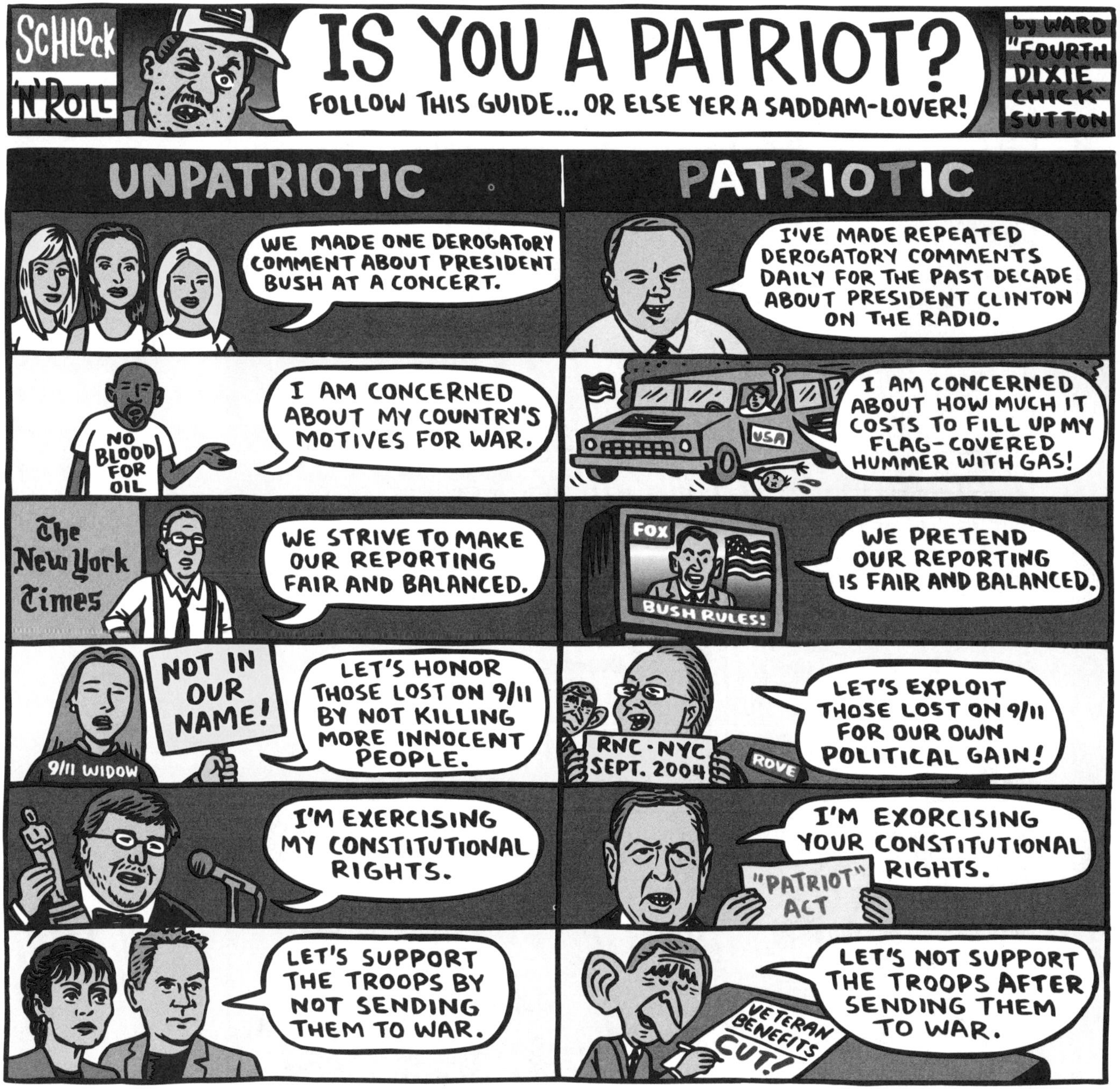
SCHLOCK 'N' ROLL
IS YOU A PATRIOT?
FOLLOW THIS GUIDE... OR ELSE YER A SADDAM-LOVER!
by WARD "FOURTH DIXIE CHICK" SUTTON
UNPATRIOTIC
PATRIOTIC
WE MADE ONE DEROGATORY COMMENT ABOUT PRESIDENT BUSH AT A CONCERT.
I'VE MADE REPEATED DEROGATORY COMMENTS DAILY FOR THE PAST DECADE ABOUT PRESIDENT CLINTON ON THE RADIO.
NO BLOOD FOR OIL
I AM CONCERNED ABOUT MY COUNTRY'S MOTIVES FOR WAR.
USA
I AM CONCERNED ABOUT HOW MUCH IT COSTS TO FILL UP MY FLAG-COVERED HUMMER WITH GAS!
The New York Times
WE STRIVE TO MAKE OUR REPORTING FAIR AND BALANCED.
FOX
BUSH RULES!
WE PRETEND OUR REPORTING IS FAIR AND BALANCED.
9/11 WIDOW
NOT IN OUR NAME!
LET'S HONOR THOSE LOST ON 9/11 BY NOT KILLING MORE INNOCENT PEOPLE.
RNC · NYC SEPT. 2004
ROVE
LET'S EXPLOIT THOSE LOST ON 9/11 FOR OUR OWN POLITICAL GAIN!
I'M EXERCISING MY CONSTITUTIONAL RIGHTS.
"PATRIOT" ACT
I'M EXORCISING YOUR CONSTITUTIONAL RIGHTS.
LET'S SUPPORT THE TROOPS BY NOT SENDING THEM TO WAR.
VETERAN BENEFITS CUT!
LET'S NOT SUPPORT THE TROOPS AFTER SENDING THEM TO WAR.

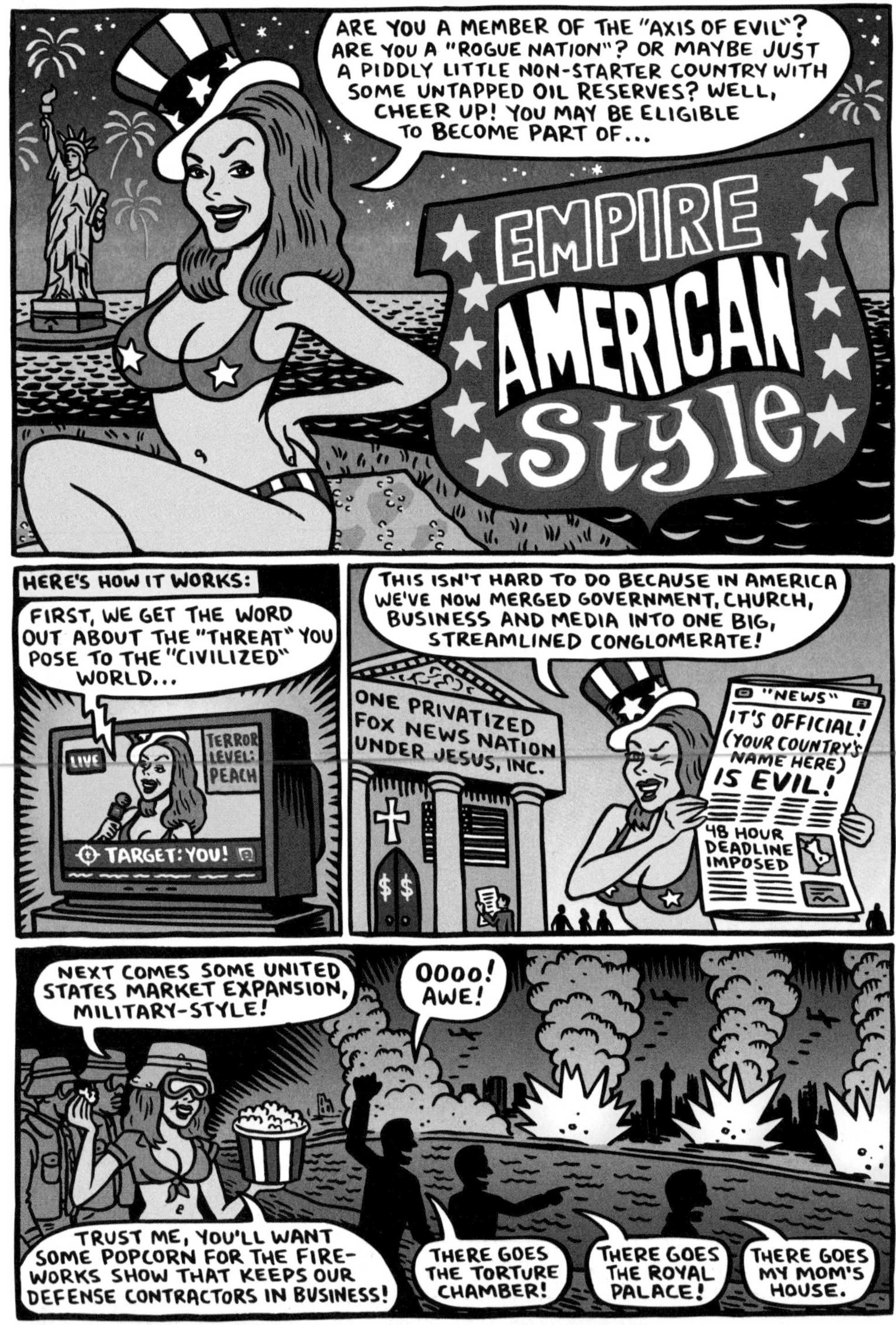
ARE YOU A MEMBER OF THE "AXIS OF EVIL"? ARE YOU A "ROGUE NATION"? OR MAYBE JUST A PIDDLY LITTLE NON-STARTER COUNTRY WITH SOME UNTAPPED OIL RESERVES? WELL, CHEER UP! YOU MAY BE ELIGIBLE TO BECOME PART OF...
EMPIRE AMERICAN STYLE
HERE'S HOW IT WORKS:
FIRST, WE GET THE WORD OUT ABOUT THE "THREAT" YOU POSE TO THE "CIVILIZED" WORLD...
TERROR LEVEL: PEACH
LIVE
TARGET: YOU!
THIS ISN'T HARD TO DO BECAUSE IN AMERICA WE'VE NOW MERGED GOVERNMENT, CHURCH, BUSINESS AND MEDIA INTO ONE BIG, STREAMLINED CONGLOMERATE!
ONE PRIVATIZED FOX NEWS NATION UNDER JESUS, INC.
"NEWS"
IT'S OFFICIAL! (YOUR COUNTRY'S NAME HERE) IS EVIL!
48 HOUR DEADLINE IMPOSED
NEXT COMES SOME UNITED STATES MARKET EXPANSION, MILITARY-STYLE!
OOOO! AWE!
TRUST ME, YOU'LL WANT SOME POPCORN FOR THE FIRE-WORKS SHOW THAT KEEPS OUR DEFENSE CONTRACTORS IN BUSINESS!
THERE GOES THE TORTURE CHAMBER!
THERE GOES THE ROYAL PALACE!
THERE GOES MY MOM'S HOUSE.

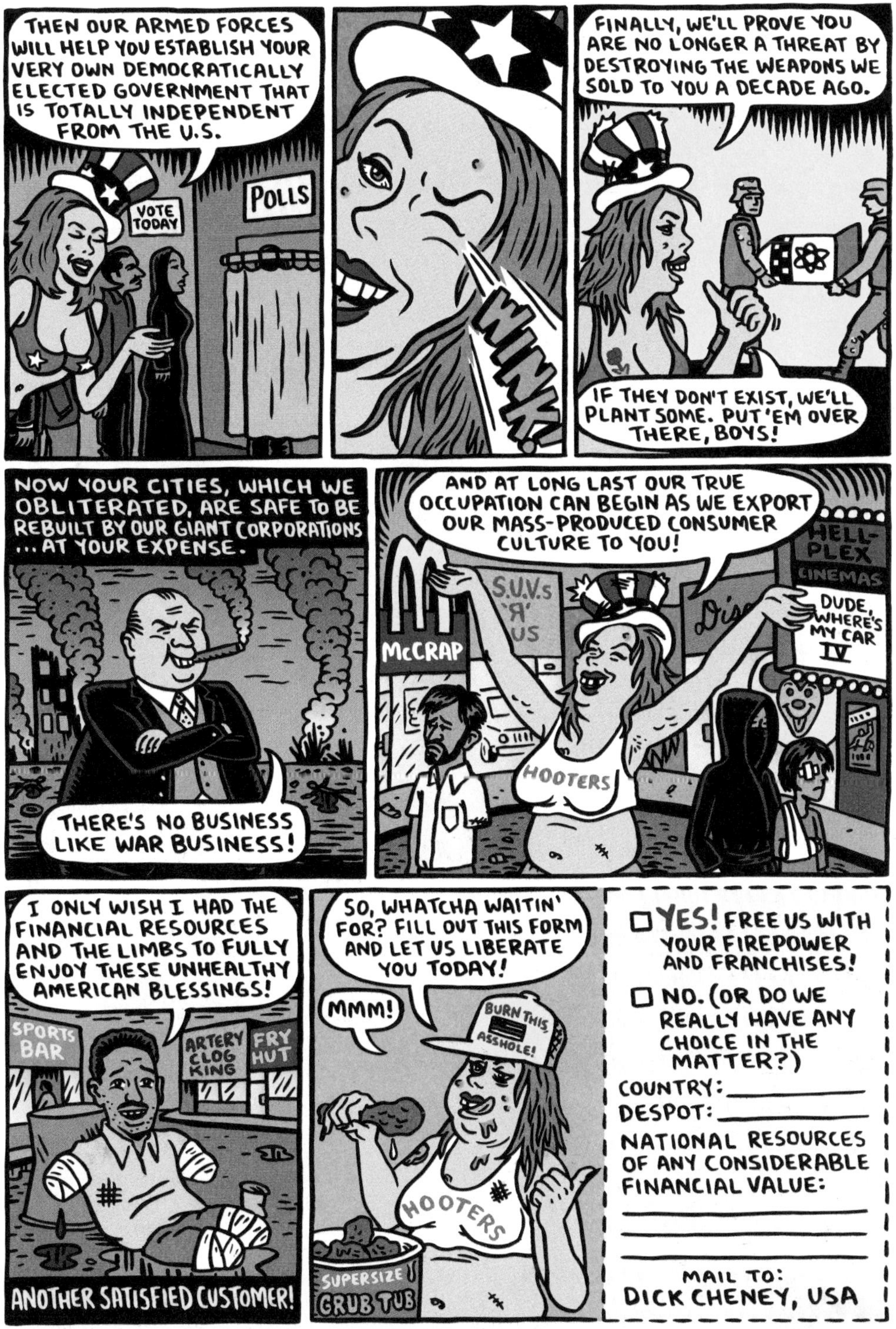
THEN OUR ARMED FORCES WILL HELP YOU ESTABLISH YOUR VERY OWN DEMOCRATICALLY ELECTED GOVERNMENT THAT IS TOTALLY INDEPENDENT FROM THE U.S.
VOTE TODAY
POLLS
WINK!
FINALLY, WE'LL PROVE YOU ARE NO LONGER A THREAT BY DESTROYING THE WEAPONS WE SOLD TO YOU A DECADE AGO.
IF THEY DON'T EXIST, WE'LL PLANT SOME. PUT 'EM OVER THERE, BOYS!
NOW YOUR CITIES, WHICH WE OBLITERATED, ARE SAFE TO BE REBUILT BY OUR GIANT CORPORATIONS ... AT YOUR EXPENSE.
THERE'S NO BUSINESS LIKE WAR BUSINESS!
AND AT LONG LAST OUR TRUE OCCUPATION CAN BEGIN AS WE EXPORT OUR MASS-PRODUCED CONSUMER CULTURE TO YOU!
McCRAP
S.U.V.s 'R' US
HELL-PLEX CINEMAS
DUDE, WHERE'S MY CAR IV
HOOTERS
I ONLY WISH I HAD THE FINANCIAL RESOURCES AND THE LIMBS TO FULLY ENJOY THESE UNHEALTHY AMERICAN BLESSINGS!
SPORTS BAR
ARTERY CLOG KING
FRY HUT
ANOTHER SATISFIED CUSTOMER!
SO, WHATCHA WAITIN' FOR? FILL OUT THIS FORM AND LET US LIBERATE YOU TODAY!
MMM!
BURN THIS, ASSHOLE!
HOOTERS
SUPERSIZE GRUB TUB
☐ YES! FREE US WITH YOUR FIREPOWER AND FRANCHISES!
☐ NO. (OR DO WE REALLY HAVE ANY CHOICE IN THE MATTER?)
COUNTRY: ________
DESPOT: ________
NATIONAL RESOURCES OF ANY CONSIDERABLE FINANCIAL VALUE:
MAIL TO: DICK CHENEY, USA

This piece originally ran in *Nozone IX: EMPIRE*, edited by Nicholas Blechman.

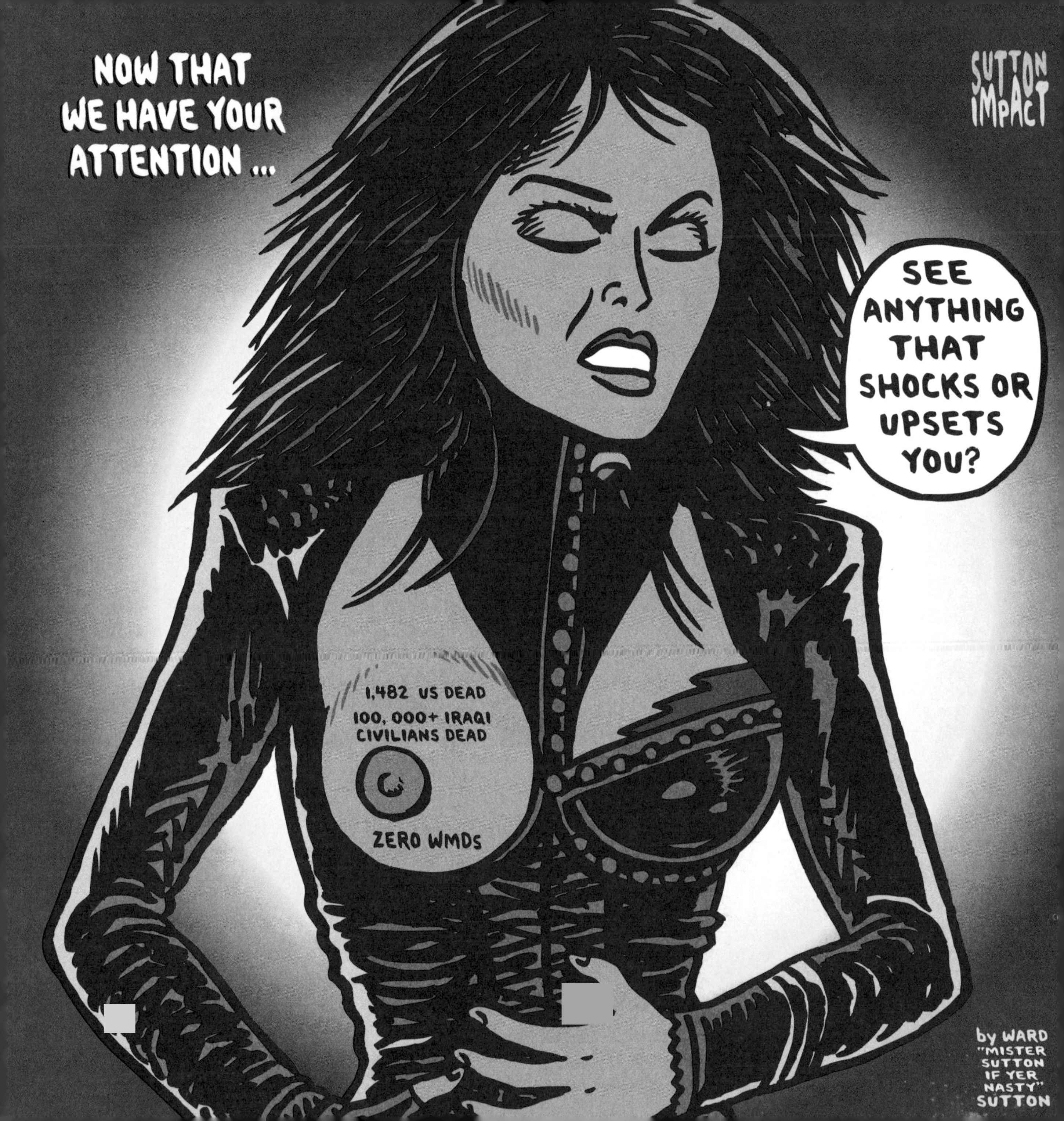
NOW THAT WE HAVE YOUR ATTENTION ...
SUTTON IMPACT
SEE ANYTHING THAT SHOCKS OR UPSETS YOU?
1,482 US DEAD
100, 000+ IRAQI CIVILIANS DEAD
ZERO WMDS
by WARD "MISTER SUTTON IF YER NASTY" SUTTON

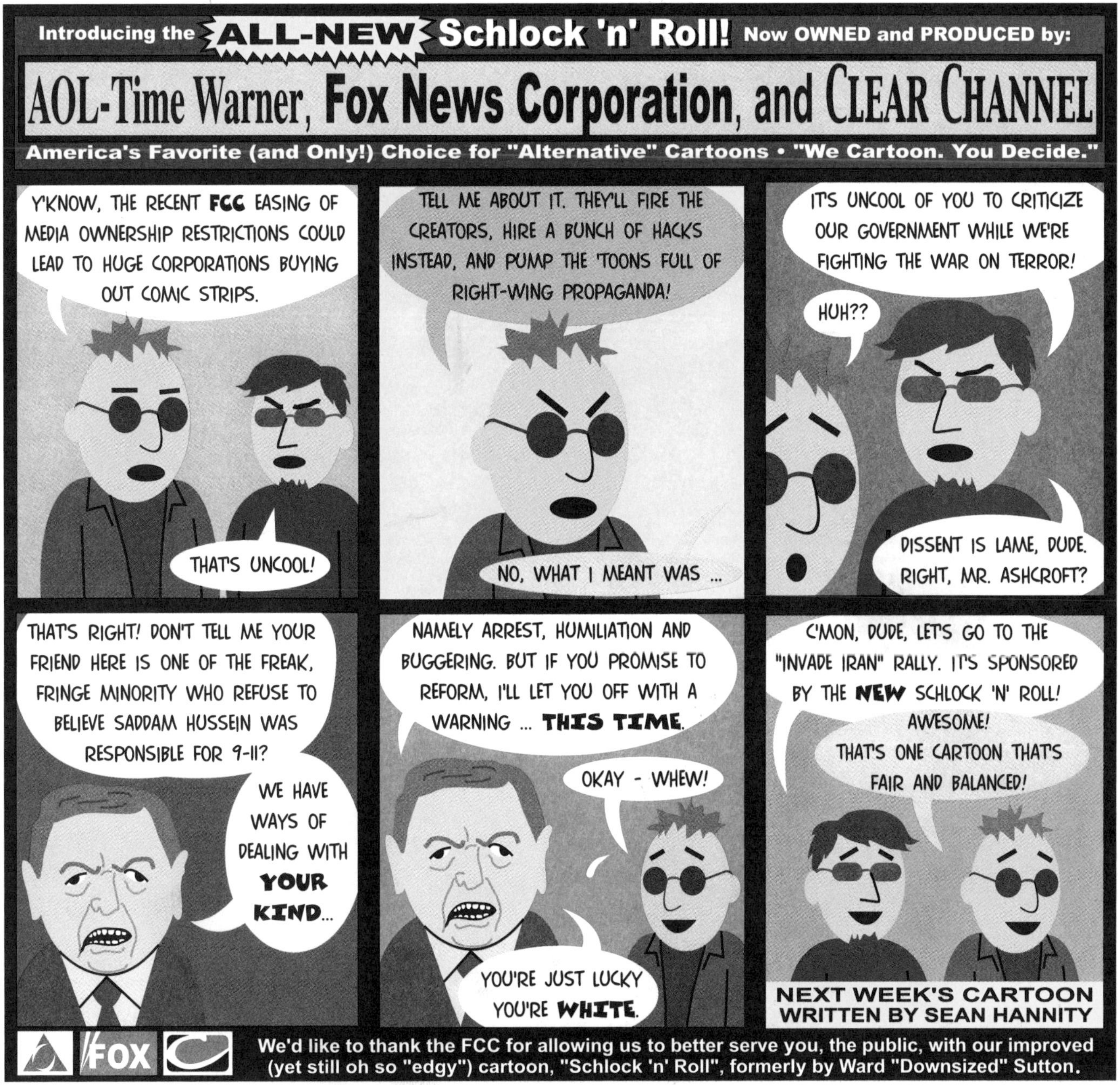
Introducing the ALL-NEW Schlock 'n' Roll! Now OWNED and PRODUCED by:
AOL-Time Warner, Fox News Corporation, and CLEAR CHANNEL
America's Favorite (and Only!) Choice for "Alternative" Cartoons • "We Cartoon. You Decide."
Y'KNOW, THE RECENT FCC EASING OF MEDIA OWNERSHIP RESTRICTIONS COULD LEAD TO HUGE CORPORATIONS BUYING OUT COMIC STRIPS.
THAT'S UNCOOL!
TELL ME ABOUT IT. THEY'LL FIRE THE CREATORS, HIRE A BUNCH OF HACKS INSTEAD, AND PUMP THE 'TOONS FULL OF RIGHT-WING PROPAGANDA!
NO, WHAT I MEANT WAS ...
IT'S UNCOOL OF YOU TO CRITICIZE OUR GOVERNMENT WHILE WE'RE FIGHTING THE WAR ON TERROR!
HUH??
DISSENT IS LAME, DUDE. RIGHT, MR. ASHCROFT?
THAT'S RIGHT! DON'T TELL ME YOUR FRIEND HERE IS ONE OF THE FREAK, FRINGE MINORITY WHO REFUSE TO BELIEVE SADDAM HUSSEIN WAS RESPONSIBLE FOR 9-11?
WE HAVE WAYS OF DEALING WITH YOUR KIND...
NAMELY ARREST, HUMILIATION AND BUGGERING. BUT IF YOU PROMISE TO REFORM, I'LL LET YOU OFF WITH A WARNING ... THIS TIME.
OKAY - WHEW!
YOU'RE JUST LUCKY YOU'RE WHITE.
C'MON, DUDE, LET'S GO TO THE "INVADE IRAN" RALLY. IT'S SPONSORED BY THE NEW SCHLOCK 'N' ROLL!
AWESOME! THAT'S ONE CARTOON THAT'S FAIR AND BALANCED!
NEXT WEEK'S CARTOON WRITTEN BY SEAN HANNITY
FOX
We'd like to thank the FCC for allowing us to better serve you, the public, with our improved (yet still oh so "edgy") cartoon, "Schlock 'n' Roll", formerly by Ward "Downsized" Sutton.

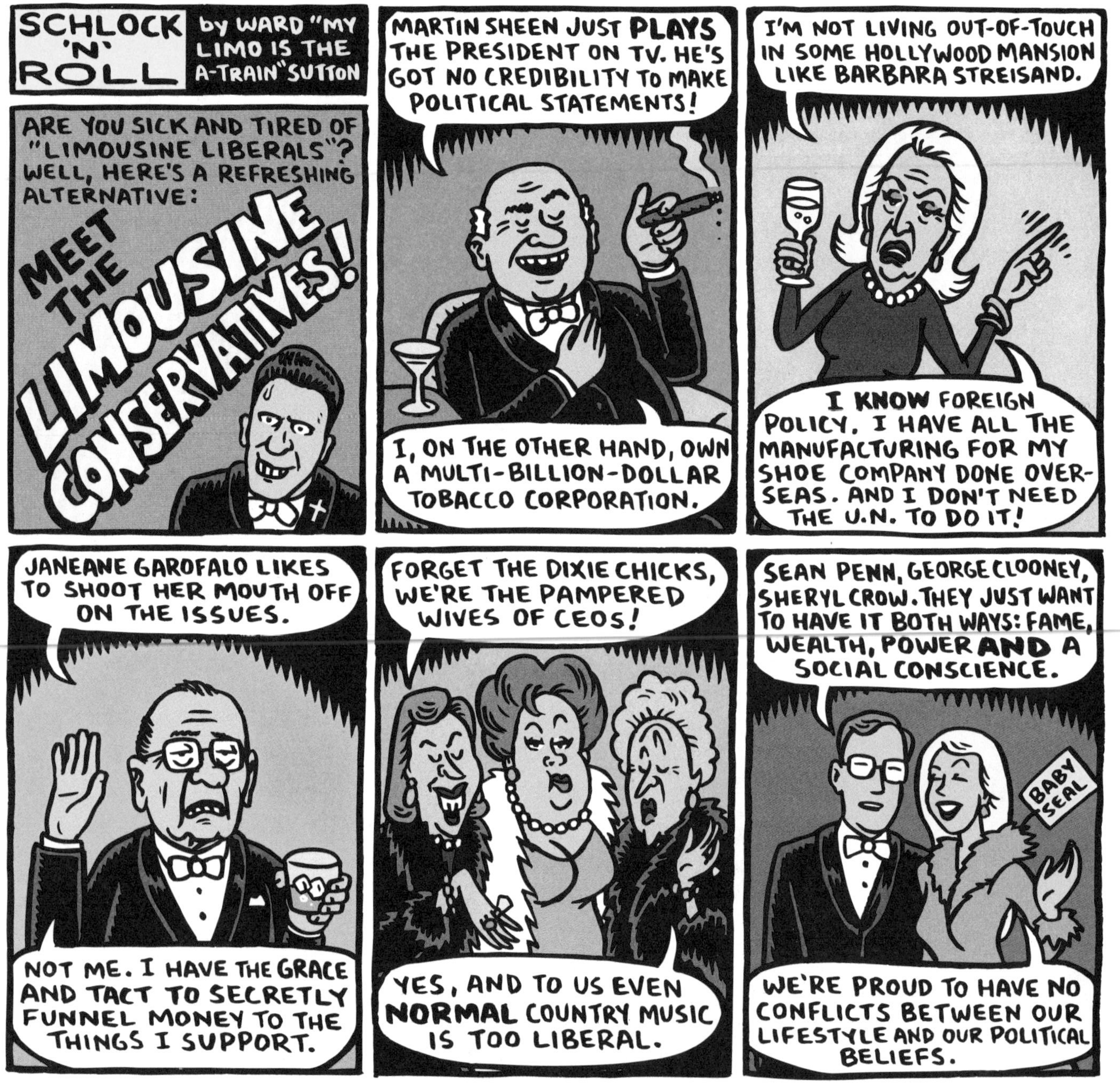
SCHLOCK 'N' ROLL
by WARD "MY LIMO IS THE A-TRAIN" SUTTON
ARE YOU SICK AND TIRED OF "LIMOUSINE LIBERALS"? WELL, HERE'S A REFRESHING ALTERNATIVE:
MEET THE LIMOUSINE CONSERVATIVES!
MARTIN SHEEN JUST PLAYS THE PRESIDENT ON TV. HE'S GOT NO CREDIBILITY TO MAKE POLITICAL STATEMENTS!
I, ON THE OTHER HAND, OWN A MULTI-BILLION-DOLLAR TOBACCO CORPORATION.
I'M NOT LIVING OUT-OF-TOUCH IN SOME HOLLYWOOD MANSION LIKE BARBARA STREISAND.
I KNOW FOREIGN POLICY. I HAVE ALL THE MANUFACTURING FOR MY SHOE COMPANY DONE OVERSEAS. AND I DON'T NEED THE U.N. TO DO IT!
JANEANE GAROFALO LIKES TO SHOOT HER MOUTH OFF ON THE ISSUES.
NOT ME. I HAVE THE GRACE AND TACT TO SECRETLY FUNNEL MONEY TO THE THINGS I SUPPORT.
FORGET THE DIXIE CHICKS, WE'RE THE PAMPERED WIVES OF CEOS!
YES, AND TO US EVEN NORMAL COUNTRY MUSIC IS TOO LIBERAL.
SEAN PENN, GEORGE CLOONEY, SHERYL CROW. THEY JUST WANT TO HAVE IT BOTH WAYS: FAME, WEALTH, POWER AND A SOCIAL CONSCIENCE.
BABY SEAL
WE'RE PROUD TO HAVE NO CONFLICTS BETWEEN OUR LIFESTYLE AND OUR POLITICAL BELIEFS.

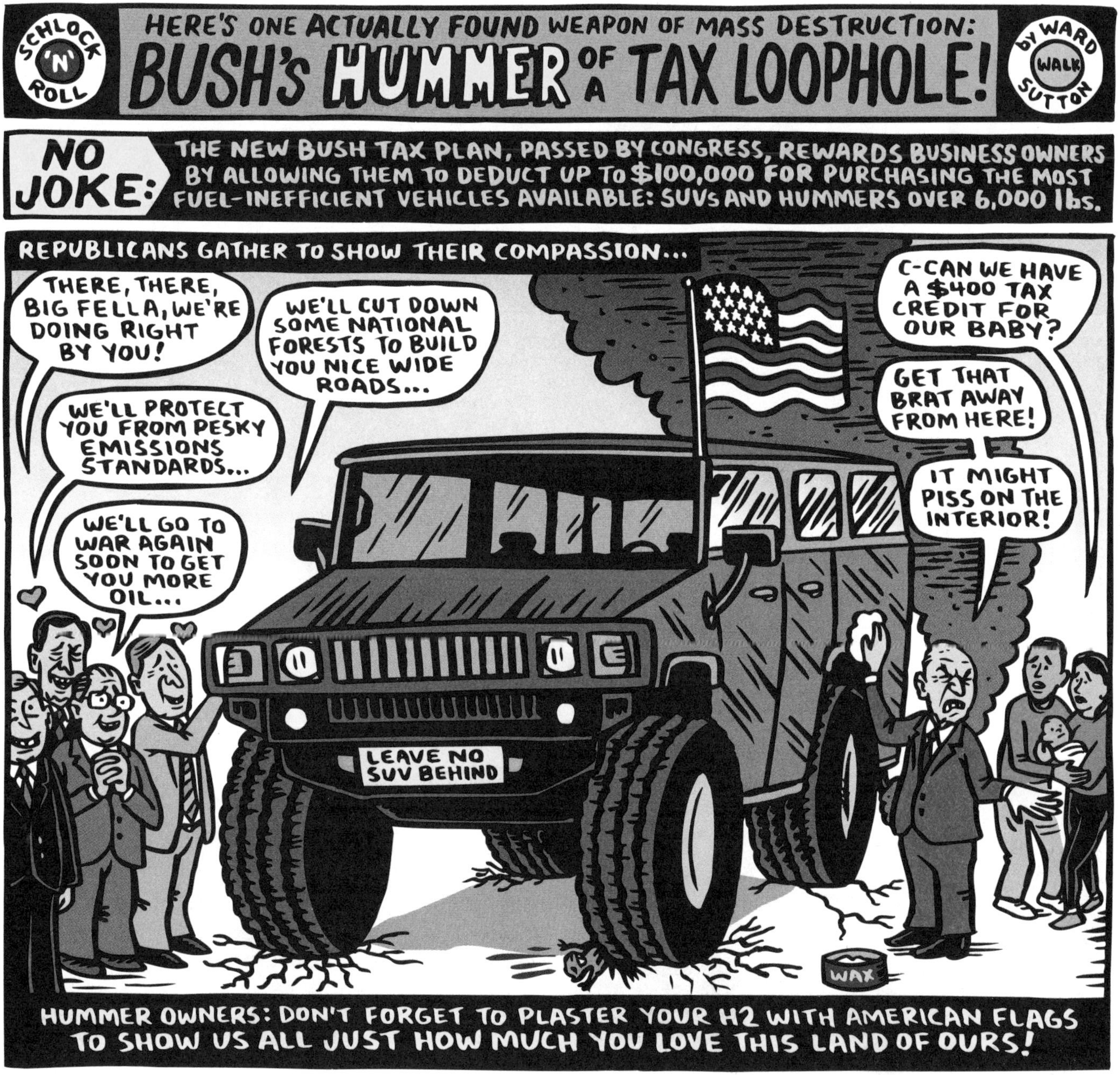
SCHLOCK 'N' ROLL
HERE'S ONE ACTUALLY FOUND WEAPON OF MASS DESTRUCTION:
BUSH'S HUMMER OF A TAX LOOPHOLE!
BY WARD WALK SUTTON
NO JOKE:
THE NEW BUSH TAX PLAN, PASSED BY CONGRESS, REWARDS BUSINESS OWNERS BY ALLOWING THEM TO DEDUCT UP TO $100,000 FOR PURCHASING THE MOST FUEL-INEFFICIENT VEHICLES AVAILABLE: SUVs AND HUMMERS OVER 6,000 lbs.
REPUBLICANS GATHER TO SHOW THEIR COMPASSION...
THERE, THERE, BIG FELLA, WE'RE DOING RIGHT BY YOU!
WE'LL PROTECT YOU FROM PESKY EMISSIONS STANDARDS...
WE'LL GO TO WAR AGAIN SOON TO GET YOU MORE OIL...
WE'LL CUT DOWN SOME NATIONAL FORESTS TO BUILD YOU NICE WIDE ROADS...
C-CAN WE HAVE A $400 TAX CREDIT FOR OUR BABY?
GET THAT BRAT AWAY FROM HERE!
IT MIGHT PISS ON THE INTERIOR!
LEAVE NO SUV BEHIND
WAX
HUMMER OWNERS: DON'T FORGET TO PLASTER YOUR H2 WITH AMERICAN FLAGS TO SHOW US ALL JUST HOW MUCH YOU LOVE THIS LAND OF OURS!

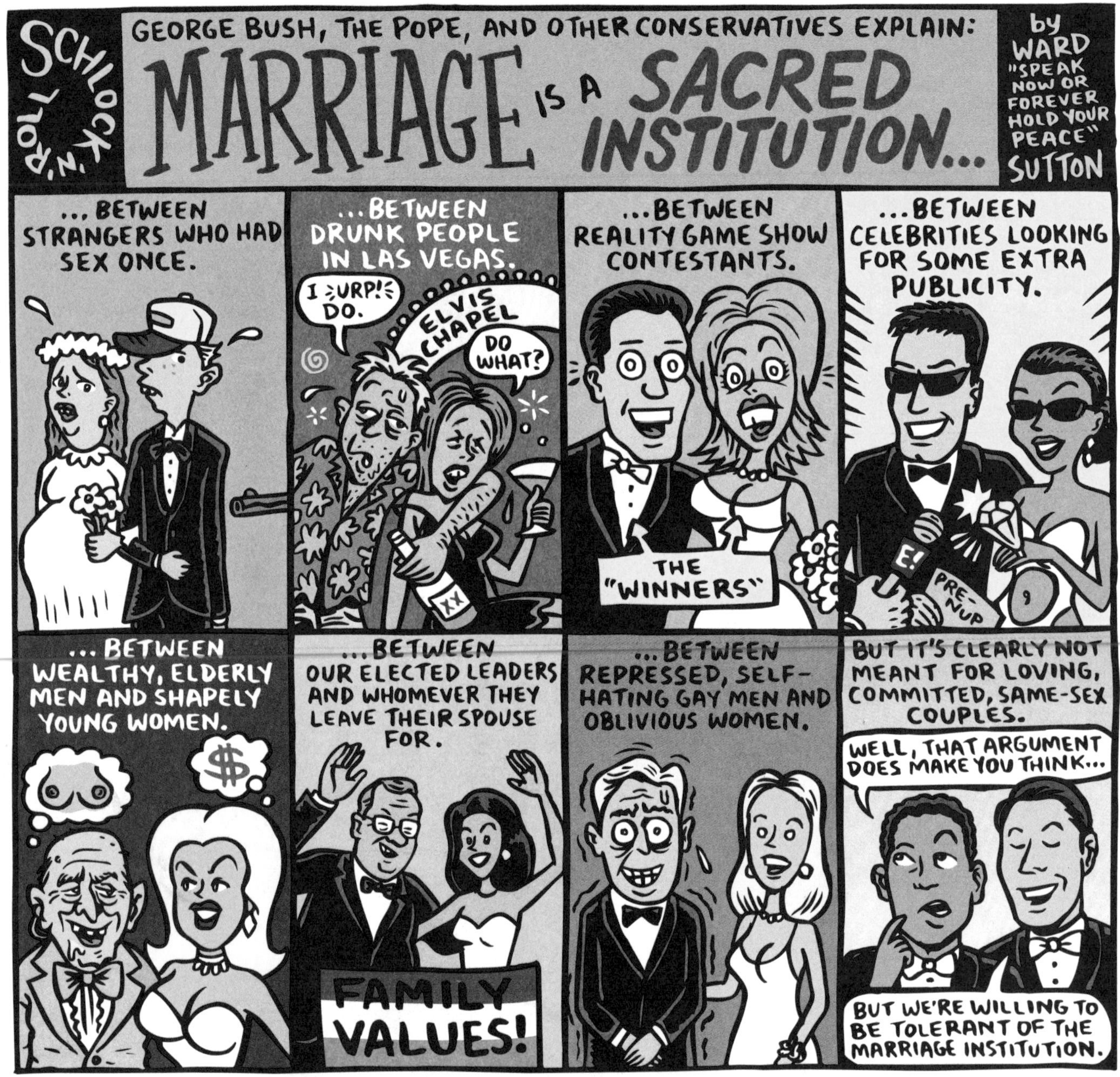
SCHLOCK 'N' ROLL
GEORGE BUSH, THE POPE, AND OTHER CONSERVATIVES EXPLAIN:
MARRIAGE IS A SACRED INSTITUTION...
by WARD "SPEAK NOW OR FOREVER HOLD YOUR PEACE" SUTTON
...BETWEEN STRANGERS WHO HAD SEX ONCE.
...BETWEEN DRUNK PEOPLE IN LAS VEGAS.
I *URP!* DO.
ELVIS CHAPEL
DO WHAT?
XX
...BETWEEN REALITY GAME SHOW CONTESTANTS.
THE "WINNERS"
...BETWEEN CELEBRITIES LOOKING FOR SOME EXTRA PUBLICITY.
E!
PRE-NUP
...BETWEEN WEALTHY, ELDERLY MEN AND SHAPELY YOUNG WOMEN.
$
...BETWEEN OUR ELECTED LEADERS AND WHOMEVER THEY LEAVE THEIR SPOUSE FOR.
FAMILY VALUES!
...BETWEEN REPRESSED, SELF-HATING GAY MEN AND OBLIVIOUS WOMEN.
BUT IT'S CLEARLY NOT MEANT FOR LOVING, COMMITTED, SAME-SEX COUPLES.
WELL, THAT ARGUMENT DOES MAKE YOU THINK...
BUT WE'RE WILLING TO BE TOLERANT OF THE MARRIAGE INSTITUTION.

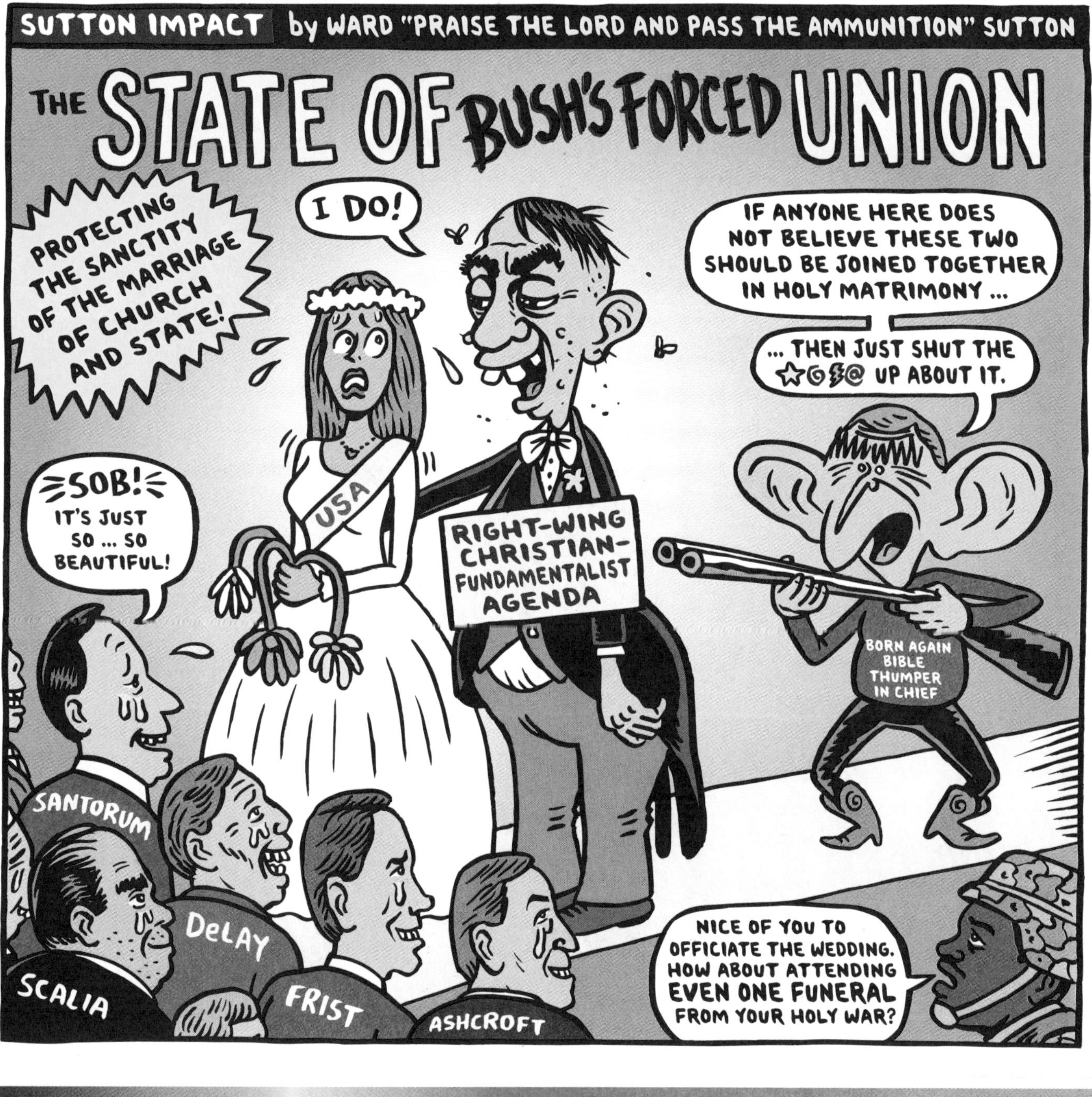
SUTTON IMPACT
by WARD "PRAISE THE LORD AND PASS THE AMMUNITION" SUTTON
THE STATE OF BUSH'S FORCED UNION
PROTECTING THE SANCTITY OF THE MARRIAGE OF CHURCH AND STATE!
I DO!
IF ANYONE HERE DOES NOT BELIEVE THESE TWO SHOULD BE JOINED TOGETHER IN HOLY MATRIMONY ...
... THEN JUST SHUT THE ☆@$@ UP ABOUT IT.
SOB! IT'S JUST SO ... SO BEAUTIFUL!
USA
RIGHT-WING CHRISTIAN-FUNDAMENTALIST AGENDA
BORN AGAIN BIBLE THUMPER IN CHIEF
SANTORUM
DeLAY
SCALIA
FRIST
ASHCROFT
NICE OF YOU TO OFFICIATE THE WEDDING. HOW ABOUT ATTENDING EVEN ONE FUNERAL FROM YOUR HOLY WAR?

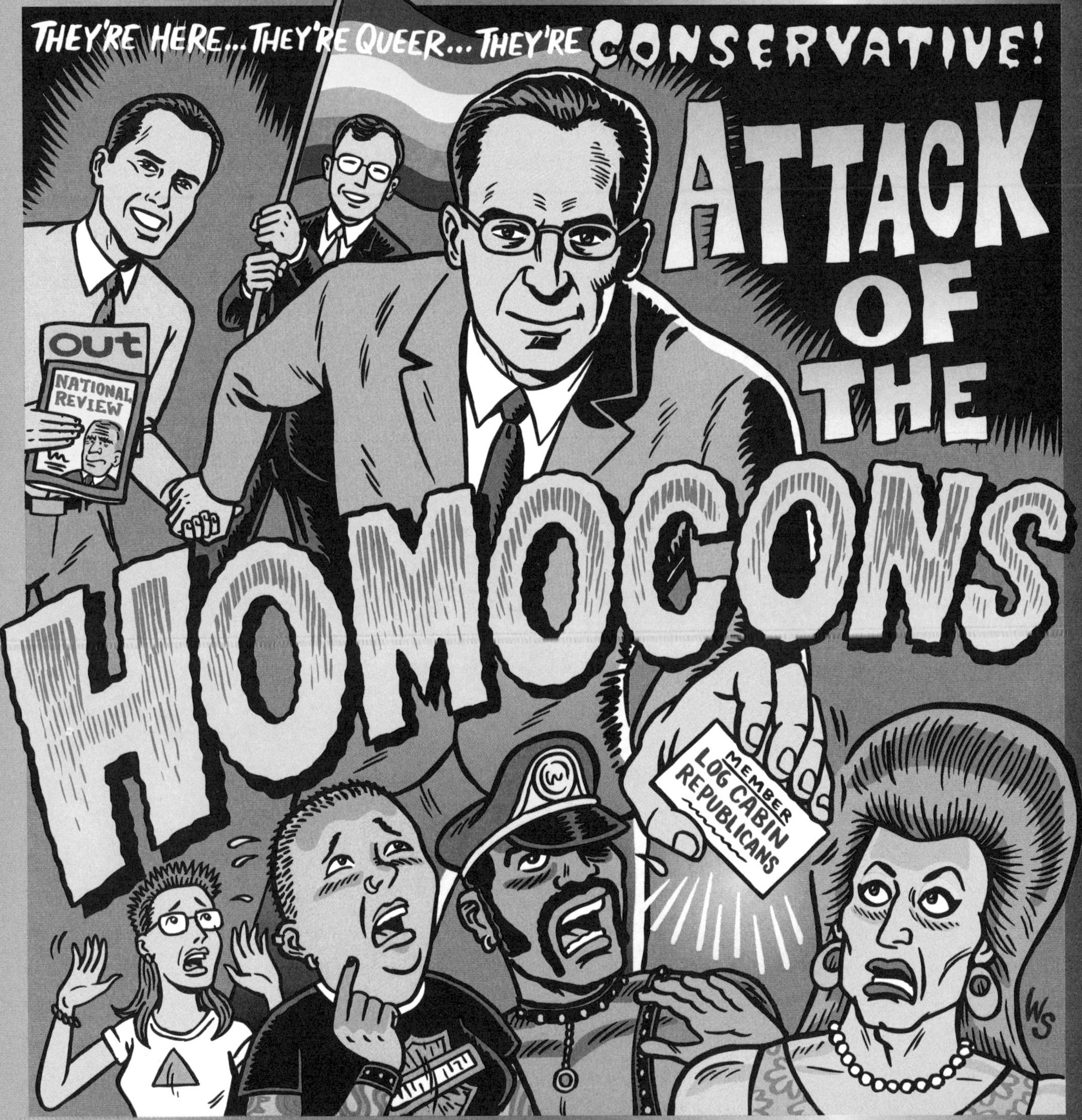

THEY'RE HERE... THEY'RE QUEER... THEY'RE CONSERVATIVE!
ATTACK OF THE HOMOCONS
OUT
NATIONAL REVIEW
MEMBER LOG CABIN REPUBLICANS
WS

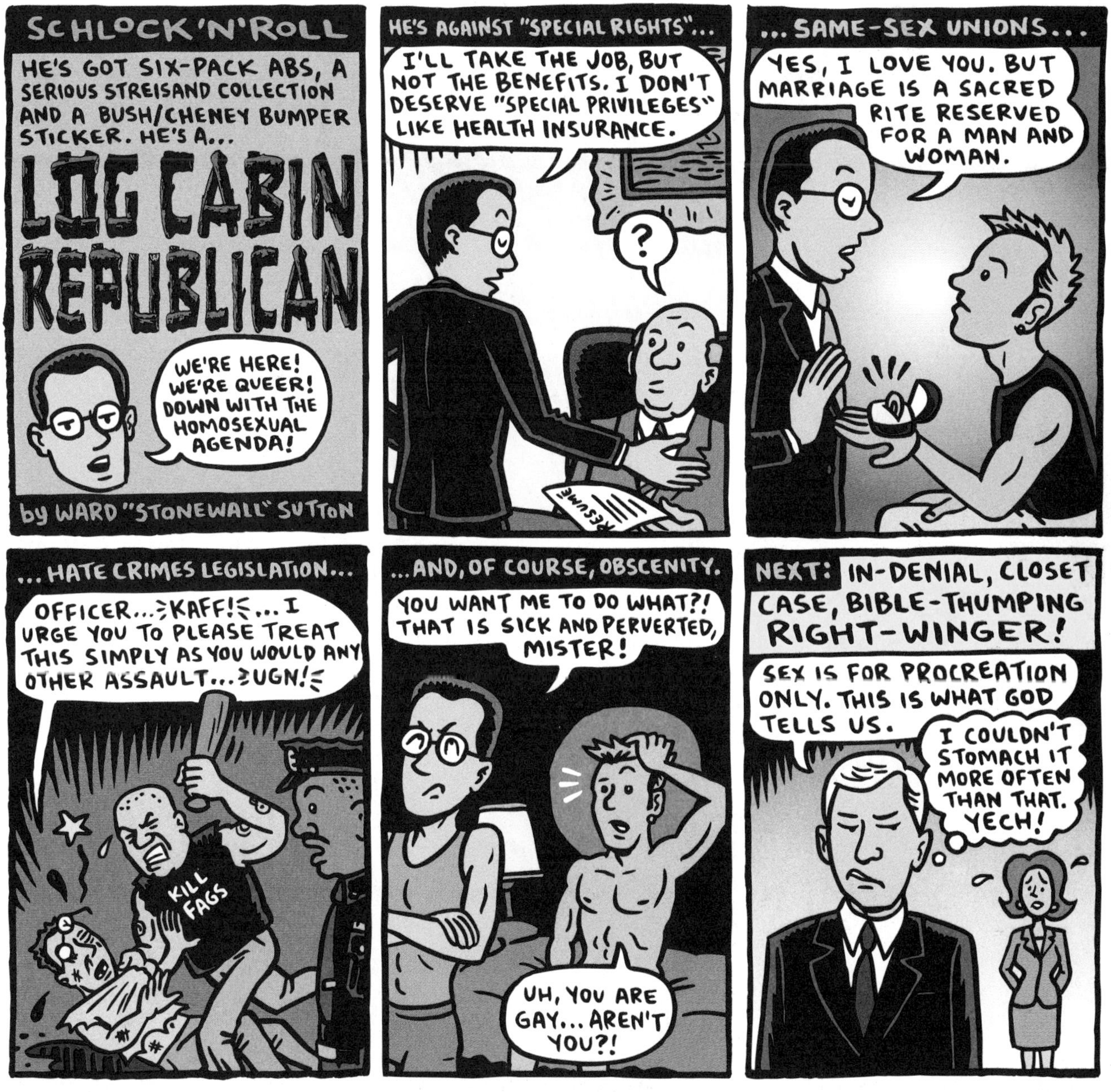
SCHLOCK'N'ROLL
HE'S GOT SIX-PACK ABS, A SERIOUS STREISAND COLLECTION AND A BUSH/CHENEY BUMPER STICKER. HE'S A...
LOG CABIN REPUBLICAN
WE'RE HERE! WE'RE QUEER! DOWN WITH THE HOMOSEXUAL AGENDA!
by WARD "STONEWALL" SUTTON
HE'S AGAINST "SPECIAL RIGHTS"...
I'LL TAKE THE JOB, BUT NOT THE BENEFITS. I DON'T DESERVE "SPECIAL PRIVILEGES" LIKE HEALTH INSURANCE.
?
RESUME
... SAME-SEX UNIONS...
YES, I LOVE YOU. BUT MARRIAGE IS A SACRED RITE RESERVED FOR A MAN AND WOMAN.
... HATE CRIMES LEGISLATION...
OFFICER... KAFF! ... I URGE YOU TO PLEASE TREAT THIS SIMPLY AS YOU WOULD ANY OTHER ASSAULT... UGN!
KILL FAGS
... AND, OF COURSE, OBSCENITY.
YOU WANT ME TO DO WHAT?! THAT IS SICK AND PERVERTED, MISTER!
UH, YOU ARE GAY... AREN'T YOU?!
NEXT: IN-DENIAL, CLOSET CASE, BIBLE-THUMPING RIGHT-WINGER!
SEX IS FOR PROCREATION ONLY. THIS IS WHAT GOD TELLS US.
I COULDN'T STOMACH IT MORE OFTEN THAN THAT. YECH!

What's worse: being despised by one group for your sexual orientation or being despised by another group for your political orientation? Log Cabin Republicans just want to have it both ways, I guess. Maybe some of them have two closets. The facing page was a cover for *The Nation*.

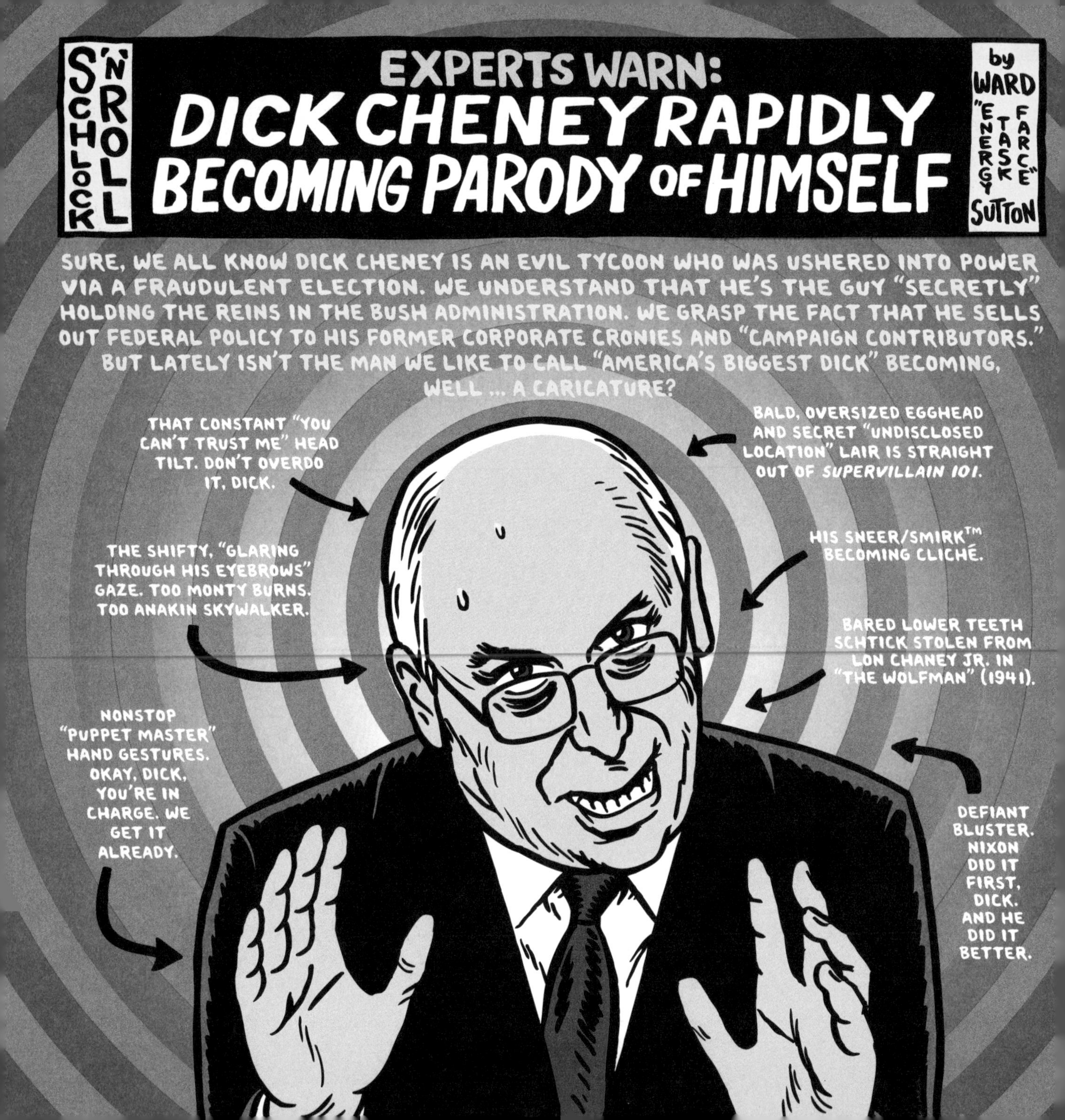
SCHLOCK 'N' ROLL
EXPERTS WARN:
DICK CHENEY RAPIDLY BECOMING PARODY OF HIMSELF
by WARD "ENERGY TASK FARCE" SUTTON
SURE, WE ALL KNOW DICK CHENEY IS AN EVIL TYCOON WHO WAS USHERED INTO POWER VIA A FRAUDULENT ELECTION. WE UNDERSTAND THAT HE'S THE GUY "SECRETLY" HOLDING THE REINS IN THE BUSH ADMINISTRATION. WE GRASP THE FACT THAT HE SELLS OUT FEDERAL POLICY TO HIS FORMER CORPORATE CRONIES AND "CAMPAIGN CONTRIBUTORS." BUT LATELY ISN'T THE MAN WE LIKE TO CALL "AMERICA'S BIGGEST DICK" BECOMING, WELL ... A CARICATURE?
THAT CONSTANT "YOU CAN'T TRUST ME" HEAD TILT. DON'T OVERDO IT, DICK.
BALD, OVERSIZED EGGHEAD AND SECRET "UNDISCLOSED LOCATION" LAIR IS STRAIGHT OUT OF SUPERVILLAIN 101.
THE SHIFTY, "GLARING THROUGH HIS EYEBROWS" GAZE. TOO MONTY BURNS. TOO ANAKIN SKYWALKER.
HIS SNEER/SMIRK™ BECOMING CLICHÉ.
BARED LOWER TEETH SCHTICK STOLEN FROM LON CHANEY JR. IN "THE WOLFMAN" (1941).
NONSTOP "PUPPET MASTER" HAND GESTURES. OKAY, DICK, YOU'RE IN CHARGE. WE GET IT ALREADY.
DEFIANT BLUSTER. NIXON DID IT FIRST, DICK. AND HE DID IT BETTER.

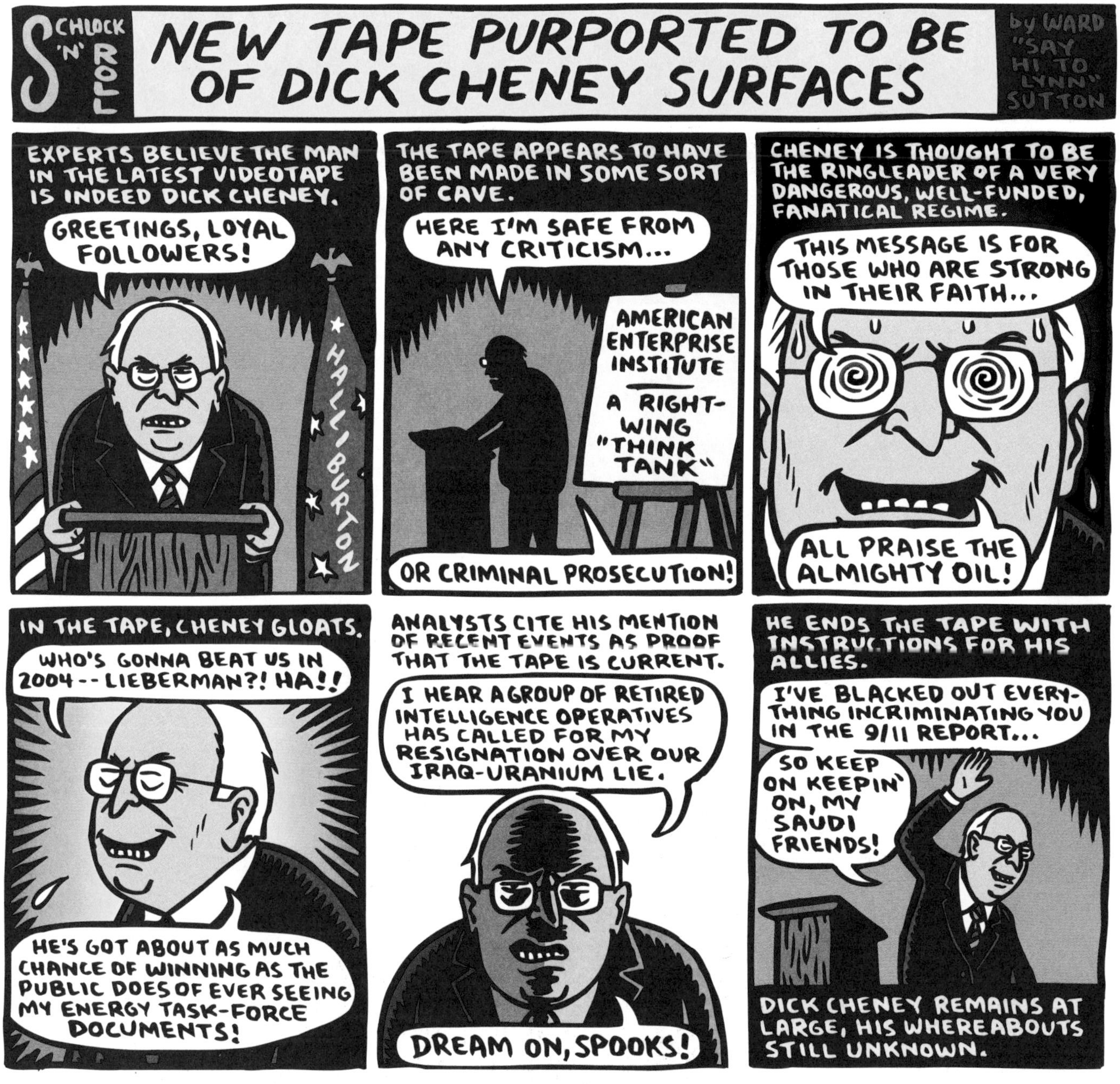
SCHLOCK 'N' ROLL
NEW TAPE PURPORTED TO BE OF DICK CHENEY SURFACES
by WARD "SAY HI TO LYNN" SUTTON
EXPERTS BELIEVE THE MAN IN THE LATEST VIDEOTAPE IS INDEED DICK CHENEY.
GREETINGS, LOYAL FOLLOWERS!
HALLIBURTON
THE TAPE APPEARS TO HAVE BEEN MADE IN SOME SORT OF CAVE.
HERE I'M SAFE FROM ANY CRITICISM...
AMERICAN ENTERPRISE INSTITUTE
A RIGHT-WING "THINK TANK"
OR CRIMINAL PROSECUTION!
CHENEY IS THOUGHT TO BE THE RINGLEADER OF A VERY DANGEROUS, WELL-FUNDED, FANATICAL REGIME.
THIS MESSAGE IS FOR THOSE WHO ARE STRONG IN THEIR FAITH...
ALL PRAISE THE ALMIGHTY OIL!
IN THE TAPE, CHENEY GLOATS.
WHO'S GONNA BEAT US IN 2004 -- LIEBERMAN?! HA!!
HE'S GOT ABOUT AS MUCH CHANCE OF WINNING AS THE PUBLIC DOES OF EVER SEEING MY ENERGY TASK-FORCE DOCUMENTS!
ANALYSTS CITE HIS MENTION OF RECENT EVENTS AS PROOF THAT THE TAPE IS CURRENT.
I HEAR A GROUP OF RETIRED INTELLIGENCE OPERATIVES HAS CALLED FOR MY RESIGNATION OVER OUR IRAQ-URANIUM LIE.
DREAM ON, SPOOKS!
HE ENDS THE TAPE WITH INSTRUCTIONS FOR HIS ALLIES.
I'VE BLACKED OUT EVERYTHING INCRIMINATING YOU IN THE 9/11 REPORT...
SO KEEP ON KEEPIN' ON, MY SAUDI FRIENDS!
DICK CHENEY REMAINS AT LARGE, HIS WHEREABOUTS STILL UNKNOWN.

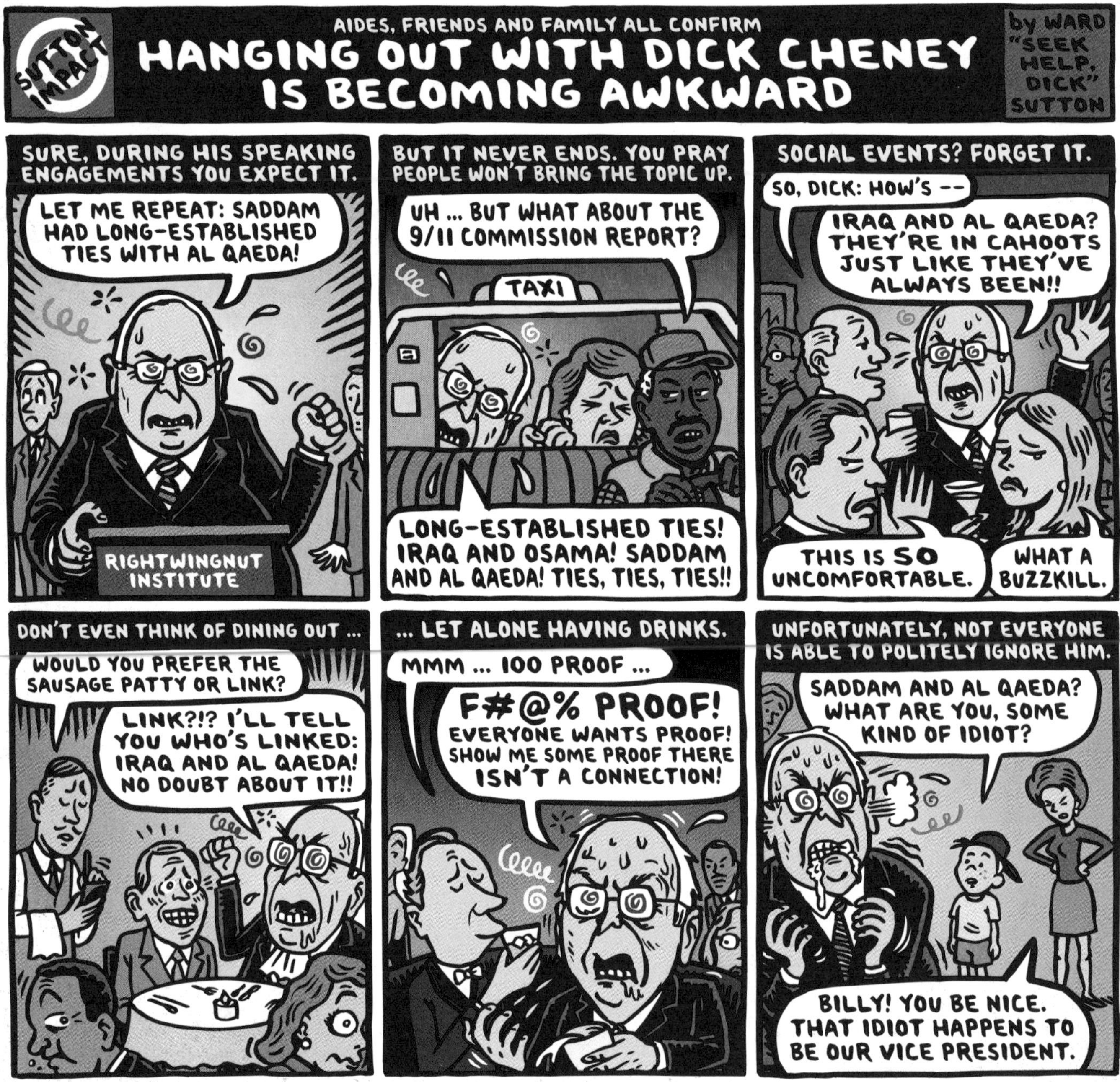
SUTTON IMPACT
AIDES, FRIENDS AND FAMILY ALL CONFIRM
HANGING OUT WITH DICK CHENEY IS BECOMING AWKWARD
by WARD "SEEK HELP, DICK" SUTTON
SURE, DURING HIS SPEAKING ENGAGEMENTS YOU EXPECT IT.
LET ME REPEAT: SADDAM HAD LONG-ESTABLISHED TIES WITH AL QAEDA!
RIGHTWINGNUT INSTITUTE
BUT IT NEVER ENDS. YOU PRAY PEOPLE WON'T BRING THE TOPIC UP.
UH ... BUT WHAT ABOUT THE 9/11 COMMISSION REPORT?
TAXI
LONG-ESTABLISHED TIES! IRAQ AND OSAMA! SADDAM AND AL QAEDA! TIES, TIES, TIES!!
SOCIAL EVENTS? FORGET IT.
SO, DICK: HOW'S --
IRAQ AND AL QAEDA? THEY'RE IN CAHOOTS JUST LIKE THEY'VE ALWAYS BEEN!!
THIS IS SO UNCOMFORTABLE.
WHAT A BUZZKILL.
DON'T EVEN THINK OF DINING OUT ...
WOULD YOU PREFER THE SAUSAGE PATTY OR LINK?
LINK?!? I'LL TELL YOU WHO'S LINKED: IRAQ AND AL QAEDA! NO DOUBT ABOUT IT!!
... LET ALONE HAVING DRINKS.
MMM ... 100 PROOF ...
F#@% PROOF! EVERYONE WANTS PROOF! SHOW ME SOME PROOF THERE ISN'T A CONNECTION!
UNFORTUNATELY, NOT EVERYONE IS ABLE TO POLITELY IGNORE HIM.
SADDAM AND AL QAEDA? WHAT ARE YOU, SOME KIND OF IDIOT?
BILLY! YOU BE NICE. THAT IDIOT HAPPENS TO BE OUR VICE PRESIDENT.

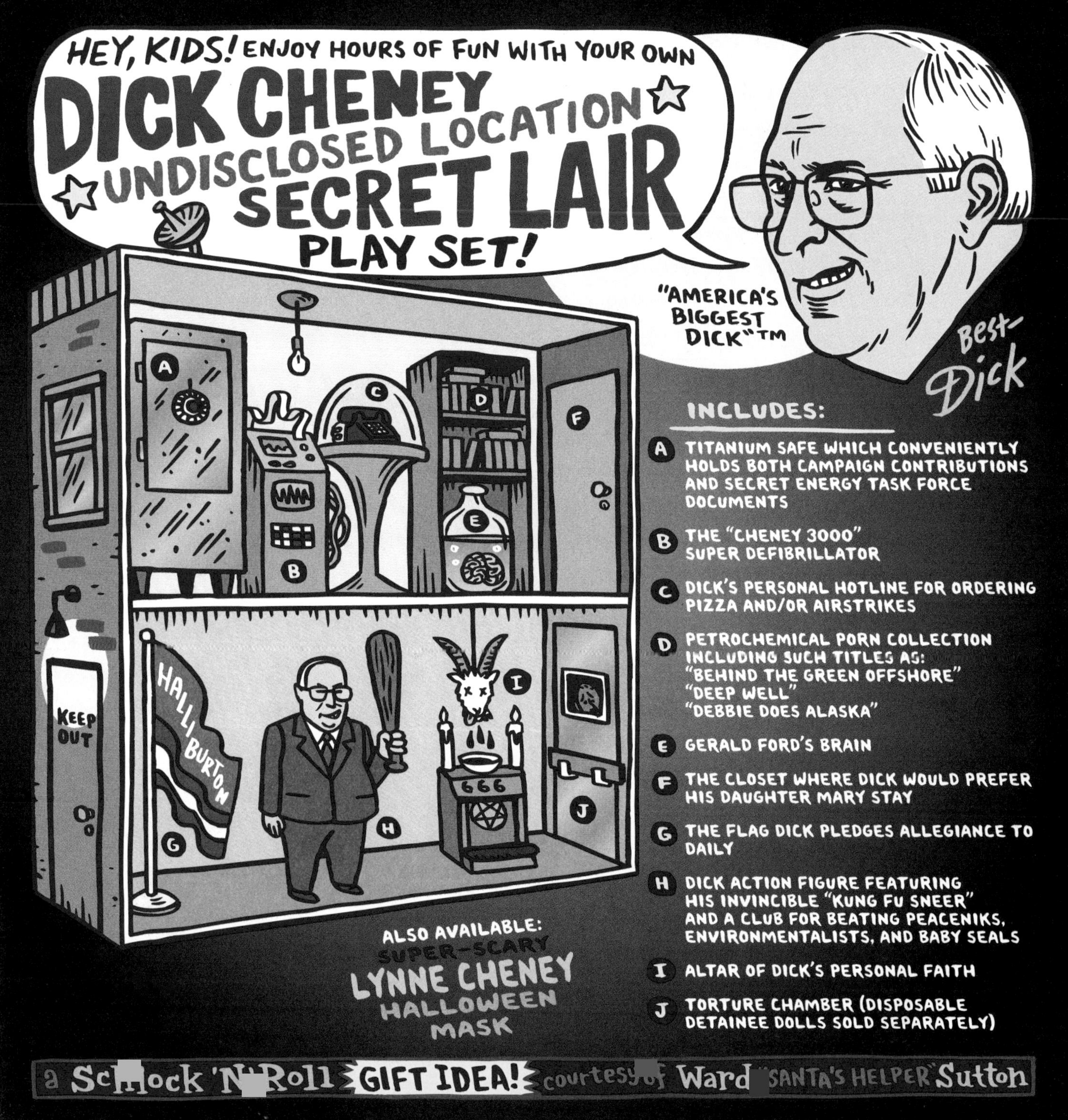
HEY, KIDS! ENJOY HOURS OF FUN WITH YOUR OWN
DICK CHENEY
UNDISCLOSED LOCATION
SECRET LAIR
PLAY SET!
"AMERICA'S BIGGEST DICK"™
Best-Dick
A
B
C
D
E
F
G
H
I
J
KEEP OUT
HALLIBURTON
666
INCLUDES:
A TITANIUM SAFE WHICH CONVENIENTLY HOLDS BOTH CAMPAIGN CONTRIBUTIONS AND SECRET ENERGY TASK FORCE DOCUMENTS
B THE "CHENEY 3000" SUPER DEFIBRILLATOR
C DICK'S PERSONAL HOTLINE FOR ORDERING PIZZA AND/OR AIRSTRIKES
D PETROCHEMICAL PORN COLLECTION INCLUDING SUCH TITLES AS: "BEHIND THE GREEN OFFSHORE" "DEEP WELL" "DEBBIE DOES ALASKA"
E GERALD FORD'S BRAIN
F THE CLOSET WHERE DICK WOULD PREFER HIS DAUGHTER MARY STAY
G THE FLAG DICK PLEDGES ALLEGIANCE TO DAILY
H DICK ACTION FIGURE FEATURING HIS INVINCIBLE "KUNG FU SNEER" AND A CLUB FOR BEATING PEACENIKS, ENVIRONMENTALISTS, AND BABY SEALS
I ALTAR OF DICK'S PERSONAL FAITH
J TORTURE CHAMBER (DISPOSABLE DETAINEE DOLLS SOLD SEPARATELY)
ALSO AVAILABLE: SUPER-SCARY LYNNE CHENEY HALLOWEEN MASK
a Schlock 'N' Roll GIFT IDEA! courtesy of Ward "SANTA'S HELPER" Sutton

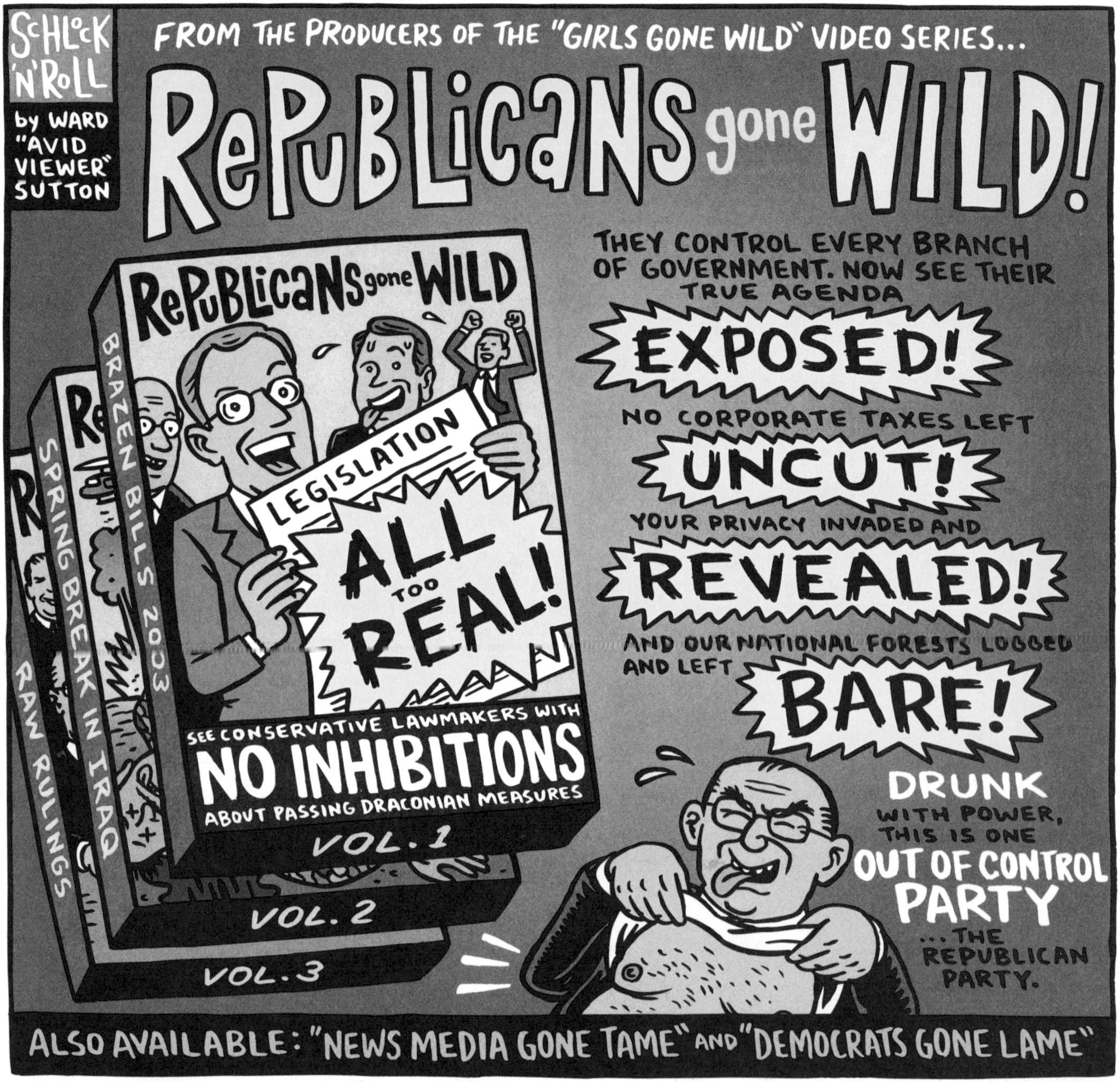
SCHLOCK 'N' ROLL
by WARD "AVID VIEWER" SUTTON
FROM THE PRODUCERS OF THE "GIRLS GONE WILD" VIDEO SERIES...
REPUBLICANS gone WILD!
REPUBLICANS gone WILD
LEGISLATION
ALL TOO REAL!
SEE CONSERVATIVE LAWMAKERS WITH
NO INHIBITIONS
ABOUT PASSING DRACONIAN MEASURES
VOL. 1
BRAZEN BILLS 2003
VOL. 2
SPRING BREAK IN IRAQ
VOL. 3
RAW RULINGS
THEY CONTROL EVERY BRANCH OF GOVERNMENT. NOW SEE THEIR TRUE AGENDA
EXPOSED!
NO CORPORATE TAXES LEFT
UNCUT!
YOUR PRIVACY INVADED AND
REVEALED!
AND OUR NATIONAL FORESTS LOGGED AND LEFT
BARE!
DRUNK WITH POWER, THIS IS ONE
OUT OF CONTROL PARTY
...THE REPUBLICAN PARTY.
ALSO AVAILABLE: "NEWS MEDIA GONE TAME" AND "DEMOCRATS GONE LAME"

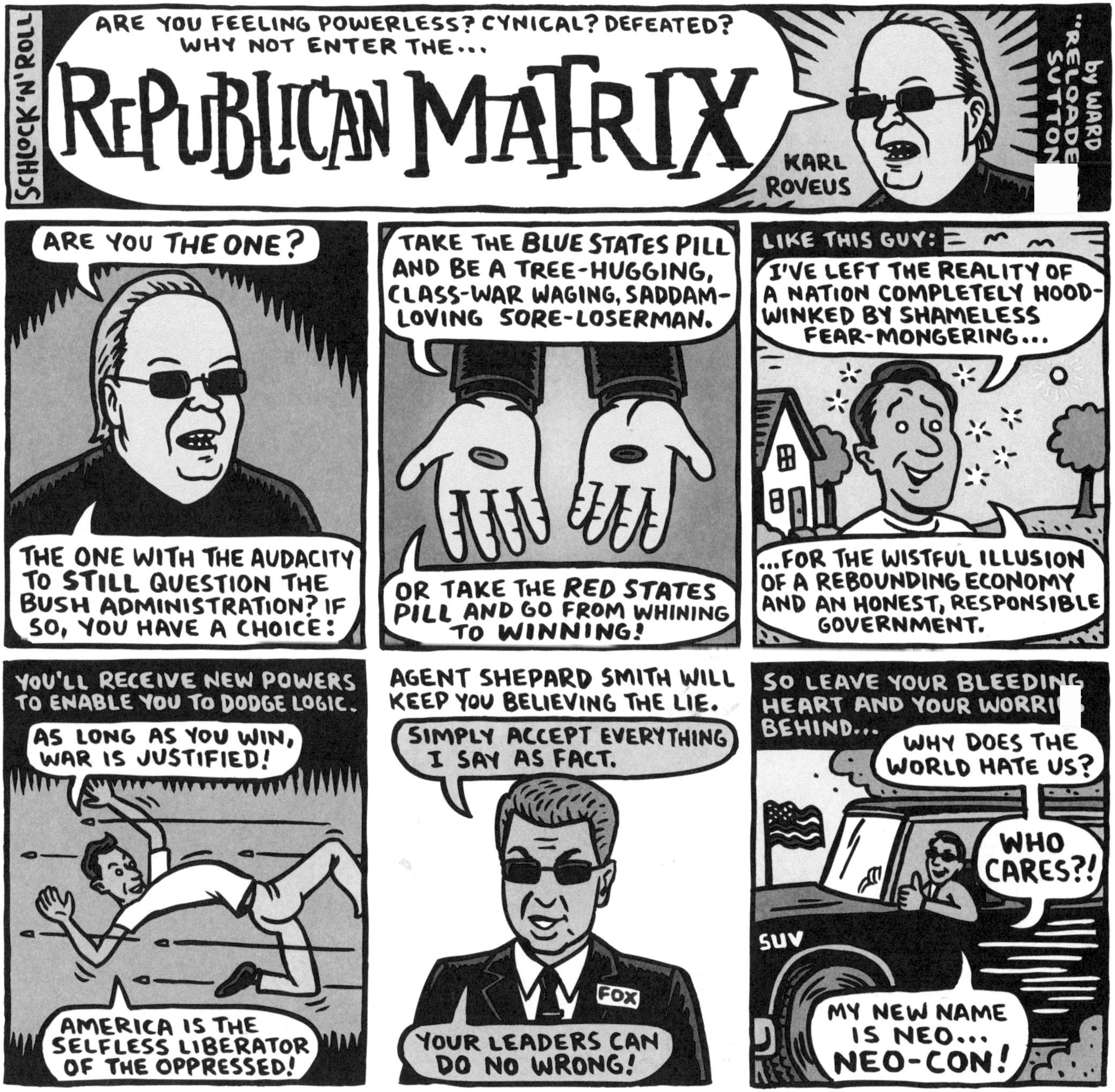
SCHLOCK 'N' ROLL
ARE YOU FEELING POWERLESS? CYNICAL? DEFEATED? WHY NOT ENTER THE...
REPUBLICAN MATRIX
KARL ROVEUS
by WARD "RELOADE SUTTON
ARE YOU THE ONE?
THE ONE WITH THE AUDACITY TO STILL QUESTION THE BUSH ADMINISTRATION? IF SO, YOU HAVE A CHOICE:
TAKE THE BLUE STATES PILL AND BE A TREE-HUGGING, CLASS-WAR WAGING, SADDAM-LOVING SORE-LOSERMAN.
OR TAKE THE RED STATES PILL AND GO FROM WHINING TO WINNING!
LIKE THIS GUY:
I'VE LEFT THE REALITY OF A NATION COMPLETELY HOOD-WINKED BY SHAMELESS FEAR-MONGERING...
...FOR THE WISTFUL ILLUSION OF A REBOUNDING ECONOMY AND AN HONEST, RESPONSIBLE GOVERNMENT.
YOU'LL RECEIVE NEW POWERS TO ENABLE YOU TO DODGE LOGIC.
AS LONG AS YOU WIN, WAR IS JUSTIFIED!
AMERICA IS THE SELFLESS LIBERATOR OF THE OPPRESSED!
AGENT SHEPARD SMITH WILL KEEP YOU BELIEVING THE LIE.
SIMPLY ACCEPT EVERYTHING I SAY AS FACT.
FOX
YOUR LEADERS CAN DO NO WRONG!
SO LEAVE YOUR BLEEDIN HEART AND YOUR WORRI BEHIND...
WHY DOES THE WORLD HATE US?
WHO CARES?!
SUV
MY NEW NAME IS NEO... NEO-CON!

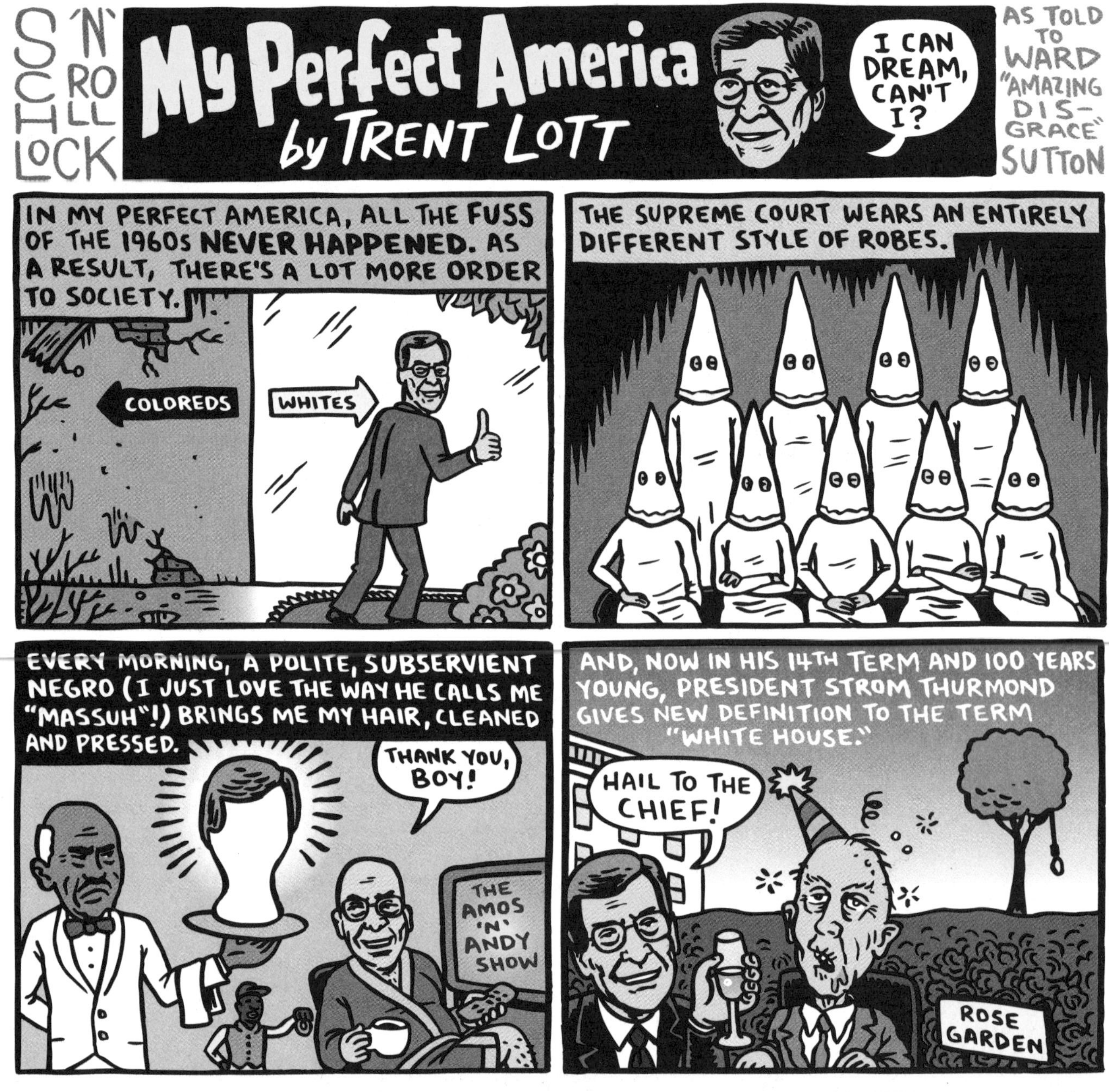
SCHLOCK 'N' ROLL
My Perfect America
by TRENT LOTT
I CAN DREAM, CAN'T I?
AS TOLD TO WARD "AMAZING DIS-GRACE" SUTTON
IN MY PERFECT AMERICA, ALL THE FUSS OF THE 1960s NEVER HAPPENED. AS A RESULT, THERE'S A LOT MORE ORDER TO SOCIETY.
COLOREDS
WHITES
THE SUPREME COURT WEARS AN ENTIRELY DIFFERENT STYLE OF ROBES.
EVERY MORNING, A POLITE, SUBSERVIENT NEGRO (I JUST LOVE THE WAY HE CALLS ME "MASSUH"!) BRINGS ME MY HAIR, CLEANED AND PRESSED.
THANK YOU, BOY!
THE AMOS 'N' ANDY SHOW
AND, NOW IN HIS 14TH TERM AND 100 YEARS YOUNG, PRESIDENT STROM THURMOND GIVES NEW DEFINITION TO THE TERM "WHITE HOUSE."
HAIL TO THE CHIEF!
ROSE GARDEN

In Washington DC a few years ago, I rounded a corner and bumped right into Trent Lott and a bunch of his henchmen. He looked inhuman – like some alien pod-person sent here to destroy the planet.

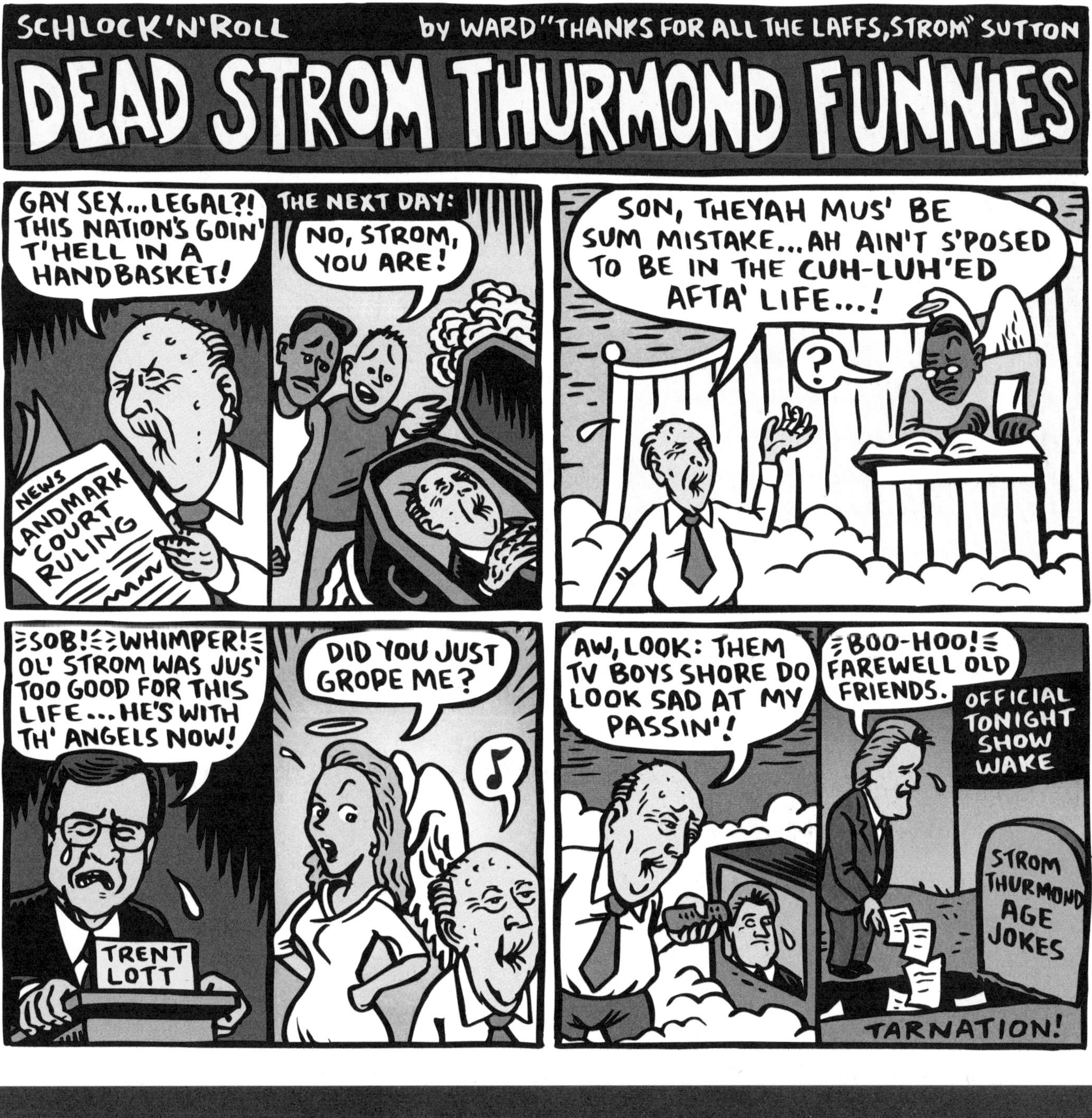
SCHLOCK'N'ROLL
by WARD "THANKS FOR ALL THE LAFFS, STROM" SUTTON
DEAD STROM THURMOND FUNNIES
GAY SEX... LEGAL?! THIS NATION'S GOIN' T'HELL IN A HANDBASKET!
NEWS
LANDMARK COURT RULING
THE NEXT DAY:
NO, STROM, YOU ARE!
SON, THEYAH MUS' BE SUM MISTAKE... AH AIN'T S'POSED TO BE IN THE CUH-LUH'ED AFTA' LIFE...!
?
SOB! WHIMPER! OL' STROM WAS JUS' TOO GOOD FOR THIS LIFE... HE'S WITH TH' ANGELS NOW!
TRENT LOTT
DID YOU JUST GROPE ME?
AW, LOOK: THEM TV BOYS SHORE DO LOOK SAD AT MY PASSIN'!
BOO-HOO! FAREWELL OLD FRIENDS.
OFFICIAL TONIGHT SHOW WAKE
STROM THURMOND AGE JOKES
TARNATION!

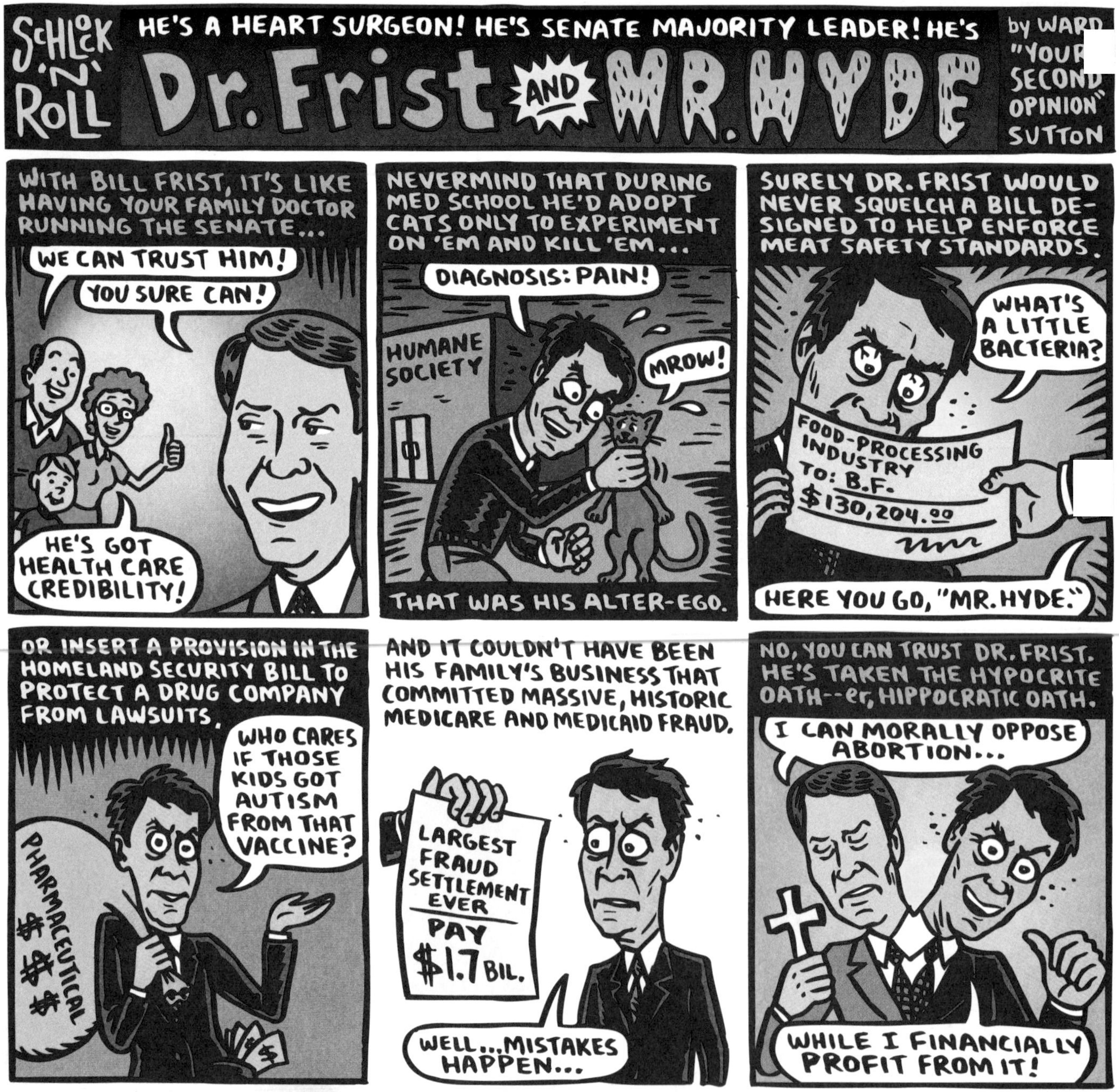
SCHLOCK 'N' ROLL
HE'S A HEART SURGEON! HE'S SENATE MAJORITY LEADER! HE'S
Dr. Frist AND MR. HYDE
by WARD "YOUR SECOND OPINION" SUTTON
WITH BILL FRIST, IT'S LIKE HAVING YOUR FAMILY DOCTOR RUNNING THE SENATE...
WE CAN TRUST HIM!
YOU SURE CAN!
HE'S GOT HEALTH CARE CREDIBILITY!
NEVERMIND THAT DURING MED SCHOOL HE'D ADOPT CATS ONLY TO EXPERIMENT ON 'EM AND KILL 'EM...
DIAGNOSIS: PAIN!
HUMANE SOCIETY
MROW!
THAT WAS HIS ALTER-EGO.
SURELY DR. FRIST WOULD NEVER SQUELCH A BILL DESIGNED TO HELP ENFORCE MEAT SAFETY STANDARDS.
WHAT'S A LITTLE BACTERIA?
FOOD-PROCESSING INDUSTRY
TO: B.F.
$130,204.00
HERE YOU GO, "MR. HYDE."
OR INSERT A PROVISION IN THE HOMELAND SECURITY BILL TO PROTECT A DRUG COMPANY FROM LAWSUITS.
WHO CARES IF THOSE KIDS GOT AUTISM FROM THAT VACCINE?
PHARMACEUTICAL $ $ $
AND IT COULDN'T HAVE BEEN HIS FAMILY'S BUSINESS THAT COMMITTED MASSIVE, HISTORIC MEDICARE AND MEDICAID FRAUD.
LARGEST FRAUD SETTLEMENT EVER
PAY $1.7 BIL.
WELL... MISTAKES HAPPEN...
NO, YOU CAN TRUST DR. FRIST. HE'S TAKEN THE HYPOCRITE OATH--er, HIPPOCRATIC OATH.
I CAN MORALLY OPPOSE ABORTION...
WHILE I FINANCIALLY PROFIT FROM IT!

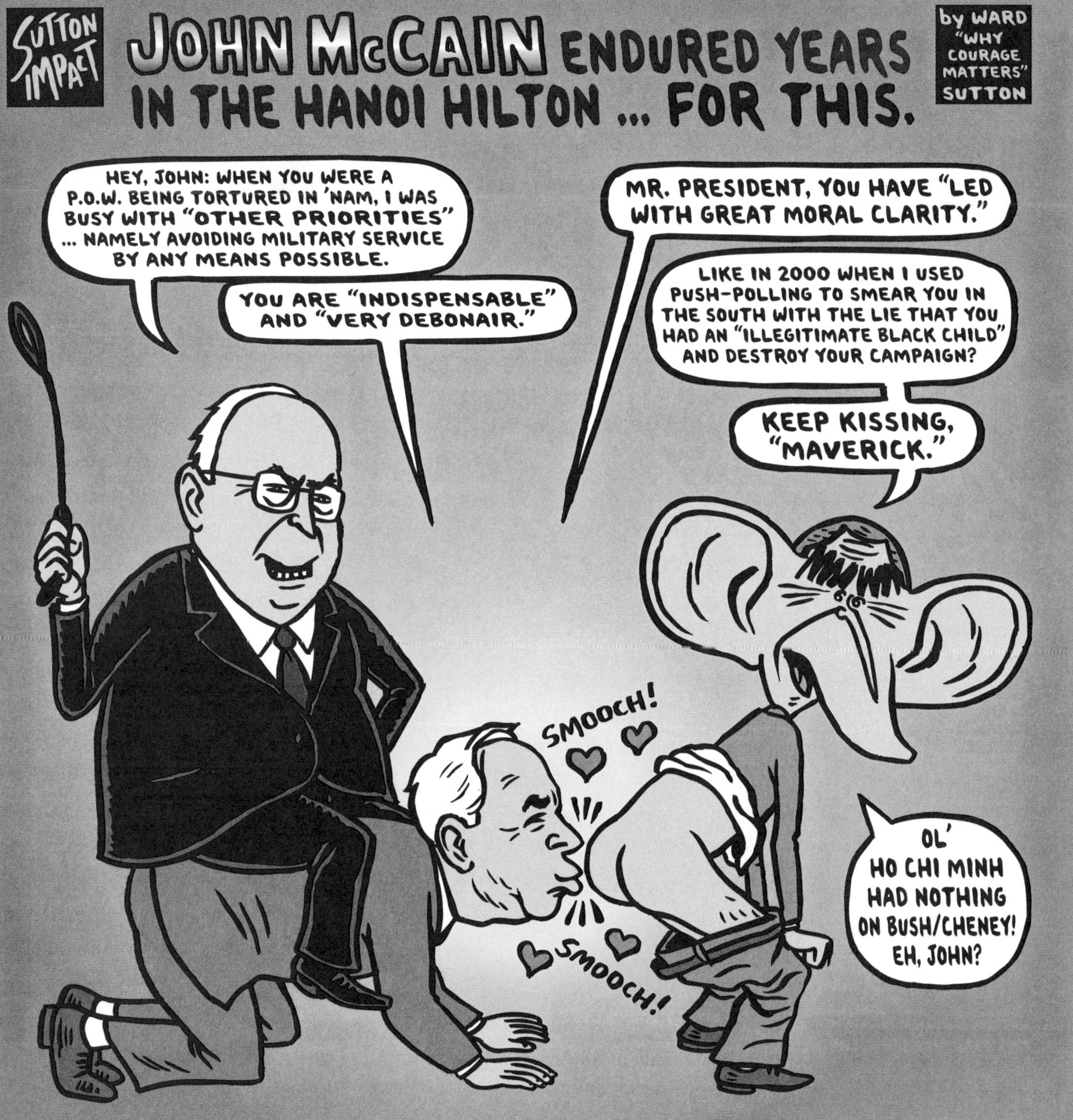
SUTTON IMPACT
JOHN McCAIN ENDURED YEARS IN THE HANOI HILTON ... FOR THIS.
by WARD "WHY COURAGE MATTERS" SUTTON
HEY, JOHN: WHEN YOU WERE A P.O.W. BEING TORTURED IN 'NAM, I WAS BUSY WITH "OTHER PRIORITIES" ... NAMELY AVOIDING MILITARY SERVICE BY ANY MEANS POSSIBLE.
YOU ARE "INDISPENSABLE" AND "VERY DEBONAIR."
MR. PRESIDENT, YOU HAVE "LED WITH GREAT MORAL CLARITY."
LIKE IN 2000 WHEN I USED PUSH-POLLING TO SMEAR YOU IN THE SOUTH WITH THE LIE THAT YOU HAD AN "ILLEGITIMATE BLACK CHILD" AND DESTROY YOUR CAMPAIGN?
KEEP KISSING, "MAVERICK."
SMOOCH!
SMOOCH!
OL' HO CHI MINH HAD NOTHING ON BUSH/CHENEY! EH, JOHN?

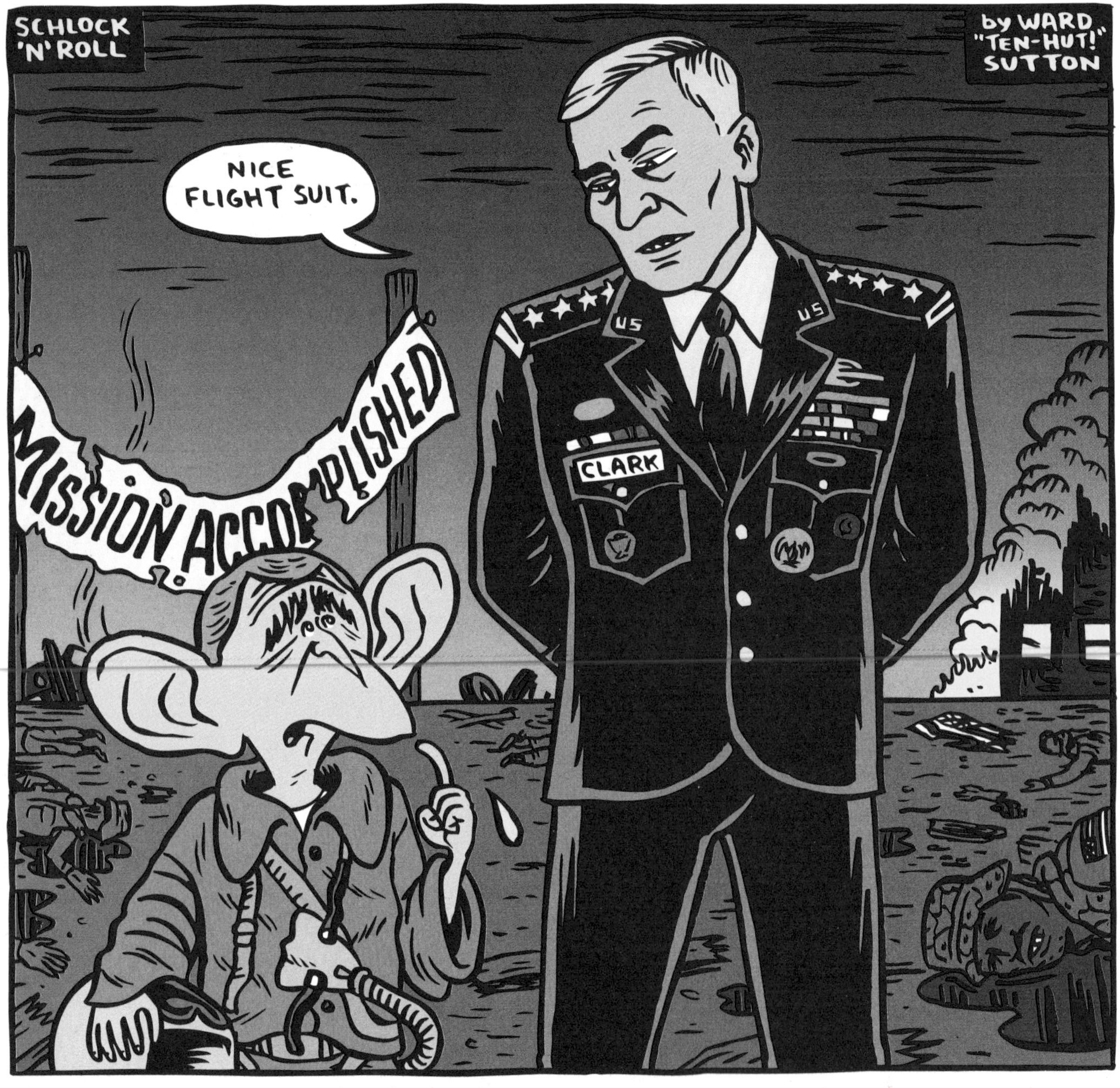
SCHLOCK 'N' ROLL
by WARD "TEN-HUT!" SUTTON
NICE FLIGHT SUIT.
MISSION ACCOMPLISHED
CLARK
US
US

While covering the 2004 Democratic Convention for the *Village Voice*, I briefly met Wesley Clark in passing and gave him a copy of this cartoon. His response? "That's cute."

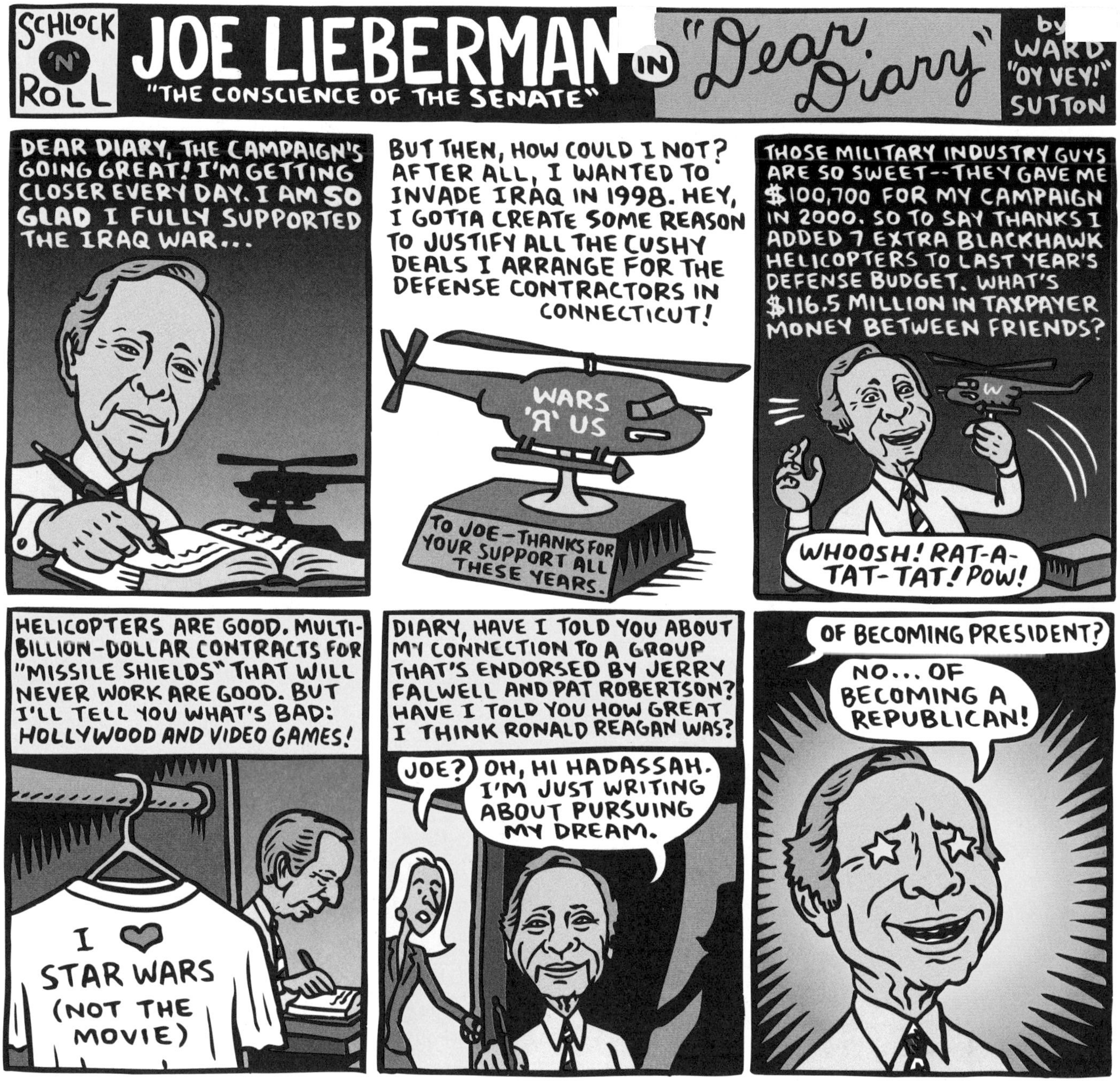
SCHLOCK 'N' ROLL
JOE LIEBERMAN
"THE CONSCIENCE OF THE SENATE"
IN "Dear Diary"
by WARD "OY VEY!" SUTTON
DEAR DIARY, THE CAMPAIGN'S GOING GREAT! I'M GETTING CLOSER EVERY DAY. I AM SO GLAD I FULLY SUPPORTED THE IRAQ WAR...
BUT THEN, HOW COULD I NOT? AFTER ALL, I WANTED TO INVADE IRAQ IN 1998. HEY, I GOTTA CREATE SOME REASON TO JUSTIFY ALL THE CUSHY DEALS I ARRANGE FOR THE DEFENSE CONTRACTORS IN CONNECTICUT!
WARS 'R' US
TO JOE—THANKS FOR YOUR SUPPORT ALL THESE YEARS.
THOSE MILITARY INDUSTRY GUYS ARE SO SWEET--THEY GAVE ME $100,700 FOR MY CAMPAIGN IN 2000. SO TO SAY THANKS I ADDED 7 EXTRA BLACKHAWK HELICOPTERS TO LAST YEAR'S DEFENSE BUDGET. WHAT'S $116.5 MILLION IN TAXPAYER MONEY BETWEEN FRIENDS?
W
WHOOSH! RAT-A-TAT-TAT! POW!
HELICOPTERS ARE GOOD. MULTI-BILLION-DOLLAR CONTRACTS FOR "MISSILE SHIELDS" THAT WILL NEVER WORK ARE GOOD. BUT I'LL TELL YOU WHAT'S BAD: HOLLYWOOD AND VIDEO GAMES!
I ♥ STAR WARS (NOT THE MOVIE)
DIARY, HAVE I TOLD YOU ABOUT MY CONNECTION TO A GROUP THAT'S ENDORSED BY JERRY FALWELL AND PAT ROBERTSON? HAVE I TOLD YOU HOW GREAT I THINK RONALD REAGAN WAS?
JOE?
OH, HI HADASSAH. I'M JUST WRITING ABOUT PURSUING MY DREAM.
OF BECOMING PRESIDENT?
NO... OF BECOMING A REPUBLICAN!

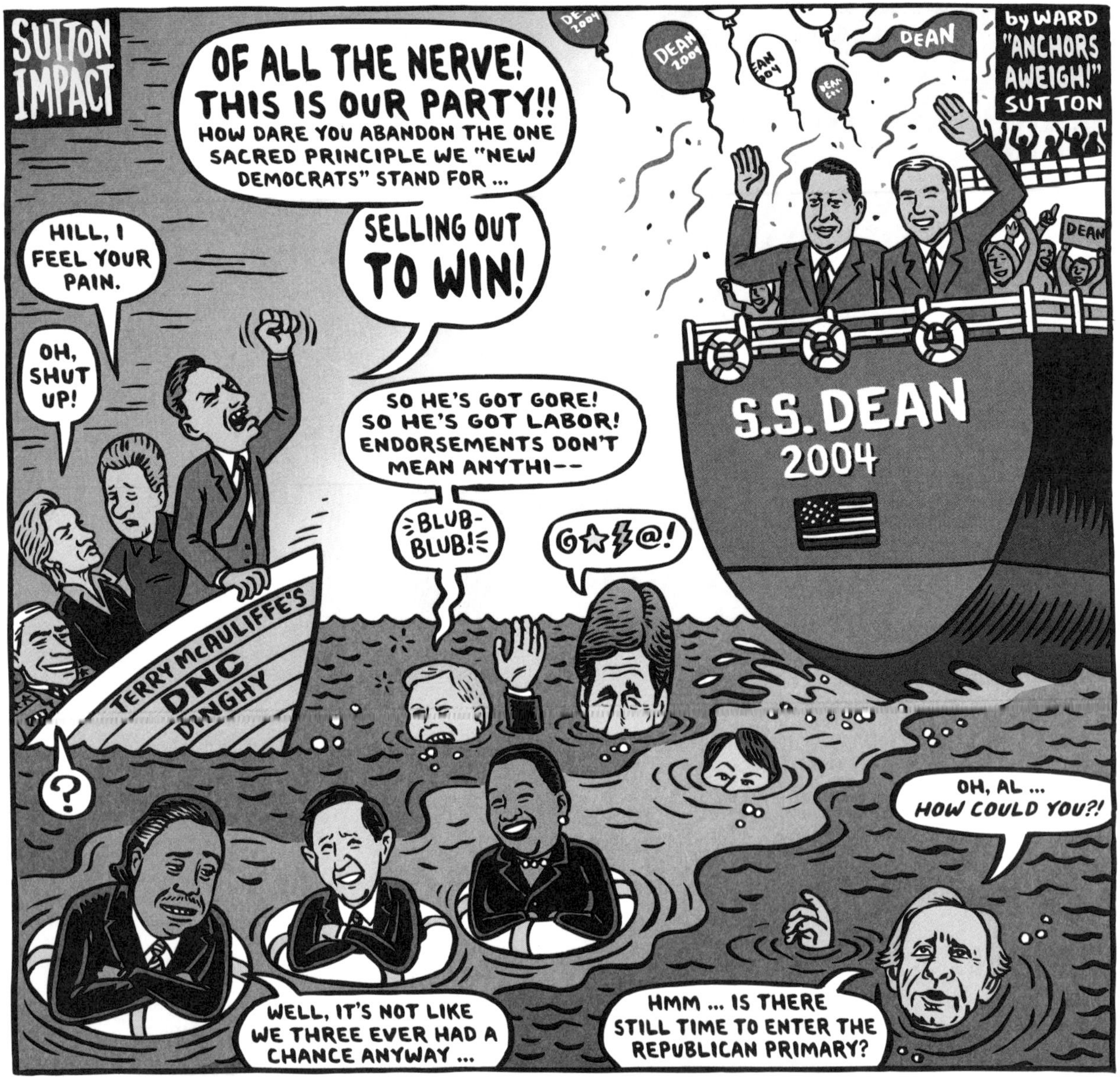
SUTTON IMPACT
by WARD "ANCHORS AWEIGH!" SUTTON
OF ALL THE NERVE! THIS IS OUR PARTY!! HOW DARE YOU ABANDON THE ONE SACRED PRINCIPLE WE "NEW DEMOCRATS" STAND FOR ...
SELLING OUT TO WIN!
HILL, I FEEL YOUR PAIN.
OH, SHUT UP!
SO HE'S GOT GORE! SO HE'S GOT LABOR! ENDORSEMENTS DON'T MEAN ANYTHI--
BLUB-BLUB!
G☆⚡@!
TERRY McAULIFFE'S DNC DINGHY
?
S.S. DEAN 2004
DEAN
OH, AL ... HOW COULD YOU?!
WELL, IT'S NOT LIKE WE THREE EVER HAD A CHANCE ANYWAY ...
HMM ... IS THERE STILL TIME TO ENTER THE REPUBLICAN PRIMARY?

At a Dean fundraiser I attended in May, 2003, the good doctor gave a speech that was right on, but the buzz of the evening was shockingly low wattage and the size of the audience was anemic (especially for Manhattan). The host, Whoopi Goldberg, gestured from the stage to the media platform (empty except for one woman with a camcorder) and said, "That's all the press we've got? Oh, shit." Nonetheless, later that year Dean had the momentum ...

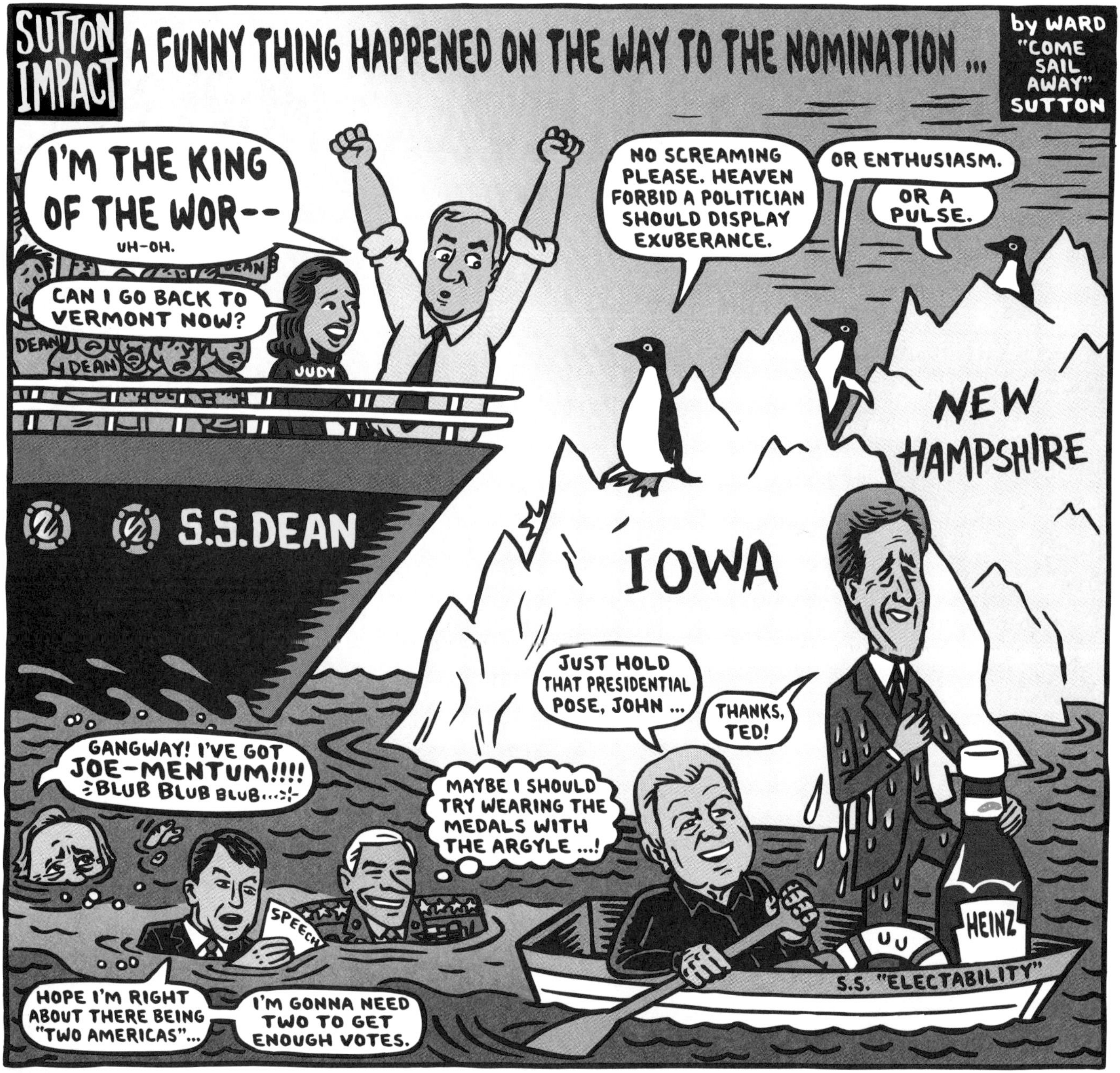
SUTTON IMPACT
A FUNNY THING HAPPENED ON THE WAY TO THE NOMINATION ...
by WARD "COME SAIL AWAY" SUTTON
I'M THE KING OF THE WOR--
UH-OH.
CAN I GO BACK TO VERMONT NOW?
DEAN
DEAN
DEAN
JUDY
S.S. DEAN
NO SCREAMING PLEASE. HEAVEN FORBID A POLITICIAN SHOULD DISPLAY EXUBERANCE.
OR ENTHUSIASM.
OR A PULSE.
IOWA
NEW HAMPSHIRE
JUST HOLD THAT PRESIDENTIAL POSE, JOHN ...
THANKS, TED!
GANGWAY! I'VE GOT JOE-MENTUM!!!! BLUB BLUB BLUB...
MAYBE I SHOULD TRY WEARING THE MEDALS WITH THE ARGYLE ...!
SPEECH
HEINZ
S.S. "ELECTABILITY"
HOPE I'M RIGHT ABOUT THERE BEING "TWO AMERICAS"...
I'M GONNA NEED TWO TO GET ENOUGH VOTES.

... at least for awhile. Kerry sailed away with the nom, and thus this sequel.

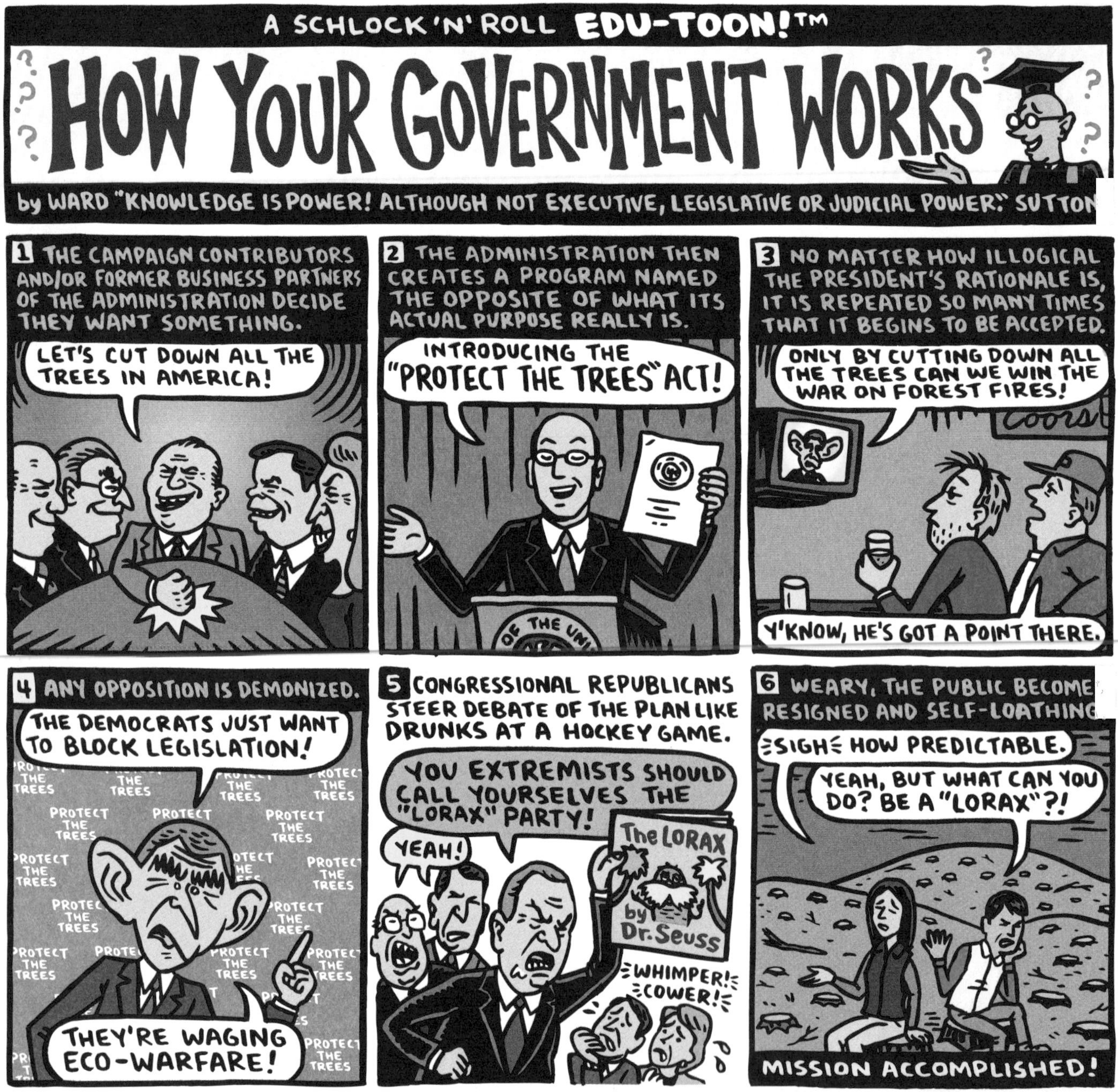
A SCHLOCK 'N' ROLL EDU-TOON!™
HOW YOUR GOVERNMENT WORKS
by WARD "KNOWLEDGE IS POWER! ALTHOUGH NOT EXECUTIVE, LEGISLATIVE OR JUDICIAL POWER." SUTTON
1 THE CAMPAIGN CONTRIBUTORS AND/OR FORMER BUSINESS PARTNERS OF THE ADMINISTRATION DECIDE THEY WANT SOMETHING.
LET'S CUT DOWN ALL THE TREES IN AMERICA!
2 THE ADMINISTRATION THEN CREATES A PROGRAM NAMED THE OPPOSITE OF WHAT ITS ACTUAL PURPOSE REALLY IS.
INTRODUCING THE "PROTECT THE TREES" ACT!
3 NO MATTER HOW ILLOGICAL THE PRESIDENT'S RATIONALE IS, IT IS REPEATED SO MANY TIMES THAT IT BEGINS TO BE ACCEPTED.
ONLY BY CUTTING DOWN ALL THE TREES CAN WE WIN THE WAR ON FOREST FIRES!
Coors
Y'KNOW, HE'S GOT A POINT THERE.
4 ANY OPPOSITION IS DEMONIZED.
THE DEMOCRATS JUST WANT TO BLOCK LEGISLATION!
PROTECT THE TREES
THEY'RE WAGING ECO-WARFARE!
5 CONGRESSIONAL REPUBLICANS STEER DEBATE OF THE PLAN LIKE DRUNKS AT A HOCKEY GAME.
YOU EXTREMISTS SHOULD CALL YOURSELVES THE "LORAX" PARTY!
YEAH!
The LORAX by Dr. Seuss
WHIMPER! COWER!
6 WEARY, THE PUBLIC BECOMES RESIGNED AND SELF-LOATHING.
SIGH HOW PREDICTABLE.
YEAH, BUT WHAT CAN YOU DO? BE A "LORAX"?!
MISSION ACCOMPLISHED!

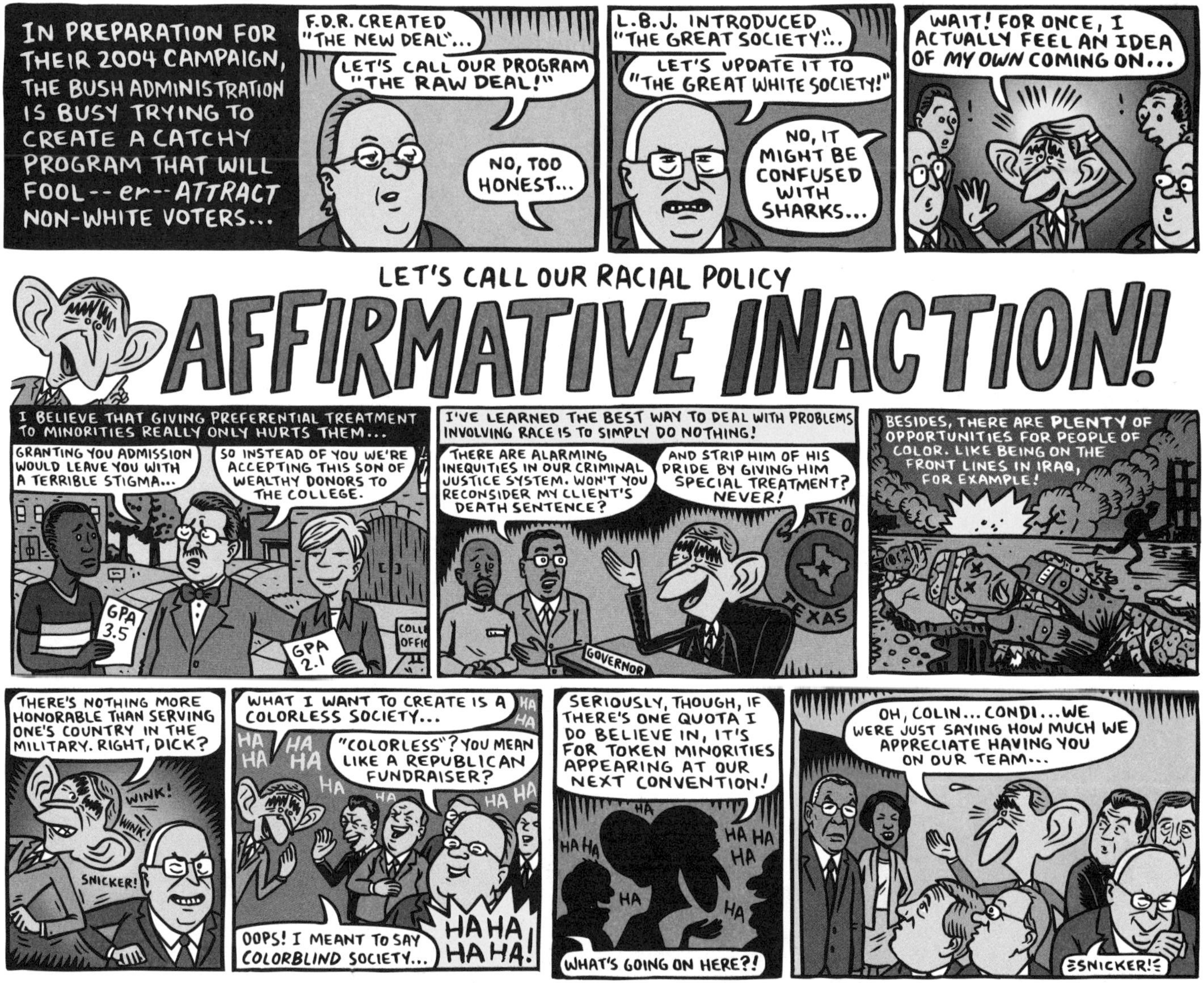
IN PREPARATION FOR THEIR 2004 CAMPAIGN, THE BUSH ADMINISTRATION IS BUSY TRYING TO CREATE A CATCHY PROGRAM THAT WILL FOOL--er--ATTRACT NON-WHITE VOTERS...
F.D.R. CREATED "THE NEW DEAL"...
LET'S CALL OUR PROGRAM "THE RAW DEAL!"
NO, TOO HONEST...
L.B.J. INTRODUCED "THE GREAT SOCIETY"...
LET'S UPDATE IT TO "THE GREAT WHITE SOCIETY!"
NO, IT MIGHT BE CONFUSED WITH SHARKS...
WAIT! FOR ONCE, I ACTUALLY FEEL AN IDEA OF MY OWN COMING ON...
LET'S CALL OUR RACIAL POLICY
AFFIRMATIVE INACTION!
I BELIEVE THAT GIVING PREFERENTIAL TREATMENT TO MINORITIES REALLY ONLY HURTS THEM...
GRANTING YOU ADMISSION WOULD LEAVE YOU WITH A TERRIBLE STIGMA...
SO INSTEAD OF YOU WE'RE ACCEPTING THIS SON OF WEALTHY DONORS TO THE COLLEGE.
GPA 3.5
GPA 2.1
I'VE LEARNED THE BEST WAY TO DEAL WITH PROBLEMS INVOLVING RACE IS TO SIMPLY DO NOTHING!
THERE ARE ALARMING INEQUITIES IN OUR CRIMINAL JUSTICE SYSTEM. WON'T YOU RECONSIDER MY CLIENT'S DEATH SENTENCE?
AND STRIP HIM OF HIS PRIDE BY GIVING HIM SPECIAL TREATMENT? NEVER!
GOVERNOR
TEXAS
BESIDES, THERE ARE PLENTY OF OPPORTUNITIES FOR PEOPLE OF COLOR. LIKE BEING ON THE FRONT LINES IN IRAQ, FOR EXAMPLE!
THERE'S NOTHING MORE HONORABLE THAN SERVING ONE'S COUNTRY IN THE MILITARY. RIGHT, DICK?
WINK! WINK!
SNICKER!
WHAT I WANT TO CREATE IS A COLORLESS SOCIETY...
"COLORLESS"? YOU MEAN LIKE A REPUBLICAN FUNDRAISER?
HA HA HA HA
OOPS! I MEANT TO SAY COLORBLIND SOCIETY...
HA HA HA HA!
SERIOUSLY, THOUGH, IF THERE'S ONE QUOTA I DO BELIEVE IN, IT'S FOR TOKEN MINORITIES APPEARING AT OUR NEXT CONVENTION!
HA HA HA
WHAT'S GOING ON HERE?!
OH, COLIN... CONDI... WE WERE JUST SAYING HOW MUCH WE APPRECIATE HAVING YOU ON OUR TEAM...
SNICKER!

This was one of a number of cartoons I created for *One World* magazine, whose Editorial Director was Hip-Hop mogul Russell Simmons. *One World* was created for a multi-ethnic, urban audience with an eye on racial inclusiveness. I liked their mission and so agreed to work for them for well below my normal rate. Unfortunately, the magazine went under ... and with it went my paychecks.

SUTTON IMPACT

IT HAS NOW BEEN REVEALED THAT WHEN PRESIDENT BUSH WENT TO IRAQ FOR THANKSGIVING, HE POSED WITH A FAKE TURKEY TO MAKE IT LOOK LIKE HE WAS SERVING THE TROOPS DINNER. LET'S LOOK AHEAD TO SOME OF HIS FUTURE ...

# PHONY PHOTO-OPS

BY WARD "SAY CHEESE" SUTTON

100% PLASTIC
MADE IN CHINA

ON ARBOR DAY HE'LL PLANT A FAKE TREE.

HEY, IT'S THE ONE KIND MY HEALTHY FORESTS INITIATIVE* WILL PROTECT FROM LOGGING!

*ACTUAL NAME OF HIS PLAN.

ON EARTH DAY HE'LL PRETEND TO RECYCLE.

I'LL JUST DUMP THIS STUFF IN A LANDFILL LATER ...

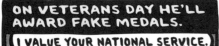

EWS

ALONG WITH ALL THOSE ENVIRONMENTAL REGULATIONS I'VE TRASHED!

ON LABOR DAY HE'LL HONOR FAKE LABORERS.

YOU CEOS WORK SO HARD TO EARN ALL THAT MONEY YOU GIVE ME. YOU SHOULD RELAX! CAN I GET YOU SOME LEMONADE? OR ANOTHER TAX BREAK?

$   $

ON VETERANS DAY HE'LL AWARD FAKE MEDALS.

I VALUE YOUR NATIONAL SERVICE.

CUT BENEFITS

ON CHRISTMAS HE'LL LEAVE OUR CHILDREN A "GIFT" ...

HO HO HO!

IT'S ALL YOURS, KIDS!

RECORD DEFICIT $$

TO: YOU!

AND ON ELECTION DAY ...?

HOW ABOUT ANOTHER FAKE VICTORY?

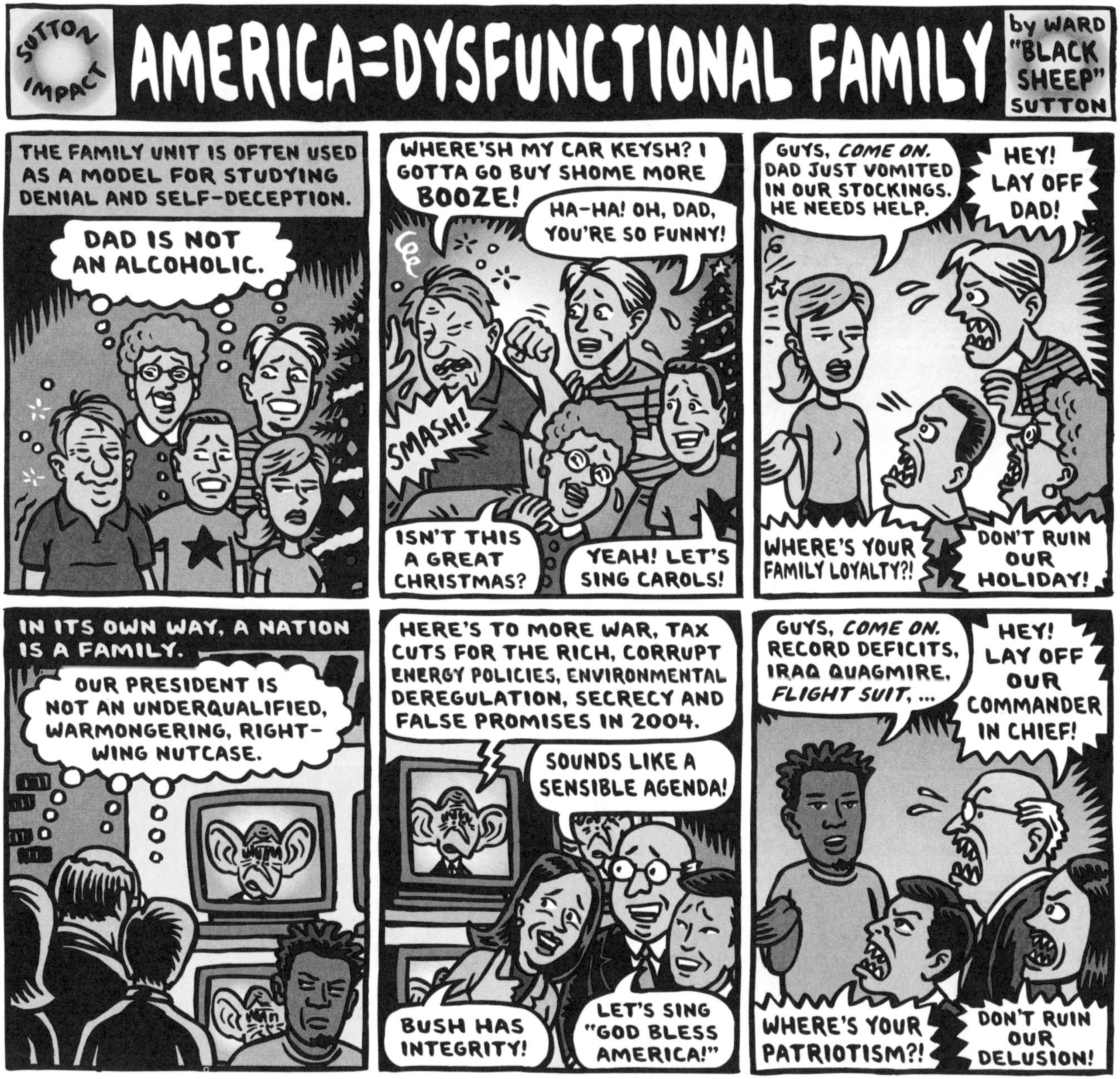
SUTTON IMPACT
AMERICA=DYSFUNCTIONAL FAMILY
by WARD "BLACK SHEEP" SUTTON
THE FAMILY UNIT IS OFTEN USED AS A MODEL FOR STUDYING DENIAL AND SELF-DECEPTION.
DAD IS NOT AN ALCOHOLIC.
WHERE'SH MY CAR KEYSH? I GOTTA GO BUY SHOME MORE BOOZE!
HA-HA! OH, DAD, YOU'RE SO FUNNY!
SMASH!
ISN'T THIS A GREAT CHRISTMAS?
YEAH! LET'S SING CAROLS!
GUYS, COME ON. DAD JUST VOMITED IN OUR STOCKINGS. HE NEEDS HELP.
HEY! LAY OFF DAD!
WHERE'S YOUR FAMILY LOYALTY?!
DON'T RUIN OUR HOLIDAY!
IN ITS OWN WAY, A NATION IS A FAMILY.
OUR PRESIDENT IS NOT AN UNDERQUALIFIED, WARMONGERING, RIGHT-WING NUTCASE.
HERE'S TO MORE WAR, TAX CUTS FOR THE RICH, CORRUPT ENERGY POLICIES, ENVIRONMENTAL DEREGULATION, SECRECY AND FALSE PROMISES IN 2004.
SOUNDS LIKE A SENSIBLE AGENDA!
BUSH HAS INTEGRITY!
LET'S SING "GOD BLESS AMERICA!"
GUYS, COME ON. RECORD DEFICITS, IRAQ QUAGMIRE, FLIGHT SUIT, ...
HEY! LAY OFF OUR COMMANDER IN CHIEF!
WHERE'S YOUR PATRIOTISM?!
DON'T RUIN OUR DELUSION!

This cartoon was inspired by a Bill Moyers program from the 1980s examining lying by public officials (ie Watergate). The program wisely pointed out that "Every lie needs a willing listener who wants to believe it's true." George Bush has a lot of willing listeners.

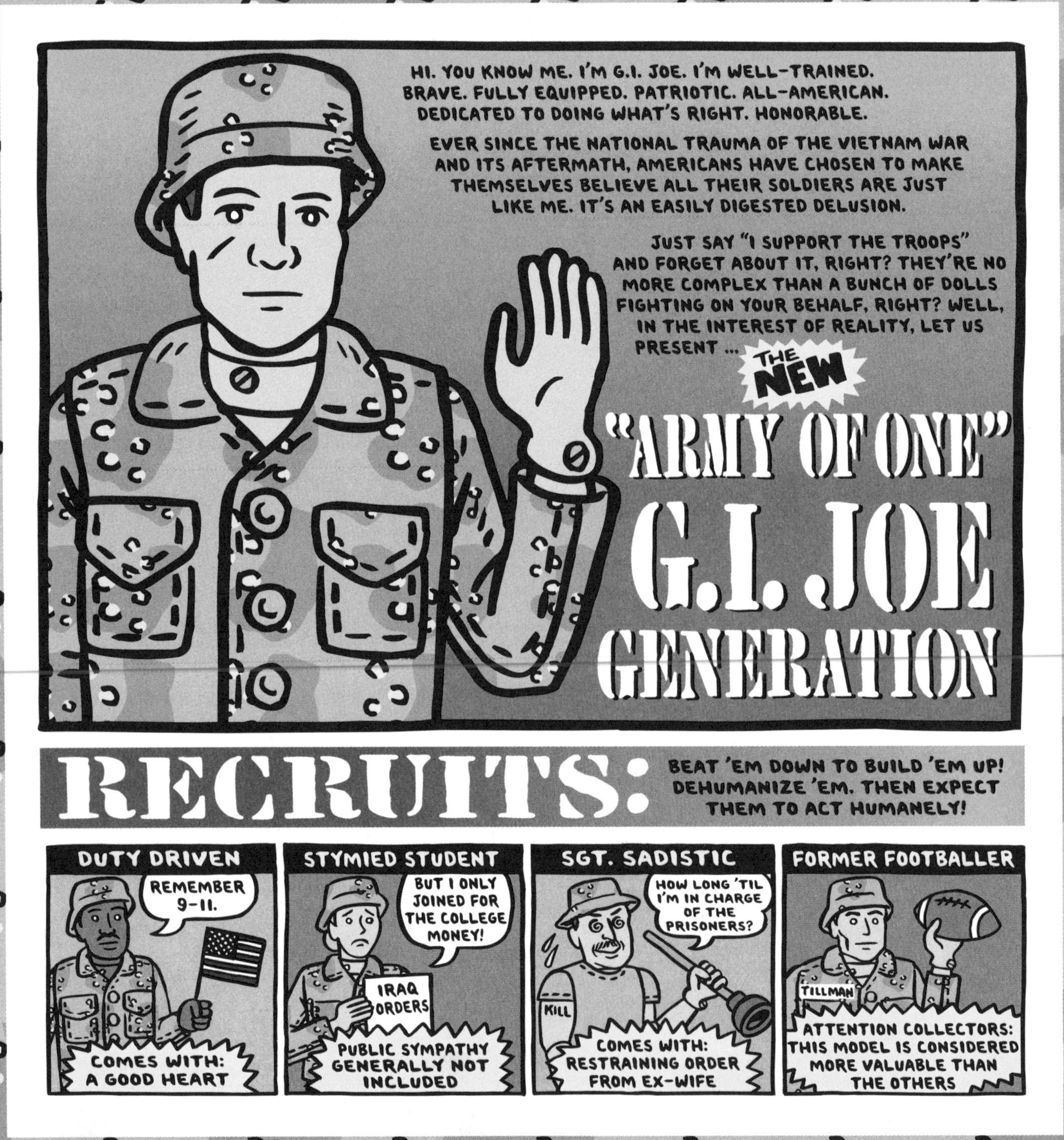
HI. YOU KNOW ME. I'M G.I. JOE. I'M WELL-TRAINED. BRAVE. FULLY EQUIPPED. PATRIOTIC. ALL-AMERICAN. DEDICATED TO DOING WHAT'S RIGHT. HONORABLE.
EVER SINCE THE NATIONAL TRAUMA OF THE VIETNAM WAR AND ITS AFTERMATH, AMERICANS HAVE CHOSEN TO MAKE THEMSELVES BELIEVE ALL THEIR SOLDIERS ARE JUST LIKE ME. IT'S AN EASILY DIGESTED DELUSION.
JUST SAY "I SUPPORT THE TROOPS" AND FORGET ABOUT IT, RIGHT? THEY'RE NO MORE COMPLEX THAN A BUNCH OF DOLLS FIGHTING ON YOUR BEHALF, RIGHT? WELL, IN THE INTEREST OF REALITY, LET US PRESENT ...
THE NEW
"ARMY OF ONE"
G.I. JOE
GENERATION
RECRUITS:
BEAT 'EM DOWN TO BUILD 'EM UP! DEHUMANIZE 'EM. THEN EXPECT THEM TO ACT HUMANELY!
DUTY DRIVEN
REMEMBER 9-11.
COMES WITH: A GOOD HEART
STYMIED STUDENT
BUT I ONLY JOINED FOR THE COLLEGE MONEY!
IRAQ ORDERS
PUBLIC SYMPATHY GENERALLY NOT INCLUDED
SGT. SADISTIC
HOW LONG 'TIL I'M IN CHARGE OF THE PRISONERS?
KILL
COMES WITH: RESTRAINING ORDER FROM EX-WIFE
FORMER FOOTBALLER
TILLMAN
ATTENTION COLLECTORS: THIS MODEL IS CONSIDERED MORE VALUABLE THAN THE OTHERS

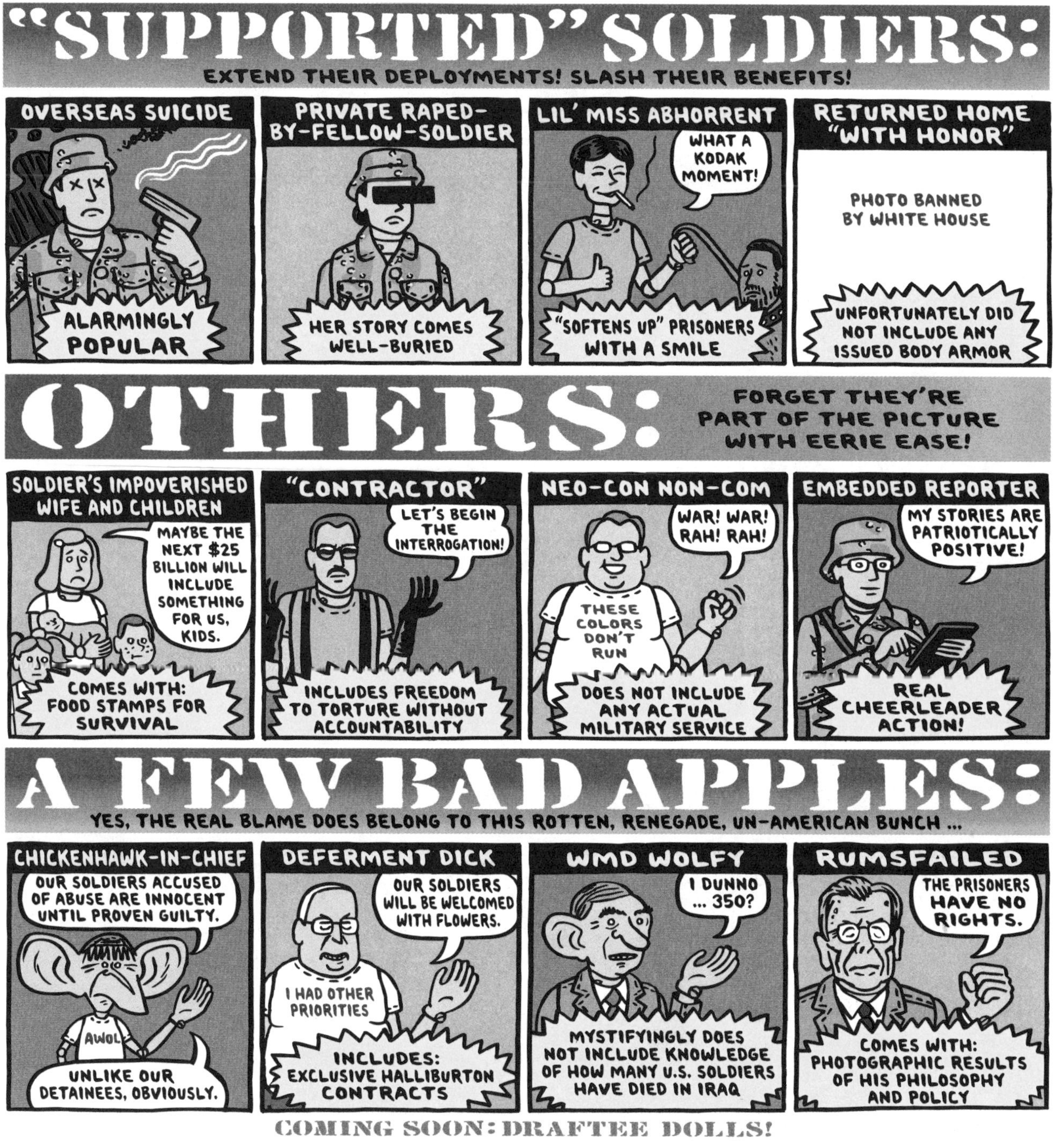
"SUPPORTED" SOLDIERS:
EXTEND THEIR DEPLOYMENTS! SLASH THEIR BENEFITS!
OVERSEAS SUICIDE
ALARMINGLY POPULAR
PRIVATE RAPED-BY-FELLOW-SOLDIER
HER STORY COMES WELL-BURIED
LIL' MISS ABHORRENT
WHAT A KODAK MOMENT!
"SOFTENS UP" PRISONERS WITH A SMILE
RETURNED HOME "WITH HONOR"
PHOTO BANNED BY WHITE HOUSE
UNFORTUNATELY DID NOT INCLUDE ANY ISSUED BODY ARMOR
OTHERS:
FORGET THEY'RE PART OF THE PICTURE WITH EERIE EASE!
SOLDIER'S IMPOVERISHED WIFE AND CHILDREN
MAYBE THE NEXT $25 BILLION WILL INCLUDE SOMETHING FOR US, KIDS.
COMES WITH: FOOD STAMPS FOR SURVIVAL
"CONTRACTOR"
LET'S BEGIN THE INTERROGATION!
INCLUDES FREEDOM TO TORTURE WITHOUT ACCOUNTABILITY
NEO-CON NON-COM
WAR! WAR! RAH! RAH!
THESE COLORS DON'T RUN
DOES NOT INCLUDE ANY ACTUAL MILITARY SERVICE
EMBEDDED REPORTER
MY STORIES ARE PATRIOTICALLY POSITIVE!
REAL CHEERLEADER ACTION!
A FEW BAD APPLES:
YES, THE REAL BLAME DOES BELONG TO THIS ROTTEN, RENEGADE, UN-AMERICAN BUNCH ...
CHICKENHAWK-IN-CHIEF
OUR SOLDIERS ACCUSED OF ABUSE ARE INNOCENT UNTIL PROVEN GUILTY.
AWOL
UNLIKE OUR DETAINEES, OBVIOUSLY.
DEFERMENT DICK
OUR SOLDIERS WILL BE WELCOMED WITH FLOWERS.
I HAD OTHER PRIORITIES
INCLUDES: EXCLUSIVE HALLIBURTON CONTRACTS
WMD WOLFY
I DUNNO ... 350?
MYSTIFYINGLY DOES NOT INCLUDE KNOWLEDGE OF HOW MANY U.S. SOLDIERS HAVE DIED IN IRAQ
RUMSFAILED
THE PRISONERS HAVE NO RIGHTS.
COMES WITH: PHOTOGRAPHIC RESULTS OF HIS PHILOSOPHY AND POLICY
COMING SOON: DRAFTEE DOLLS!

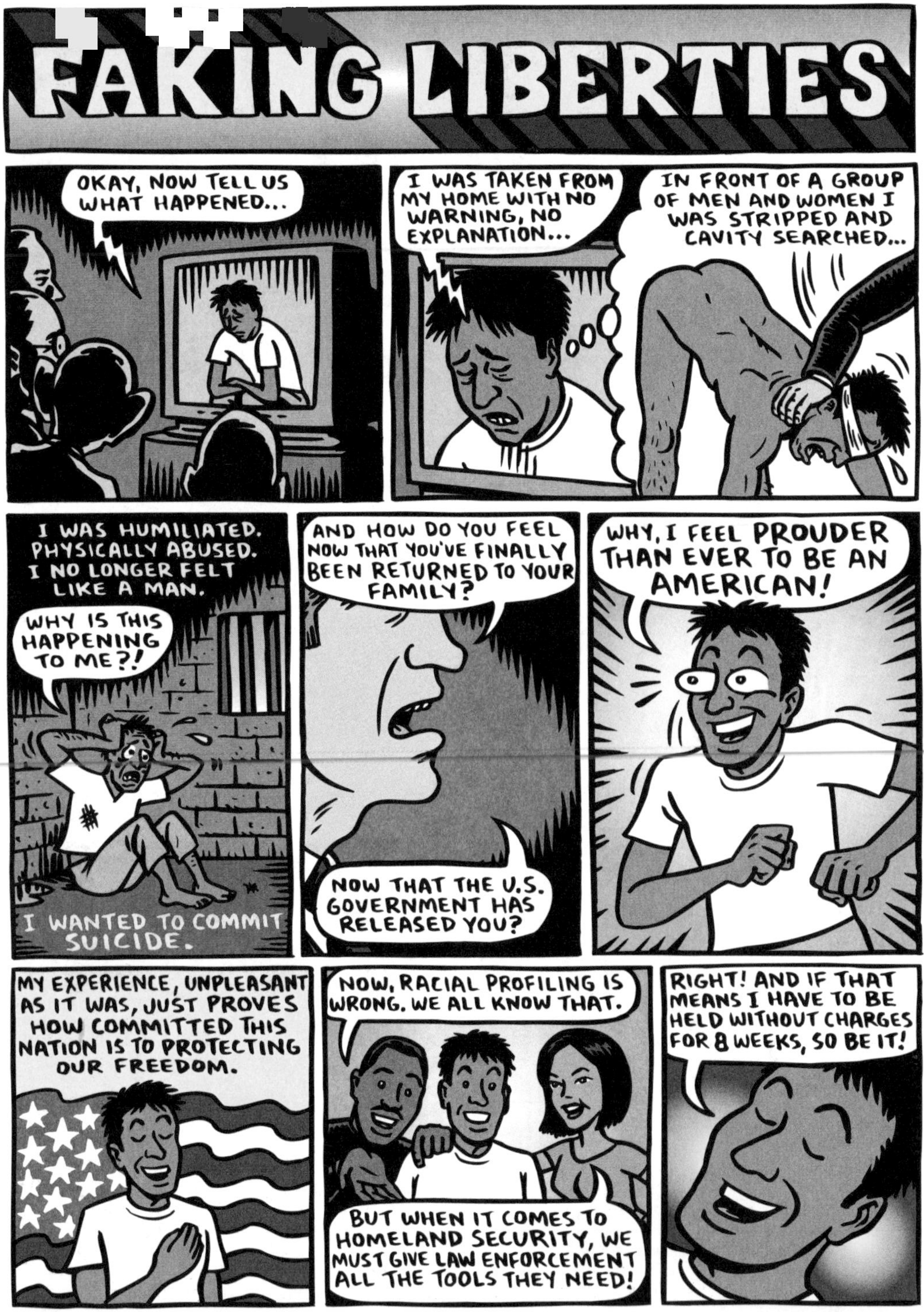
FAKING LIBERTIES
OKAY, NOW TELL US WHAT HAPPENED...
I WAS TAKEN FROM MY HOME WITH NO WARNING, NO EXPLANATION...
IN FRONT OF A GROUP OF MEN AND WOMEN I WAS STRIPPED AND CAVITY SEARCHED...
I WAS HUMILIATED. PHYSICALLY ABUSED. I NO LONGER FELT LIKE A MAN.
WHY IS THIS HAPPENING TO ME?!
I WANTED TO COMMIT SUICIDE.
AND HOW DO YOU FEEL NOW THAT YOU'VE FINALLY BEEN RETURNED TO YOUR FAMILY?
NOW THAT THE U.S. GOVERNMENT HAS RELEASED YOU?
WHY, I FEEL PROUDER THAN EVER TO BE AN AMERICAN!
MY EXPERIENCE, UNPLEASANT AS IT WAS, JUST PROVES HOW COMMITTED THIS NATION IS TO PROTECTING OUR FREEDOM.
NOW, RACIAL PROFILING IS WRONG. WE ALL KNOW THAT.
BUT WHEN IT COMES TO HOMELAND SECURITY, WE MUST GIVE LAW ENFORCEMENT ALL THE TOOLS THEY NEED!
RIGHT! AND IF THAT MEANS I HAVE TO BE HELD WITHOUT CHARGES FOR 8 WEEKS, SO BE IT!

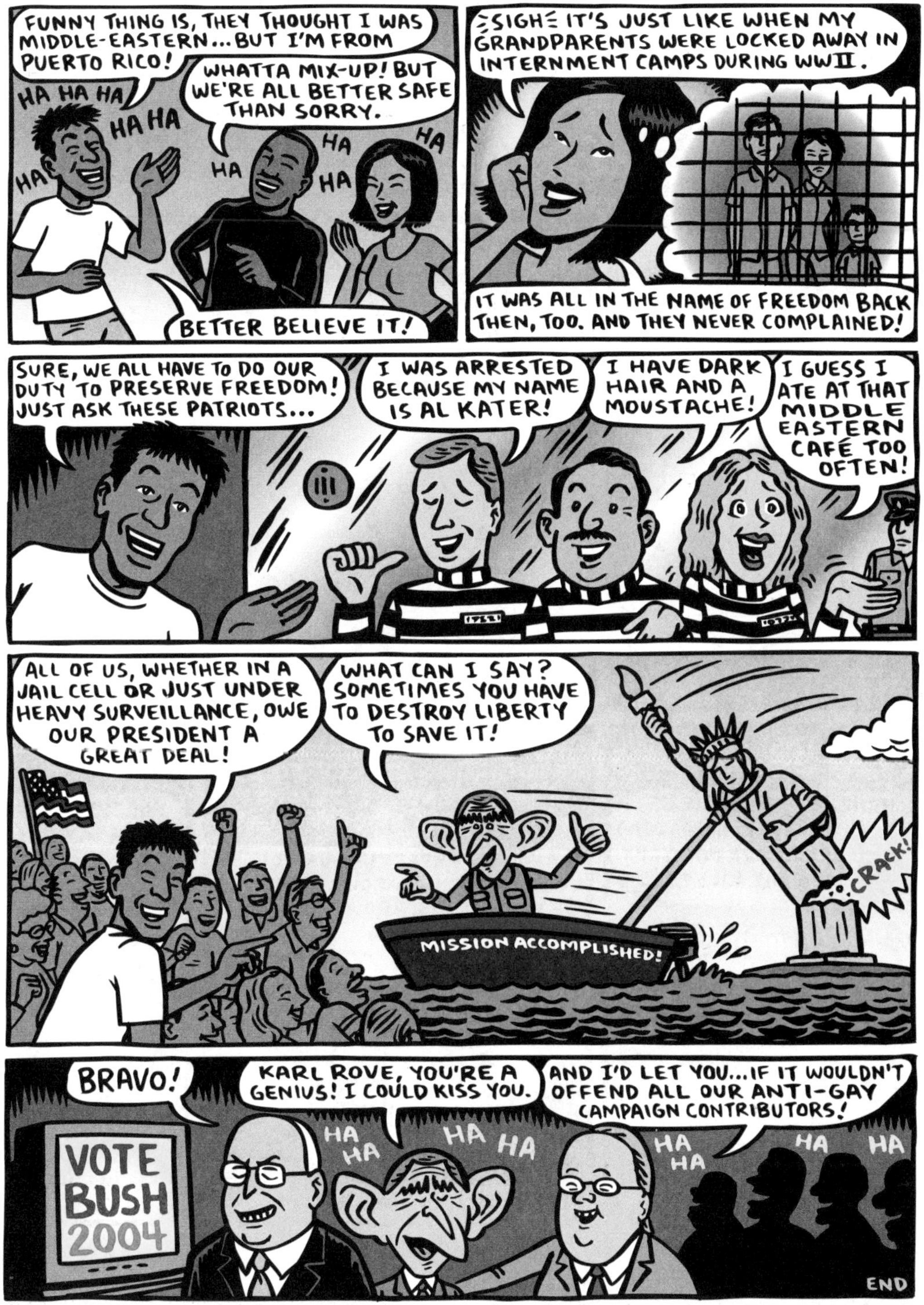
FUNNY THING IS, THEY THOUGHT I WAS MIDDLE-EASTERN... BUT I'M FROM PUERTO RICO!
HA HA HA
HA HA
HA
WHATTA MIX-UP! BUT WE'RE ALL BETTER SAFE THAN SORRY.
HA
HA
HA
HA
BETTER BELIEVE IT!
≡SIGH≡ IT'S JUST LIKE WHEN MY GRANDPARENTS WERE LOCKED AWAY IN INTERNMENT CAMPS DURING WWII.
IT WAS ALL IN THE NAME OF FREEDOM BACK THEN, TOO. AND THEY NEVER COMPLAINED!
SURE, WE ALL HAVE TO DO OUR DUTY TO PRESERVE FREEDOM! JUST ASK THESE PATRIOTS...
I WAS ARRESTED BECAUSE MY NAME IS AL KATER!
I HAVE DARK HAIR AND A MOUSTACHE!
I GUESS I ATE AT THAT MIDDLE EASTERN CAFÉ TOO OFTEN!
ALL OF US, WHETHER IN A JAIL CELL OR JUST UNDER HEAVY SURVEILLANCE, OWE OUR PRESIDENT A GREAT DEAL!
WHAT CAN I SAY? SOMETIMES YOU HAVE TO DESTROY LIBERTY TO SAVE IT!
MISSION ACCOMPLISHED!
CRACK!
BRAVO!
KARL ROVE, YOU'RE A GENIUS! I COULD KISS YOU.
AND I'D LET YOU... IF IT WOULDN'T OFFEND ALL OUR ANTI-GAY CAMPAIGN CONTRIBUTORS!
VOTE BUSH 2004
HA HA
HA HA
HA HA
HA
HA
END

This piece originally ran in *World War 3 Illustrated*, edited by Peter Kuper, among others.

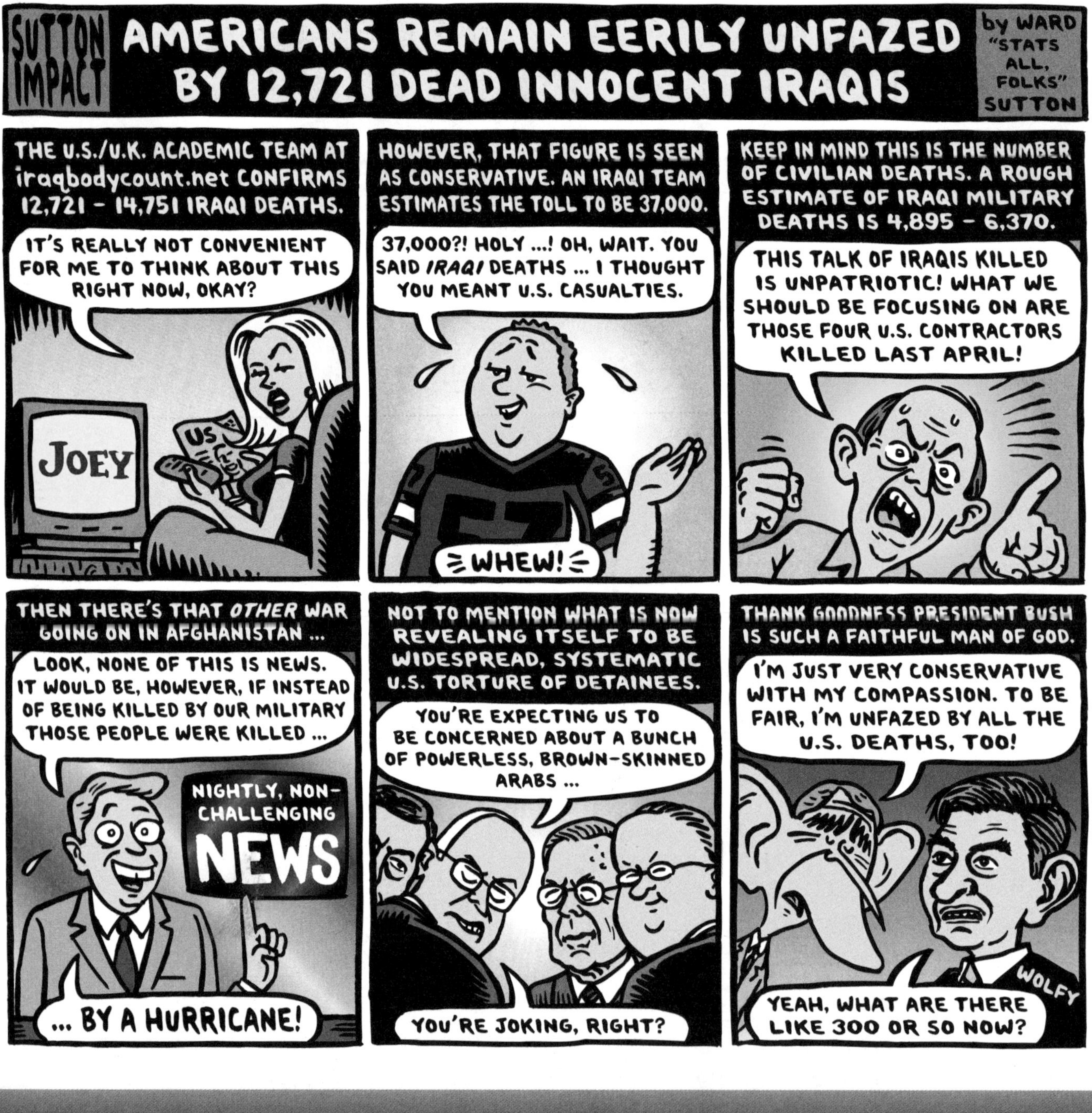
SUTTON IMPACT
AMERICANS REMAIN EERILY UNFAZED BY 12,721 DEAD INNOCENT IRAQIS
by WARD "STATS ALL, FOLKS" SUTTON
THE U.S./U.K. ACADEMIC TEAM AT iraqbodycount.net CONFIRMS 12,721 – 14,751 IRAQI DEATHS.
IT'S REALLY NOT CONVENIENT FOR ME TO THINK ABOUT THIS RIGHT NOW, OKAY?
JOEY
US
HOWEVER, THAT FIGURE IS SEEN AS CONSERVATIVE. AN IRAQI TEAM ESTIMATES THE TOLL TO BE 37,000.
37,000?! HOLY ...! OH, WAIT. YOU SAID *IRAQI* DEATHS ... I THOUGHT YOU MEANT U.S. CASUALTIES.
WHEW!
KEEP IN MIND THIS IS THE NUMBER OF CIVILIAN DEATHS. A ROUGH ESTIMATE OF IRAQI MILITARY DEATHS IS 4,895 – 6,370.
THIS TALK OF IRAQIS KILLED IS UNPATRIOTIC! WHAT WE SHOULD BE FOCUSING ON ARE THOSE FOUR U.S. CONTRACTORS KILLED LAST APRIL!
THEN THERE'S THAT *OTHER* WAR GOING ON IN AFGHANISTAN ...
LOOK, NONE OF THIS IS NEWS. IT WOULD BE, HOWEVER, IF INSTEAD OF BEING KILLED BY OUR MILITARY THOSE PEOPLE WERE KILLED ...
NIGHTLY, NON-CHALLENGING NEWS
... BY A HURRICANE!
NOT TO MENTION WHAT IS NOW REVEALING ITSELF TO BE WIDESPREAD, SYSTEMATIC U.S. TORTURE OF DETAINEES.
YOU'RE EXPECTING US TO BE CONCERNED ABOUT A BUNCH OF POWERLESS, BROWN-SKINNED ARABS ...
YOU'RE JOKING, RIGHT?
THANK GOODNESS PRESIDENT BUSH IS SUCH A FAITHFUL MAN OF GOD.
I'M JUST VERY CONSERVATIVE WITH MY COMPASSION. TO BE FAIR, I'M UNFAZED BY ALL THE U.S. DEATHS, TOO!
YEAH, WHAT ARE THERE LIKE 300 OR SO NOW?
WOLFY

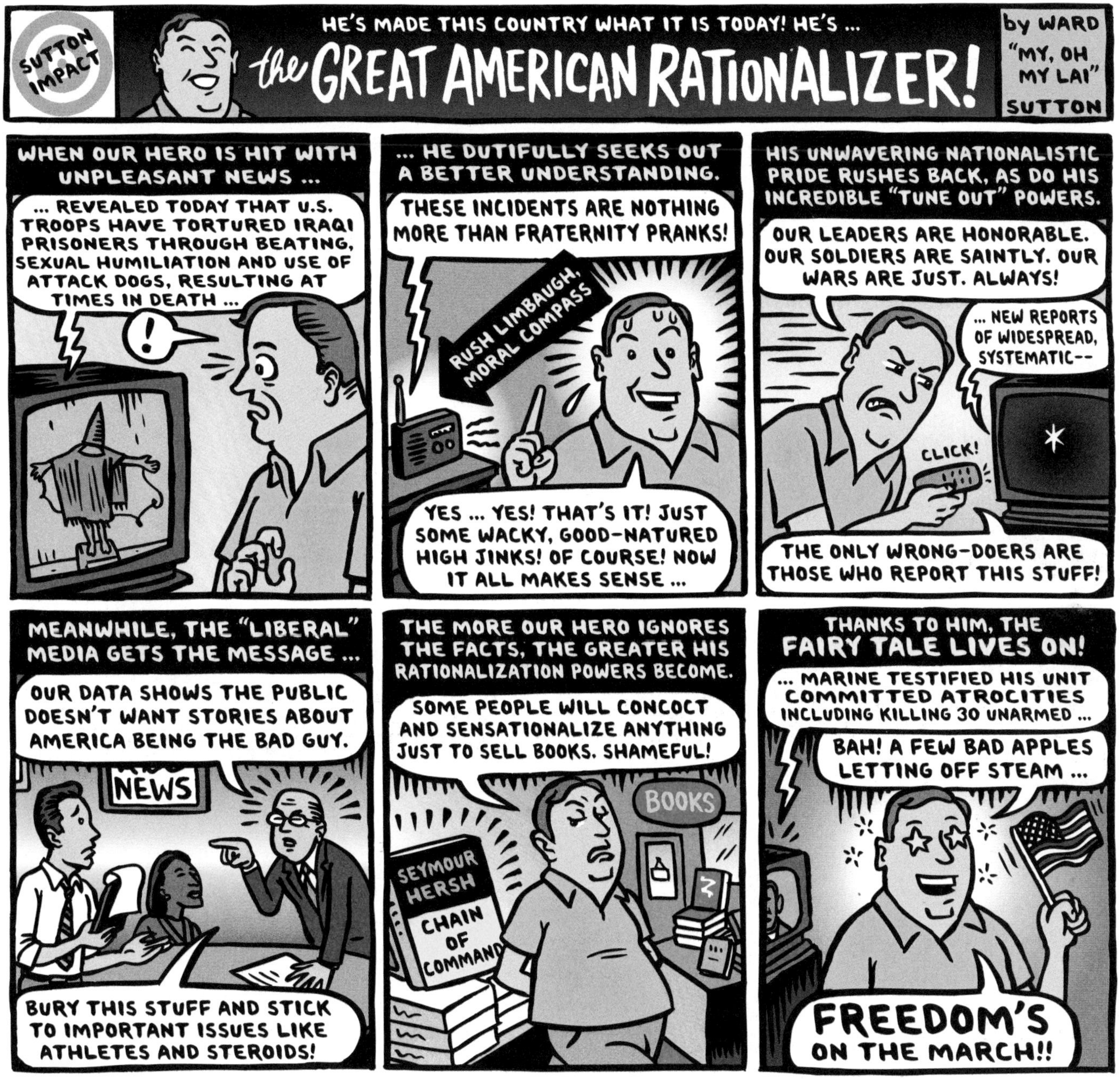
SUTTON IMPACT
HE'S MADE THIS COUNTRY WHAT IT IS TODAY! HE'S ...
the GREAT AMERICAN RATIONALIZER!
by WARD "MY, OH MY LAI" SUTTON
WHEN OUR HERO IS HIT WITH UNPLEASANT NEWS ...
... REVEALED TODAY THAT U.S. TROOPS HAVE TORTURED IRAQI PRISONERS THROUGH BEATING, SEXUAL HUMILIATION AND USE OF ATTACK DOGS, RESULTING AT TIMES IN DEATH ...
!
... HE DUTIFULLY SEEKS OUT A BETTER UNDERSTANDING.
THESE INCIDENTS ARE NOTHING MORE THAN FRATERNITY PRANKS!
RUSH LIMBAUGH, MORAL COMPASS
YES ... YES! THAT'S IT! JUST SOME WACKY, GOOD-NATURED HIGH JINKS! OF COURSE! NOW IT ALL MAKES SENSE ...
HIS UNWAVERING NATIONALISTIC PRIDE RUSHES BACK, AS DO HIS INCREDIBLE "TUNE OUT" POWERS.
OUR LEADERS ARE HONORABLE. OUR SOLDIERS ARE SAINTLY. OUR WARS ARE JUST. ALWAYS!
... NEW REPORTS OF WIDESPREAD, SYSTEMATIC--
CLICK!
THE ONLY WRONG-DOERS ARE THOSE WHO REPORT THIS STUFF!
MEANWHILE, THE "LIBERAL" MEDIA GETS THE MESSAGE ...
OUR DATA SHOWS THE PUBLIC DOESN'T WANT STORIES ABOUT AMERICA BEING THE BAD GUY.
NEWS
BURY THIS STUFF AND STICK TO IMPORTANT ISSUES LIKE ATHLETES AND STEROIDS!
THE MORE OUR HERO IGNORES THE FACTS, THE GREATER HIS RATIONALIZATION POWERS BECOME.
SOME PEOPLE WILL CONCOCT AND SENSATIONALIZE ANYTHING JUST TO SELL BOOKS. SHAMEFUL!
BOOKS
SEYMOUR HERSH CHAIN OF COMMAND
THANKS TO HIM, THE FAIRY TALE LIVES ON!
... MARINE TESTIFIED HIS UNIT COMMITTED ATROCITIES INCLUDING KILLING 30 UNARMED ...
BAH! A FEW BAD APPLES LETTING OFF STEAM ...
FREEDOM'S ON THE MARCH!!

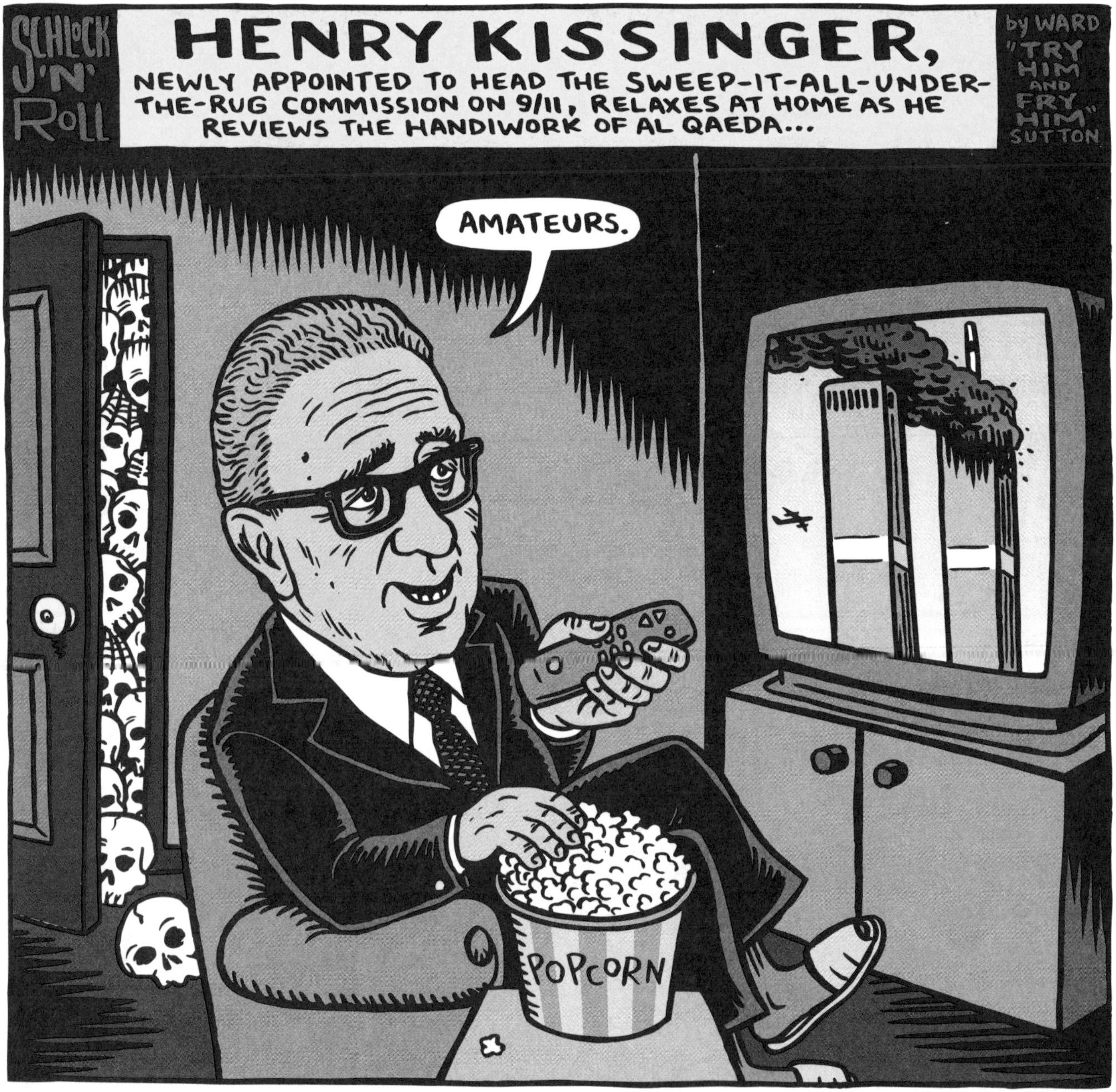
SCHLOCK 'N' ROLL
HENRY KISSINGER,
NEWLY APPOINTED TO HEAD THE SWEEP-IT-ALL-UNDER-THE-RUG COMMISSION ON 9/11, RELAXES AT HOME AS HE REVIEWS THE HANDIWORK OF AL QAEDA...
by WARD "TRY HIM AND FRY HIM" SUTTON
AMATEURS.
POPCORN

Such a shame ol' Henry resigned as head of the commission, pillar of ethics that he is.

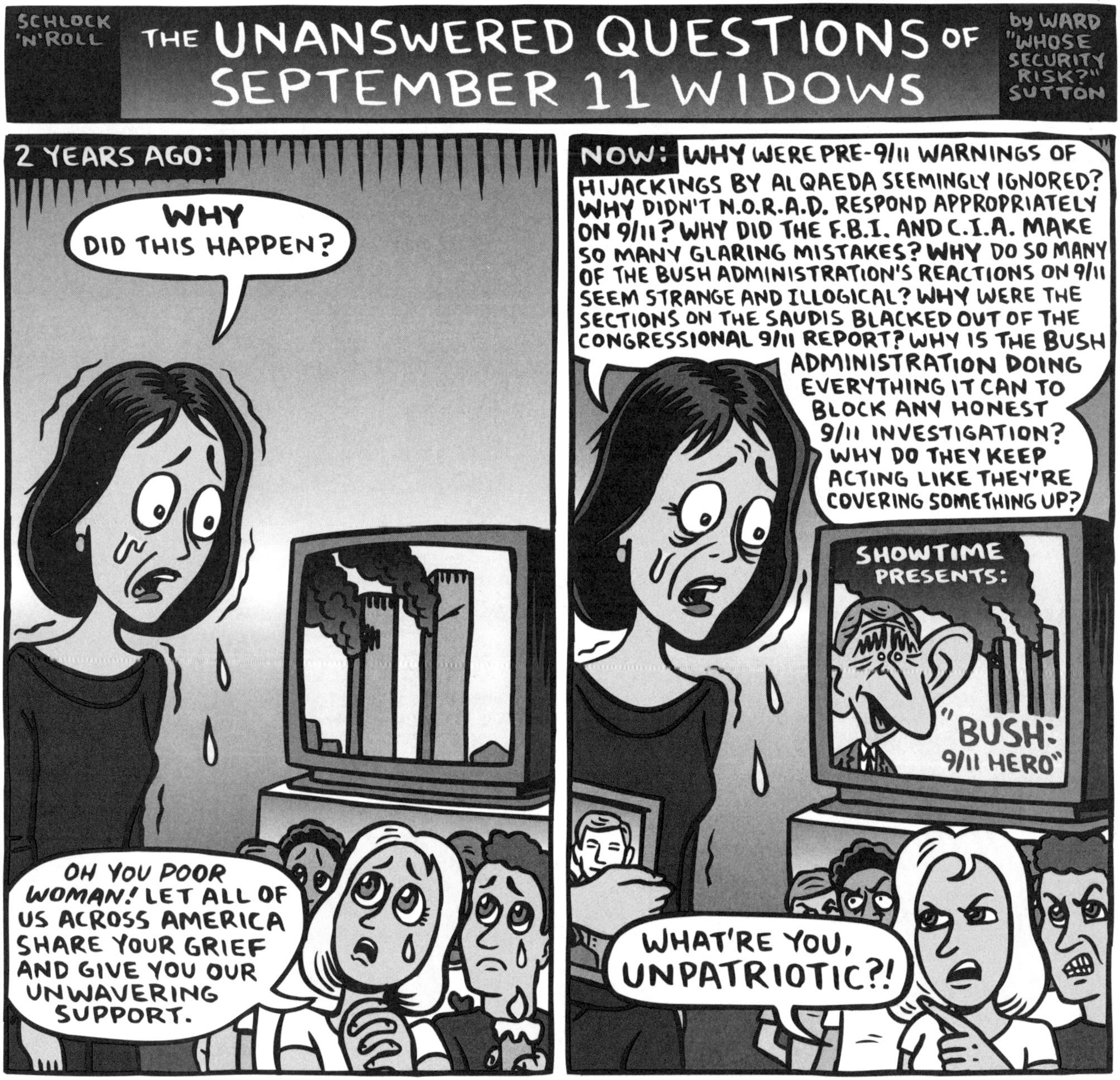
SCHLOCK 'N' ROLL
THE UNANSWERED QUESTIONS OF SEPTEMBER 11 WIDOWS
by WARD "WHOSE SECURITY RISK?" SUTTON
2 YEARS AGO:
WHY DID THIS HAPPEN?
OH YOU POOR WOMAN! LET ALL OF US ACROSS AMERICA SHARE YOUR GRIEF AND GIVE YOU OUR UNWAVERING SUPPORT.
NOW:
WHY WERE PRE-9/11 WARNINGS OF HIJACKINGS BY AL QAEDA SEEMINGLY IGNORED? WHY DIDN'T N.O.R.A.D. RESPOND APPROPRIATELY ON 9/11? WHY DID THE F.B.I. AND C.I.A. MAKE SO MANY GLARING MISTAKES? WHY DO SO MANY OF THE BUSH ADMINISTRATION'S REACTIONS ON 9/11 SEEM STRANGE AND ILLOGICAL? WHY WERE THE SECTIONS ON THE SAUDIS BLACKED OUT OF THE CONGRESSIONAL 9/11 REPORT? WHY IS THE BUSH ADMINISTRATION DOING EVERYTHING IT CAN TO BLOCK ANY HONEST 9/11 INVESTIGATION? WHY DO THEY KEEP ACTING LIKE THEY'RE COVERING SOMETHING UP?
SHOWTIME PRESENTS:
"BUSH: 9/11 HERO"
WHAT'RE YOU, UNPATRIOTIC?!

Tsk! Why can't those 9/11 widows just shut their mouths and salute the president?

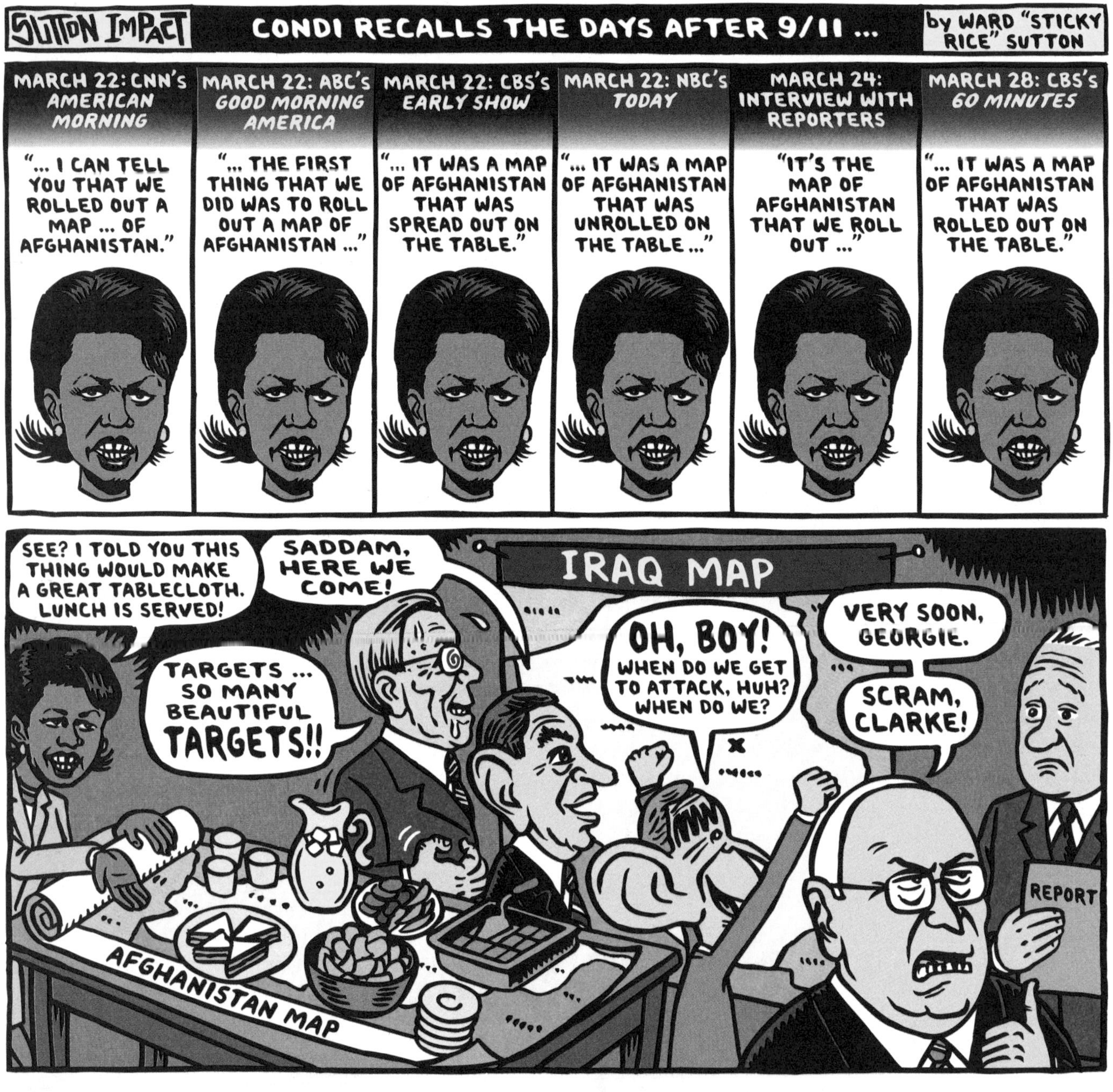
SUTTON IMPACT
CONDI RECALLS THE DAYS AFTER 9/11 ...
by WARD "STICKY RICE" SUTTON
MARCH 22: CNN's AMERICAN MORNING
"... I CAN TELL YOU THAT WE ROLLED OUT A MAP ... OF AFGHANISTAN."
MARCH 22: ABC's GOOD MORNING AMERICA
"... THE FIRST THING THAT WE DID WAS TO ROLL OUT A MAP OF AFGHANISTAN ..."
MARCH 22: CBS's EARLY SHOW
"... IT WAS A MAP OF AFGHANISTAN THAT WAS SPREAD OUT ON THE TABLE."
MARCH 22: NBC's TODAY
"... IT WAS A MAP OF AFGHANISTAN THAT WAS UNROLLED ON THE TABLE ..."
MARCH 24: INTERVIEW WITH REPORTERS
"IT'S THE MAP OF AFGHANISTAN THAT WE ROLL OUT ..."
MARCH 28: CBS's 60 MINUTES
"... IT WAS A MAP OF AFGHANISTAN THAT WAS ROLLED OUT ON THE TABLE."
SEE? I TOLD YOU THIS THING WOULD MAKE A GREAT TABLECLOTH. LUNCH IS SERVED!
SADDAM, HERE WE COME!
IRAQ MAP
TARGETS ... SO MANY BEAUTIFUL TARGETS!!
OH, BOY! WHEN DO WE GET TO ATTACK, HUH? WHEN DO WE?
VERY SOON, GEORGIE.
SCRAM, CLARKE!
REPORT
AFGHANISTAN MAP

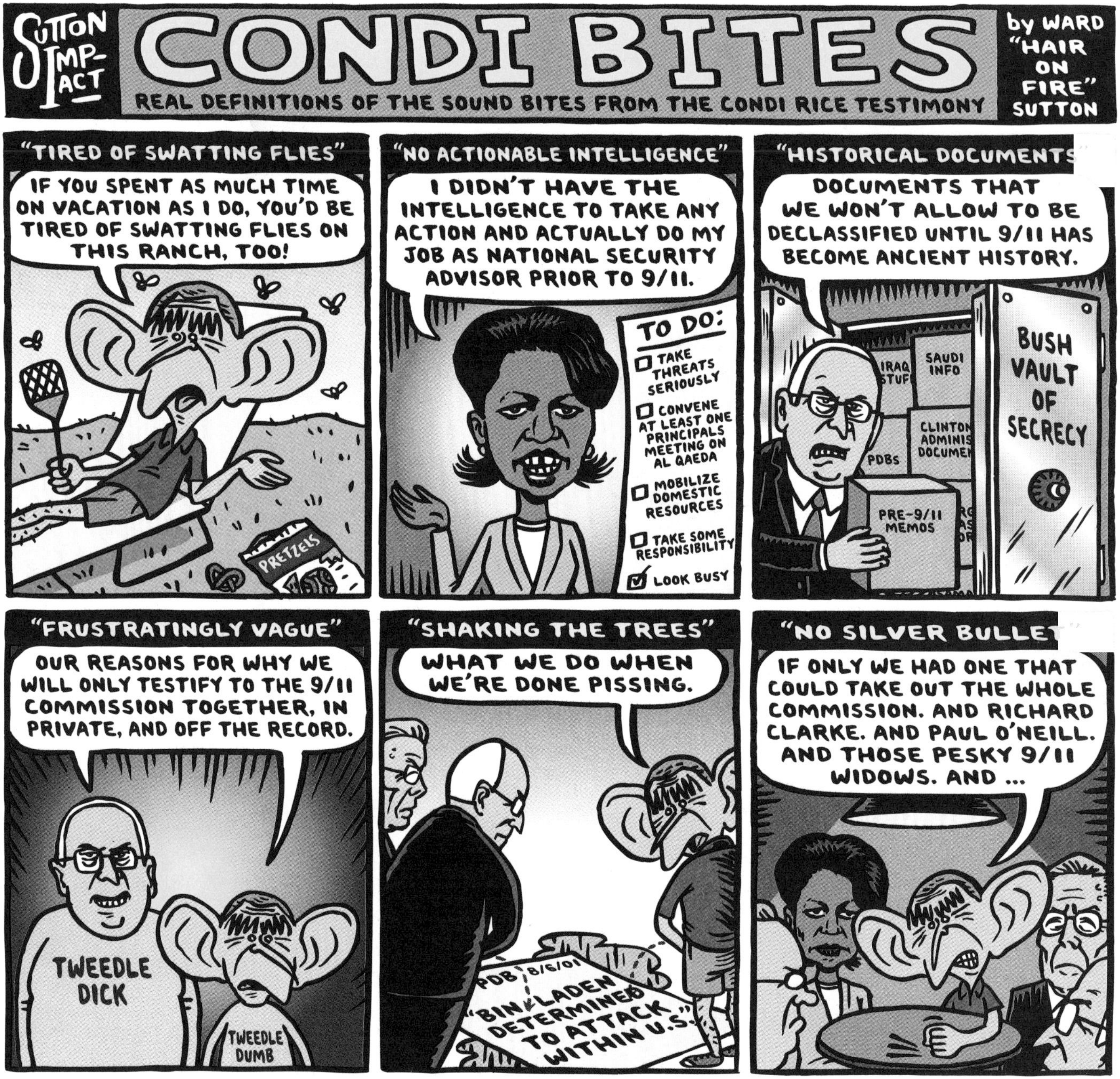
SUTTON IMP-ACT
CONDI BITES
REAL DEFINITIONS OF THE SOUND BITES FROM THE CONDI RICE TESTIMONY
by WARD "HAIR ON FIRE" SUTTON
"TIRED OF SWATTING FLIES"
IF YOU SPENT AS MUCH TIME ON VACATION AS I DO, YOU'D BE TIRED OF SWATTING FLIES ON THIS RANCH, TOO!
PRETZELS
"NO ACTIONABLE INTELLIGENCE"
I DIDN'T HAVE THE INTELLIGENCE TO TAKE ANY ACTION AND ACTUALLY DO MY JOB AS NATIONAL SECURITY ADVISOR PRIOR TO 9/11.
TO DO:
TAKE THREATS SERIOUSLY
CONVENE AT LEAST ONE PRINCIPALS MEETING ON AL QAEDA
MOBILIZE DOMESTIC RESOURCES
TAKE SOME RESPONSIBILITY
LOOK BUSY
"HISTORICAL DOCUMENTS"
DOCUMENTS THAT WE WON'T ALLOW TO BE DECLASSIFIED UNTIL 9/11 HAS BECOME ANCIENT HISTORY.
BUSH VAULT OF SECRECY
SAUDI INFO
PDBS
PRE-9/11 MEMOS
"FRUSTRATINGLY VAGUE"
OUR REASONS FOR WHY WE WILL ONLY TESTIFY TO THE 9/11 COMMISSION TOGETHER, IN PRIVATE, AND OFF THE RECORD.
TWEEDLE DICK
TWEEDLE DUMB
"SHAKING THE TREES"
WHAT WE DO WHEN WE'RE DONE PISSING.
PDB 8/6/01
"BIN LADEN DETERMINED TO ATTACK WITHIN U.S."
"NO SILVER BULLET"
IF ONLY WE HAD ONE THAT COULD TAKE OUT THE WHOLE COMMISSION. AND RICHARD CLARKE. AND PAUL O'NEILL. AND THOSE PESKY 9/11 WIDOWS. AND ...

**SUTTON IMPACT**

# BUSH STRONG ON DEFENSE

by WARD "BOMBS AND BOMB-SHELLS" SUTTON

**Panel 1:** WHEN WE RECEIVE INFORMATION ON DANGEROUS THREATS, MY ADMINISTRATION ALWAYS REACTS **SWIFTLY AND DECISIVELY.**

FOR EXAMPLE ...

**Panel 2:** WHEN MY FORMER TREASURY SECRETARY STRUCK, I RESPONDED IMMEDIATELY.

BUSH WAS OBSESSED WITH IRAQ FROM DAY ONE IN OFFICE.

**ATTACK** HIS CREDIBILITY!

PAUL O'NEILL

**Panel 3:** I LAUNCHED A PREEMPTIVE STRIKE AGAINST CHIEF MEDICARE ACTUARY RICHARD FOSTER.

IF YOU DISCLOSE THE REAL MEDICARE COST ESTIMATES, YOU WILL SUFFER "EXTREMELY SEVERE" CONSEQUENCES.

**Panel 4:** DIFFERENT DANGERS REQUIRE DIFFERENT STRATEGIES. LIKE WHEN AMBASSADOR JOSEPH WILSON REVEALED THE FALSE STATEMENTS IN MY 2003 STATE OF THE UNION SPEECH ...

NEWS

WHITE HOUSE LEAKS INFO THAT WILSON'S WIFE IS A CIA OPERATIVE. ILLEGAL MOVE ENDANGERS HER LIFE AND ENDS HER CAREER.

**Panel 5:** AND NOW I'VE DEPLOYED MY TROOPS AGAINST MY FORMER COUNTERTERRORISM CHIEF.

BUSH HAS DONE A TERRIBLE JOB IN THE WAR ON TERROR.

**ASSASSINATE** HIS CHARACTER!

RICHARD CLARKE

**Panel 6:** REMEMBER, AMERICANS: **I'M A WAR PRESIDENT.**

... AT WAR WITH THE TRUTH.

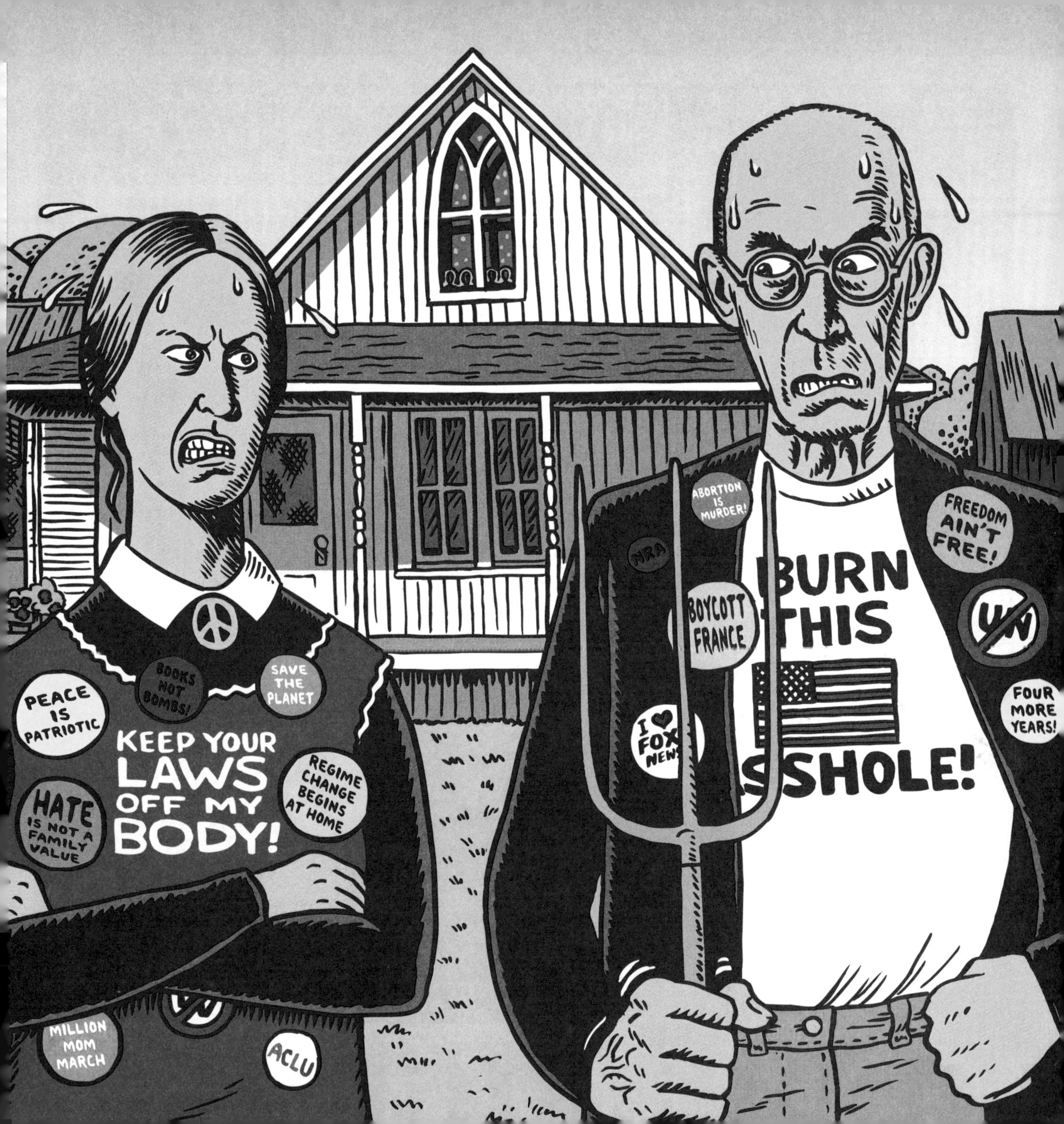
BOOKS NOT BOMBS!
SAVE THE PLANET
PEACE IS PATRIOTIC
KEEP YOUR LAWS OFF MY BODY!
HATE IS NOT A FAMILY VALUE
REGIME CHANGE BEGINS AT HOME
MILLION MOM MARCH
ACLU
ABORTION IS MURDER!
NRA
BOYCOTT FRANCE
I ♥ FOX NEW
BURN THIS
SSHOLE!
FREEDOM AIN'T FREE!
UN
FOUR MORE YEARS!

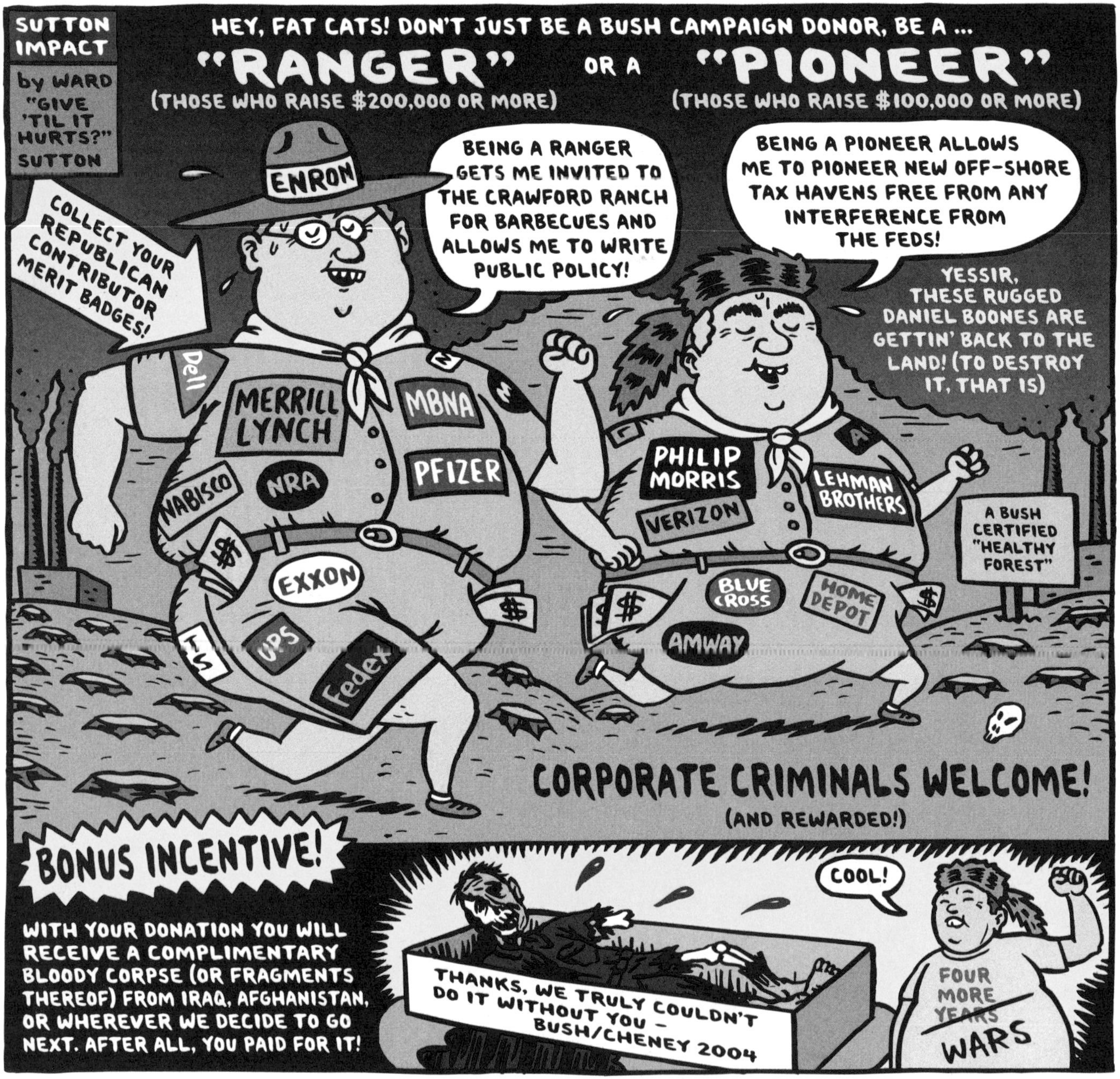
SUTTON IMPACT
by WARD "GIVE 'TIL IT HURTS?" SUTTON
HEY, FAT CATS! DON'T JUST BE A BUSH CAMPAIGN DONOR, BE A ...
"RANGER" OR A "PIONEER"
(THOSE WHO RAISE $200,000 OR MORE)
(THOSE WHO RAISE $100,000 OR MORE)
ENRON
BEING A RANGER GETS ME INVITED TO THE CRAWFORD RANCH FOR BARBECUES AND ALLOWS ME TO WRITE PUBLIC POLICY!
BEING A PIONEER ALLOWS ME TO PIONEER NEW OFF-SHORE TAX HAVENS FREE FROM ANY INTERFERENCE FROM THE FEDS!
COLLECT YOUR REPUBLICAN CONTRIBUTOR MERIT BADGES!
YESSIR, THESE RUGGED DANIEL BOONES ARE GETTIN' BACK TO THE LAND! (TO DESTROY IT, THAT IS)
Dell
MERRILL LYNCH
MBNA
NABISCO
NRA
PFIZER
EXXON
UPS
Fedex
PHILIP MORRIS
VERIZON
LEHMAN BROTHERS
BLUE CROSS
HOME DEPOT
AMWAY
A BUSH CERTIFIED "HEALTHY FOREST"
CORPORATE CRIMINALS WELCOME!
(AND REWARDED!)
BONUS INCENTIVE!
WITH YOUR DONATION YOU WILL RECEIVE A COMPLIMENTARY BLOODY CORPSE (OR FRAGMENTS THEREOF) FROM IRAQ, AFGHANISTAN, OR WHEREVER WE DECIDE TO GO NEXT. AFTER ALL, YOU PAID FOR IT!
COOL!
THANKS, WE TRULY COULDN'T DO IT WITHOUT YOU – BUSH/CHENEY 2004
FOUR MORE YEARS WARS

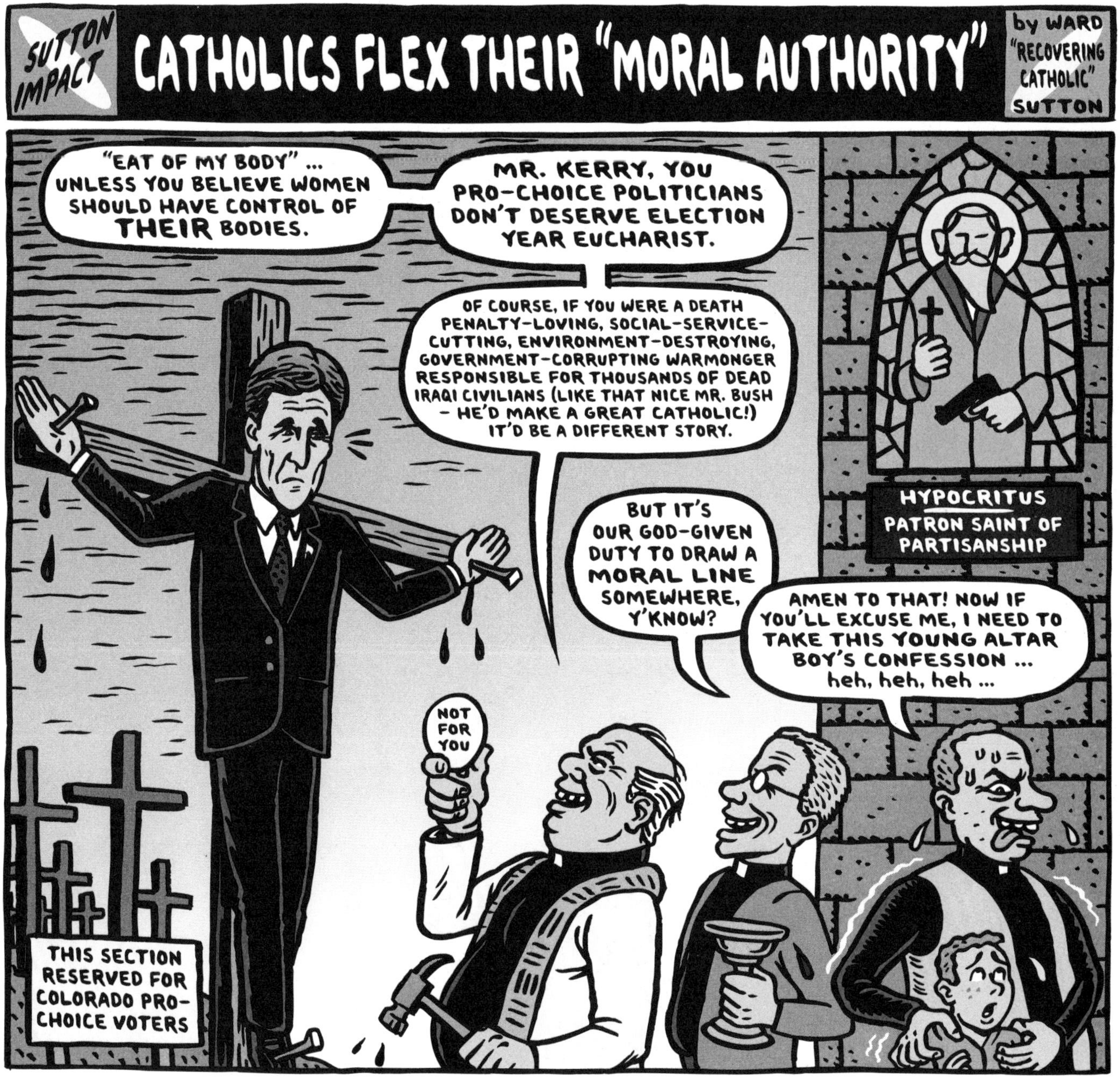
SUTTON IMPACT
CATHOLICS FLEX THEIR "MORAL AUTHORITY"
by WARD "RECOVERING CATHOLIC" SUTTON
"EAT OF MY BODY" ... UNLESS YOU BELIEVE WOMEN SHOULD HAVE CONTROL OF THEIR BODIES.
MR. KERRY, YOU PRO-CHOICE POLITICIANS DON'T DESERVE ELECTION YEAR EUCHARIST.
OF COURSE, IF YOU WERE A DEATH PENALTY-LOVING, SOCIAL-SERVICE-CUTTING, ENVIRONMENT-DESTROYING, GOVERNMENT-CORRUPTING WARMONGER RESPONSIBLE FOR THOUSANDS OF DEAD IRAQI CIVILIANS (LIKE THAT NICE MR. BUSH - HE'D MAKE A GREAT CATHOLIC!) IT'D BE A DIFFERENT STORY.
HYPOCRITUS
PATRON SAINT OF PARTISANSHIP
BUT IT'S OUR GOD-GIVEN DUTY TO DRAW A MORAL LINE SOMEWHERE, Y'KNOW?
AMEN TO THAT! NOW IF YOU'LL EXCUSE ME, I NEED TO TAKE THIS YOUNG ALTAR BOY'S CONFESSION ... heh, heh, heh ...
NOT FOR YOU
THIS SECTION RESERVED FOR COLORADO PRO-CHOICE VOTERS

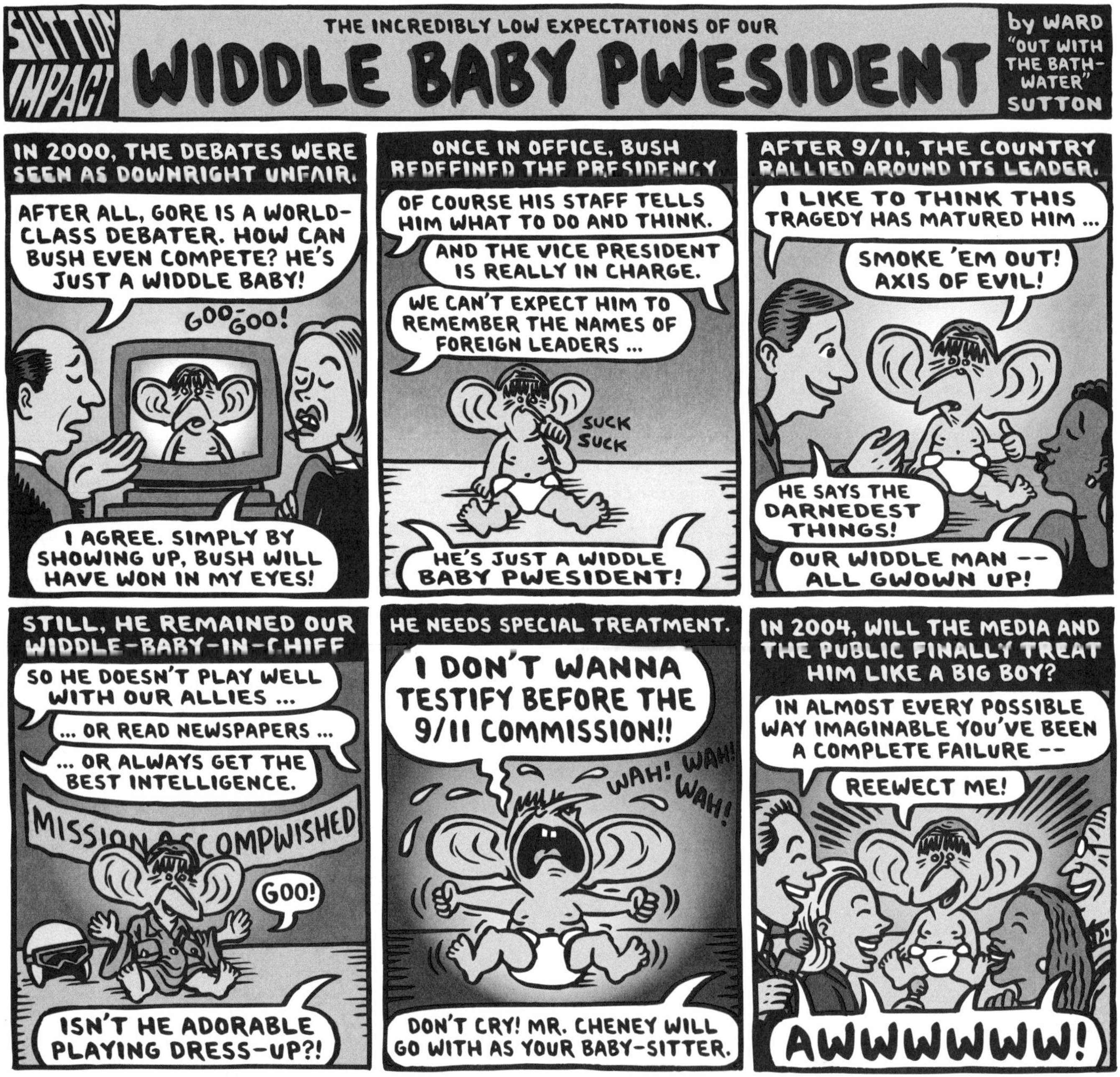
SUTTON IMPACT
THE INCREDIBLY LOW EXPECTATIONS OF OUR
WIDDLE BABY PWESIDENT
by WARD "OUT WITH THE BATH-WATER" SUTTON
IN 2000, THE DEBATES WERE SEEN AS DOWNRIGHT UNFAIR.
AFTER ALL, GORE IS A WORLD-CLASS DEBATER. HOW CAN BUSH EVEN COMPETE? HE'S JUST A WIDDLE BABY!
GOO-GOO!
I AGREE. SIMPLY BY SHOWING UP, BUSH WILL HAVE WON IN MY EYES!
ONCE IN OFFICE, BUSH REDEFINED THE PRESIDENCY.
OF COURSE HIS STAFF TELLS HIM WHAT TO DO AND THINK.
AND THE VICE PRESIDENT IS REALLY IN CHARGE.
WE CAN'T EXPECT HIM TO REMEMBER THE NAMES OF FOREIGN LEADERS ...
SUCK SUCK
HE'S JUST A WIDDLE BABY PWESIDENT!
AFTER 9/11, THE COUNTRY RALLIED AROUND ITS LEADER.
I LIKE TO THINK THIS TRAGEDY HAS MATURED HIM ...
SMOKE 'EM OUT! AXIS OF EVIL!
HE SAYS THE DARNEDEST THINGS!
OUR WIDDLE MAN -- ALL GWOWN UP!
STILL, HE REMAINED OUR WIDDLE-BABY-IN-CHIEF.
SO HE DOESN'T PLAY WELL WITH OUR ALLIES ...
... OR READ NEWSPAPERS ...
... OR ALWAYS GET THE BEST INTELLIGENCE.
MISSION ACCOMPWISHED
GOO!
ISN'T HE ADORABLE PLAYING DRESS-UP?!
HE NEEDS SPECIAL TREATMENT.
I DON'T WANNA TESTIFY BEFORE THE 9/11 COMMISSION!!
WAH! WAH! WAH! WAH!
DON'T CRY! MR. CHENEY WILL GO WITH AS YOUR BABY-SITTER.
IN 2004, WILL THE MEDIA AND THE PUBLIC FINALLY TREAT HIM LIKE A BIG BOY?
IN ALMOST EVERY POSSIBLE WAY IMAGINABLE YOU'VE BEEN A COMPLETE FAILURE --
REEWECT ME!
AWWWWWWW!

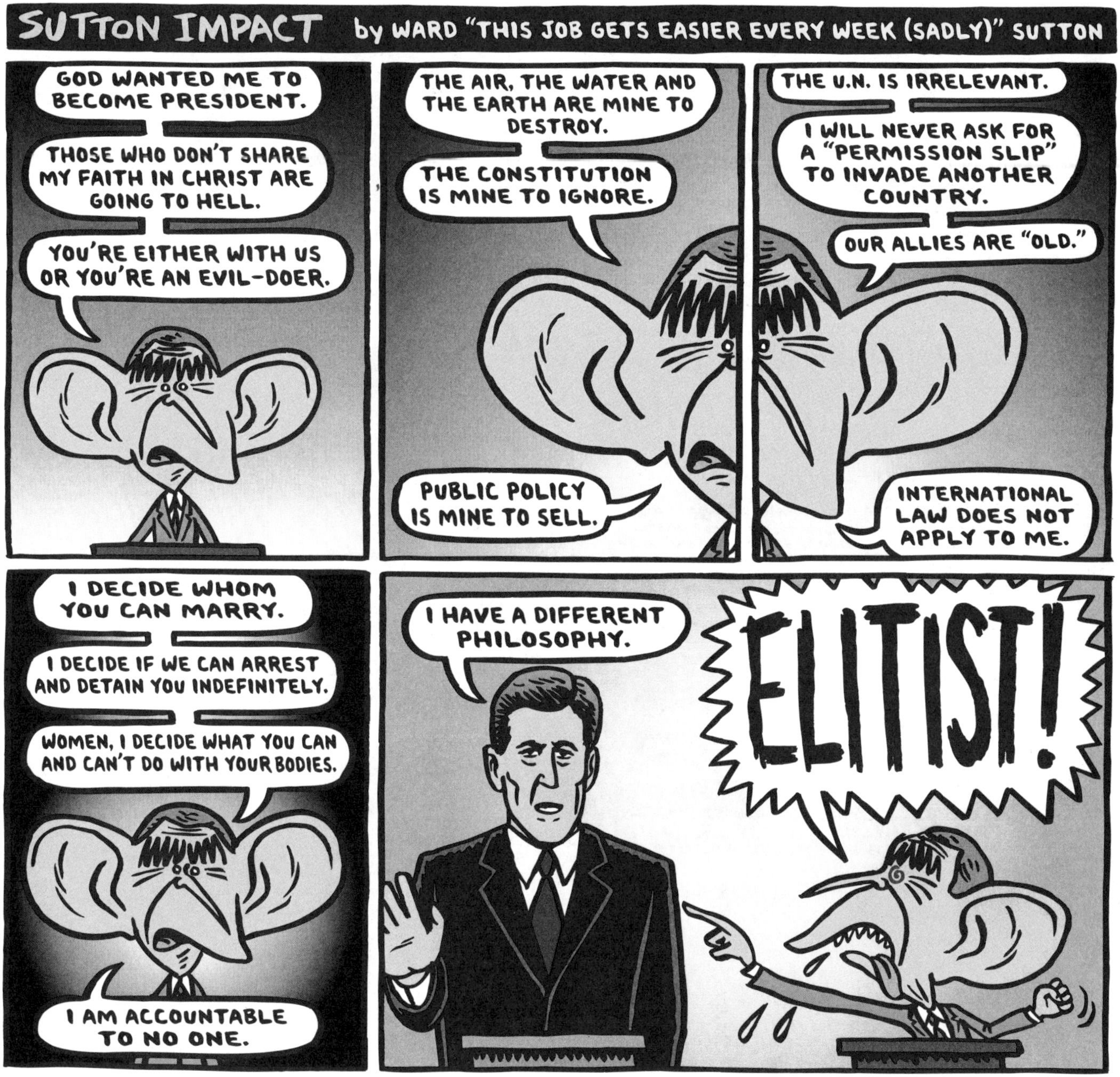
SUTTON IMPACT by WARD "THIS JOB GETS EASIER EVERY WEEK (SADLY)" SUTTON
GOD WANTED ME TO BECOME PRESIDENT.
THOSE WHO DON'T SHARE MY FAITH IN CHRIST ARE GOING TO HELL.
YOU'RE EITHER WITH US OR YOU'RE AN EVIL-DOER.
THE AIR, THE WATER AND THE EARTH ARE MINE TO DESTROY.
THE CONSTITUTION IS MINE TO IGNORE.
PUBLIC POLICY IS MINE TO SELL.
THE U.N. IS IRRELEVANT.
I WILL NEVER ASK FOR A "PERMISSION SLIP" TO INVADE ANOTHER COUNTRY.
OUR ALLIES ARE "OLD."
INTERNATIONAL LAW DOES NOT APPLY TO ME.
I DECIDE WHOM YOU CAN MARRY.
I DECIDE IF WE CAN ARREST AND DETAIN YOU INDEFINITELY.
WOMEN, I DECIDE WHAT YOU CAN AND CAN'T DO WITH YOUR BODIES.
I AM ACCOUNTABLE TO NO ONE.
I HAVE A DIFFERENT PHILOSOPHY.
ELITIST!

# COVERING THE RNC

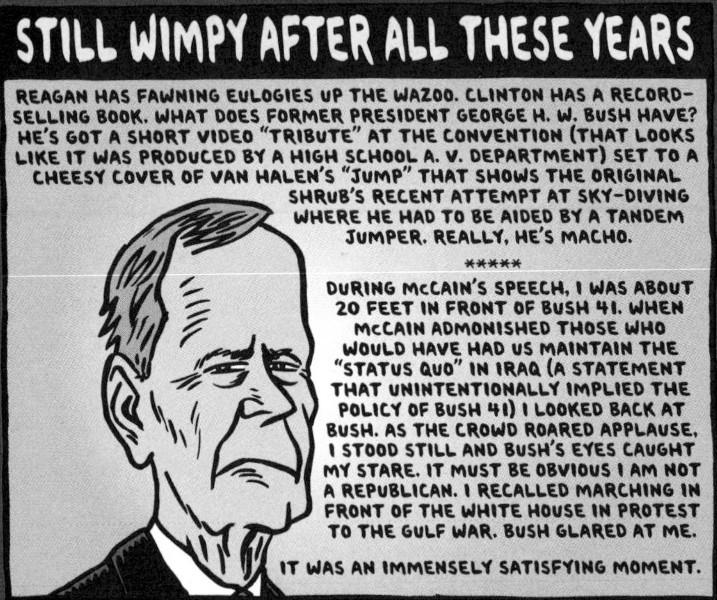
STILL WIMPY AFTER ALL THESE YEARS
REAGAN HAS FAWNING EULOGIES UP THE WAZOO. CLINTON HAS A RECORD-SELLING BOOK. WHAT DOES FORMER PRESIDENT GEORGE H. W. BUSH HAVE? HE'S GOT A SHORT VIDEO "TRIBUTE" AT THE CONVENTION (THAT LOOKS LIKE IT WAS PRODUCED BY A HIGH SCHOOL A. V. DEPARTMENT) SET TO A CHEESY COVER OF VAN HALEN'S "JUMP" THAT SHOWS THE ORIGINAL SHRUB'S RECENT ATTEMPT AT SKY-DIVING WHERE HE HAD TO BE AIDED BY A TANDEM JUMPER. REALLY, HE'S MACHO.
*****
DURING McCAIN'S SPEECH, I WAS ABOUT 20 FEET IN FRONT OF BUSH 41. WHEN McCAIN ADMONISHED THOSE WHO WOULD HAVE HAD US MAINTAIN THE "STATUS QUO" IN IRAQ (A STATEMENT THAT UNINTENTIONALLY IMPLIED THE POLICY OF BUSH 41) I LOOKED BACK AT BUSH. AS THE CROWD ROARED APPLAUSE, I STOOD STILL AND BUSH'S EYES CAUGHT MY STARE. IT MUST BE OBVIOUS I AM NOT A REPUBLICAN. I RECALLED MARCHING IN FRONT OF THE WHITE HOUSE IN PROTEST TO THE GULF WAR. BUSH GLARED AT ME.
IT WAS AN IMMENSELY SATISFYING MOMENT.

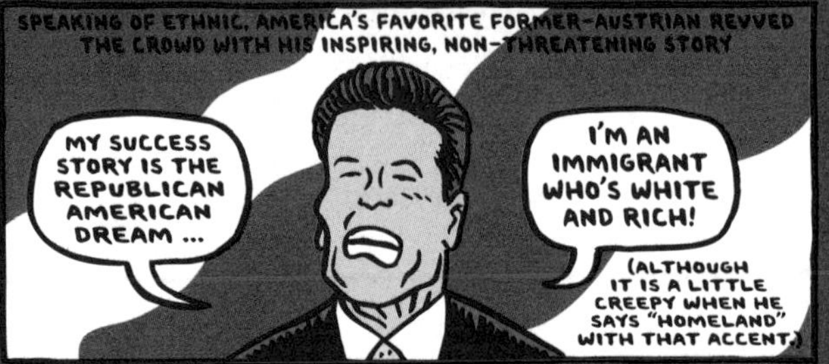
SPEAKING OF ETHNIC, AMERICA'S FAVORITE FORMER-AUSTRIAN REVVED THE CROWD WITH HIS INSPIRING, NON-THREATENING STORY
MY SUCCESS STORY IS THE REPUBLICAN AMERICAN DREAM ...
I'M AN IMMIGRANT WHO'S WHITE AND RICH!
(ALTHOUGH IT IS A LITTLE CREEPY WHEN HE SAYS "HOMELAND" WITH THAT ACCENT.)

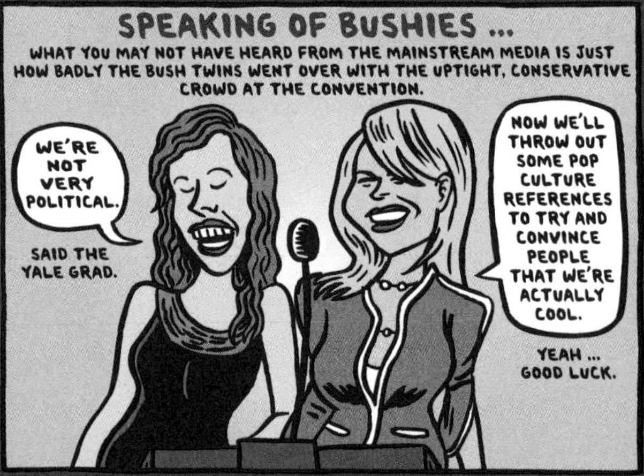
SPEAKING OF BUSHIES ...
WHAT YOU MAY NOT HAVE HEARD FROM THE MAINSTREAM MEDIA IS JUST HOW BADLY THE BUSH TWINS WENT OVER WITH THE UPTIGHT, CONSERVATIVE CROWD AT THE CONVENTION.
WE'RE NOT VERY POLITICAL.
SAID THE YALE GRAD.
NOW WE'LL THROW OUT SOME POP CULTURE REFERENCES TO TRY AND CONVINCE PEOPLE THAT WE'RE ACTUALLY COOL.
YEAH ... GOOD LUCK.

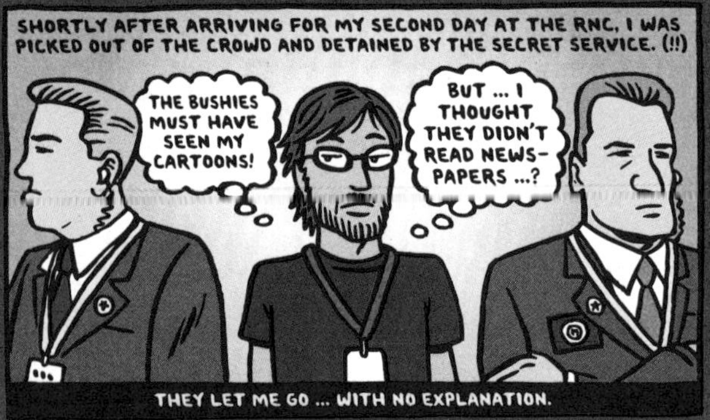
SHORTLY AFTER ARRIVING FOR MY SECOND DAY AT THE RNC, I WAS PICKED OUT OF THE CROWD AND DETAINED BY THE SECRET SERVICE. (!!)
THE BUSHIES MUST HAVE SEEN MY CARTOONS!
BUT ... I THOUGHT THEY DIDN'T READ NEWS-PAPERS ...?
THEY LET ME GO ... WITH NO EXPLANATION.

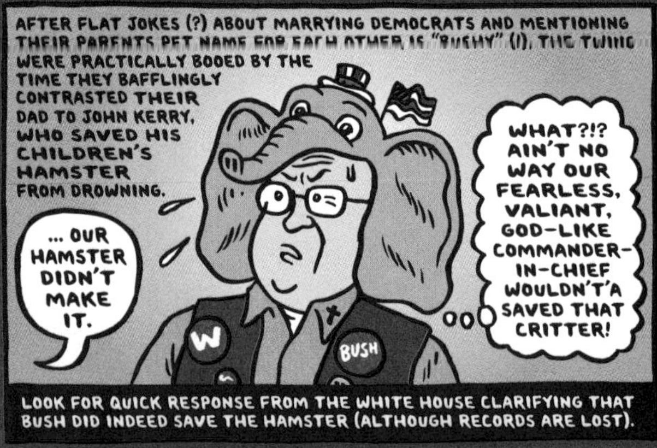
AFTER FLAT JOKES (?) ABOUT MARRYING DEMOCRATS AND MENTIONING THEIR PARENTS PET NAME FOR EACH OTHER IS "BUSHY" (!), THE TWINS WERE PRACTICALLY BOOED BY THE TIME THEY BAFFLINGLY CONTRASTED THEIR DAD TO JOHN KERRY, WHO SAVED HIS CHILDREN'S HAMSTER FROM DROWNING.
... OUR HAMSTER DIDN'T MAKE IT.
WHAT?!? AIN'T NO WAY OUR FEARLESS, VALIANT, GOD-LIKE COMMANDER-IN-CHIEF WOULDN'T'A SAVED THAT CRITTER!
W
BUSH
LOOK FOR QUICK RESPONSE FROM THE WHITE HOUSE CLARIFYING THAT BUSH DID INDEED SAVE THE HAMSTER (ALTHOUGH RECORDS ARE LOST).

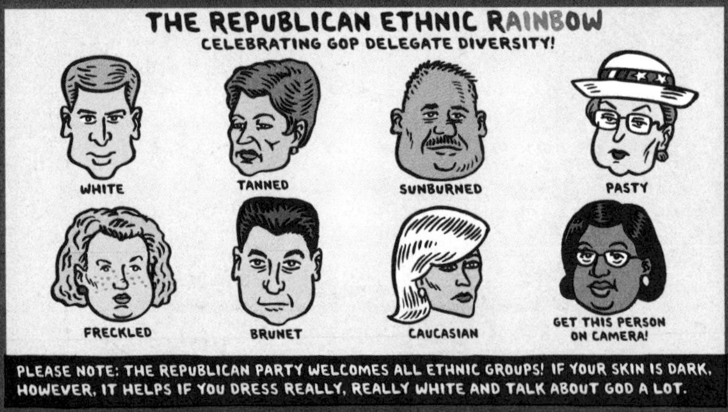
THE REPUBLICAN ETHNIC RAINBOW
CELEBRATING GOP DELEGATE DIVERSITY!
WHITE
TANNED
SUNBURNED
PASTY
FRECKLED
BRUNET
CAUCASIAN
GET THIS PERSON ON CAMERA!
PLEASE NOTE: THE REPUBLICAN PARTY WELCOMES ALL ETHNIC GROUPS! IF YOUR SKIN IS DARK, HOWEVER, IT HELPS IF YOU DRESS REALLY, REALLY WHITE AND TALK ABOUT GOD A LOT.

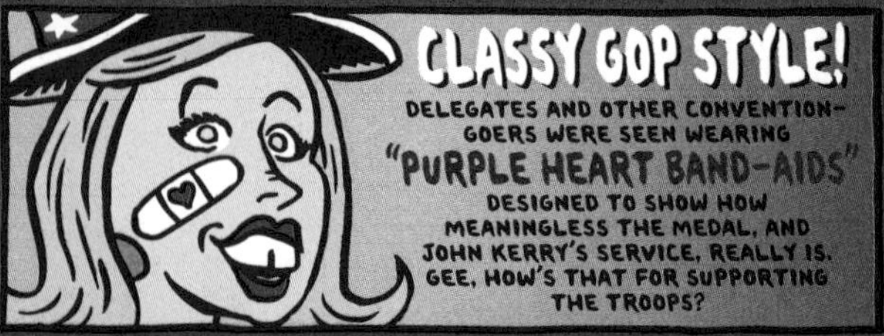
CLASSY GOP STYLE!
DELEGATES AND OTHER CONVENTION-GOERS WERE SEEN WEARING
"PURPLE HEART BAND-AIDS"
DESIGNED TO SHOW HOW MEANINGLESS THE MEDAL, AND JOHN KERRY'S SERVICE, REALLY IS. GEE, HOW'S THAT FOR SUPPORTING THE TROOPS?

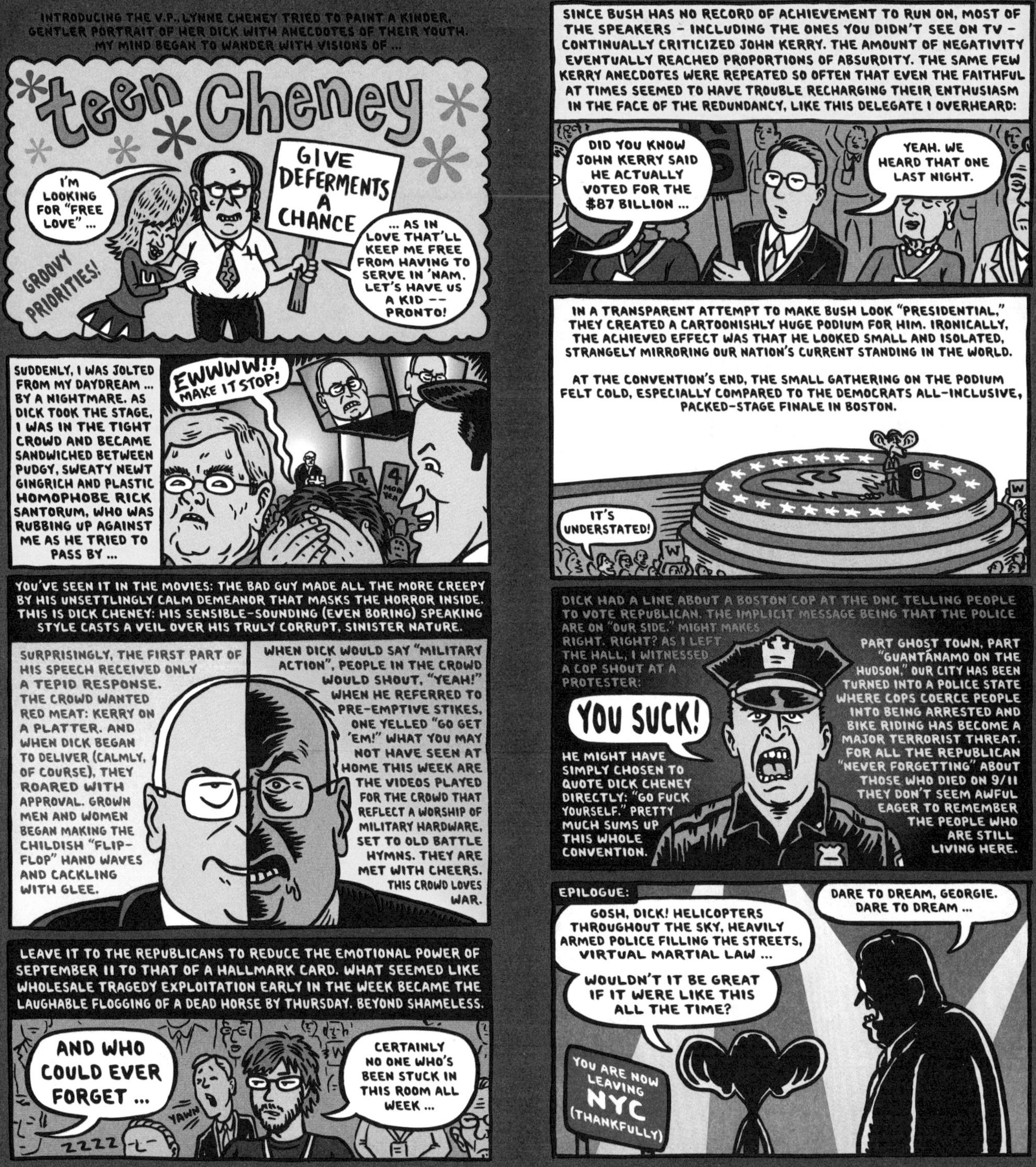
INTRODUCING THE V.P., LYNNE CHENEY TRIED TO PAINT A KINDER, GENTLER PORTRAIT OF HER DICK WITH ANECDOTES OF THEIR YOUTH. MY MIND BEGAN TO WANDER WITH VISIONS OF ...
teen Cheney
I'M LOOKING FOR "FREE LOVE" ...
GIVE DEFERMENTS A CHANCE
... AS IN LOVE THAT'LL KEEP ME FREE FROM HAVING TO SERVE IN 'NAM. LET'S HAVE US A KID -- PRONTO!
GROOVY PRIORITIES!
SUDDENLY, I WAS JOLTED FROM MY DAYDREAM ... BY A NIGHTMARE. AS DICK TOOK THE STAGE, I WAS IN THE TIGHT CROWD AND BECAME SANDWICHED BETWEEN PUDGY, SWEATY NEWT GINGRICH AND PLASTIC HOMOPHOBE RICK SANTORUM, WHO WAS RUBBING UP AGAINST ME AS HE TRIED TO PASS BY ...
EWWWW!! MAKE IT STOP!
YOU'VE SEEN IT IN THE MOVIES: THE BAD GUY MADE ALL THE MORE CREEPY BY HIS UNSETTLINGLY CALM DEMEANOR THAT MASKS THE HORROR INSIDE. THIS IS DICK CHENEY: HIS SENSIBLE-SOUNDING (EVEN BORING) SPEAKING STYLE CASTS A VEIL OVER HIS TRULY CORRUPT, SINISTER NATURE.
SURPRISINGLY, THE FIRST PART OF HIS SPEECH RECEIVED ONLY A TEPID RESPONSE. THE CROWD WANTED RED MEAT: KERRY ON A PLATTER. AND WHEN DICK BEGAN TO DELIVER (CALMLY, OF COURSE), THEY ROARED WITH APPROVAL. GROWN MEN AND WOMEN BEGAN MAKING THE CHILDISH "FLIP-FLOP" HAND WAVES AND CACKLING WITH GLEE.
WHEN DICK WOULD SAY "MILITARY ACTION", PEOPLE IN THE CROWD WOULD SHOUT, "YEAH!" WHEN HE REFERRED TO PRE-EMPTIVE STIKES, ONE YELLED "GO GET 'EM!" WHAT YOU MAY NOT HAVE SEEN AT HOME THIS WEEK ARE THE VIDEOS PLAYED FOR THE CROWD THAT REFLECT A WORSHIP OF MILITARY HARDWARE, SET TO OLD BATTLE HYMNS. THEY ARE MET WITH CHEERS. THIS CROWD LOVES WAR.
LEAVE IT TO THE REPUBLICANS TO REDUCE THE EMOTIONAL POWER OF SEPTEMBER 11 TO THAT OF A HALLMARK CARD. WHAT SEEMED LIKE WHOLESALE TRAGEDY EXPLOITATION EARLY IN THE WEEK BECAME THE LAUGHABLE FLOGGING OF A DEAD HORSE BY THURSDAY. BEYOND SHAMELESS.
AND WHO COULD EVER FORGET ...
CERTAINLY NO ONE WHO'S BEEN STUCK IN THIS ROOM ALL WEEK ...
YAWN
ZZZZ
SINCE BUSH HAS NO RECORD OF ACHIEVEMENT TO RUN ON, MOST OF THE SPEAKERS – INCLUDING THE ONES YOU DIDN'T SEE ON TV – CONTINUALLY CRITICIZED JOHN KERRY. THE AMOUNT OF NEGATIVITY EVENTUALLY REACHED PROPORTIONS OF ABSURDITY. THE SAME FEW KERRY ANECDOTES WERE REPEATED SO OFTEN THAT EVEN THE FAITHFUL AT TIMES SEEMED TO HAVE TROUBLE RECHARGING THEIR ENTHUSIASM IN THE FACE OF THE REDUNDANCY, LIKE THIS DELEGATE I OVERHEARD:
DID YOU KNOW JOHN KERRY SAID HE ACTUALLY VOTED FOR THE $87 BILLION ...
YEAH. WE HEARD THAT ONE LAST NIGHT.
IN A TRANSPARENT ATTEMPT TO MAKE BUSH LOOK "PRESIDENTIAL," THEY CREATED A CARTOONISHLY HUGE PODIUM FOR HIM. IRONICALLY, THE ACHIEVED EFFECT WAS THAT HE LOOKED SMALL AND ISOLATED, STRANGELY MIRRORING OUR NATION'S CURRENT STANDING IN THE WORLD.
AT THE CONVENTION'S END, THE SMALL GATHERING ON THE PODIUM FELT COLD, ESPECIALLY COMPARED TO THE DEMOCRATS ALL-INCLUSIVE, PACKED-STAGE FINALE IN BOSTON.
IT'S UNDERSTATED!
DICK HAD A LINE ABOUT A BOSTON COP AT THE DNC TELLING PEOPLE TO VOTE REPUBLICAN. THE IMPLICIT MESSAGE BEING THAT THE POLICE ARE ON "OUR SIDE." MIGHT MAKES RIGHT. RIGHT? AS I LEFT THE HALL, I WITNESSED A COP SHOUT AT A PROTESTER:
YOU SUCK!
HE MIGHT HAVE SIMPLY CHOSEN TO QUOTE DICK CHENEY DIRECTLY: "GO FUCK YOURSELF." PRETTY MUCH SUMS UP THIS WHOLE CONVENTION.
PART GHOST TOWN, PART "GUANTÁNAMO ON THE HUDSON," OUR CITY HAS BEEN TURNED INTO A POLICE STATE WHERE COPS COERCE PEOPLE INTO BEING ARRESTED AND BIKE RIDING HAS BECOME A MAJOR TERRORIST THREAT. FOR ALL THE REPUBLICAN "NEVER FORGETTING" ABOUT THOSE WHO DIED ON 9/11 THEY DON'T SEEM AWFUL EAGER TO REMEMBER THE PEOPLE WHO ARE STILL LIVING HERE.
EPILOGUE:
GOSH, DICK! HELICOPTERS THROUGHOUT THE SKY, HEAVILY ARMED POLICE FILLING THE STREETS, VIRTUAL MARTIAL LAW ...
WOULDN'T IT BE GREAT IF IT WERE LIKE THIS ALL THE TIME?
DARE TO DREAM, GEORGIE. DARE TO DREAM ...
YOU ARE NOW LEAVING NYC (THANKFULLY)

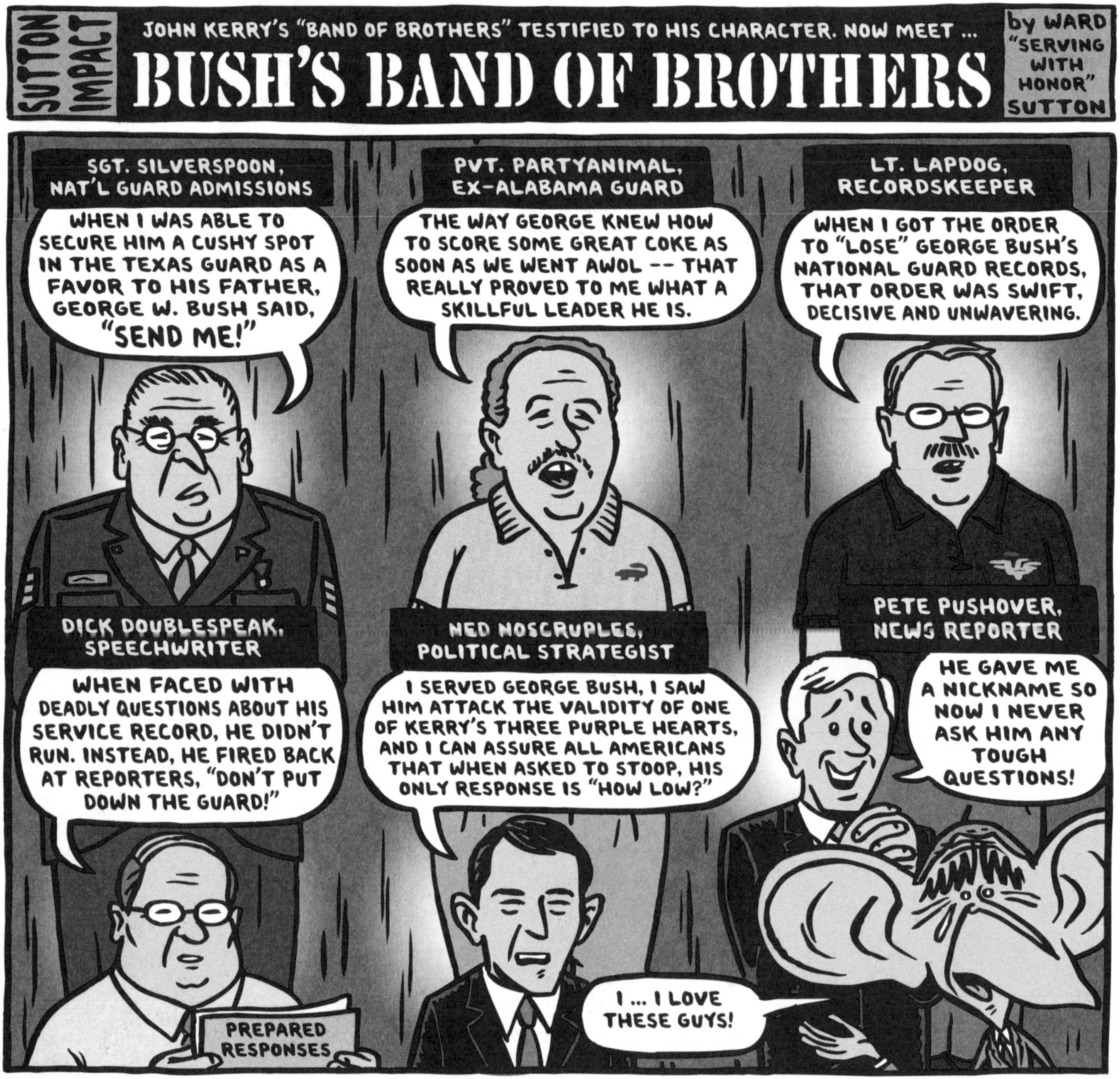
SUTTON IMPACT
JOHN KERRY'S "BAND OF BROTHERS" TESTIFIED TO HIS CHARACTER. NOW MEET ...
BUSH'S BAND OF BROTHERS
by WARD "SERVING WITH HONOR" SUTTON
SGT. SILVERSPOON, NAT'L GUARD ADMISSIONS
WHEN I WAS ABLE TO SECURE HIM A CUSHY SPOT IN THE TEXAS GUARD AS A FAVOR TO HIS FATHER, GEORGE W. BUSH SAID, "SEND ME!"
PVT. PARTYANIMAL, EX-ALABAMA GUARD
THE WAY GEORGE KNEW HOW TO SCORE SOME GREAT COKE AS SOON AS WE WENT AWOL -- THAT REALLY PROVED TO ME WHAT A SKILLFUL LEADER HE IS.
LT. LAPDOG, RECORDSKEEPER
WHEN I GOT THE ORDER TO "LOSE" GEORGE BUSH'S NATIONAL GUARD RECORDS, THAT ORDER WAS SWIFT, DECISIVE AND UNWAVERING.
DICK DOUBLESPEAK, SPEECHWRITER
WHEN FACED WITH DEADLY QUESTIONS ABOUT HIS SERVICE RECORD, HE DIDN'T RUN. INSTEAD, HE FIRED BACK AT REPORTERS, "DON'T PUT DOWN THE GUARD!"
NED NOSCRUPLES, POLITICAL STRATEGIST
I SERVED GEORGE BUSH, I SAW HIM ATTACK THE VALIDITY OF ONE OF KERRY'S THREE PURPLE HEARTS, AND I CAN ASSURE ALL AMERICANS THAT WHEN ASKED TO STOOP, HIS ONLY RESPONSE IS "HOW LOW?"
PETE PUSHOVER, NEWS REPORTER
HE GAVE ME A NICKNAME SO NOW I NEVER ASK HIM ANY TOUGH QUESTIONS!
PREPARED RESPONSES
I ... I LOVE THESE GUYS!

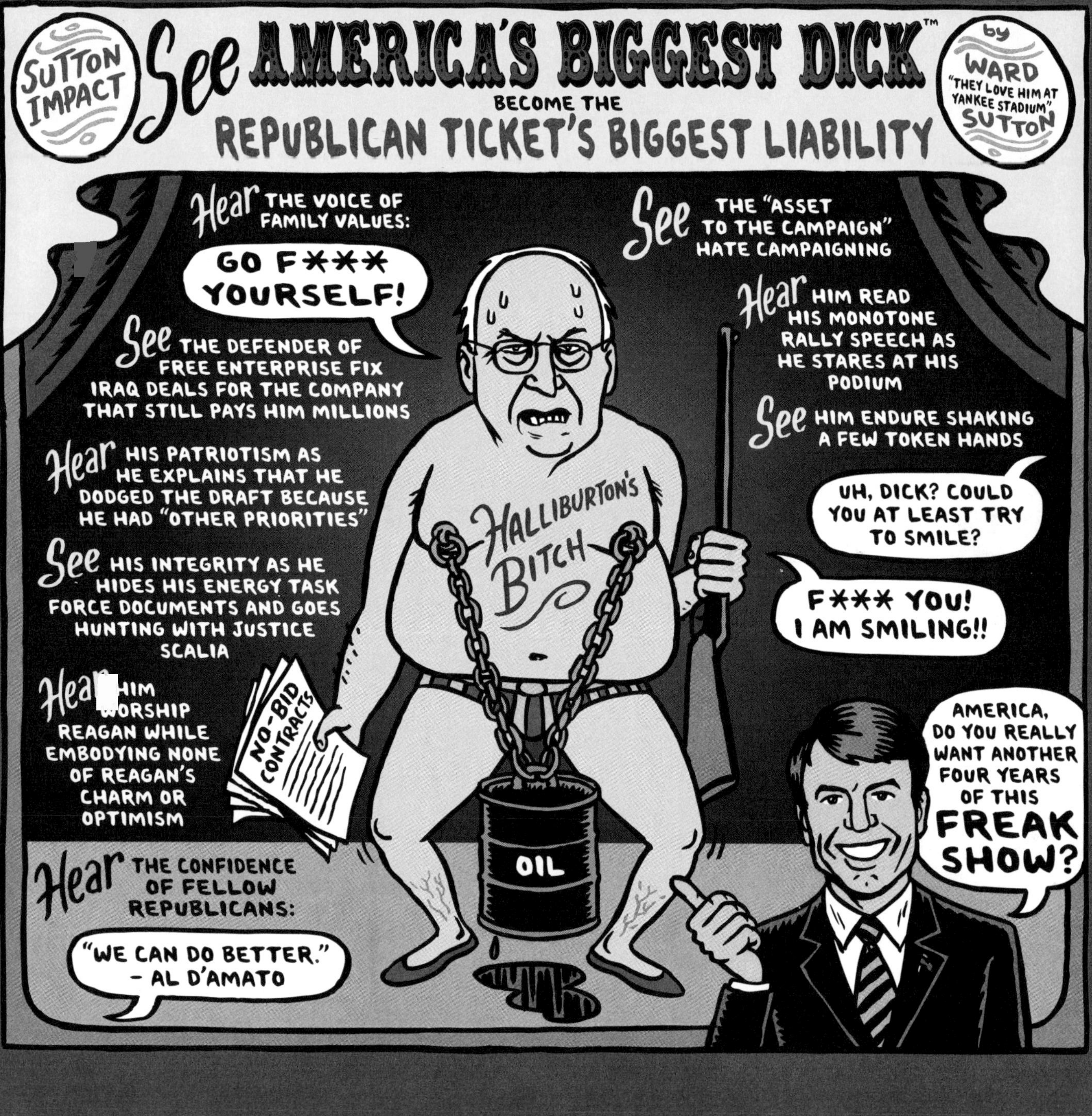
SUTTON IMPACT
See AMERICA'S BIGGEST DICK™
BECOME THE
REPUBLICAN TICKET'S BIGGEST LIABILITY
by WARD "THEY LOVE HIM AT YANKEE STADIUM" SUTTON
Hear THE VOICE OF FAMILY VALUES:
GO F*** YOURSELF!
See THE DEFENDER OF FREE ENTERPRISE FIX IRAQ DEALS FOR THE COMPANY THAT STILL PAYS HIM MILLIONS
Hear HIS PATRIOTISM AS HE EXPLAINS THAT HE DODGED THE DRAFT BECAUSE HE HAD "OTHER PRIORITIES"
See HIS INTEGRITY AS HE HIDES HIS ENERGY TASK FORCE DOCUMENTS AND GOES HUNTING WITH JUSTICE SCALIA
Hea HIM WORSHIP REAGAN WHILE EMBODYING NONE OF REAGAN'S CHARM OR OPTIMISM
HALLIBURTON'S BITCH
NO-BID CONTRACTS
OIL
See THE "ASSET TO THE CAMPAIGN" HATE CAMPAIGNING
Hear HIM READ HIS MONOTONE RALLY SPEECH AS HE STARES AT HIS PODIUM
See HIM ENDURE SHAKING A FEW TOKEN HANDS
UH, DICK? COULD YOU AT LEAST TRY TO SMILE?
F*** YOU! I AM SMILING!!
Hear THE CONFIDENCE OF FELLOW REPUBLICANS:
"WE CAN DO BETTER." - AL D'AMATO
AMERICA, DO YOU REALLY WANT ANOTHER FOUR YEARS OF THIS FREAK SHOW?

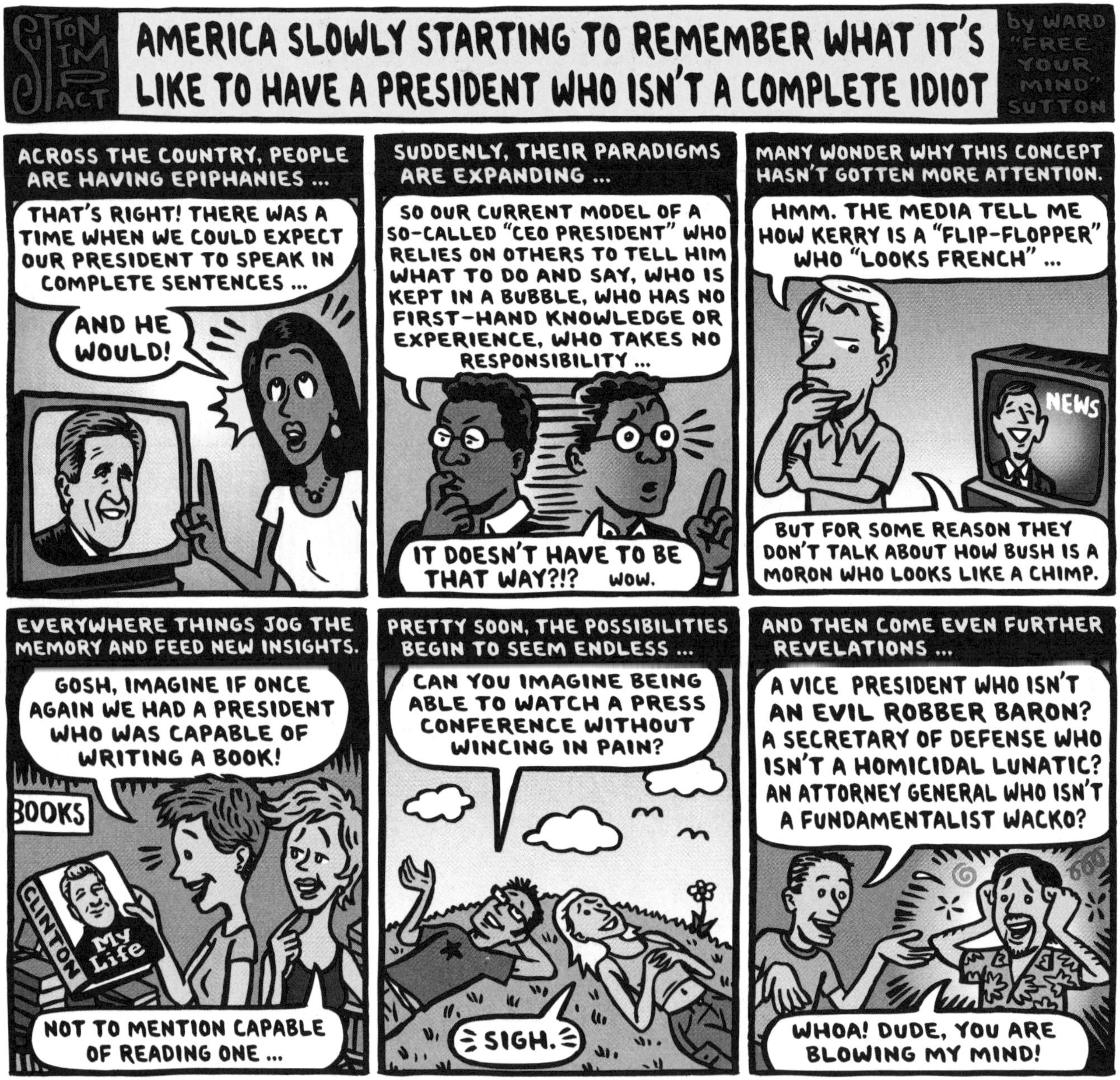
SUTTON IMPACT
AMERICA SLOWLY STARTING TO REMEMBER WHAT IT'S LIKE TO HAVE A PRESIDENT WHO ISN'T A COMPLETE IDIOT
by WARD "FREE YOUR MIND" SUTTON
ACROSS THE COUNTRY, PEOPLE ARE HAVING EPIPHANIES ...
THAT'S RIGHT! THERE WAS A TIME WHEN WE COULD EXPECT OUR PRESIDENT TO SPEAK IN COMPLETE SENTENCES ...
AND HE WOULD!
SUDDENLY, THEIR PARADIGMS ARE EXPANDING ...
SO OUR CURRENT MODEL OF A SO-CALLED "CEO PRESIDENT" WHO RELIES ON OTHERS TO TELL HIM WHAT TO DO AND SAY, WHO IS KEPT IN A BUBBLE, WHO HAS NO FIRST-HAND KNOWLEDGE OR EXPERIENCE, WHO TAKES NO RESPONSIBILITY ...
IT DOESN'T HAVE TO BE THAT WAY?!?
WOW.
MANY WONDER WHY THIS CONCEPT HASN'T GOTTEN MORE ATTENTION.
HMM. THE MEDIA TELL ME HOW KERRY IS A "FLIP-FLOPPER" WHO "LOOKS FRENCH" ...
NEWS
BUT FOR SOME REASON THEY DON'T TALK ABOUT HOW BUSH IS A MORON WHO LOOKS LIKE A CHIMP.
EVERYWHERE THINGS JOG THE MEMORY AND FEED NEW INSIGHTS.
GOSH, IMAGINE IF ONCE AGAIN WE HAD A PRESIDENT WHO WAS CAPABLE OF WRITING A BOOK!
BOOKS
CLINTON
My Life
NOT TO MENTION CAPABLE OF READING ONE ...
PRETTY SOON, THE POSSIBILITIES BEGIN TO SEEM ENDLESS ...
CAN YOU IMAGINE BEING ABLE TO WATCH A PRESS CONFERENCE WITHOUT WINCING IN PAIN?
SIGH.
AND THEN COME EVEN FURTHER REVELATIONS ...
A VICE PRESIDENT WHO ISN'T AN EVIL ROBBER BARON? A SECRETARY OF DEFENSE WHO ISN'T A HOMICIDAL LUNATIC? AN ATTORNEY GENERAL WHO ISN'T A FUNDAMENTALIST WACKO?
WHOA! DUDE, YOU ARE BLOWING MY MIND!

It's almost cruel to reprint this one. So close and yet ... painful.

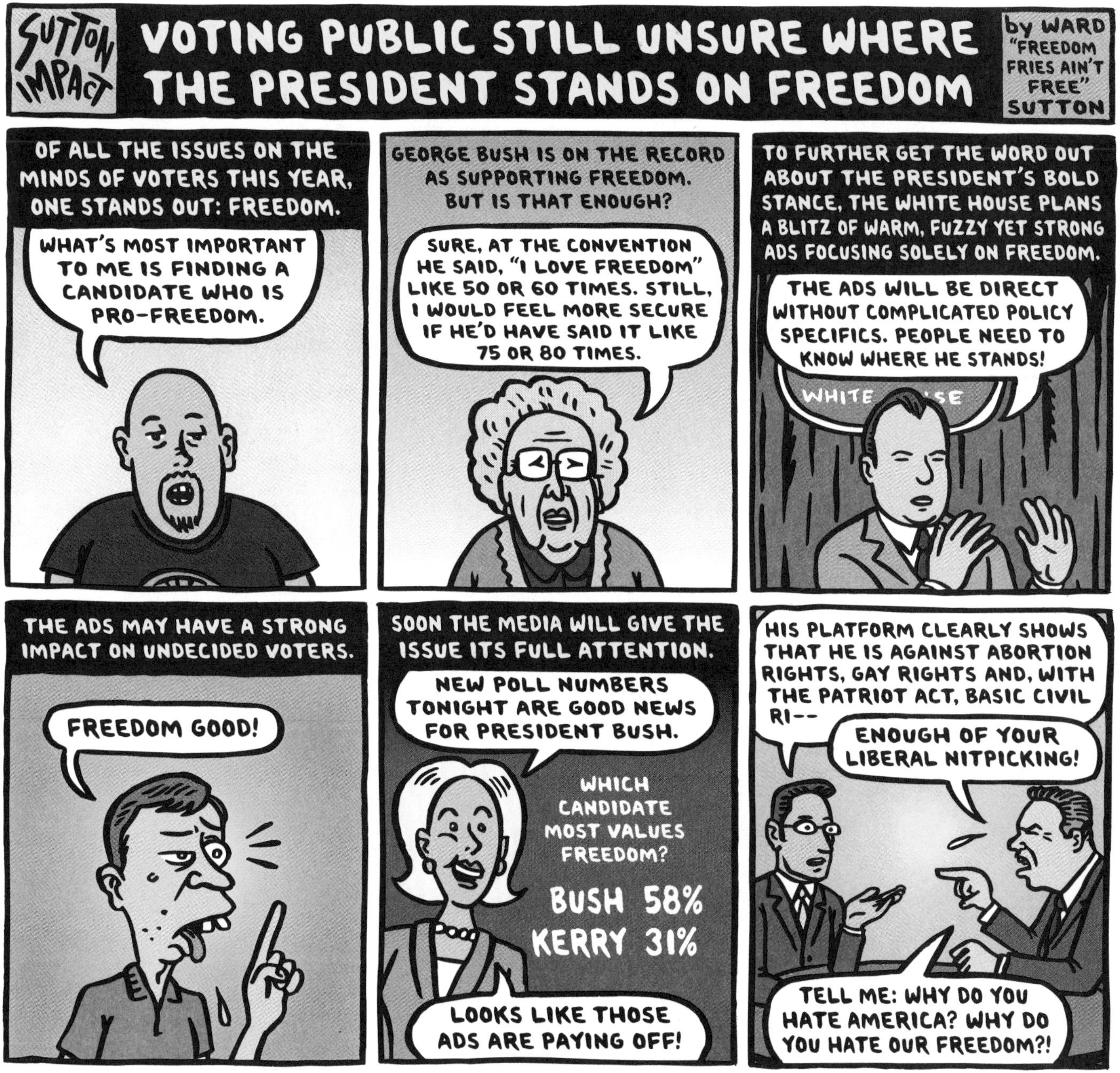
SUTTON IMPACT
VOTING PUBLIC STILL UNSURE WHERE THE PRESIDENT STANDS ON FREEDOM
by WARD "FREEDOM FRIES AIN'T FREE" SUTTON
OF ALL THE ISSUES ON THE MINDS OF VOTERS THIS YEAR, ONE STANDS OUT: FREEDOM.
WHAT'S MOST IMPORTANT TO ME IS FINDING A CANDIDATE WHO IS PRO-FREEDOM.
GEORGE BUSH IS ON THE RECORD AS SUPPORTING FREEDOM. BUT IS THAT ENOUGH?
SURE, AT THE CONVENTION HE SAID, "I LOVE FREEDOM" LIKE 50 OR 60 TIMES. STILL, I WOULD FEEL MORE SECURE IF HE'D HAVE SAID IT LIKE 75 OR 80 TIMES.
TO FURTHER GET THE WORD OUT ABOUT THE PRESIDENT'S BOLD STANCE, THE WHITE HOUSE PLANS A BLITZ OF WARM, FUZZY YET STRONG ADS FOCUSING SOLELY ON FREEDOM.
THE ADS WILL BE DIRECT WITHOUT COMPLICATED POLICY SPECIFICS. PEOPLE NEED TO KNOW WHERE HE STANDS!
THE ADS MAY HAVE A STRONG IMPACT ON UNDECIDED VOTERS.
FREEDOM GOOD!
SOON THE MEDIA WILL GIVE THE ISSUE ITS FULL ATTENTION.
NEW POLL NUMBERS TONIGHT ARE GOOD NEWS FOR PRESIDENT BUSH.
WHICH CANDIDATE MOST VALUES FREEDOM?
BUSH 58%
KERRY 31%
LOOKS LIKE THOSE ADS ARE PAYING OFF!
HIS PLATFORM CLEARLY SHOWS THAT HE IS AGAINST ABORTION RIGHTS, GAY RIGHTS AND, WITH THE PATRIOT ACT, BASIC CIVIL RI--
ENOUGH OF YOUR LIBERAL NITPICKING!
TELL ME: WHY DO YOU HATE AMERICA? WHY DO YOU HATE OUR FREEDOM?!

SCHLOCK 'N' ROLL

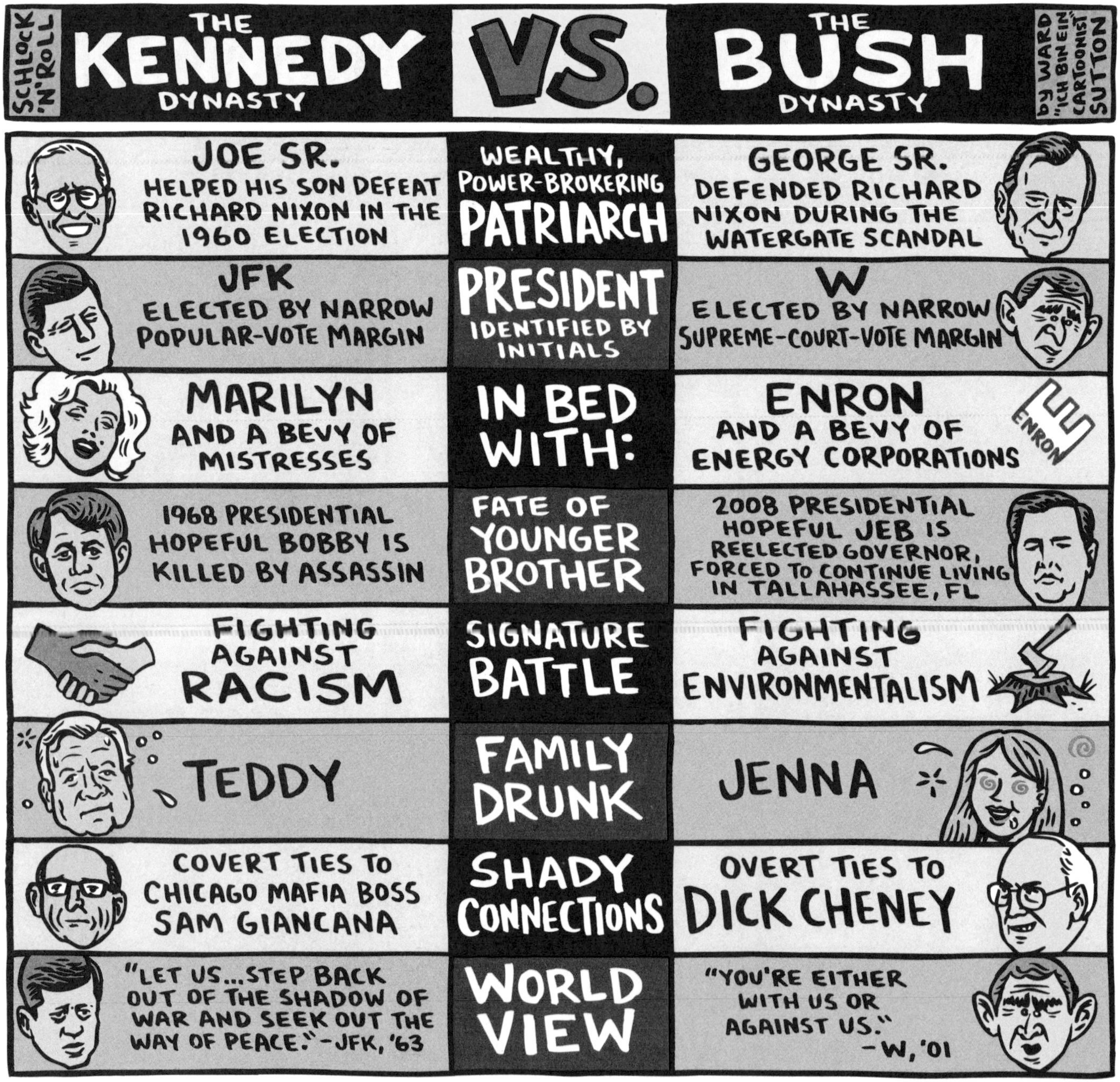

# THE KENNEDY DYNASTY  VS. THE BUSH DYNASTY

 by WARD "ICH BIN EIN" CARTOONIST SUTTON

| KENNEDY | | BUSH |
|---|---|---|
|  **JOE SR.** HELPED HIS SON DEFEAT RICHARD NIXON IN THE 1960 ELECTION | WEALTHY, POWER-BROKERING **PATRIARCH** | **GEORGE SR.** DEFENDED RICHARD NIXON DURING THE WATERGATE SCANDAL  |
|  wait | | |
| **JFK** ELECTED BY NARROW POPULAR-VOTE MARGIN | **PRESIDENT** IDENTIFIED BY INITIALS | **W** ELECTED BY NARROW SUPREME-COURT-VOTE MARGIN  |
| **MARILYN** AND A BEVY OF MISTRESSES | **IN BED WITH:** | **ENRON** AND A BEVY OF ENERGY CORPORATIONS |
| 1968 PRESIDENTIAL HOPEFUL BOBBY IS KILLED BY ASSASSIN | FATE OF **YOUNGER BROTHER** | 2008 PRESIDENTIAL HOPEFUL JEB IS REELECTED GOVERNOR, FORCED TO CONTINUE LIVING IN TALLAHASSEE, FL  |
| **FIGHTING** AGAINST **RACISM** | SIGNATURE **BATTLE** | **FIGHTING** AGAINST **ENVIRONMENTALISM** |
|  **TEDDY** | **FAMILY DRUNK** | **JENNA**  |
|  COVERT TIES TO CHICAGO MAFIA BOSS SAM GIANCANA | **SHADY CONNECTIONS** | OVERT TIES TO **DICK CHENEY**  |
| "LET US...STEP BACK OUT OF THE SHADOW OF WAR AND SEEK OUT THE WAY OF PEACE." -JFK, '63 | **WORLD VIEW** | "YOU'RE EITHER WITH US OR AGAINST US." -W, '01  |

**SUTTON IMPACT**

# LBJ VS. W

by WARD
"HEARTS
AND
MINDS"
SUTTON

| GOOD OL' BOY FROM TEXAS | FAUX GOOD OL' BOY FROM YALE |
|---|---|
| BEFORE PRESIDENCY WAS KNOWN AS "MASTER OF THE SENATE" | BEFORE PRESIDENCY WAS KNOWN AS "FAILURE AT BUSINESS" |
| TRAGICALLY BECAME PRESIDENT WHEN JOHN KENNEDY SHOULD HAVE BEEN | TRAGICALLY BECAME PRESIDENT WHEN AL GORE SHOULD HAVE BEEN |
| DESPITE HISTORIC ELECTION LANDSLIDE, HE WAS PESSIMISTIC AND DEPRESSED | DESPITE HISTORIC ELECTION CONTROVERSY, HE WAS COCKY AND SMUG |
| OBSESSED WITH BOBBY KENNEDY | OBSESSED WITH SADDAM HUSSEIN |
| PLAYED DOWN WAR IN VIETNAM IN ORDER TO PASS HIS INCREDIBLY PROGRESSIVE LEGISLATIVE AGENDA | PLAYS UP WAR ON TERROR IN ORDER TO PASS HIS INCREDIBLY REGRESSIVE LEGISLATIVE AGENDA |
| CONTROLLED HIS VICE PRESIDENT | IS CONTROLLED BY HIS VICE PRESIDENT |
| ENACTED BOLD PROGRAM TO AID THE POOR | ENACTING BOLD PROGRAMS TO AID THE RICH |
| WAS DISTURBINGLY PREOCCUPIED WITH WHAT NEWSPAPER COLUMNISTS WROTE ABOUT HIM | DISTURBINGLY, DOESN'T READ NEWSPAPERS |
| CREATED MEDICARE TO BENEFIT SENIORS | CHANGED MEDICARE TO BENEFIT DRUG COMPANIES |
| WAS FURIOUS WITH THOSE ON HIS STAFF THAT LEAKED SENSITIVE INFORMATION | PROTECTS THOSE ON HIS STAFF THAT LEAKED SENSITIVE INFORMATION |
| LED NATION INTO A WAR ON BASIS OF AN ATTACK THAT NEVER HAPPENED | LED NATION INTO A WAR ON BASIS OF WEAPONS THAT NEVER EXISTED |
| EMPOWERED VOTERS WITH 1965 CIVIL RIGHTS ACT | DISENFRANCHISED VOTERS WITH 2000, 2004 DIRTY TRICKS |

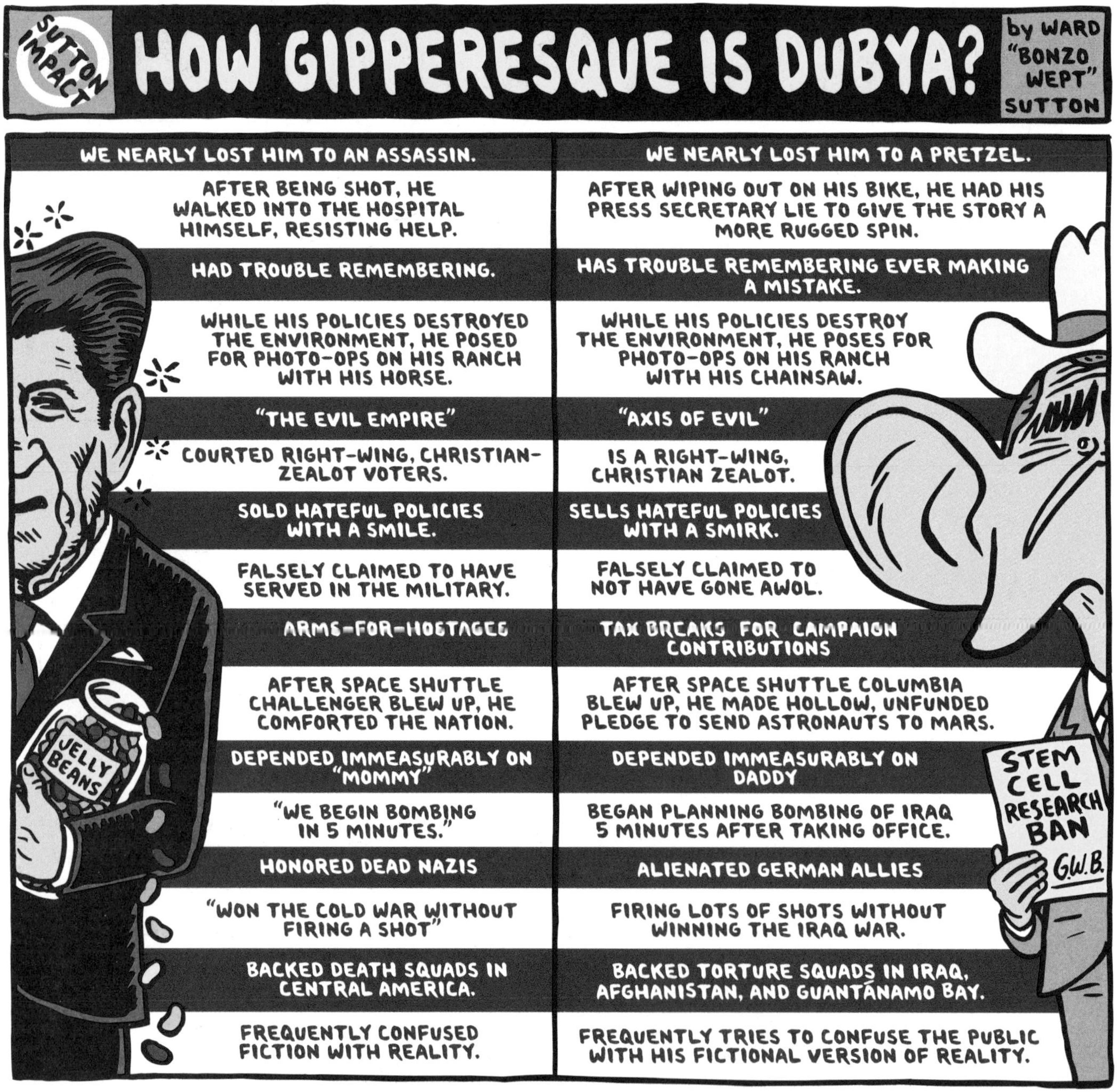

# HOW GIPPERESQUE IS DUBYA?

by WARD "BONZO WEPT" SUTTON

| WE NEARLY LOST HIM TO AN ASSASSIN. | WE NEARLY LOST HIM TO A PRETZEL. |
|---|---|
| AFTER BEING SHOT, HE WALKED INTO THE HOSPITAL HIMSELF, RESISTING HELP. | AFTER WIPING OUT ON HIS BIKE, HE HAD HIS PRESS SECRETARY LIE TO GIVE THE STORY A MORE RUGGED SPIN. |
| HAD TROUBLE REMEMBERING. | HAS TROUBLE REMEMBERING EVER MAKING A MISTAKE. |
| WHILE HIS POLICIES DESTROYED THE ENVIRONMENT, HE POSED FOR PHOTO-OPS ON HIS RANCH WITH HIS HORSE. | WHILE HIS POLICIES DESTROY THE ENVIRONMENT, HE POSES FOR PHOTO-OPS ON HIS RANCH WITH HIS CHAINSAW. |
| "THE EVIL EMPIRE" | "AXIS OF EVIL" |
| COURTED RIGHT-WING, CHRISTIAN-ZEALOT VOTERS. | IS A RIGHT-WING, CHRISTIAN ZEALOT. |
| SOLD HATEFUL POLICIES WITH A SMILE. | SELLS HATEFUL POLICIES WITH A SMIRK. |
| FALSELY CLAIMED TO HAVE SERVED IN THE MILITARY. | FALSELY CLAIMED TO NOT HAVE GONE AWOL. |
| ARMS-FOR-HOSTAGES | TAX BREAKS FOR CAMPAIGN CONTRIBUTIONS |
| AFTER SPACE SHUTTLE CHALLENGER BLEW UP, HE COMFORTED THE NATION. | AFTER SPACE SHUTTLE COLUMBIA BLEW UP, HE MADE HOLLOW, UNFUNDED PLEDGE TO SEND ASTRONAUTS TO MARS. |
| DEPENDED IMMEASURABLY ON "MOMMY" | DEPENDED IMMEASURABLY ON DADDY |
| "WE BEGIN BOMBING IN 5 MINUTES." | BEGAN PLANNING BOMBING OF IRAQ 5 MINUTES AFTER TAKING OFFICE. |
| HONORED DEAD NAZIS | ALIENATED GERMAN ALLIES |
| "WON THE COLD WAR WITHOUT FIRING A SHOT" | FIRING LOTS OF SHOTS WITHOUT WINNING THE IRAQ WAR. |
| BACKED DEATH SQUADS IN CENTRAL AMERICA. | BACKED TORTURE SQUADS IN IRAQ, AFGHANISTAN, AND GUANTÁNAMO BAY. |
| FREQUENTLY CONFUSED FICTION WITH REALITY. | FREQUENTLY TRIES TO CONFUSE THE PUBLIC WITH HIS FICTIONAL VERSION OF REALITY. |

JELLY BEANS

STEM CELL RESEARCH BAN G.W.B.

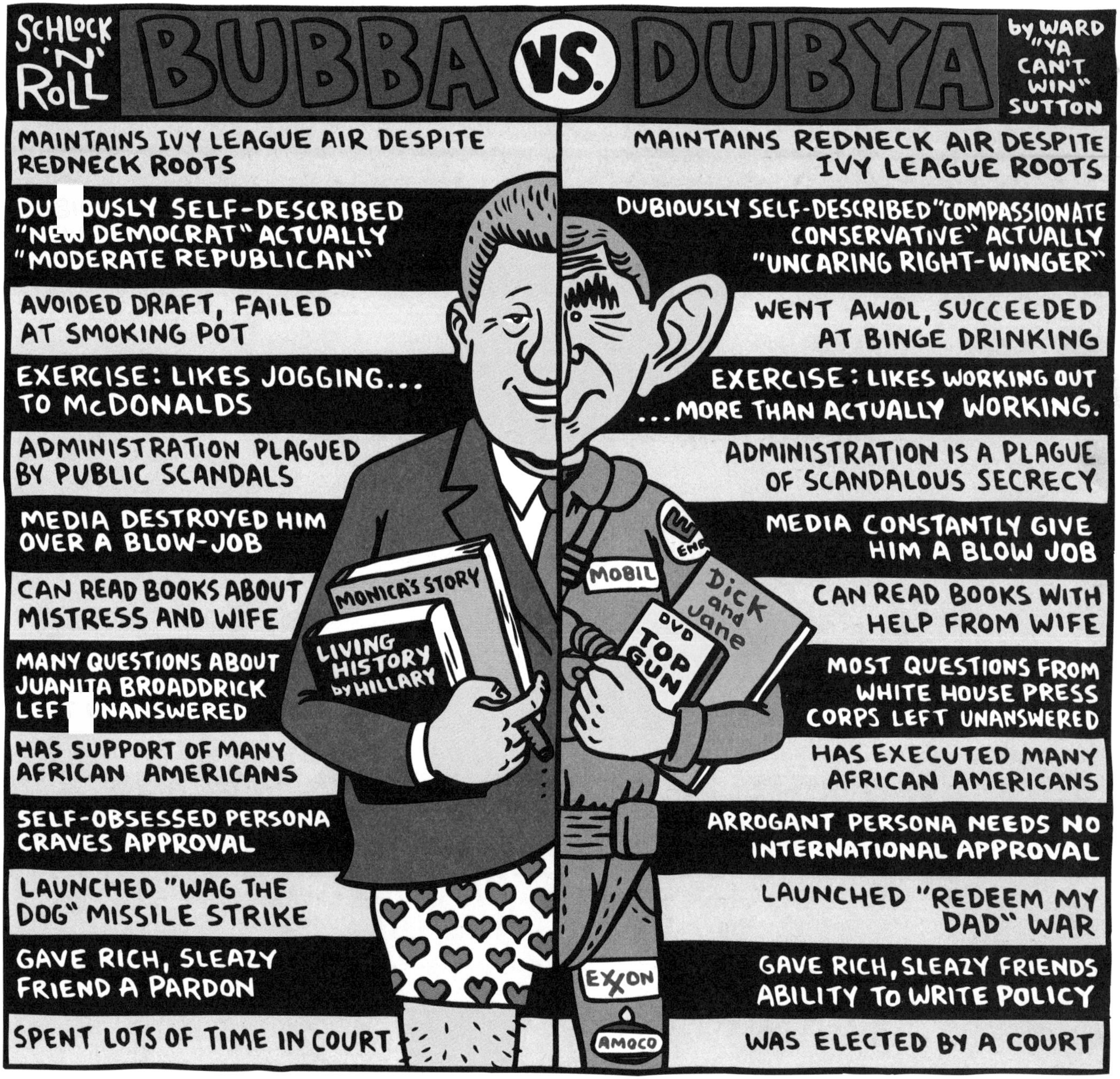
SCHLOCK 'N' ROLL
BUBBA VS. DUBYA
by WARD "YA CAN'T WIN" SUTTON
MAINTAINS IVY LEAGUE AIR DESPITE REDNECK ROOTS
MAINTAINS REDNECK AIR DESPITE IVY LEAGUE ROOTS
DUBIOUSLY SELF-DESCRIBED "NEW DEMOCRAT" ACTUALLY "MODERATE REPUBLICAN"
DUBIOUSLY SELF-DESCRIBED "COMPASSIONATE CONSERVATIVE" ACTUALLY "UNCARING RIGHT-WINGER"
AVOIDED DRAFT, FAILED AT SMOKING POT
WENT AWOL, SUCCEEDED AT BINGE DRINKING
EXERCISE: LIKES JOGGING... TO McDONALDS
EXERCISE: LIKES WORKING OUT ...MORE THAN ACTUALLY WORKING.
ADMINISTRATION PLAGUED BY PUBLIC SCANDALS
ADMINISTRATION IS A PLAGUE OF SCANDALOUS SECRECY
MEDIA DESTROYED HIM OVER A BLOW-JOB
MEDIA CONSTANTLY GIVE HIM A BLOW JOB
CAN READ BOOKS ABOUT MISTRESS AND WIFE
CAN READ BOOKS WITH HELP FROM WIFE
MONICA'S STORY
LIVING HISTORY by HILLARY
MOBIL
Dick and Jane
DVD TOP GUN
MANY QUESTIONS ABOUT JUANITA BROADDRICK LEFT UNANSWERED
MOST QUESTIONS FROM WHITE HOUSE PRESS CORPS LEFT UNANSWERED
HAS SUPPORT OF MANY AFRICAN AMERICANS
HAS EXECUTED MANY AFRICAN AMERICANS
SELF-OBSESSED PERSONA CRAVES APPROVAL
ARROGANT PERSONA NEEDS NO INTERNATIONAL APPROVAL
LAUNCHED "WAG THE DOG" MISSILE STRIKE
LAUNCHED "REDEEM MY DAD" WAR
GAVE RICH, SLEAZY FRIEND A PARDON
GAVE RICH, SLEAZY FRIENDS ABILITY TO WRITE POLICY
EXXON
AMOCO
SPENT LOTS OF TIME IN COURT
WAS ELECTED BY A COURT

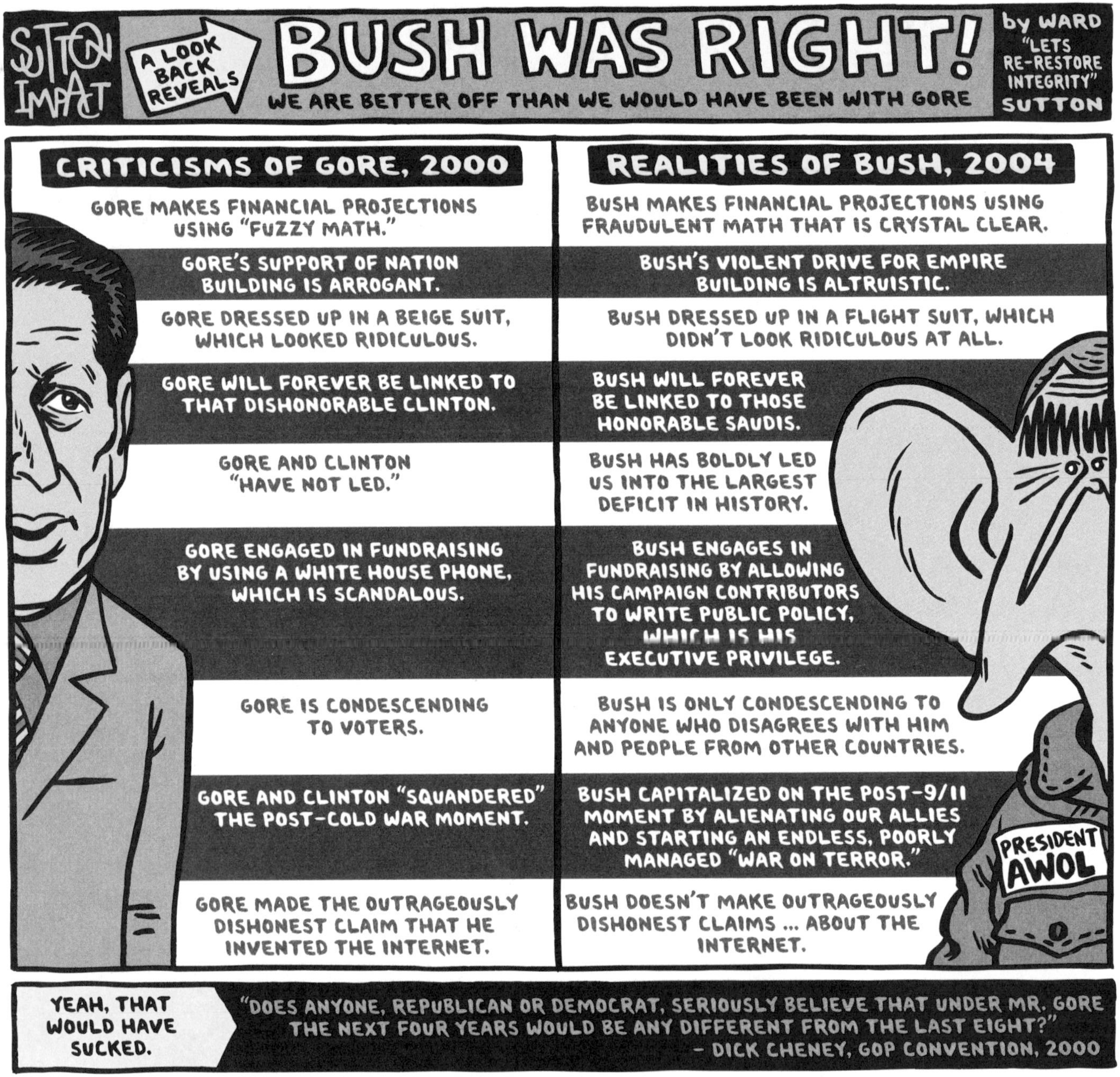

# BUSH WAS RIGHT!

SUTTON IMPACT · A LOOK BACK REVEALS

WE ARE BETTER OFF THAN WE WOULD HAVE BEEN WITH GORE

by WARD "LETS RE-RESTORE INTEGRITY" SUTTON

| CRITICISMS OF GORE, 2000 | REALITIES OF BUSH, 2004 |
| --- | --- |
| GORE MAKES FINANCIAL PROJECTIONS USING "FUZZY MATH." | BUSH MAKES FINANCIAL PROJECTIONS USING FRAUDULENT MATH THAT IS CRYSTAL CLEAR. |
| GORE'S SUPPORT OF NATION BUILDING IS ARROGANT. | BUSH'S VIOLENT DRIVE FOR EMPIRE BUILDING IS ALTRUISTIC. |
| GORE DRESSED UP IN A BEIGE SUIT, WHICH LOOKED RIDICULOUS. | BUSH DRESSED UP IN A FLIGHT SUIT, WHICH DIDN'T LOOK RIDICULOUS AT ALL. |
| GORE WILL FOREVER BE LINKED TO THAT DISHONORABLE CLINTON. | BUSH WILL FOREVER BE LINKED TO THOSE HONORABLE SAUDIS. |
| GORE AND CLINTON "HAVE NOT LED." | BUSH HAS BOLDLY LED US INTO THE LARGEST DEFICIT IN HISTORY. |
| GORE ENGAGED IN FUNDRAISING BY USING A WHITE HOUSE PHONE, WHICH IS SCANDALOUS. | BUSH ENGAGES IN FUNDRAISING BY ALLOWING HIS CAMPAIGN CONTRIBUTORS TO WRITE PUBLIC POLICY, WHICH IS HIS EXECUTIVE PRIVILEGE. |
| GORE IS CONDESCENDING TO VOTERS. | BUSH IS ONLY CONDESCENDING TO ANYONE WHO DISAGREES WITH HIM AND PEOPLE FROM OTHER COUNTRIES. |
| GORE AND CLINTON "SQUANDERED" THE POST-COLD WAR MOMENT. | BUSH CAPITALIZED ON THE POST-9/11 MOMENT BY ALIENATING OUR ALLIES AND STARTING AN ENDLESS, POORLY MANAGED "WAR ON TERROR." |
| GORE MADE THE OUTRAGEOUSLY DISHONEST CLAIM THAT HE INVENTED THE INTERNET. | BUSH DOESN'T MAKE OUTRAGEOUSLY DISHONEST CLAIMS ... ABOUT THE INTERNET. |

PRESIDENT AWOL

YEAH, THAT WOULD HAVE SUCKED.

"DOES ANYONE, REPUBLICAN OR DEMOCRAT, SERIOUSLY BELIEVE THAT UNDER MR. GORE THE NEXT FOUR YEARS WOULD BE ANY DIFFERENT FROM THE LAST EIGHT?"
— DICK CHENEY, GOP CONVENTION, 2000

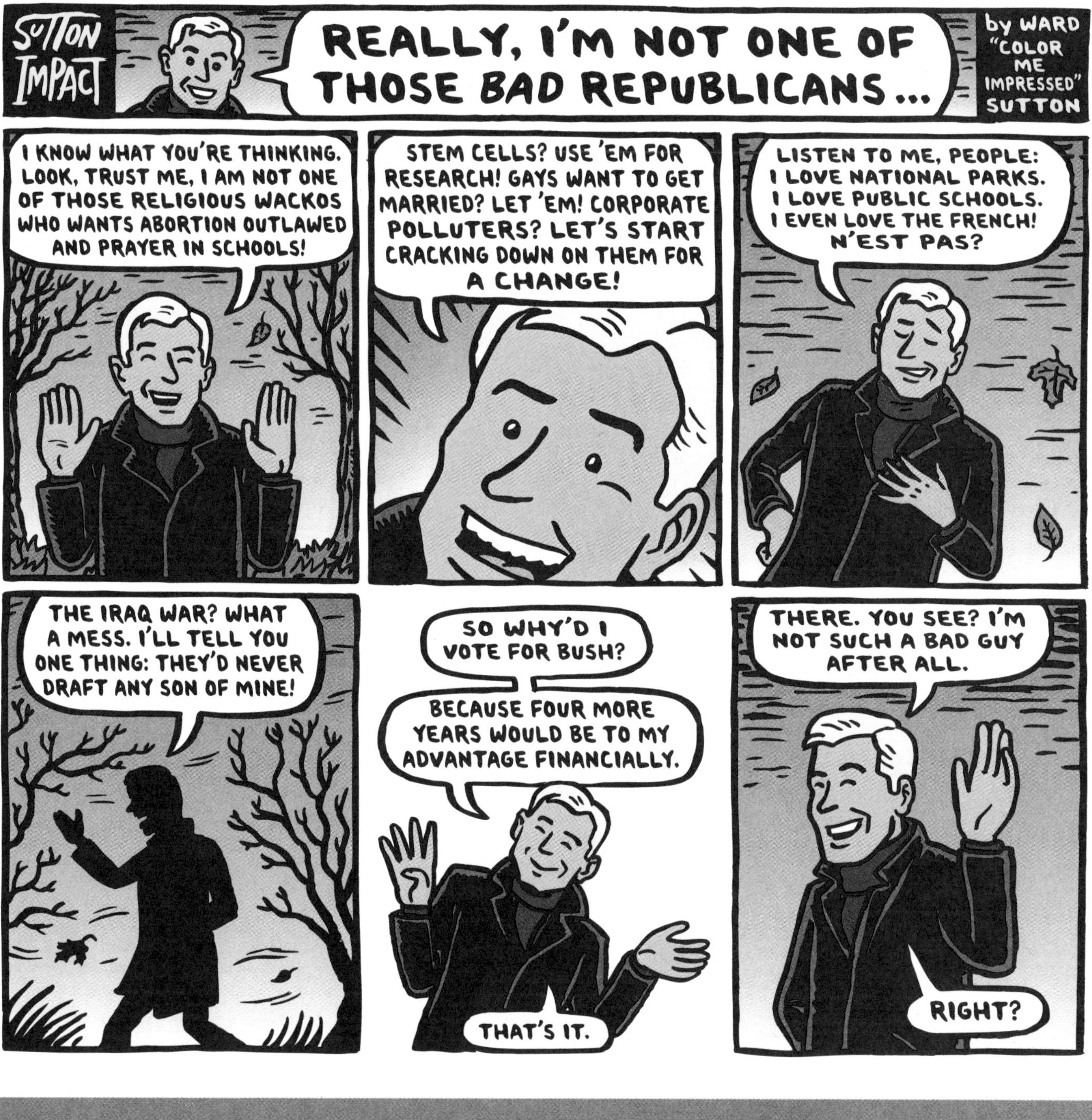
SUTTON IMPACT
REALLY, I'M NOT ONE OF THOSE BAD REPUBLICANS...
by WARD "COLOR ME IMPRESSED" SUTTON
I KNOW WHAT YOU'RE THINKING. LOOK, TRUST ME, I AM NOT ONE OF THOSE RELIGIOUS WACKOS WHO WANTS ABORTION OUTLAWED AND PRAYER IN SCHOOLS!
STEM CELLS? USE 'EM FOR RESEARCH! GAYS WANT TO GET MARRIED? LET 'EM! CORPORATE POLLUTERS? LET'S START CRACKING DOWN ON THEM FOR A CHANGE!
LISTEN TO ME, PEOPLE: I LOVE NATIONAL PARKS. I LOVE PUBLIC SCHOOLS. I EVEN LOVE THE FRENCH! N'EST PAS?
THE IRAQ WAR? WHAT A MESS. I'LL TELL YOU ONE THING: THEY'D NEVER DRAFT ANY SON OF MINE!
SO WHY'D I VOTE FOR BUSH?
BECAUSE FOUR MORE YEARS WOULD BE TO MY ADVANTAGE FINANCIALLY.
THAT'S IT.
THERE. YOU SEE? I'M NOT SUCH A BAD GUY AFTER ALL.
RIGHT?

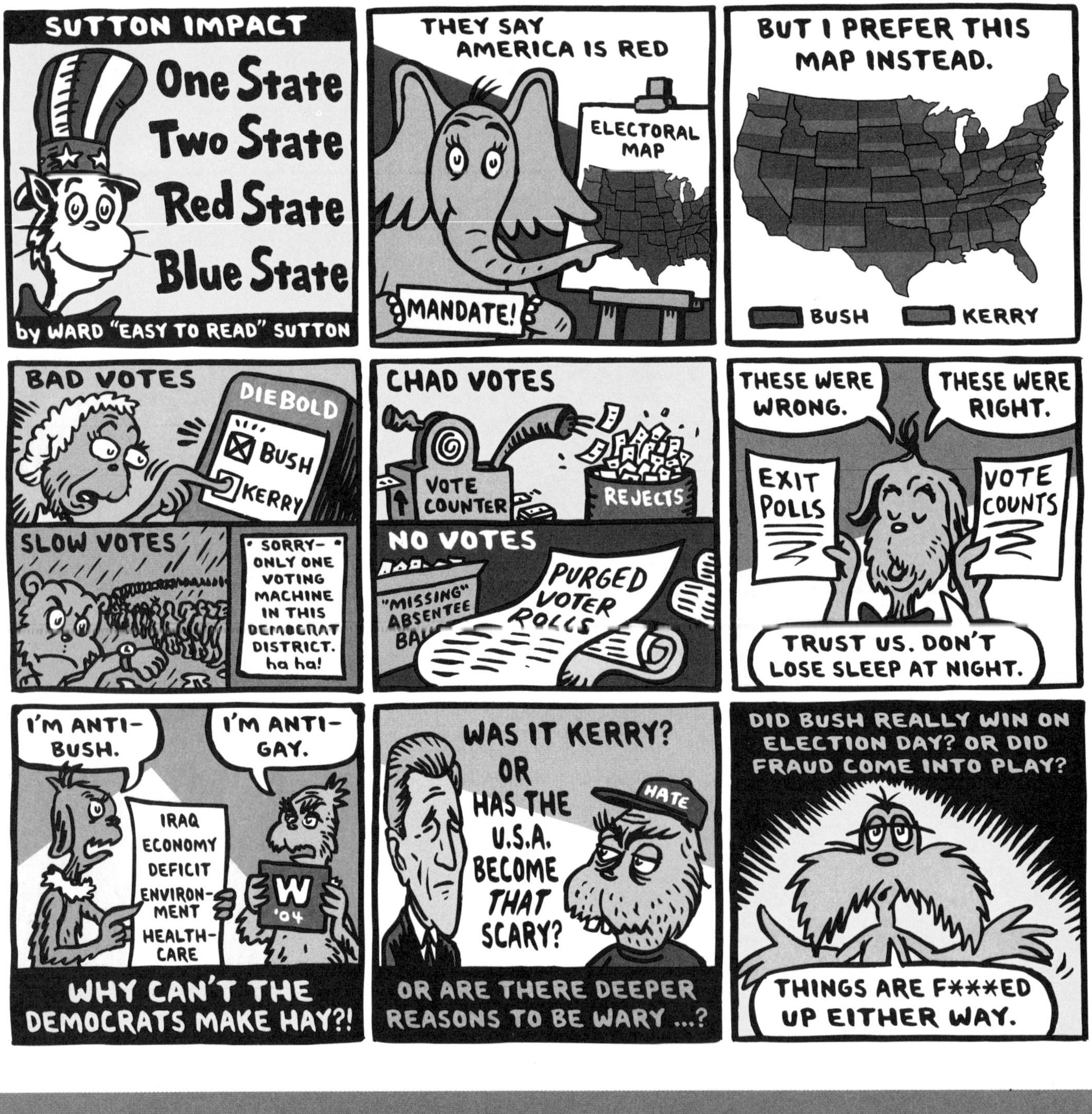
SUTTON IMPACT
One State
Two State
Red State
Blue State
by WARD "EASY TO READ" SUTTON
THEY SAY AMERICA IS RED
ELECTORAL MAP
MANDATE!
BUT I PREFER THIS MAP INSTEAD.
BUSH
KERRY
BAD VOTES
DIEBOLD
BUSH
KERRY
CHAD VOTES
VOTE COUNTER
REJECTS
SLOW VOTES
SORRY—ONLY ONE VOTING MACHINE IN THIS DEMOCRAT DISTRICT. ha ha!
NO VOTES
"MISSING" ABSENTEE BA
PURGED VOTER ROLLS
THESE WERE WRONG.
THESE WERE RIGHT.
EXIT POLLS
VOTE COUNTS
TRUST US. DON'T LOSE SLEEP AT NIGHT.
I'M ANTI-BUSH.
I'M ANTI-GAY.
IRAQ
ECONOMY
DEFICIT
ENVIRON-MENT
HEALTH-CARE
W '04
WHY CAN'T THE DEMOCRATS MAKE HAY?!
WAS IT KERRY? OR HAS THE U.S.A. BECOME THAT SCARY?
HATE
OR ARE THERE DEEPER REASONS TO BE WARY ...?
DID BUSH REALLY WIN ON ELECTION DAY? OR DID FRAUD COME INTO PLAY?
THINGS ARE F***ED UP EITHER WAY.

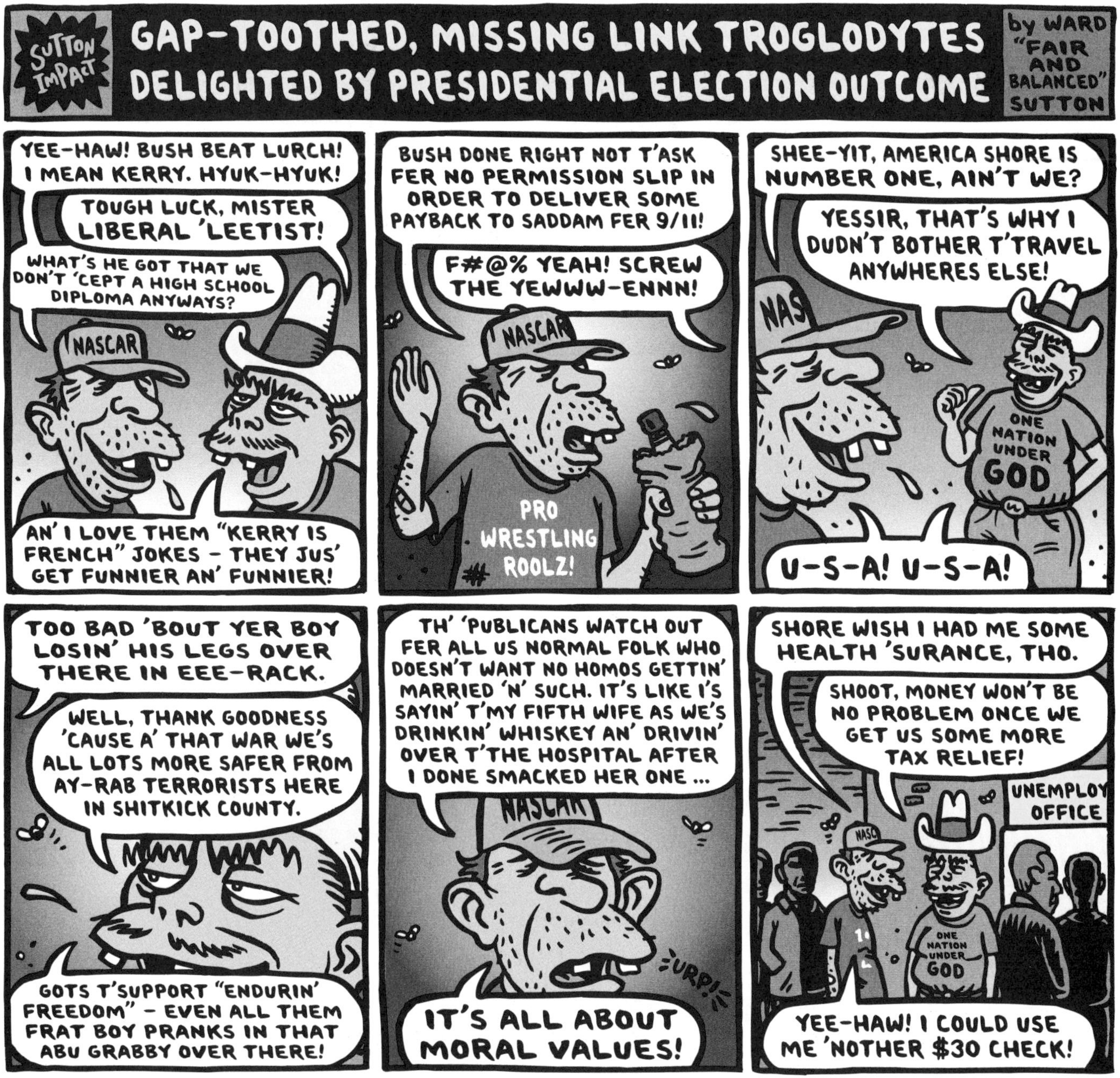
SUTTON IMPACT
GAP-TOOTHED, MISSING LINK TROGLODYTES DELIGHTED BY PRESIDENTIAL ELECTION OUTCOME
by WARD "FAIR AND BALANCED" SUTTON
YEE-HAW! BUSH BEAT LURCH! I MEAN KERRY. HYUK-HYUK!
TOUGH LUCK, MISTER LIBERAL 'LEETIST!
WHAT'S HE GOT THAT WE DON'T 'CEPT A HIGH SCHOOL DIPLOMA ANYWAYS?
NASCAR
AN' I LOVE THEM "KERRY IS FRENCH" JOKES – THEY JUS' GET FUNNIER AN' FUNNIER!
BUSH DONE RIGHT NOT T'ASK FER NO PERMISSION SLIP IN ORDER TO DELIVER SOME PAYBACK TO SADDAM FER 9/11!
F#@% YEAH! SCREW THE YEWWW-ENNN!
NASCAR
PRO WRESTLING ROOLZ!
SHEE-YIT, AMERICA SHORE IS NUMBER ONE, AIN'T WE?
YESSIR, THAT'S WHY I DUDN'T BOTHER T'TRAVEL ANYWHERES ELSE!
ONE NATION UNDER GOD
U-S-A! U-S-A!
TOO BAD 'BOUT YER BOY LOSIN' HIS LEGS OVER THERE IN EEE-RACK.
WELL, THANK GOODNESS 'CAUSE A' THAT WAR WE'S ALL LOTS MORE SAFER FROM AY-RAB TERRORISTS HERE IN SHITKICK COUNTY.
GOTS T'SUPPORT "ENDURIN' FREEDOM" – EVEN ALL THEM FRAT BOY PRANKS IN THAT ABU GRABBY OVER THERE!
TH' 'PUBLICANS WATCH OUT FER ALL US NORMAL FOLK WHO DOESN'T WANT NO HOMOS GETTIN' MARRIED 'N' SUCH. IT'S LIKE I'S SAYIN' T'MY FIFTH WIFE AS WE'S DRINKIN' WHISKEY AN' DRIVIN' OVER T'THE HOSPITAL AFTER I DONE SMACKED HER ONE ...
NASCAR
URP!
IT'S ALL ABOUT MORAL VALUES!
SHORE WISH I HAD ME SOME HEALTH 'SURANCE, THO.
SHOOT, MONEY WON'T BE NO PROBLEM ONCE WE GET US SOME MORE TAX RELIEF!
UNEMPLOY OFFICE
ONE NATION UNDER GOD
YEE-HAW! I COULD USE ME 'NOTHER $30 CHECK!

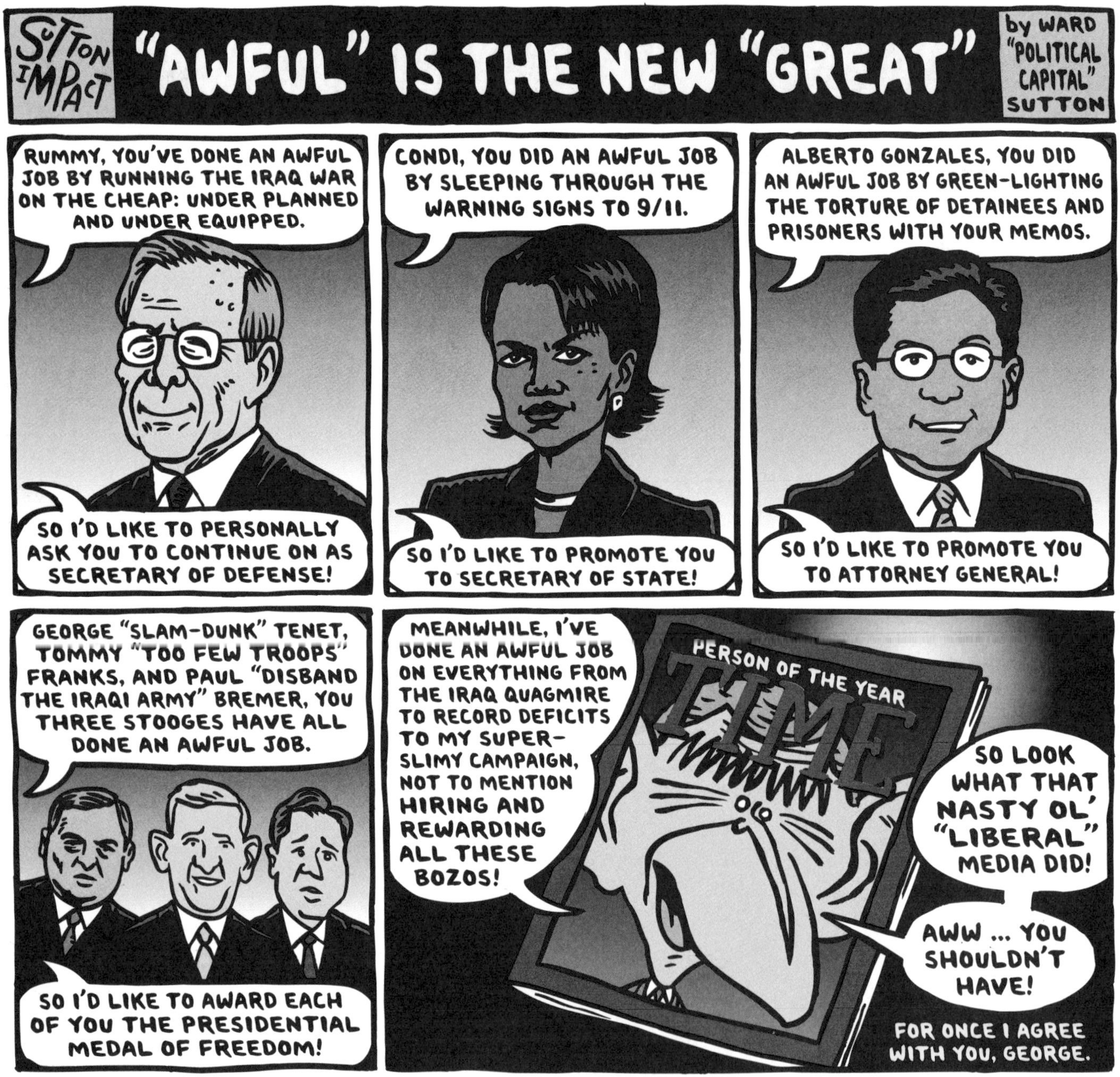
SUTTON IMPACT
"AWFUL" IS THE NEW "GREAT"
by WARD "POLITICAL CAPITAL" SUTTON
RUMMY, YOU'VE DONE AN AWFUL JOB BY RUNNING THE IRAQ WAR ON THE CHEAP: UNDER PLANNED AND UNDER EQUIPPED.
SO I'D LIKE TO PERSONALLY ASK YOU TO CONTINUE ON AS SECRETARY OF DEFENSE!
CONDI, YOU DID AN AWFUL JOB BY SLEEPING THROUGH THE WARNING SIGNS TO 9/11.
SO I'D LIKE TO PROMOTE YOU TO SECRETARY OF STATE!
ALBERTO GONZALES, YOU DID AN AWFUL JOB BY GREEN-LIGHTING THE TORTURE OF DETAINEES AND PRISONERS WITH YOUR MEMOS.
SO I'D LIKE TO PROMOTE YOU TO ATTORNEY GENERAL!
GEORGE "SLAM-DUNK" TENET, TOMMY "TOO FEW TROOPS" FRANKS, AND PAUL "DISBAND THE IRAQI ARMY" BREMER, YOU THREE STOOGES HAVE ALL DONE AN AWFUL JOB.
SO I'D LIKE TO AWARD EACH OF YOU THE PRESIDENTIAL MEDAL OF FREEDOM!
MEANWHILE, I'VE DONE AN AWFUL JOB ON EVERYTHING FROM THE IRAQ QUAGMIRE TO RECORD DEFICITS TO MY SUPER-SLIMY CAMPAIGN, NOT TO MENTION HIRING AND REWARDING ALL THESE BOZOS!
PERSON OF THE YEAR
TIME
SO LOOK WHAT THAT NASTY OL' "LIBERAL" MEDIA DID!
AWW ... YOU SHOULDN'T HAVE!
FOR ONCE I AGREE WITH YOU, GEORGE.

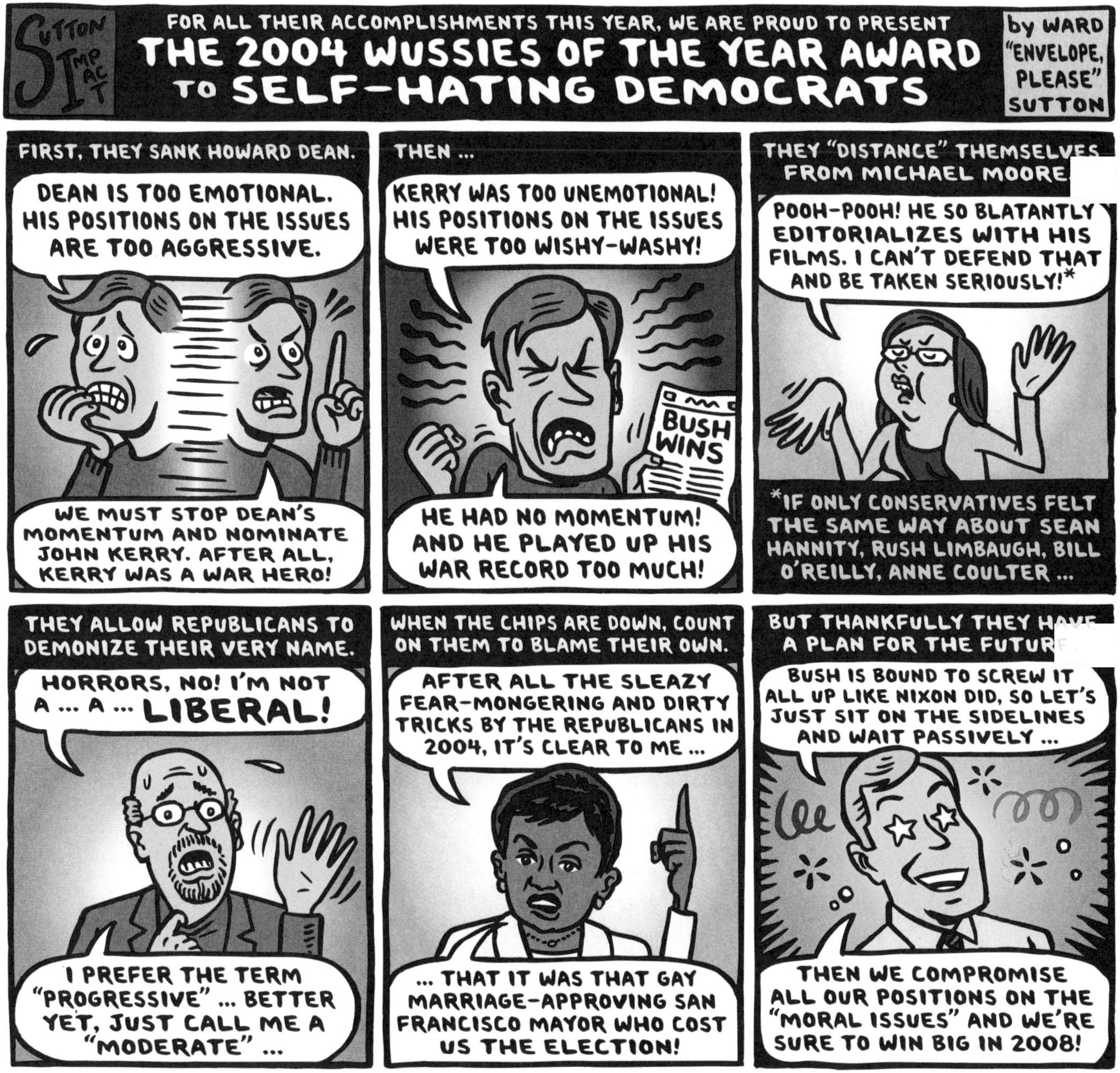
SUTTON IMPACT
FOR ALL THEIR ACCOMPLISHMENTS THIS YEAR, WE ARE PROUD TO PRESENT
THE 2004 WUSSIES OF THE YEAR AWARD TO SELF-HATING DEMOCRATS
by WARD "ENVELOPE, PLEASE" SUTTON
FIRST, THEY SANK HOWARD DEAN.
DEAN IS TOO EMOTIONAL. HIS POSITIONS ON THE ISSUES ARE TOO AGGRESSIVE.
WE MUST STOP DEAN'S MOMENTUM AND NOMINATE JOHN KERRY. AFTER ALL, KERRY WAS A WAR HERO!
THEN ...
KERRY WAS TOO UNEMOTIONAL! HIS POSITIONS ON THE ISSUES WERE TOO WISHY-WASHY!
BUSH WINS
HE HAD NO MOMENTUM! AND HE PLAYED UP HIS WAR RECORD TOO MUCH!
THEY "DISTANCE" THEMSELVES FROM MICHAEL MOORE.
POOH-POOH! HE SO BLATANTLY EDITORIALIZES WITH HIS FILMS. I CAN'T DEFEND THAT AND BE TAKEN SERIOUSLY!*
*IF ONLY CONSERVATIVES FELT THE SAME WAY ABOUT SEAN HANNITY, RUSH LIMBAUGH, BILL O'REILLY, ANNE COULTER ...
THEY ALLOW REPUBLICANS TO DEMONIZE THEIR VERY NAME.
HORRORS, NO! I'M NOT A ... A ... LIBERAL!
I PREFER THE TERM "PROGRESSIVE" ... BETTER YET, JUST CALL ME A "MODERATE" ...
WHEN THE CHIPS ARE DOWN, COUNT ON THEM TO BLAME THEIR OWN.
AFTER ALL THE SLEAZY FEAR-MONGERING AND DIRTY TRICKS BY THE REPUBLICANS IN 2004, IT'S CLEAR TO ME ...
... THAT IT WAS THAT GAY MARRIAGE-APPROVING SAN FRANCISCO MAYOR WHO COST US THE ELECTION!
BUT THANKFULLY THEY HAVE A PLAN FOR THE FUTURE.
BUSH IS BOUND TO SCREW IT ALL UP LIKE NIXON DID, SO LET'S JUST SIT ON THE SIDELINES AND WAIT PASSIVELY ...
THEN WE COMPROMISE ALL OUR POSITIONS ON THE "MORAL ISSUES" AND WE'RE SURE TO WIN BIG IN 2008!

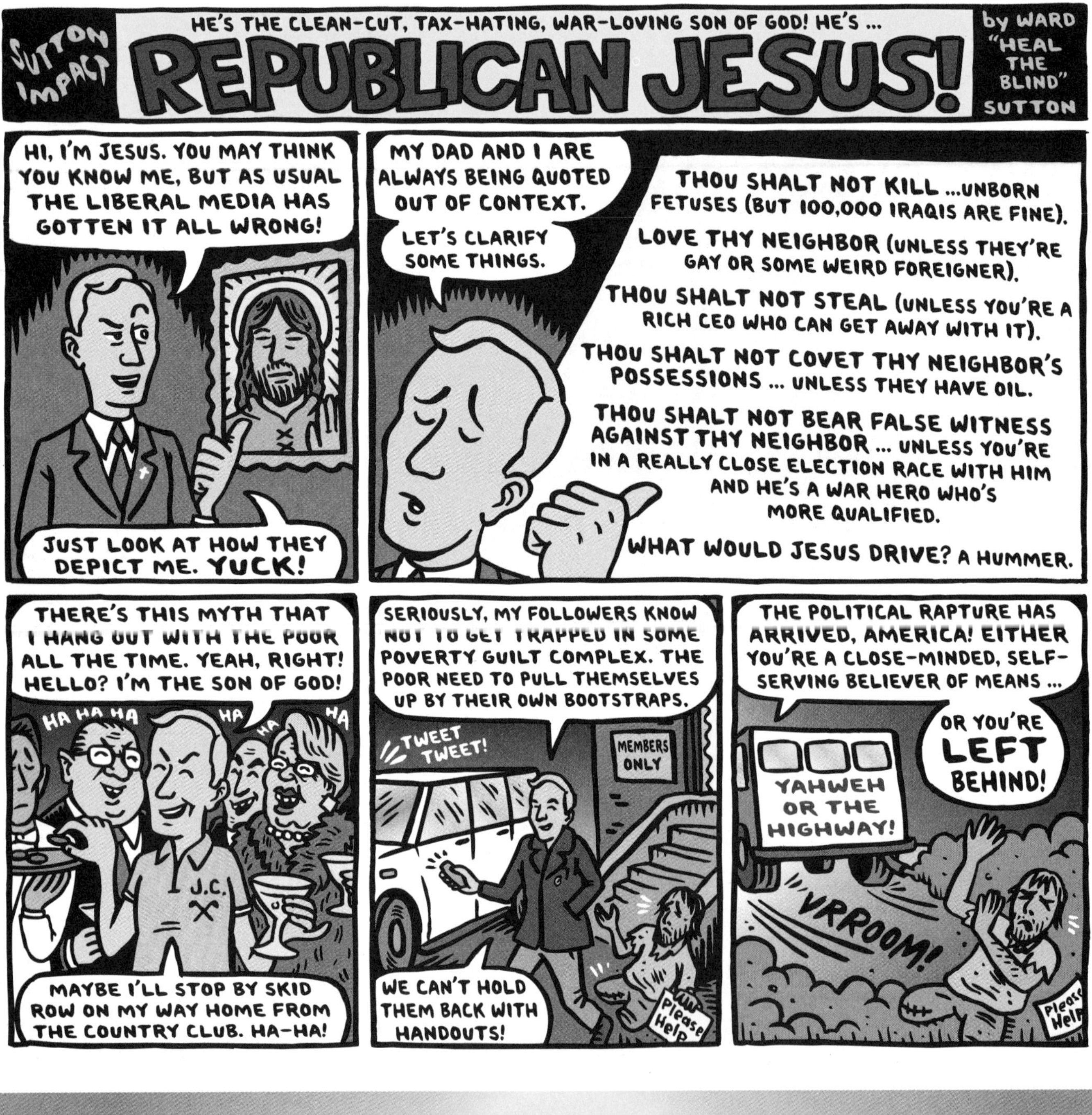
SUTTON IMPACT
HE'S THE CLEAN-CUT, TAX-HATING, WAR-LOVING SON OF GOD! HE'S ...
REPUBLICAN JESUS!
by WARD "HEAL THE BLIND" SUTTON
HI, I'M JESUS. YOU MAY THINK YOU KNOW ME, BUT AS USUAL THE LIBERAL MEDIA HAS GOTTEN IT ALL WRONG!
JUST LOOK AT HOW THEY DEPICT ME. YUCK!
MY DAD AND I ARE ALWAYS BEING QUOTED OUT OF CONTEXT.
LET'S CLARIFY SOME THINGS.
THOU SHALT NOT KILL ...UNBORN FETUSES (BUT 100,000 IRAQIS ARE FINE).
LOVE THY NEIGHBOR (UNLESS THEY'RE GAY OR SOME WEIRD FOREIGNER).
THOU SHALT NOT STEAL (UNLESS YOU'RE A RICH CEO WHO CAN GET AWAY WITH IT).
THOU SHALT NOT COVET THY NEIGHBOR'S POSSESSIONS ... UNLESS THEY HAVE OIL.
THOU SHALT NOT BEAR FALSE WITNESS AGAINST THY NEIGHBOR ... UNLESS YOU'RE IN A REALLY CLOSE ELECTION RACE WITH HIM AND HE'S A WAR HERO WHO'S MORE QUALIFIED.
WHAT WOULD JESUS DRIVE? A HUMMER.
THERE'S THIS MYTH THAT I HANG OUT WITH THE POOR ALL THE TIME. YEAH, RIGHT! HELLO? I'M THE SON OF GOD!
HA HA HA
HA
HA
HA
J.C.
MAYBE I'LL STOP BY SKID ROW ON MY WAY HOME FROM THE COUNTRY CLUB. HA-HA!
SERIOUSLY, MY FOLLOWERS KNOW NOT TO GET TRAPPED IN SOME POVERTY GUILT COMPLEX. THE POOR NEED TO PULL THEMSELVES UP BY THEIR OWN BOOTSTRAPS.
TWEET TWEET!
MEMBERS ONLY
WE CAN'T HOLD THEM BACK WITH HANDOUTS!
Please Help
THE POLITICAL RAPTURE HAS ARRIVED, AMERICA! EITHER YOU'RE A CLOSE-MINDED, SELF-SERVING BELIEVER OF MEANS ...
OR YOU'RE LEFT BEHIND!
YAHWEH OR THE HIGHWAY!
VRROOM!
Please Help

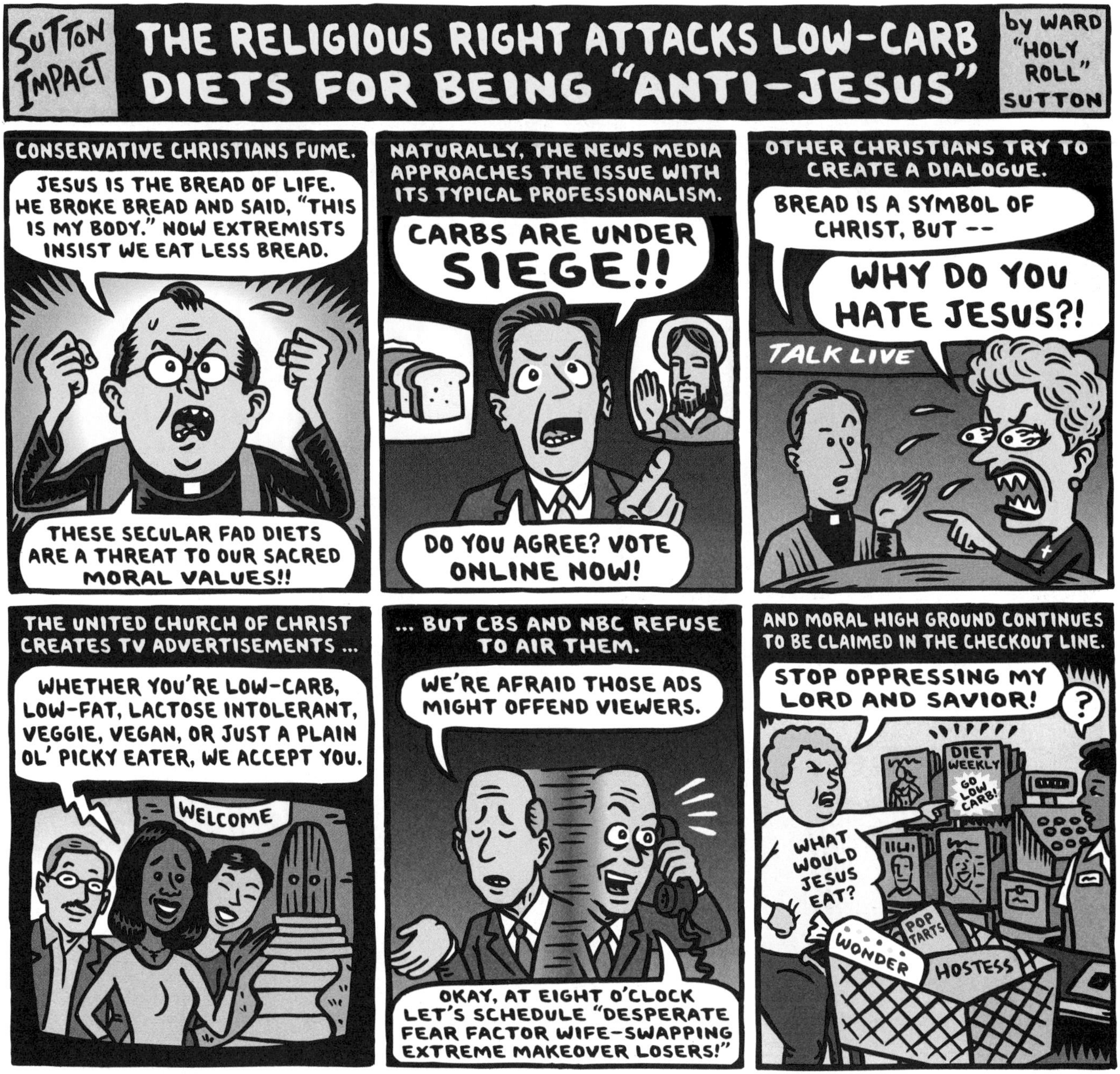
SUTTON IMPACT
THE RELIGIOUS RIGHT ATTACKS LOW-CARB DIETS FOR BEING "ANTI-JESUS"
by WARD "HOLY ROLL" SUTTON
CONSERVATIVE CHRISTIANS FUME.
JESUS IS THE BREAD OF LIFE. HE BROKE BREAD AND SAID, "THIS IS MY BODY." NOW EXTREMISTS INSIST WE EAT LESS BREAD.
THESE SECULAR FAD DIETS ARE A THREAT TO OUR SACRED MORAL VALUES!!
NATURALLY, THE NEWS MEDIA APPROACHES THE ISSUE WITH ITS TYPICAL PROFESSIONALISM.
CARBS ARE UNDER SIEGE!!
DO YOU AGREE? VOTE ONLINE NOW!
OTHER CHRISTIANS TRY TO CREATE A DIALOGUE.
BREAD IS A SYMBOL OF CHRIST, BUT --
WHY DO YOU HATE JESUS?!
TALK LIVE
THE UNITED CHURCH OF CHRIST CREATES TV ADVERTISEMENTS ...
WHETHER YOU'RE LOW-CARB, LOW-FAT, LACTOSE INTOLERANT, VEGGIE, VEGAN, OR JUST A PLAIN OL' PICKY EATER, WE ACCEPT YOU.
WELCOME
... BUT CBS AND NBC REFUSE TO AIR THEM.
WE'RE AFRAID THOSE ADS MIGHT OFFEND VIEWERS.
OKAY, AT EIGHT O'CLOCK LET'S SCHEDULE "DESPERATE FEAR FACTOR WIFE-SWAPPING EXTREME MAKEOVER LOSERS!"
AND MORAL HIGH GROUND CONTINUES TO BE CLAIMED IN THE CHECKOUT LINE.
STOP OPPRESSING MY LORD AND SAVIOR!
?
DIET WEEKLY
GO LOW CARB!
WHAT WOULD JESUS EAT?
POP TARTS
WONDER
HOSTESS

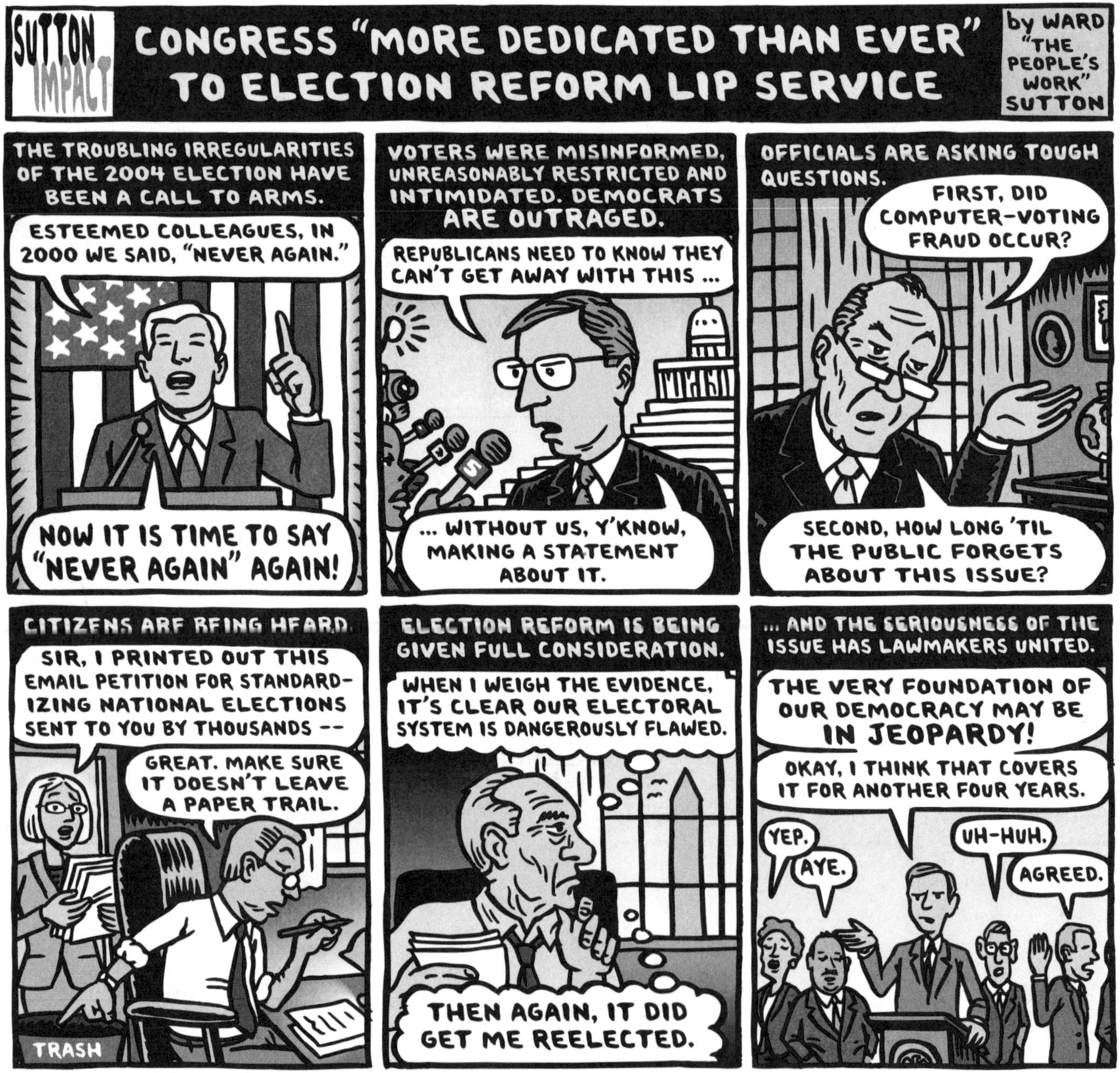
SUTTON IMPACT
CONGRESS "MORE DEDICATED THAN EVER" TO ELECTION REFORM LIP SERVICE
by WARD "THE PEOPLE'S WORK" SUTTON
THE TROUBLING IRREGULARITIES OF THE 2004 ELECTION HAVE BEEN A CALL TO ARMS.
ESTEEMED COLLEAGUES, IN 2000 WE SAID, "NEVER AGAIN."
NOW IT IS TIME TO SAY "NEVER AGAIN" AGAIN!
VOTERS WERE MISINFORMED, UNREASONABLY RESTRICTED AND INTIMIDATED. DEMOCRATS ARE OUTRAGED.
REPUBLICANS NEED TO KNOW THEY CAN'T GET AWAY WITH THIS ...
... WITHOUT US, Y'KNOW, MAKING A STATEMENT ABOUT IT.
OFFICIALS ARE ASKING TOUGH QUESTIONS.
FIRST, DID COMPUTER-VOTING FRAUD OCCUR?
SECOND, HOW LONG 'TIL THE PUBLIC FORGETS ABOUT THIS ISSUE?
CITIZENS ARE BEING HEARD.
SIR, I PRINTED OUT THIS EMAIL PETITION FOR STANDARDIZING NATIONAL ELECTIONS SENT TO YOU BY THOUSANDS --
GREAT. MAKE SURE IT DOESN'T LEAVE A PAPER TRAIL.
TRASH
ELECTION REFORM IS BEING GIVEN FULL CONSIDERATION.
WHEN I WEIGH THE EVIDENCE, IT'S CLEAR OUR ELECTORAL SYSTEM IS DANGEROUSLY FLAWED.
THEN AGAIN, IT DID GET ME REELECTED.
... AND THE SERIOUSNESS OF THE ISSUE HAS LAWMAKERS UNITED.
THE VERY FOUNDATION OF OUR DEMOCRACY MAY BE IN JEOPARDY!
OKAY, I THINK THAT COVERS IT FOR ANOTHER FOUR YEARS.
YEP.
AYE.
UH-HUH.
AGREED.

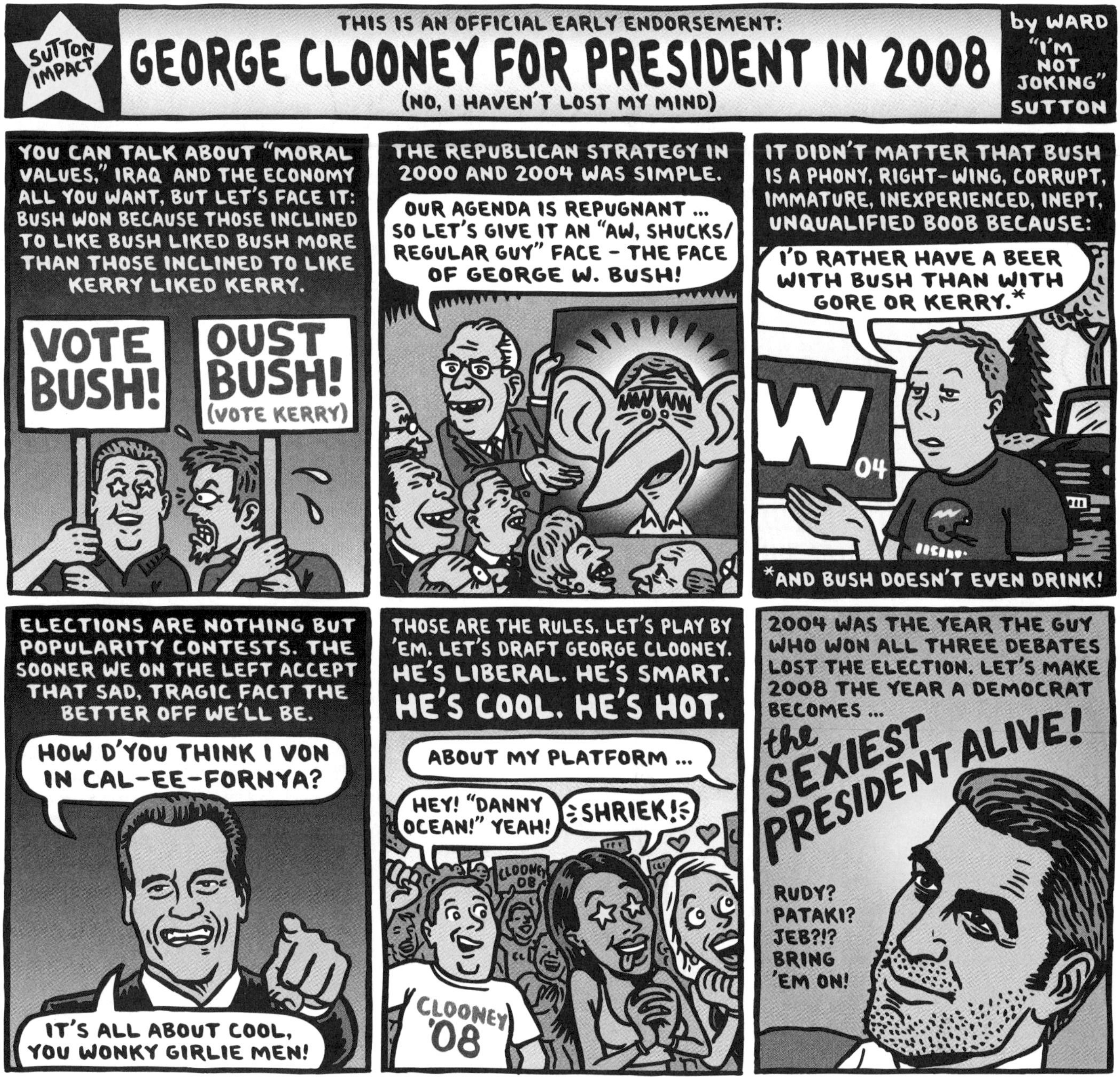
SUTTON IMPACT
THIS IS AN OFFICIAL EARLY ENDORSEMENT:
GEORGE CLOONEY FOR PRESIDENT IN 2008
(NO, I HAVEN'T LOST MY MIND)
by WARD "I'M NOT JOKING" SUTTON
YOU CAN TALK ABOUT "MORAL VALUES," IRAQ AND THE ECONOMY ALL YOU WANT, BUT LET'S FACE IT: BUSH WON BECAUSE THOSE INCLINED TO LIKE BUSH LIKED BUSH MORE THAN THOSE INCLINED TO LIKE KERRY LIKED KERRY.
VOTE BUSH!
OUST BUSH! (VOTE KERRY)
THE REPUBLICAN STRATEGY IN 2000 AND 2004 WAS SIMPLE.
OUR AGENDA IS REPUGNANT ... SO LET'S GIVE IT AN "AW, SHUCKS/REGULAR GUY" FACE – THE FACE OF GEORGE W. BUSH!
IT DIDN'T MATTER THAT BUSH IS A PHONY, RIGHT-WING, CORRUPT, IMMATURE, INEXPERIENCED, INEPT, UNQUALIFIED BOOB BECAUSE:
I'D RATHER HAVE A BEER WITH BUSH THAN WITH GORE OR KERRY.*
W 04
*AND BUSH DOESN'T EVEN DRINK!
ELECTIONS ARE NOTHING BUT POPULARITY CONTESTS. THE SOONER WE ON THE LEFT ACCEPT THAT SAD, TRAGIC FACT THE BETTER OFF WE'LL BE.
HOW D'YOU THINK I VON IN CAL-EE-FORNYA?
IT'S ALL ABOUT COOL, YOU WONKY GIRLIE MEN!
THOSE ARE THE RULES. LET'S PLAY BY 'EM. LET'S DRAFT GEORGE CLOONEY. HE'S LIBERAL. HE'S SMART. HE'S COOL. HE'S HOT.
ABOUT MY PLATFORM ...
HEY! "DANNY OCEAN!" YEAH!
SHRIEK!
CLOONEY 08
CLOONEY '08
2004 WAS THE YEAR THE GUY WHO WON ALL THREE DEBATES LOST THE ELECTION. LET'S MAKE 2008 THE YEAR A DEMOCRAT BECOMES ...
the SEXIEST PRESIDENT ALIVE!
RUDY? PATAKI? JEB?!? BRING 'EM ON!

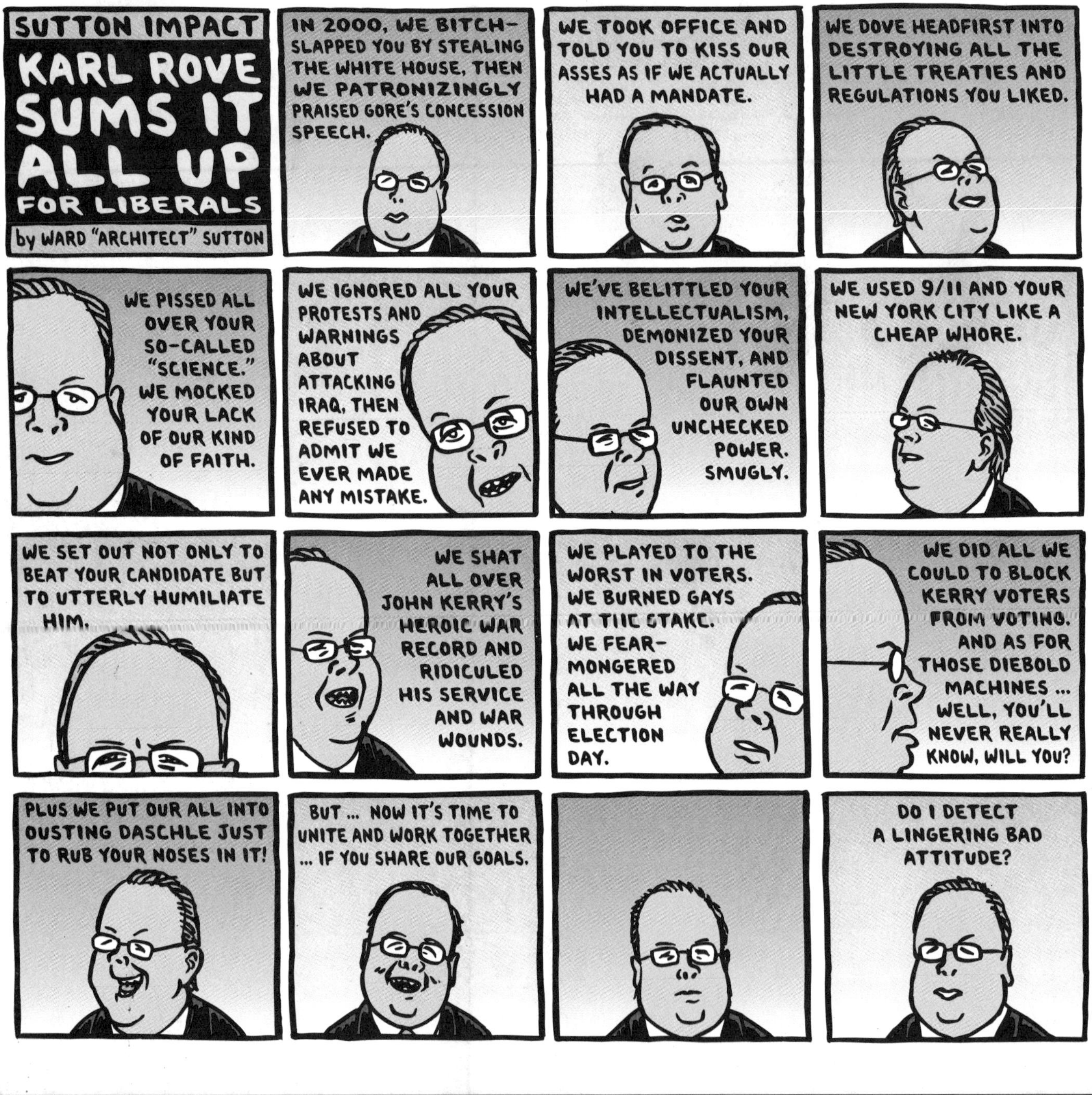
SUTTON IMPACT
KARL ROVE SUMS IT ALL UP FOR LIBERALS
by WARD "ARCHITECT" SUTTON
IN 2000, WE BITCH-SLAPPED YOU BY STEALING THE WHITE HOUSE, THEN WE PATRONIZINGLY PRAISED GORE'S CONCESSION SPEECH.
WE TOOK OFFICE AND TOLD YOU TO KISS OUR ASSES AS IF WE ACTUALLY HAD A MANDATE.
WE DOVE HEADFIRST INTO DESTROYING ALL THE LITTLE TREATIES AND REGULATIONS YOU LIKED.
WE PISSED ALL OVER YOUR SO-CALLED "SCIENCE." WE MOCKED YOUR LACK OF OUR KIND OF FAITH.
WE IGNORED ALL YOUR PROTESTS AND WARNINGS ABOUT ATTACKING IRAQ, THEN REFUSED TO ADMIT WE EVER MADE ANY MISTAKE.
WE'VE BELITTLED YOUR INTELLECTUALISM, DEMONIZED YOUR DISSENT, AND FLAUNTED OUR OWN UNCHECKED POWER. SMUGLY.
WE USED 9/11 AND YOUR NEW YORK CITY LIKE A CHEAP WHORE.
WE SET OUT NOT ONLY TO BEAT YOUR CANDIDATE BUT TO UTTERLY HUMILIATE HIM.
WE SHAT ALL OVER JOHN KERRY'S HEROIC WAR RECORD AND RIDICULED HIS SERVICE AND WAR WOUNDS.
WE PLAYED TO THE WORST IN VOTERS. WE BURNED GAYS AT THE STAKE. WE FEAR-MONGERED ALL THE WAY THROUGH ELECTION DAY.
WE DID ALL WE COULD TO BLOCK KERRY VOTERS FROM VOTING. AND AS FOR THOSE DIEBOLD MACHINES ... WELL, YOU'LL NEVER REALLY KNOW, WILL YOU?
PLUS WE PUT OUR ALL INTO OUSTING DASCHLE JUST TO RUB YOUR NOSES IN IT!
BUT ... NOW IT'S TIME TO UNITE AND WORK TOGETHER ... IF YOU SHARE OUR GOALS.
DO I DETECT A LINGERING BAD ATTITUDE?